MW01029120

NEW DEMOCRACY

NEW DEMOCRACY

The Creation of the Modern American State

WILLIAM J. NOVAK

Harvard University Press
Cambridge, Massachusetts
London, England
2022

Library of Congress Cataloging-in-Publication Data

Names: Novak, William J., 1961– author.
Title: New democracy : the creation of the modern American state / William J. Novak.
Description: Cambridge, Massachusetts : Harvard University Press, 2022. |
Includes bibliographical references and index.
Identifiers: LCCN 2021036818 | ISBN 9780674260443 (cloth)
Subjects: LCSH: Democracy—United States—History—19th century. | Democracy—
United States—History—20th century. | United States—Politics and government—
19th century. | United States—Politics and government—20th century.
Classification: LCC JK31 .N68 2022 | DDC 320.973—dc23/eng/20211007
LC record available at https://lccn.loc.gov/2021036818

For Margie

CONTENTS

CONTENTS   *viii*

NEW DEMOCRACY

INTRODUCTION

The Progressive Pursuit of a Social Democratic State

―――

In America, democracy follows its own inclination.
We are being daily carried along by an irresistible movement
toward—what? Despotism perhaps, perhaps a republic,
but certainly toward a democratic social state.

—ALEXIS DE TOCQUEVILLE

The cure for the ills of Democracy is more Democracy.

—JANE ADDAMS

Between 1866 and 1932—between the Civil War and the New Deal—the American system of governance was fundamentally transformed, with momentous implications for modern American social and economic life. Nineteenth-century traditions of local self-government and associative citizenship were replaced by a modern approach to positive statecraft, social legislation, economic regulation, and public administration still with us today. The last such formative transformation in the structure of American public life occurred in the late eighteenth century and was dubbed by Gordon Wood as "the creation of the American republic."[1] This later turn-of-the-century revolution in governance is best characterized as "the creation of the modern American state." It was the second great act in the legal-political history of American democracy.

This book is a history of that transformation. Its main thesis is explicit in its title. This era witnessed not just an "age of reform" or a "response to industrialism" or a "search for order."[2] Rather, it was marked by the specific and unambiguous emergence of a new regime of American governance—a modern democratic state. The nineteenth-century patterns of associational governance, common law, and local regulation I described in *The People's Welfare* as "the well-regulated society" were displaced by a decisive reconfiguration of the relationship between state, law, economy, and society in the United States.[3] A central nation-state built on new positive—and,

I will argue, *new democratic*—conceptions of politics and administration radically extended its reach into American social and economic life. In the social sphere, new definitions of national citizenship, rights, and belonging, coupled with new forms of cultural policing and social policy making, transformed the basic relationships of state and society. Social legislation and social welfare emerged as new objects of state and national governments actively committed to guaranteeing social rights while also insuring and policing populations. In the economic sphere, the relationship of government and the market underwent a similar restructuring. The state regulation of modern business and mass production and consumption ushered in a new understanding of the interdependence of statecraft and economic development in a mixed economy and a new political-economic vision of the democratic control of capitalism. Together these changes amounted to a fundamental reworking of American governance that was arguably the most significant legal-political development of the twentieth century. It moved to the center of American history a modern legislative, administrative, and regulatory state of a vastness and complexity still being reckoned with in new law school courses on legislation and regulation.[4] This juridical, governmental, and political revolution left no aspect of modern American life untouched or the same. To the contrary, it ushered in an American political modernity with which many Americans remain profoundly unreconciled to this very day.

This book explores in detail the basic building blocks of this second American Revolution. New conceptions of citizenship, constitution, nationhood, statecraft, police power, public utility, social police, antimonopoly, unfair competition, and social provision will be examined in turn for the insights they provide into this great transformation in public law and public policy. And the many lists and thicker descriptions of a multitude of laws, policies, and reforms that dot these chapters add historical concreteness and particularity to the general social and economic impact of this governmental revolution. The great legal historian Willard Hurst dubbed this transformation a "significant watershed in the history of public policy in the United States," producing "a country which by the nineteen-twenties bore little resemblance to its forbear. . . . Public policy took on a content that was distinctive to the twentieth century." Though Hurst did not write a full-scale history of this legal, administrative, and regulatory revolution, he provided a short list of four broad areas of policy change that evoked the scale and scope of this modern transformation: (a) the new economy with its demands for more legal interventions in the marketplace: public utility regulation, collective bargaining, consumer protections, fiscal policy, and state planning; (b) the new scarcity generated by population increases, crowded conditions, and growing resource demands requiring "greater attention to conserving human and natural resources"; (c) the new security—physical, social, emotional, and consumer—apparent in such diverse policies as criminal law, welfare and insurance law, antidiscrimination law, and quality control; and (d) the new science and technology requiring a public policy more attuned to issues of education, private research foundations, and communications. The present book includes many other lists of social and economic policy innovation, but Hurst's short one provides a fitting introductory glimpse into the new reach and range of the modern American state.[5]

Now, of course, historical transformations of this size and significance do not escape the attention of modern historians and social scientists for very long. Consequently, the history of this particular period is the subject of an enormous and ever-expanding scholarly literature. The history of late nineteenth- and early twentieth-century law, state, and politics has never been more complete or sophisticated (as well as contested).[6] But despite recent advances, important interpretive problems remain.

Some of these interpretive problems have long been on my scholarly agenda.[7] *New Democracy* is the book I committed to writing in the conclusion to *People's Welfare,* and it is fair to see it as something of a sequel to that earlier volume, completing a legal history of the American regulatory state from the first days of the new republic to the onset of the New Deal. There is thus a necessary continuity of theme across the work as a whole. This book continues my long-term effort to debunk persistent and dangerous fallacies about an original American historical tradition defined primarily by transcendent precommitments to private individual rights, formalistic constitutional limitations, and laissez-faire political economy. In contrast, this project excavates an alternative American historical reality where public rights, popular lawmaking, and robust regulatory technologies take center stage in a narrative grounded in an examination of the actual practical workings and pragmatic public policy demands of a rapidly expanding and modernizing polity, society, and economy. Four interpretive themes are integral to this project as a whole: (1) the workings of the American state; (2) the substance of American democracy; (3) the pragmatic concept of the political; and (4) the consequence of American public law.

The American State. This project continues my effort to probe the distinctive and changing core features of the American state, showing concretely when and how the modern American state took shape and what made it different from what came before and after. Taking a more synthetic approach to statecraft and governance, it attempts to push past more partial views of the American state, limited to specific policy areas, individual state builders, administrative bureaucracies, or the federal government. It simultaneously attempts to move beyond abstract discussions or conceptual definitions of "the American state" per se. As John Dewey warned, "The concept of the state, like most concepts which are introduced by 'The,' is both too rigid and too tied up with controversies to be of ready use. . . . The moment we utter the words 'The State,' a score of intellectual ghosts rise to obscure our vision."[8] The goal of this foray is not to define or debate the state but to show it as closely as possible in its minute operations at multiple levels of governance, in its changing technologies, and in its legacy of practical socioeconomic consequences. Legal change was absolutely central to this historical development—as American statecraft was pulled from beneath the weight of common-law practice and gifted a more modern pedigree in legislation, regulation, and administration.

This pragmatic attempt to describe how the state actually works and changes takes explicit aim at the tendency to talk about the American state primarily in terms of its "nature" or "essence." Too frequently such discussions quickly devolve into rather exceptionalist treatments of American state laggardness, backwardness, or comparative underdevelopment. I have discussed this elsewhere as the myth of a distinctly "weak" American state, emphasizing an original tradition of political self-abnegation, legal constraint, and distributed countervailing power: federalism, checks and balances, separation of powers, constitutional limitations, private individual rights, a competitive market, and a voluntaristic civil society.[9] From Alexis de Tocqueville's musings on a federal government tending to "get daily weaker" to G. W. F. Hegel's famous doubt that the United States was a "real State" at all, a distinguished genealogy has grown up around the idea that the American state was a lesser and lighter form.[10] Ernst Cassirer viewed such conceptions as residues of ancient mythic and symbolic forms of thought out of sync with the autonomous, reflexive, and critical reason that he viewed as the modern achievement of enlightenment.[11] Without underestimating the force of fiction, myth, and ideal in history, Cassirer endorsed instead the constructive and creative energies unleashed in those more disenchanted historical periods when, eyes wide open, human beings embraced their own productive powers and critical intelligence.

The epoch covered by this book—what Vernon Parrington discussed as "the beginnings of critical realism in America"—was one such historic period.[12] Indeed, as early as 1887, Albert Shaw attempted to clear away some of the myth and folderol surrounding "the American state and the American man." "The average American has an unequaled capacity for the entertainment of legal fictions and kindred delusions," Shaw critically argued. "Never for a moment relinquishing their theory [of laissez-faire], the people of the United States have assiduously pursued and cherished a practical policy utterly inconsistent with that theory." Surveying the thousands of regulatory laws passed by state legislatures in the late nineteenth century, Shaw concluded that "the one common and striking characteristic of this huge collection of new statutes is its utter disregard of the laissez-faire principle. . . . They seem to have left nothing for future Legislatures to regulate."[13]

As Shaw suggested, the power of American cultural myths like laissez-faire or statelessness could render invisible even radical government, state, and regulatory interventions. Arthur Schlesinger's defanging of progressive reform was typical: "After the American fashion it was a doctrineless conviction, the product of an adjustment to new times for the sake of preserving the traditional spirit of self-reliance and free competition."[14] As this book hopes to make clear, the era of progressive reform reflected neither "doctrineless convictions" nor the "traditional spirit" of American "self-reliance and free competition." Rather it was permeated by a fundamental reconsideration of almost every basic doctrine in American law, politics, and governance. It culminated in the creation of a new, modern, and powerful democratic state. That state was neither an anachronistic patchwork nor the exceptional creature of a mythic American antistatism. To the contrary, it was built directly on a long and continuous tradition of American popular lawmaking, public policy making, and statecraft that has only recently become the focus of a burgeoning historiographical revision.[15] In sync with this more recent American history, this book documents the self-conscious construction of new social forms of democratic and state power at the turn of the twentieth century. As we will see, "new" liberalism and "public" law played key roles in the production of this new regime. But as Franz Neumann warned, one should not "fall victim to a historical fallacy" of associating liberal or legal elements with weakness. "The liberal state," he noted, "has always been as strong as the political and social situation and the interests of society demanded. It has conducted warfare and crushed strikes; with the help of strong navies it has protected its investment, with the help of strong armies it has defended and extended its boundaries, with the help of the police it has restored 'peace and order.'"[16]

The Eclipse of Democracy. Franz Neumann was half right. Like fellow Frankfurt School theorists interested in ideas of "state capitalism," Neumann understood the new power and force unleashed by the early twentieth-century reconfiguration of the basic relation of modern states and modern economies and societies.[17] But like many theorists and scholars, he erred in overlooking a central component of this modern revolution in statecraft—its inescapable democratic dimension.

The present account of the creation of the modern American state centers democracy in a way that other works have too frequently neglected when deploying dominant interpretive frameworks like classical liberalism or classical republicanism. This book prioritizes and interrogates the broader and substantive democratic commitments at the very heart of the production of the modern American state. Modern democracy was a core value and practice of such state reformers as John Dewey, Jane Addams, and Walter Weyl. They understood the challenge of modern statecraft in the unprecedented popular demand for public provisioning and popular administration in an increasingly mass society and economy. Local and common-law techniques—from existing poor law to corporation law—were no longer up to the task of modern public provision, infrastructure, and police and, indeed, were themselves sources of new inequalities. Modern modes of governance were self-consciously pioneered in new efforts to meet the needs and solve the problems of rapidly expanding democratic publics. The revolutionary (if incomplete) shift from aristocratic to democratic techniques of governance—across the spectrum of public policy making—would simultaneously foreground the all-important issue of determining who *was* and who *was not* a member, a participant, and ultimately a citizen in that newly created conception of an American demos. By foregrounding democracy, this book emphasizes both the unprecedented aspirations as well as the distinctively proscribed limitations—the inclusion and the exclusion—at the very heart of modern American history.

Conventional theories and histories of the modern state have had a rather torturous relationship to the complex phenomenon that is modern democracy. Rather than investigating the modern interrelationship of the state and democracy, the general trend in the history and theory of the state has moved in the opposite direction—eclipsing democracy as an important piece of the puzzle altogether. The democratic state thus remains something of an enigma even as it wields greater and more consequent force into the modern period. The history of the American state in particular continues to sound in a strangely antidemocratic key (as do equally problematic aspirations to some kind of "stateless democracy" or civil society without a state).[18] Rather than integrate themes of political and socioeconomic democracy, chroniclers of the modern American state have emphasized instead liberalism and bureaucracy.

For most commentators, the modern American state is still best understood as a classically *liberal* state. As Louis Hartz put it in *The Liberal Tra-*

dition in America, a basic liberal individualism drove Americans to the ineluctable and fateful political conclusion "that the power of the state must be limited."[19] For a legion of like-minded authors and social scientists, Hartz's synthesis cemented a common impression of the American state as a so-called neutral or night-watchman state always doing the minimum in subservience to the higher ideals of private civil society and liberal rights theories. Pierre Bourdieu dubbed this "initial definition" of the state as a neutral-site "optimistic functionalism"—"the discourse that agents of the state produce about the state." Bourdieu noted its deep roots in the liberal social-contract and state-of-nature theories of Thomas Hobbes and John Locke.[20] And indeed, liberal interpretations of the American state remain chained to a pervasive nomenclature of individual rights, contract, property, market, and civil society as well as an overreliance on the pantheon of British political theorizing: Hobbes, Locke, John Stuart Mill, Herbert Spencer, Isaiah Berlin. The liberal theory of the state suffers from a deficit both democratic as well as American. As Michel Foucault observed, "In political analysis, we have still not cut off the king's head."[21] Consequently, the democratic state remains elusive.

The problems with the classical liberal account of a neutral and night-watchman state are manifest. Originalist liberal renderings of the fundamental limitations constraining the American state simply cannot account for what we now know in detail about that state's prolific subsequent development. Recent histories of the American state have all strived to grasp an inescapable fact about modern American history—the development of a legal-economic and geopolitical hegemon. Most obviously, slavery, segregation, the removal of Indigenous peoples, and immigration restriction and policing were simply not products of laissez-faire or an exceptional American predisposition to leave people alone or a constitutional imperative to protect individual rights. From the now well-documented development of a modern fiscal and welfare state to the equally momentous rise of a modern warfare and carceral state, the historical record of American statecraft is different, and the classical liberal account, implausible. Unsurprisingly, the explanatory limits of the liberal paradigm quickly spawned a quest for alternatives. The turn to "classical republicanism" in the history of political thought was one such development.[22] The "republican synthesis" constructively recovered an alternative intellectual genealogy of the American founding and rehabilitated important and ongoing political languages of "public virtue," "common good," and "civic humanism" with much potential for historical revision. In the end, however, the "republican turn" offered comparatively less insight into the changing contours of the American state or the actual conduct of American governance. Driven by a more intellectualist and contextualist methodology—and drawn backward in time to the ideas and texts of seventeenth- and eighteenth-century "commonwealthmen"—republicanism was perhaps as ill equipped to explain the future direction of American statecraft and democracy as the thin, negative vision of Lockean liberalism it sought to supplant. Moments of the American political have always owed more to majorities and magistrates than to either Milton or Machiavelli.

An alternative approach to the modern American state takes explicit issue with some of the limitations of both the liberal and republican traditions, striving for a more objective and social-scientific appraisal. Of late, this position has established itself as a powerful new orthodoxy. In place of Locke or Machiavelli, the patron saint of this most recent synthesis is Max Weber—social theorist of the modern state par excellence. Indeed, the modern study and theory of the state continues to labor beneath the long shadow of Weber's classic conception of the state—defined most succinctly in "Politics as a Vocation" as "a human community that (successfully) claims the monopoly of the legitimate use of physical force within a given territory."[23] In place of traditional American emphases on liberalism or republicanism, Weber offered up *bureaucracy* as the hallmark of the modern state. For Weber, the rational development of what he described in detail as "legal authority with a bureaucratic administrative staff" was the sine qua non of modern statecraft and the social-scientific standard through which to assess states past and present.[24] It was this distinctly Weberian vision of a nineteenth-century Continental European state that captured American historical-sociological imagination well into the late twentieth century. Despite an extraordinarily rich American vernacular literature on the state and democracy—from Emerson and Whitman to James and Dewey to the original development of modern social science (Ward, Mead, Ely, Commons, Goodnow, Freund, Addams, Breckinridge)—American efforts to "bring the state back in" inexplicably turned back instead to the nineteenth-century ideal types of Max Weber.[25]

This Weberian inheritance plunged a comparatively aristocratic (if not monarchical) conception of the state into the very heart of an American political tradition already hobbled by a striking democratic deficit. Despite its seeming theoretical sophistication, the basic bureaucratic state idea harkened back to the conservative and moderating role that a professional class of ennobled civil servants supposedly played in the wake of the popular upheavals of the French Revolution and its aftermath. Unsurprisingly, the Prussian bureaucracy—what one historian dubbed "Plato's guardian class"—was the model.[26] Hegel's *Philosophy of Right* was an early locus classicus concerning both the crucial role of executive power and the crucial task of bureaucratic "civil servants" in upholding "the universal interest of the state." The higher administrative bodies, he concluded, "converge in their supreme heads who are in touch with the monarch himself."[27]

The persistence of this basically bureaucratic and aristocratic conception of the state is a significant obstacle to modern understanding. Indeed the whole notion of assessing the American state by turning back to Hintze and Weber and Hegel and the lost priorities of nineteenth-century Prussian fiscal-military bureaucracy only exacerbated the dominant tendency to evacuate considerations of democracy from the history of the American political. This was a state concept focused on the particular traits of elites at the center of power, emphasizing the rulers at the expense of the ruled, the government rather than the governed, and the few rather than the many. It thus conjures up something of the unsettling, antidemocratic image of what G. R. Elton once described as "the old-fashioned political historian, on his knees before the thrones of kings."[28]

Of course, the antidemocratic flaws in a largely bureaucratic conception of modern statecraft have been apparent for some time. In his original and still powerful *Critique of Hegel's Doctrine of the State*, Karl Marx made the classic case. The conscious elision of democracy, Marx contended, was the central flaw in the Hegelian state project and in all such state theories written, as he put it, "as if the actual state were not the people." Marx attacked the "state formalism" of the bureaucratic theory as an "apologia" rather than an analysis of the modern state, calling bureaucrats "theologians of the state." Democracy, in contrast, was both form and substance—"the people's own creation" wherein "man does not exist for the sake of the law, but the law exists for the sake of man." "Democracy," Marx prophetically concluded, "relates to all other forms of state as its Old Testament."[29]

The basic eclipse of democracy in reigning theories of the modern American state remains the fundamental defect. It is a problem in general, obscuring the actual functioning of democratic states into the twenty-first century. But it poses a particular problem for coming to terms with the nature of modern American state development. The period between the Civil War and the New Deal did witness major transformations in liberalism and law. It also saw dramatic changes in bureaucracy, central authority, administrative hierarchies, and the expansion of officialdom. But when commentators at the time drew back to assess the nature of the whole—both form and substance—they saw it as nothing less than the beginning of a new and modern democracy. In the crucial political year of 1912, Walter Weyl drew attention to recent transformations in both state and democracy, citing (a) "the evolution in many States and cities" of "popular control," subjecting industry and "business to a governmental supervision"; as well as (b) "the new democratic movement in its innumerable ramifications; in ordinances, laws, judicial decisions, group actions, and individual labors." Weyl witnessed firsthand the creation of the modern American state, and he branded its consequences as well as its aspiration nothing less than "the New Democracy."[30]

Toward a Pragmatic Concept of the American Political. The need for an interpretive integration of the modern state and modern democracy also forces a reconsideration of the basic concept of the political in American history. Since Richard Hofstadter's epics *The Age of Reform* and *The American Political Tradition,* American political history has served up endless new attempts to reckon more fully with the American political.[31] To date, however, the concept of the political in the United States continues to lag theoretical development elsewhere, especially in France, where Pierre Rosanvallon, Claude Lefort, and Marcel Gauchet—what Stephen Sawyer has dubbed the "Paris school"—have been productively rethinking the interconnection of the modern political-governmental and the socioeconomic for more than a generation.[32] In Germany too, the legacy of the Frankfurt school continues to fuel fresh thinking on modern politics, police, law, and society in the hands of such capacious and creative innovators as Jürgen Habermas and Axel Honneth.[33]

In contrast, American treatment of the political continues to cling to conventional renderings of established interpretive orthodoxies. Indeed, American study of the state continues to oscillate between the poles of society-centered versus polity-centered analysis.[34] In the former, the state and mainstream politics are treated as epiphenomenal, dependent variables—separate from, less significant than, and reflexive of prime movements in the foundational spheres of social, cultural, or economic life. Here, a critical social history of politics predominates, where the lineaments of the political are traced far away from the central corridors of power—in the everyday social, cultural, and economic conflicts of ordinary folk and subaltern groups.[35] In extreme forms, American society-centered approaches can exhibit an intransigence to political questions of state and democracy that borders on what Michel Foucault talked about as "state phobia."[36]

In this harshly dichotomous framing, polity-centered analysis offers up the alternative where "state autonomy" replaces "state phobia." Here, politics is still viewed as separate from society. Only now causal arrows—and frequently normative appraisals—point in the opposite direction as elite and independent state builders, politicians, and bureaucrats exert power, pressure, and policies on all aspects of society and economy. In the tradition of

American political development, the state is seen as "a central actor in its own right" and "an autonomous force" to be reckoned with on its own resolutely political terms.[37] This perspective self-consciously brings new attention to the subject of American statecraft per se. But Tony Judt effectively captured the limitations of such a basic "divorce" of political history from social history. "Describing the behaviour of the ruling classes," Judt argued, "this remains, as ever, a form of historical writing adapted to the preservation of the status quo."[38]

In the end, the formal bifurcation of polity and society purchased analytical clarity at the expense of historical explanation. The separation of the political from the social and the state from society simply defied the nature of a modern history notable for the increased interdependence of public and private, individual and collective, the state and the market. Indeed, since the pioneering inquiries of Benjamin Constant, Tocqueville, and J. S. Mill, it has been apparent that what separated modern from ancient conditions of freedom was the arrival of a new kind of distinctly *social state*—a state consumed by the problem of socioeconomic policy making and social provisioning on a diverse and general scale beyond the parochialism of traditional local self-government. The rise of modern democratic states quickly outstripped the explanatory powers of traditional, formalist schemas positing the separate and autonomous powers of public sovereign authority counterposed to the liberties of private civil society. Such juridical and bourgeois conceptions of the formal separations of power elided the very revolution that brought state and society, political life and social life, into irretrievably constant contact and conversation. As contemporary theorists as diverse as Hannah Arendt and Carl Schmitt argued for some time, a defining characteristic of recent history and a hallmark of modern times is the dense interpenetration of the political and the social. "The equation state = politics," Schmitt noted, "becomes erroneous and deceptive at exactly the moment when state and society penetrate each other. What had been up to that point affairs of state become thereby social matters, and vice versa."[39] A proper conception of the political in the modern period thoroughly implicates the social relation in all its manifestations as the very core of the political modernity to be explained.

Pierre Rosanvallon recognized this fundamental fact when he recommended a turn to "the political as a noun" rather than as an adjective—highlighting the modern political and social as "indissociable." Referring to "the political" rather than to "politics," Rosanvallon concluded, "is to speak of power and law, state and nation, equality and justice, identity and difference, citizenship and civility."[40] Such a synthetic approach highlighted the state as something more than an administrative mechanism or an instrumental governmental apparatus just as the political involved so much more than partisan competition for institutionalized power. For Rosanvallon, the state was a "form of social representation"—the very "crossroads of the social and the political"—the consequence of "continuous interaction with that society."[41] Such a capacious and open-ended rendering of the state and the political has special implications for the history of democratic societies—that is, "those societies in which the conditions of life in common are not defined a priori." Rosanvallon noted an open and "indeterminate" quality in democratic as opposed to totalitarian states that rendered the state/society relation especially fungible—resisting final closure. The modern democratic state, thus, could only be apprehended through its ever-changing history. Or as Rosanvallon concluded, "One must see that democracy *is* a history."[42]

Or a genealogy. Michel Foucault too predicated his revolutionary genealogy of modern police powers on a similar great refusal to reinscribe the formal, juridical, and quintessentially liberal architecture of sovereignty, state, and politics versus society and economy.[43] Foucault's welcome new focus on "the mesh" and "the technologies" of power—"dispositions, manoeuvres, tactics, techniques, functionings"—was a critical and pragmatic alternative to the more classical "juridical" and "formal" ideas of power from which, he repeatedly contended, "we must now free ourselves." In Foucault's analysis, neither the state nor the society was an autonomous or "unitary body, in which one and only one power is exercised." Rather, drawing on the actual police histories of a Jeremy Bentham and Marx rather than the abstract legal categories of a Hugo Grotius and Samuel von Pufendorf, Foucault emphasized the "archipelago of power" and the "network of relations" that routinely transgressed the conventionally drawn boundary lines "between the state and its citizen" or "the frontier between classes."[44] Axel Honneth's conceptions of social freedom and a struggle for recognition also transcended conventional state/society divisions. Explicitly rejecting the supposed philosophical clarity and jurisprudential confidence that sprang from formally detaching the political subject from the concrete social and historical contexts of modern life, Honneth built instead on the thoroughgoing historicality and sociality of Hegel's concept of reason (and its critique of the "atomistic principles" of natural law) and George Herbert Mead's idea of "the social self" (and its critique of abstract individualism), as well as John Dewey's more critical, pragmatic, and democratic rendering of the political and its problems (and its total critique of naturalized concepts of law, liberalism, and state).[45]

The invocation of Mead and Dewey makes clear just how important antiformalism was to the creation of the modern democratic state.[46] Indeed, two generations of American historians have now definitively established the significance of pragmatism, sociological jurisprudence, and legal realism in underwriting a progressive reform mentality as well as modern social science. This book attempts to demonstrate the degree to which critical realism and antiformalism also had direct effects transforming the instrumentalities of modern law and governance, as the likes of Ernst Freund constructed a modern police power, Felix Frankfurter crafted modern public utility, and Sophonisba Breckinridge built modern social service administration.[47] A pragmatic conception of the political places emphasis directly on the actual conduct of governance and the fungible workings and potentialities of modern democratic states. It approaches the state not definitionally in terms of what *it* essentially *is* but in terms of what it realistically *does* and *how* it practically works, taking special note of when and how the diverse modalities, technologies, and capacities of statecraft changed over time. "What really matters," John Dewey contended, "is not the inner nature of objects but their mutual relations"—not the "inhering essence" but the "analysis of facts" concerning the "social consequences" and changing extrinsic effects that objects, things, institutions, rules, and laws produce on the ground in the real world.[48] Such a synthetic, pragmatic, postmetaphysical concept of the practical, everyday interrelations of state, democracy, politics, and society was at the very center of the progressive pursuit of a social democratic state.

The Instrumentalities of American Public Law. A more pragmatic concept of the political creates the room necessary to see the centrality of law in producing the dramatic social effects and consequences associated with American political modernity. This book is a work of modern sociolegal history. As such, it realistically and critically takes issue with more classical and formalistic treatments of a "higher" liberal rule-of-law tradition supposedly operating somewhere outside of and above politics and the state. Within conventional liberal constitutional interpretation, judges are still too frequently portrayed not as officers and agents of the state but as something akin to disinterested, apolitical, and neutral umpires just calling balls and strikes, protecting private rights and private interests from the illiberal interferences of an inherently coercive government. Rooted in classical ideals of a *Rechtsstaat,* or a distinctly legal or jural state, American exceptionalism elevated the "spirit of the common law" and an originalist Constitution to preferred positions in defining, controlling, and legitimating the American state. For Edward Corwin, "the 'Higher Law' background" of the United States stretched "from Demosthenes to Calvin Coolidge and beyond," enshrining a unique set of American legal doctrines—judicial review, vested rights, and substantive due process of law—that prioritized private right and enforced constitutional limitations against the overexertions of state regulatory authority.[49] Julius Goebel channeled that basic ideal (with special homage to its English pedigree) in the opening pages of volume 1 of *The Oliver Wendell Holmes Devise History of the Supreme Court of the United States:* "When the first colonies were planted on the North American continent, *the judicial* had come to occupy a position of preeminence in the *English constitution.*" Goebel viewed the entire colonial project as an effort "to establish a rule of law" independent of "the laws of men," what he called "the suzerainty of the great fundamentals—the supremacy of the law, the prescription of certainty, the orderly determination of controversies and, above all, the dominating concept of due process."[50] Henry Maine, A. V. Dicey, and Friedrich Hayek, among countless other commentators, would continue to find the key to American political development not in historic or vernacular traditions of democracy or popular self-government but in "constitutional limitations"—the special juridical forms that reined in the American state and underwrote a "constitution of liberty."[51] Contemporary conservative invocations of the "original" or "lost" or "exiled" Constitution are thus only the last in a long line of endorsements of the power of judges, courts, and legal doctrine to protect the spirit of law from the power of the people.[52]

Much of the critical-realist energy in the so-called new legal history pioneered by James Willard Hurst and Morton Horwitz came from a self-conscious rejection of the conventional sources, methods, and topics that encrusted such sclerotic constitutional conceptions—great cases, high courts, herculean judges, and the comparatively infrequent incidence of judicial review.[53] Emphasizing the previously neglected historical development of the doctrinal categories of private law, the new sociolegal history opened a wider horizon for surveying what Hurst called "the living interplay of law and social growth." This new perspective moved beyond the crabbed understanding of law as a fundamentally limiting power (a series of "thou shalt nots" addressed to power holders) so as to investigate law's forceful creative efficacy—for good or for ill—in modern society and economy.[54] My own first book followed in that tradition, stressing the distinctive common-law underpinnings of the early American well-regulated society, albeit devoting more attention to the public and regulatory consequences of doctrines like public nuisance. The present book, however, redirects attention elsewhere—to the monumental impact of the rise of modern *public law* in American sociolegal development. This book emphasizes the public restructuring of governance that attended the modern ascendancy of legislation, regulation, and administration in American law at the turn of the twentieth century. In contrast to conventional accounts featuring law primarily as a negative check on American political development, this history recovers the creative and constitutive (what some have called juris-generative) power of public law in the making of a modern democratic state. The chapters of this volume bear witness to this alternative emphasis. In place of contract, property, and tort as the central building blocks of American legal modernity, *New Democracy* is built around the public law categories of citizenship, police power, public utility, social legislation, antimonopoly, and administrative law.

These instrumentalities of public law were crucial to the progressive project of democratizing the state. The progressives' distinctly pragmatic vision of democracy—focused as it was on the ends, outcomes, and consequences of effectuating social change, equalizing resources, and enhancing human life in a modernizing society and economy—hinged on generalizing the capacities of the American state. What Michael Mann called the state's "infrastructural power"—its practical capacity to permeate social life and logistically implement policy decisions—became more important than elucidating the formal and juridical boundaries of "stateness" that preoccupied a Corwin or a Goebel.[55] *Potentia*—a power rooted in the government's practical ability to "control the disposition of things"—trumped abstract conceptual debates about *potestas,* the rightful nature of rule.[56] The actual tools and techniques of an expanding public law established the contested site for this era's most impactful socioeconomic policy initiatives. At stake in these debates and struggles over the public's law was nothing less than the salus populi—the ability of a modernizing state to continue to provide for a democratic people's welfare. The modern reform effort to reassert popular and public legal control over "a vastly expanded and enriched world" was in the end an effort to reestablish the welfare of the people as the all-important object of a true democracy.[57] "For a long period, we acted as if our democracy were something that perpetuated itself automatically," John Dewey argued, but "the creation of democracy" was now just "as urgent as it was a hundred and fifty years ago." A new and modern democracy now required popular re-creation "by deliberate and determined endeavor"—a re-creation of "the political structure of a self-governing society" during a modern crisis of legitimacy.

A Crisis in Democratic Theory

In less than seventy years, the United States passed from a world of Civil War and Reconstruction to the world of Franklin Roosevelt's New Deal. And whereas some constitutional scholars prefer to emphasize and magnify those especially salient "constitutional moments," this book concentrates on the momentous legal-political developments in between.[58] Moreover, in contrast to conventional accounts that split this historical era into two separate and competing phases of Gilded Age conservative reaction versus Progressive Era liberal reform, this book insists on examining this period as of a piece.[59] Here the creation of the modern American administrative and regulatory state—across both social and economic fields— is viewed as more than one hand clapping in seemingly endless cycles of conservative orthodoxy versus liberal activism. Rather, this governmental revolution is presented as nothing less than the American response to modernity.[60]

Across diverse and competing struggles, issues, and events, the basic legal-political changes that created the modern democratic state from 1866 to 1932 represented a reassessment of existing American values and institutions amid a full-blown legitimation crisis. The diverse citizens, reformers, jurists, and social scientists that animate these pages were not merely an old middle class wrestling with status anxiety or a new professional elite eager to get on in a changed world. They were neither simple anticorruption fighters (mugwumps or muckrakers) nor just foot soldiers in the latest rendition of ideological battle (old conservative/new conservative, maternalist/paternalist, corporate liberal/radical socialist). They were American moderns struggling with the underlying problem of reconciling individuals to the challenges of an onrushing modernity along its deepest and most confounding dimensions. They were wrestling seriously with the problem of how to make institutions more rational and individuals more free in a crisis environment—with *rational* and *free* both taking on new social and democratic meaning and possibility in modern times. In the process, they reinvented the American state and reworked the basic terms of American democracy. They fully grasped the double-edged nature of the modern predicament—the unprecedented new capacities for rational governance and collective freedom (the dream of the Enlightenment) as well as the dire new threats and acute socioeconomic problems that would continue to haunt modern history into the twentieth and twenty-first centuries (the nightmare dialectic of that one and the same Enlightenment).[61] It is thus vital to think about this period as a whole and to approach it with this wider interpretive lens—not Anglo-American rule of law versus a Continental general-welfare state but the philosophical conditions of modernity and the nature of modern historical change. At the center of those modern conditions was a veritable "crisis of democracy."[62]

Critiques of democracy, of course, proliferated even before the dust settled on the age of revolution. But they become more common, conservative, and strident in the decades surrounding the turn of the twentieth century. Typical in England was W. E. H. Lecky's *Democracy and Liberty* (1899)—a question that he broke down along the simple lines of whether "the world should be governed by its ignorance or its intelligence." Lecky attributed many "evils" to the specifically "democratic" form of the American state, which lowered "the tone of public life and the character of public men."[63] Anthony M. Ludovici's *A Defense of Aristocracy: A Text Book for Tories* (1915) was less subtle, broadcasting the simple conclusion that "Aristocracy means Life and that Democracy means Death." In the *Nemesis of Mediocrity* (1917), Ralph Adams Cram imported such sentiments into the United States: "Democracy has achieved its perfect work and has now reduced all mankind to a dead level of incapacity. . . . It is now not a blessing but a menace." For Cram, like so many others, democracy's "menace" was distinctly racialized in an American democratic society that he now deemed "completely mongrel."[64]

But in the development of new democracy, two aristocratic critics were especially significant adversaries—Sir Henry Maine and William Graham Sumner. As early as 1886, Maine's *Popular Government* consolidated and popularized a pervasive British legal-constitutional critique of democracy that stretched from John Austin's "plea for the constitution" against Benthamite "radical politics" to A. V. Dicey's rule of law versus droit administratif to Ernest Barker's assault on "the discredited state" in favor of a "law-state."[65] Maine's contempt for the masses burned brightly: "We may say generally that the gradual establishment of the masses in power is of the blackest omen for all legislation founded on scientific opinion." Taking explicit aim at the lyrical notions of Walt Whitman and George Bancroft that democracy was "the tendency of the ages . . . which no human policy could hold back," Maine recommended "a healthful douche of cold water." Maine held that democracy was "simply and solely a form of government" with exactly the same functions and obligations as monarchy and aristocracy, namely, "maintaining national existence" and "securing national greatness and dignity." Should a choice ever come between nationalism and democracy, for Maine, it would be "better to remain a nation capable of displaying the virtues of a nation than even to be free."[66]

As William Graham Sumner made a career transporting English conservatism across the Atlantic, it should come as no surprise that he was an early adopter and popularizer of the aristocratic critique of American democracy. In an opinion-laden volume entitled *The Challenge of Facts* (1914), Sumner began by constricting the demos—limiting "who shall be the people to rule." "Even in the widest democracies," he approvingly noted, "the 'people' for political purposes, does not include women, or minors, or felons, or idiots." The "pathos of democracy in the United States" was "provincial" and "philistine," founded on the "worn and common-place opinions" of the masses—"fallacies, half-truths, and glib general-izations." Sumner held that "democracy cannot last," comparing it to pair marriage as mere contingent and transitory "folkways" doomed to extinction. "When life becomes harder," he predicted—and his social Darwinism aimed to make it so—"it will become aristocratic, and concu-binage may be expected to rise again."[67] Sumner made his brash predic-tion that aristocracy and concubinage would "rise again" in 1906 amid a surging tide of worry about the future of democracy.[68] Indeed, from the 1890s to the 1920s, almost every aspect of the democratic regime was picked apart for alleged weakness and excess: the distortions of the party system, the limits of the legislature, the corruption of the interests, the spoils system, the rise of the bosses, the problem of minority rights, the iron law of oligarchy, and the phantom of public opinion.[69] Many sin-cerely argued that democracy had run its course or, worse, in the words of Sumner, that democracy was creating "a short road to Caesarism."[70]

The critics of democracy certainly had their day. But what is less fre-quently acknowledged is the monumental response—in thought, action, and policy—to this turn-of-the-century assault on democracy. In the con-text of overwhelming evidence of crises within American democracy—from plutocratic machine politics to the disfranchisement of women to the sweeping exclusionary practices of Jim Crow and Chinese exclusion—a new democratic response was slowly but surely fashioned. Albion Small anticipated the critique of the critique when he quipped that an "attorney for absolutism" could not have presented "a more scathing indictment of democracy."[71] But it was John Dewey who spent a lifetime detailing the most complete substantive rejoinder for a new generation. Dewey's un-yielding rebuttal was rooted in the deceptively simple progressive mantra of Jane Addams, Al Smith, and so many other reformers, that "the cure for the ills of Democracy [was] more Democracy."[72] Rather than follow so many of democracy's critics down a road of liberal, legal, bureaucratic, or even aristocratic retreat, Deweyan progressives beat a path forward bent on enhancing rather than constraining *more* democracy—attempting to make modern American democracy more egalitarian, more critical, more substantive, and more public.

The progressive rejoinder began with a condemnation of aristocracy and a recommitment to democracy's most egalitarian aspirations. Dewey deemed the pretension that "history is a sound aristocracy" as "suicidal." "The aristocratic ideal" of "the elect few," he asserted, left "the many out-side the pale with no real share in the commonwealth," resulting in "the

assertion of privilege and status to the detriment of the common good."
Aristocracy worked a basic "blasphemy against personality," he argued,
while the new "democratic movement" broadened "the circle of the state" to
include every human "personality" according to the "ideal of "equality" in
which "democracy lives and moves."[73] How far was new democracy prepared to go with such an anti-aristocratic and egalitarian ideal? In theory,
all the way to a broad ethic of inclusion and nondiscrimination. At the core
of Deweyan democracy was a working faith in the potentialities "exhib-
ited in every human being irrespective of race, color, sex, birth and family,
of material or cultural wealth." Dewey held that "intolerance, abuse, calling
of names . . . because of differences of race, color, wealth, or degree of culture" were simply "treason to the democratic way of life."[74] As democracy was originally born in revolution against an old regime of monarchy,
aristocracy, and baseline social inequality, new democracy aimed to reju-
venate that revolutionary anti-aristocratic, anti-oligarchic, and equalitarian
impulse embracing every human personality.

Also true to its original roots in revolution, new democracy involved a
critical rather than a mere celebratory democracy. Morton White long ago
identified "a revolt against formalism" as a key aspect of this era's social
thought.[75] Progressives were thus well primed to go after the empty caricature of democracy in the aristocratic constitutional tradition. Dewey's "revision of the theory" of democracy began with a devastating antiformalist
critique of Sir Henry Maine auspiciously entitled "The Ethics of Democracy" (1888).[76] Dewey contended there that Maine made a mistake common
to almost all conventional treatments that considered democracy to be just
another "form" of government like monarchy or aristocracy, where the key
differences were mere matters of arithmetic: governance by the one, the few,
or the many. "To define democracy simply as the rule of the many, as sovereignty chopped up into mincemeat," Dewey held, was the product of an
"abstract and purely mechanical" formalism. Instead of viewing democracy
as a simple matter of constitutional structure, representational arithmetic,
or electoral instrumentalities, new democracy held that voting and officeholding were but tools for serving greater democratic objectives. Dewey
was emphatic on this point: "The problem of democracy was seen to be
not solved, hardly more than externally touched, by the establishment of universal suffrage and representative government." The elimination of the
monarch, the extension of the suffrage, and the institutions of popular self-
government were significant—indeed, revolutionary—political accomplishments. But "universal suffrage [and] recurring elections" were only formal
means for achieving a more complete and substantive democracy. They
were not in and of themselves "a final end and a final value." Progressive

democracy implied "something more"—something beyond the "quantitative or numerical" characteristics of "a special political form," beyond "a method of conducting government," beyond "something that took place mainly at Washington and Albany." To hold otherwise—"to erect means into the end which they serve"—was to defend an empty formalism, what Dewey ultimately deemed democratic "idolatry."[77]

So what was that "something more"—the larger element and end to be served by a new and more substantive democracy? For James Russell Lowell, Henry Carter Adams, John Dewey, and countless others, that something more was contained in a phrase that resonated throughout the period: democracy was a "way of life."[78] Deweyan progressives advocated an ends-oriented democracy that turned not just on procedural inputs but on the substantive policy outputs that more equitably and effectively secured the people's health, safety, and well-being. No mere paper democracy here. No mere formal or fugitive or phantom democracy. The "political and governmental phase of democracy," Dewey contended, was but a vehicle for "realizing ends that lie in the wide domain of human relationships and the development of human personality."[79] Democracy as a way of life implicated due regard for the welfare of each and every member of the community in the active, ongoing creation of the conditions of collective life together. As Robert Westbrook summed up this more substantive vision: "Democracy as an ethical ideal [called] upon men and women to build communities in which the necessary opportunities and resources are available for every individual to realize fully his or her particular capacities and powers through participation in political, social, and cultural life."[80] In *Democracy and Social Ethics,* Jane Addams forcefully endorsed this new perspective: democracy inhered in no "mere governmental contrivance" or "method of administration" but in nothing less than "the ultimate purpose of securing the welfare of the people."[81] All the people.

As opposed to the more conventional conflation of democracy with things like majority rule, this new capacious democratic vision was intimately bound up with social welfare and equitable governance in all aspects of a collective life democratic. And it ultimately resided in the sweeping, positive public policy-making agenda that is the subject of this book. Indeed, the proof of new democracy was in the record of public provisioning and public accomplishments that could lift all people in securing a substantively democratic way of life. New democracy thus had broad implications for political economy as institutional economists and legal-political reformers endorsed a broad program of policy reforms against economic inequality and economic domination. Social and economic inequality were not exogenous concerns to a formal electoral democratic tally; rather they were the chief problems that substantive democracy had to solve lest democratic means serve undemocratic ends. Walter Weyl's *The New Democracy* aimed directly at plutocracy and oligarchy—"our political 'bosses,' our railroad 'kings,' and our Senate 'oligarchies'"—as he assembled the case against the evils of economic want and stratification: sensational inequalities of wealth, insane extravagances, strident ostentations, wretched slums, pauperism, vice, crime, insanity, degeneration, disregard of the lives of workmen, women in dangerous factories, an industrial army created by cruel conscription, child labor, unemployment, the premature death of American babies, the ravages of "poor men's diseases," aged workingmen, the collusion of politicians, "malefactors of great wealth," hunger, crime, social vice, physical want.[82] In response, Deweyan progressives endorsed the necessity of "a democracy of wealth" wherein "all industrial relations are to be regarded as subordinate to human relations."[83] They insisted on the priority of democracy over economy, through which the power and inequality of both market and corporate systems were deemed subject to public and democratic oversight, regulation, and control.

Ultimately then, the substantive democratic end of equal and effective consideration of the welfare of all required a powerful democratic state. Prioritizing the democratic public—the demos—over and against private-sector privilege and inequality, new democracy embraced the state as an important appurtenance of democratic possibility. As Dewey's collaborator James Tufts put it in *Our Democracy,* "The finest and largest meaning of democracy is that all people should share as largely as possible in the best life. This is a view not so much about government itself as about what government is for."[84] New democracy required active governance in the service of important democratic ends—the solving of public problems, the construction of public infrastructure, the management of public resources, the provision of public services. The creation of what Graham Wallas called "the Great Society" or what John Dewey dubbed "the Great Community" required expanded public provision, public utilities, and police powers.[85] A new democratic state provided the central mechanism for the realization of greater individual and collective freedom in modern social life. In 1908, Dewey and Tufts prepared a textbook entitled *Ethics* that explicitly wedded the broad ethical vision of new democracy to the architecture of a modern administrative and regulatory state across an encyclopedia of concrete policy-making initiatives. There they defended "the moral value of the state" and its public "comprehensive laws": "The moral importance of the development of this *public* point of view, with its extensive common purposes and with a general will for maintaining them, can hardly be overestimated."[86]

A modern state joined to new ideals of substantive democracy, social welfare, and public provision was the basic vision that fueled a generation of radical reform and legal and policy transformation in this period. Modern processes and programs of democratization quickly outstripped the local, legal, and federated technologies of nineteenth-century common-law, associative, and municipal self-regulation. New democratic projects guaranteeing national citizenship, regulating industries and corporations, and policing, provisioning, and servicing a burgeoning population required the implementation and enforcement abilities of a new kind of state. The actual policy substance that resulted was specific, detailed, sprawling, and consequential. In the end, the meaning and purchase of new democracy inhabited the massive changes in constitution, policy, law, economy, and society documented in the following chapters of this book. The modern crisis of democracy was met with more than words. It was met with a cascade of social and political action reworking the American democratic system from top to bottom. The six substantive chapters that follow attempt to capture the historic content and achievements of that new democracy across the public law fields of modern citizenship, police power, public utility, social legislation, antimonopoly, and administration. Together they convey something of the general trajectory of the self-conscious American effort to reinvent and recreate democracy and statecraft at the turn of the twentieth century. John Dewey viewed this as nothing less than a second American Revolution. Walter Weyl deemed it an equally radical and revolutionary undertaking: "It [was] a new spirit, critical, concrete, insurgent." Out of a crisis of democracy challenging the relevance of all our "old-time" ideals, Weyl observed, "a new democracy" was born.[87]

New Democracy: Aspirations and Limitations

The period from 1866 to 1932 is famous for some notable procedural democratic reforms: initiative and referendum, campaign finance and lobbying regulation, the direct election of senators, women's suffrage. But, of course, the period is even more infamous for egregiously antidemocratic catastrophes like disfranchisement, racial segregation, Chinese exclusion, a war on Indigenous peoples, imperialism, and eugenics. The title of this book, *New Democracy*, should not be mistaken for a normative argument about the ultimate actualization or realization of a democratic ideal in this period. Rather, more empirically, descriptively, and historically, the aim is to chart the rise and significance of the lasting mechanisms and technologies of law, state, and policy that transformed democratic governance in this historic period. As will be seen in the close examination of particular areas of social and economic legislation and regulation, frequently those new instrumentalities were harnessed for initiatives that reflected Dewey's and Addams's ambitions to realize greater opportunity and to extend public goods and services to more people than ever before. But as will also be seen in chapters on the limitations of citizenship and the invention of social police, there was no guarantee that those technologies could not also be used for distinctly less salutary or antidemocratic ends. Increased state capacity brought unprecedented opportunities for both inclusion and exclusion, social welfare and social discipline, public provision and private expropriation— a new democracy or a new despotism. New democracy involved an always unfinished aspiration rather than a final realization. Democracy is an unfinished history. As John Dewey put it, the democratic state "must always be rediscovered."[88]

Indeed, it is against the backdrop of the terrible limitations and exclusionary practices of this historical era that something of the radicalness of the agenda of new democracy stands out in stark relief. In contrast to ideological accounts that only see in progressivism either a "road to eugenics" or a "triumph of conservatism," this book hopes to recover a more complex historical reality and a rather audacious horizon of possibility.[89] The word "progressivism" does not do justice to the radicalness and range of the reforms and causes discussed in this book between Reconstruction and the New Deal: four new amendments to the Constitution, the invention of the public utility idea, modern antimonopoly, workers' compensation and social insurance, the invention of the modern independent regulatory commission (the Interstate Commerce Commission, Federal Reserve Board, Federal Trade Commission, US Shipping Board, Federal Power Commission, Federal Radio Commission), and simply innumerable transformations in state and local public policy making. In 1887, Florence Kelley translated Friedrich Engels's *The Condition of the Working Class in England* into English, and Engels added this: "We find in America the same struggles for a shorter working-day, for a legal limitation of the working time, especially of women and children in factories; we find the truck-system in full blossom, and the cottage-system, in rural districts, made use of by the 'bosses' as a means of domination over workers."[90] In 1909 after the Springfield Race Riot, a "call" was made for a Lincoln Emancipation Conference "to discuss Means for Securing Political and Civil Equality for the Negro." The call would ultimately lead to the formation of the NAACP. There were sixty original signatories—a unique coalition of white progressives, Black activists, secular and religious leaders, men and women. In addition to W. E. B. Du Bois and Ida B. Wells, signatories included Jane Addams, Ray Stannard

Baker, John Dewey, Florence Kelley, Lincoln Steffens, Lillian Wald, Brand Whitlock, Mary Drier, and Frances Kellor. A similar coalition of diverse reformers would band together after World War I to oppose the wartime excesses of the Woodrow Wilson administration and to lead the American Civil Liberties Union (ACLU). In 1930, ACLU officers Jane Addams, Sophonisba Breckinridge, Crystal Eastman, Felix Frankfurter, Fred Howe, Harold Laski, Scott Nearing, Ernst Freund, Julia Lathrop, and Peter Witt, among others, were included in a US House "Investigation of Communist Propaganda."[91]

It is a conceit of this book that we have only begun to uncover the radical potentialities of progressive social democracy during a historical era when so much was working against it. Modern democracy is ever a historical work in progress under the clear and present danger that the demos can always be undone.[92] The modern public and its enormous problems, ongoing challenges, and sometimes overwhelming limitations are the never-ending workshop of historical democracy. There is no assurance of ultimate achievement or final realization, only the historical necessity of moving imperfectly forward to ever new beginnings. New democracy began its own difficult history with nothing less than the legacy of slavery, the problem of racial inclusion, and the constitutional invention of a new American citizenship.

1

CITIZENSHIP

The Origins of Modern American Constitutionalism

The question of citizenship strikes deeper;
deny a man this, and his personal rights are not safe.
—WILLIAM YATES

Modern American history begins with the abolition of the slaveholders' constitution. Had the Confederacy won the Civil War or had the Southern states (or select sections, groups, or individuals) been able to maintain their peculiarly inegalitarian sovereignty over a bonded people, it becomes difficult to imagine the emergence of a distinctly modern United States. History matters.

The abolition of a sectionalist, slaveholding constitution was no mean feat. Indeed, in terms of its historic scope and significance, it surpassed the Union military victory in war. It is, after all, one thing to physically defeat an enemy in battle, or to occupy another's ground, or even to cut off the king's head, but it is quite another thing to actually extinguish an old social, economic, and constitutional regime. Yet that is precisely what happened in the United States in the second half of the nineteenth century—one way of life (just as much Northern as Southern) surrendered to another. This great transformation was not the product of subterranean sociocultural forces or teleological processes of modernization. Rather, to a surprising extent, it was the consequence of a quite self-conscious and systematic deconstruction of the central pillars of the old regime. Politics matters.

A new American democratic state was consciously reconstructed on foundations that radically separated it from things "antebellum." The first American Revolution was now clearly over. As Abraham Lincoln prophesied in Peoria in 1854, "Our republican robe is soiled, and trailed in the dust. Let us repurify it. Let us turn and wash it white, in the spirit, if not the blood, of the Revolution."[1] Revolutionary ideal and antebellum actuality had clashed. And out of a deeply fraught past, there emerged a modern future for the United States.

As Alexis de Tocqueville recognized long ago about even the most revolutionary of events, countless particular continuities are always detectable within the stream of change that accompanies historical transformation. It is no more possible for nations than for individuals to wholly "obliterate their former selves . . . to make, as it were a scission in their life line and to create an unbridgeable gulf between all they had hitherto been and all they now aspired to be."[2] But despite always present historical continuities and recrudescences, there are moments in historical time when conceptually and symbolically, as much as practically and instrumentally, the terms of debate shift; where the way people make sense of their lives and the way communities derive meaning from their collective histories breaks through the hard crust of habit, custom, experience, and tradition with special ferocity. And there is no going back. The era of Civil War, emancipation, and Reconstruction was one such historical time.

Indeed, one of the most uncontroversial and widely accepted ideas in American history is the notion that the Civil War marked a fundamental transformation in American law, politics, society, and economy. Sometimes referred to as the "Second American Revolution," the Civil War was a total event—a primal struggle—that has cast a shadow over American history and life second only to the influence of the French Revolution on the subsequent history and politics of France.[3] On one side of the great divide marked by the Civil War, an uncertain, conflicted land of small, self-governing localities and decentralized economic and political rivalries still predominated. On the other side arose a bewildering new world of large cities, mass society, unprecedented economic consolidation, and new national political direction—the beginnings of modern times. The historian George Ticknor testified in 1869 that the war's effects created "a great gulf between what happened before it in our century and what has happened since." He captured the common sense of enormous rupture on the ground when he concluded, "It does not seem to me as if I were living in the country in which I was born."[4]

Three dramatic and interrelated changes in American public life were particularly salient. First, the Civil War conclusively settled the issue of secession. States, groups, or other civil subdivisions of the country could not secede from the Union. States' rights and sectionalist interpretations of the nature of the American Constitution distinctly lost. American governing traditions of local autonomy, popular sovereignty, and federalism could no longer be stretched so far as to include the power to secede from the Union. It is easy to overlook the far-reaching implications of that simple resolution. For secession not only threatened the American nation in terms of territoriality, geographical unity, and natural resources; it posed fundamental questions about the constitutional foundation of the polity as a whole. Delegitimizing the act of secession (and the constitutional conventions through which Southern states seceded) established clear limits to voluntarism and local self-government in the United States.[5] Ruling out the possibility of secession was a major victory for the forces of union and the consolidation of American law-making authority. It marked the beginnings of an ascendant nationalism in the United States.

The second decisive transformation that resulted directly from the Civil War was the simpler but even more profound proposition that it was no longer legal or constitutional in the United States to enslave people—to claim another human being as one's own property. Slavery was abolished, and a significant portion of the American population was dramatically released from bondage. Again, it is worth underscoring the obvious wider ramifications of this historic act of abolition. Just as the abolition of secession reworked traditional American conceptions of governing powers, the abolition of slavery transformed existing American notions of rights. Indeed, the legal end of slavery involved the recognition of a new foundational right—a right in all persons to be free from direct bondage. Such a kind of right was something surprisingly rare in American history to this point—a new and absolute right; a right, in principle, without any limitations; a prohibition without any exceptions.[6] This was a right applicable to all people in the United States regardless of race, gender, status, class, or state action—a right that limited federal and state governments as well as private actors, associations, and institutions. The right not to be enslaved thus joined a fairly restricted pantheon of absolute and universal prohibitions in American public and private law. The right was extended to more people than had ever before been contemplated as within the same rights-bearing public. The abolition of slavery thus launched a momentous change in established American notions of freedom, rights, and liberties. It marked the beginnings of a new era of modern rights consciousness.

Finally, there is also a consensus that the Civil War initiated some important changes in a third area of American public life—the US Constitution itself. From the immediate postwar treatises of Sidney George Fisher, John Alexander Jameson, and Orestes Brownson to the most recent histories of Eric Foner, Bruce Ackerman, and Akhil Amar, public law scholarship has remained remarkably consistent on the role of the Civil War in fundamentally reshaping the terms of the original American constitutional settlement.[7] Most transparently, the Civil War and its aftermath added three new and transformative amendments to the nation's original founding document—the first amendments since the earliest years of the republic. Though the substantive legal implications of the Thirteenth, Fourteenth, and Fifteenth Amendments have been the subject of over a century of debate and interpretation, there is no argument that they profoundly changed the American legal-political landscape. Charles Merriam understood the import of altering the founding document: "For two generations the Constitution remained unamended, and finally came to be considered an end in itself instead of a means, a thing in itself, rather than an instrument designed for a purpose, a terminus rather than a starting point." The Civil War forever changed this dynamic.[8] A new, active American constitutionalism—what Harold Hyman dubbed an "adequate constitution"—became a bold new source of legal innovation and public legitimacy.[9] As the new amendments seemed to indicate, this was a law more public, more democratic, more instrumental, and more connected to the development of the modern nation state than the settled, judge-made principles of an ancient common-law tradition. Indeed, the formal amendment of the original constitutional settlement was but the initial step in a broader legal reconstitution of the nation as a whole—as great changes in constitutionalism gave way to even broader transformations in legislation, regulation, administration, police power, public utility, and public service. What Robert Kaczorowski described as the constitutional effort to "begin the nation anew" was but the inauguration of this larger revolution in American public law.[10]

Though these changes seem simple and self-evident, together they initiated a great transformation in the overall nature, power, and reach of American governance. They ushered in a new era in the history of the American state—a new governmental regime. The defense of the national union, the advancement of new rights against enslavement (and other badges and incidents of servitude), and the amendment of the original constitutional charter together redefined the general relationship of government to the governed and created a new foundation for positive American economic and social policy making. Indeed, within these commonly accepted indicators of sociolegal change, one can detect the first outlines of the emergence of a modern democratic state in the United States. Nationalism, rights, and constitutionalism triumphed over older, competing ideals—namely, sectionalism, local self-government, and the private ordering principles of common law. For the first time, the American polity was organized around recognizably modern categories: a modern state with increasingly plenary forms of governing power addressing national citizens possessed of more generalized socioeconomic needs as well as new legal-constitutional rights. Importantly, the expansion of new state powers and new constitutional rights were simultaneous and complementary developments in this historic era. Though it is common in political theory to think of public power and private right as unalterably opposed forces in a zero-sum game, the fact of the matter is that power and rights grew up inextricably bound together in the creation of a modern American democratic state. The Civil War, emancipation, and Reconstruction forged a new constitutional relationship between the individual and the state in which unmistakable increases in state power accompanied unprecedented extensions of public policies as well as public rights.[11] This new constitutional dialectic of power and liberty, state and citizen, policy and right set up the main dynamic of modern American public law for the next 150 years.

Now, obviously, the myriad of meanings, manifestations, and implications of this constitutional revolution spilled out rapidly in every conceivable direction. But one especially good place to begin to take stock of the scale and scope of this revolution is the transformation in American citizenship inaugurated by the Civil War and Reconstruction. A new concept of the rights of national citizens protected by the revised constitutionalism of the Fourteenth Amendment, and for the moment an equally assertive Reconstruction Congress, was one of the building blocks of the new American state. The question of citizenship per se became a focal point for first working through the implications of postbellum changes in nation, citizen, constitution, power, and rights. The making of modern American citizenship is thus a perfect place to witness the beginnings of a transformation from one governmental regime to another.

Indeed, understood in broad historical and philosophical context, the citizenship struggles of the nineteenth century raised in incipient form most of the crucial issues confronting modernizing democratic states. At the top of that list were contests over the very content and meaning of political equality and the measure of social inclusion and exclusion. Citizenship, after all, entailed more than a bundle of mechanical political privileges like voting, officeholding, or jury service (things all too frequently denied many citizens in the nineteenth century). As William Yates contended as early as 1838 in his remarkable treatise *Rights of Colored Men to Suffrage, Citizenship and Trial by Jury,* "citizenship strikes deeper."[12] As a crucial site in the larger struggle for political equality and social inclusion in the wake of democratic revolution, citizenship involved a new kind of right— a threshold, constitutive right to be considered an equal and relevant member of the body politic. For Pierre Rosanvallon, democratic political citizenship produced a "revolution in equality," creating an "unprecedented relation between persons" and "a new social relation" in democratic states—reconstructing society itself.[13] The formal assertion of the political "equivalence of individuals" in constitutional vehicles like the Fourteenth Amendment produced an expanded vision of the demos thoroughly implicating the underlying socioeconomic relations linking individuals as citizens and as Americans. Democracy matters.

Since T. H. Marshall's influential essay "Citizenship and Social Class," it has become common to think about modern citizenship as evolutionary and mechanical, featuring the gradual, stage-by-stage accretion of civil, political, and, finally, socioeconomic rights.[14] In the United States, however, the making of modern citizenship involved a radical extension of the concept of equal rights across civil, political, and socioeconomic fields. Modern American citizenship established a new scale of generality for imagining the purview of state power as new national claims challenged the particularized, sectional prerogatives of old. Sectionalism has been defined as the "restriction of interest to a narrow sphere" or "undue concern with local interests or petty distinctions at the expense of general well-being."[15] The postwar retreat of just such a sectionalized notion of local, particular, and exceedingly divergent citizenships created a new generalized vision of society and body politic as well as a new national imaginary for thinking about inclusion, participation, equal treatment, and nondiscrimination. In contrast to Marshall's stage theory, the making of modern American citizenship featured the simultaneous renegotiation of civil, political, and even socioeconomic and redistributive rights, from the aspiration of the Freedmen's Bureau bills to the reform of poor law administration. Modern American citizenship was the entering wedge of a broader vision of general welfare that transformed the American state and its subsequent history.

Now of course, as demonstrated by a series of recent histories, the real, practical, and legal gains of modern American citizenship on the ground in this historical period were modest and all too frequently restricted, distorted, rolled back, and denied. Long before the infamous constitutional retreats of the *Slaughter-House Cases, Bradwell v. State of Illinois, United States v. Cruikshank,* the *Civil Rights Cases,* and *Plessy v. Ferguson,* the former Confederate general Robert V. Richardson perhaps anticipated as much when he mused in 1865, "The emancipated slaves own nothing, because nothing but freedom has been given to them."[16] A multitude of discrete and insular minorities would continue to bear the badges and incidences of discrimination, domination, and servitude, perhaps justifying a more pessimistic and tragic reading of Fourteenth Amendment citizenship as a false promise or an empty formalism. Indeed, Bethany Berger, Maggie Blackhawk, and Ian Haney López have persuasively established the real limits of this postwar revolution in citizenship law—describing in detail how a "potential emancipatory moment" for Native peoples and people of color also "laid the groundwork for future patterns of subordination."[17]

Recognizing these historic and sometimes calamitous consequences, a new vehicle of national citizenship was nonetheless forcefully created in this period, and it had immediate public policy consequences across the disparate fields of civil rights, national administration, and even social-welfare policy making. It propelled a new relation between the state and the citizen as well as between citizens themselves that ultimately transformed earlier American habits and traditions of governance and statecraft. Modern American citizenship inaugurated nothing less than a new horizon for social and political transformation and a still unfinished democratic aspiration for national inclusion and belonging.

But though a modern conception of citizenship arrived in the United States in the context of Civil War and radical Reconstruction, it would be a mistake to view it as a completely unanticipated departure. To the contrary, the concrete fight for national citizenship stretched across the long nineteenth century, from the American Revolution to this second American Revolution. It was the conscious object of social and political struggle at the grassroots as well as in the formal halls of governance. As Hannah Arendt reminded us, "Equality, in contrast to all that is involved in mere existence, is not given us, but is the result of human organization insofar as it is guided by the principle of justice. We are not born equal; we become equal as members of a group on the strength of our decision to guarantee ourselves mutually equal rights."[18] Nineteenth-century Americans were neither born free nor the natural heirs of some kind of democratic equality of condition. Rather, they became modern citizens through intense political struggle and momentous historical change.[19] As Kate Masur, Martha Jones, and Rebecca Scott have most recently reminded us, citizenship in the nineteenth century was a concept under construction—a distinctively constructed as well as constructive right, rooted in the contested equality claims that ultimately redefined the collective interrelationship of all citizens in a modern American state.[20]

The historical "lesson of the concept," as Hegel put it, was that it was "only when actuality has reached maturity that the ideal appears opposite the real and reconstructs this real world."[21] With respect to the concept of citizenship, something like that is the story behind the Fourteenth Amendment. Its formal, constitutional creation of "citizens of the United States" provided a new ideal. But it was simultaneously the culmination of a much longer and contentious actual American history. This owl of Minerva, in other words, flew only at dusk.

The Limits of Antebellum Citizenship

Though modern Americans are very much products of the Fourteenth Amendment's new beginning, there is still a prevailing tendency to view national citizenship rights as having always been there—naturally coincident with the origins of the republic. In contrast to Arendt's understanding of equality as made rather than found, human artifice rather than beneficent nature, Louis Hartz contended that Americans were simply "born equal." Hartz's idea of a single "liberal tradition" in America began with Tocqueville's observation: "The great advantage of the Americans is, that they have arrived at a state of democracy without having to endure a democratic revolution; and that they are born equal, instead of becoming so."[22] Even historians more attuned to conflict over consensus have sometimes placed the origin of modern citizenship somewhere near the American founding. Rogers Smith posited a set of "citizenship laws . . . crafted by political elites" since the Revolution that formed a consistent and coherent national law of constitutional identity regulating the rights claims of citizens.[23] With an important emphasis on obligations as well as rights of citizens, Linda Kerber too has argued for the early development of a modern citizenship framework: "Modern citizenship was created as part of the new political order courageously constructed in the era of the American Revolution. Reaching back to the Greeks and reinventing what they discovered, the founding generation produced a new and reciprocal relationship between state and citizen."[24]

Some difficulties, however, confront the conception of modern citizenship as a clean, central ordering principle of American law from the beginning. For one thing, early nineteenth-century Americans were in the process of constituting a new governmental regime in which they wrote endlessly about first principles of American government and constitutionalism—from formal charters, declarations, and constitutions, to the extensive commentaries of Federalists and Anti-Federalists, to an extraordinary legal and political treatise tradition covering almost every corner of American private and public law. And yet the fact of the matter is that before *Dred Scott* and the Civil War, national citizenship did not figure as a particularly significant part of that formal discussion of American public law. Indeed, national citizenship per se is one of the puzzling absences—nonbarking dogs—in early American public law writing.[25]

From the beginning, in fact, the idea of citizenship was deployed rather loosely and indiscriminately even in official constitutional documents. Notably, article 4 of the Articles of Confederation was the important founding statement of the privileges and immunities of "citizens." But the language of that charter was classically elusive: "The free inhabitants of each of these states, paupers, vagabonds, and fugitives from Justice excepted, shall be entitled to all privileges and immunities of free citizens in the several states; and the people of each state . . . shall enjoy therein all the privileges of trade and commerce, subject to the same duties, impositions, and restrictions, as the inhabitants thereof respectively."[26] As James Madison noted in *Federalist* no. 42, "There is a confusion of language here which is remarkable." Not only did article 4 establish a national tradition of deference to the states on the substantive content of citizenship, but the loose interchangeability of the terms "free inhabitants" and "free citizens," "people" and "inhabitants," opened the peculiar possibility that aliens (but "free inhabitants") of one state might be entitled to the privileges of citizens (thus being practically "naturalized") in another.[27] The ambiguous language of the Articles of Confederation was an early indicator that citizenship was not yet the fundamental test of freedom and unfreedom in the early United States.

Even at this early stage, however, American citizenship was already a concept under contested construction. George Bancroft detected a principle of "inter-citizenship" in article 4 that gave "reality to the union": "Inter-citizenship and mutual equality of rights between all its members gave to it a new character and enduring unity. . . . The Americans became not only one people, but one nation."[28] But not all Americans agreed. Indeed, even under the Articles of Confederation, the crucial issue that would dominate the antebellum citizenship struggle to *Dred Scott* and Civil War was already joined. South Carolina had originally objected to article 4, proposing to limit such privileges and immunities of intercitizenship to *whites only*. William Henry Drayton argued in 1778 that article 4 was "absolutely inadmissible": "I think there ought to be no doubt, but that the free inhabitants" entitled to such privileges and immunities "should be white."[29] South Carolina formally moved to add the word "white" after "free" in article 4, but such amendment was rejected by eleven of the thirteen states. In his argument in *Lemmon v. People* (1860), the attorney Joseph Blunt viewed this particular outcome as evidence of an early and broad equal citizenship commitment: "It therefore appears that 11 out of the original 13 States recognized no distinction between free blacks and free whites. The conclusion is therefore clear that at the era of the Revolution free negroes were deemed citizens."[30]

Thus already in the contest over the reach of citizenship under the Articles of Confederation, we get a template for the entire nineteenth-century citizenship debate. In formal legal usage, the concept was analytically and conceptually ambiguous. There was no clear consensus about what citizenship generally meant as this founding application of privileges and immunities moved rather indiscriminately between states, citizens, persons, and inhabitants. Despite this conceptual opacity, however, the portentous debate was also clearly joined between forces like those in South Carolina hoping to constitutionalize an unequal, exclusionary, and racist vision linking citizenship rights exclusively to whiteness and forces exemplified by Bancroft and Blunt just as determined to make sure that the aspiration for a more egalitarian, inclusive, and national citizenship persisted as a legal-historical possibility.

Ambiguity and tension accompanied this formative citizenship debate into the Constitutional Convention. At Philadelphia, the US Constitution transcended the Confederation's preference for talking in terms of "people of the different States" and "people of each State" with its bold preambulatory "We the People of the United States." "Citizens of the United States," however, was a different matter—still very much a work in progress. Despite added rigor and power in establishing a new nation, the US Constitution did not overly rely on a national citizenship concept to ground its elaborate structure of powers, limitations, and rights. Congress was granted the authority to establish a uniform law of naturalization, and citizenship was also cited three times as a prerequisite for federal office, including the requirement that the president of the United States be a "natural born citizen." Diversity of state citizenship also became a constitutional cornerstone for the jurisdiction of federal courts. But after those important stipulations, substantive discussion of citizenship was once again limited to the issue of interstate comity. Article 4, section 2 did establish a more precise citizen-to-citizen relationship concerning the different states—"the citizens of each state shall be entitled to all privileges and immunities of citizens in the several states"—in which Alexander Hamilton rooted the esteemed "basis of the Union" as opposed to Confederation.[31] But, like the articles, the Constitution provided no further formal definition of citizenship, no listing of the privileges and immunities of citizens, nor even an express description of the relationship between national and state citizenship. All that could be immediately derived from the revised privileges and immunities clause was that citizens of different states should not be made aliens to one another—that is, that out-of-state citizens were entitled to all of the state citizenship protections of in-state citizens. The Constitutional Convention again blunted South Carolina's preference for an explicitly racialized comity clause but yielded little more substance on the privileges and immunities of citizens.[32] As Alexander Bickel concluded, "The concept of citizenship play[ed] only the most minimal role in the American constitutional scheme. . . . The original Constitution . . . held itself out as bound by certain standards of conduct in its relations with people and persons, not with some legal construct called citizen."[33] As if to underscore the preamble's "We the People," the Bill of Rights was not constructed around the explicit language of "citizen" but the rights of "people," "persons," "owners," and even "the accused."[34]

So too in the extraordinary legal treatises that dominated early American political and constitutional discourse, the idea of citizenship remained a concept under development. Though William Blackstone famously devoted the first book of his *Commentaries on the Laws of England* (1765–1769) to the "Rights of Persons," the concept of citizenship was not predominant. It was the "natural-born subject," not the national citizen, that was the focus of Blackstone's inquiry, involving not a discussion of individual *right* but of political jurisdiction and the *duty* of ligeance: "Allegiance is the tie, or *ligamen*, which binds the subject to the king, in return for that protection which the king affords the subject."[35] Leading early American treatises more routinely embraced the language of citizen over subject, but like the original constitutional discussion, they offered comparatively little substantive elaboration. Joseph Story's *Commentaries on the Constitution* (1833) mustered the definitional truism: "Every citizen of a state is, *ipso facto,* a citizen of the United States. And a person, who is a naturalized citizen of the United States, by a like residence in any state in the Union, becomes, *ipso facto*, a citizen of that state."[36] The "American Blackstone" James Kent provided more substance on the stakes of citizenship in a discussion of aliens in his *Commentaries on American Law* (1826). But that formative text only reinforced the sense that one must look well beyond national citizenship to really understand the basic substantive rights and duties, privileges and penalties, and inclusions and exclusions involved in early American public life. Kent enumerated a series of real disabilities affecting noncitizens as aliens, including the inability "to have a stable freehold interest in land, or to hold any civil office, or vote at elections, or take any active share in the administration of the government."[37] While such disabilities were serious, of course, many of them also applied to certain classes of citizens in antebellum America, particularly married women and free persons of color. Moreover, many of the particular disabilities of alienage could be (and frequently were) overridden by special or general state statute.[38]

Frequent public law references to citizenship as primarily a matter for individual states and for national comity suggest the difficulty of importing modern assumptions about citizenship rights into early American history. Federalism and localism wreaked havoc on the substantive articulation of a coherent conception of national citizenship rights. Consequently most rights, duties, privileges, and immunities remained products of a complicated recipe of federalism, sectionalism, state differentiation, jurisdictional preference, and local control. As a national matter, the exact nature of privileges and immunities was left largely unspecified. In *Connor v. Elliott* (1856), the US Supreme Court explicitly refused to describe and define such privileges and immunities, preferring a slow, case-by-case elaboration. In classic dicta in the case of *Corfield v. Coryell* (1823), Justice Bushrod Washington produced the most explicit, extensive, and oft-cited enumeration of "the privileges and immunities of citizens in the several states."[39] He did so, however, in the context of upholding a New Jersey statute that granted the exclusive right to take oysters from state waters only to New Jersey residents: "We cannot accede to the proposition . . . that, under this provision of the constitution, the citizens of the several states are permitted to participate in all the rights which belong exclusively to the citizens of any other particular state, merely upon the ground that they are enjoyed by those citizens."[40]

The early American law of citizenship thus remained profoundly disparate and diverse—a law of multiple and competing jurisdictions. As Chancellor Kent noted, "The privileges thus conferred are local and necessarily territorial in their nature. The laws and usages of one state cannot be permitted to prescribe qualifications for citizens, to be claimed and exercised in other states, in contravention to their local polity."[41] But even such jurisdictional multiplicity did not fully capture just how segmented and confused rights claims remained in the early nineteenth century. Below the level of state statutes and constitutional provisions, most American rights and obligations remained products of local governments, associations, and courts elaborating highly differentiated local bylaws and common-law rules of status, membership, and association. The sectional, local, and common-law nature of nineteenth-century American rule precluded the emergence of a more universal or uniform conception of citizenship rights. Strangely and rather notoriously in this period, many noncitizens (primarily white and male noncitizens) ended up enjoying far more rights, entitlements, privileges, and immunities (ranging from voting to property ownership to the right to sue and be sued to procedural due process) than a great many citizens of the United States (especially married women and free persons of color). So what exactly does it mean to deploy the category of citizenship to talk about things enjoyed by noncitizens and denied certain citizens? Occam's razor suggests that such things were not primarily matters of citizenship.

Hence, a preliminary examination of the formal constitutional definitions of early American citizenship ends up much where Attorney General Edward Bates did in his famous 1862 opinion on citizenship on the cusp of the modern era:

> Who is a citizen? What constitutes a citizen of the United States? I have often been pained by the fruitless search in our law books and the records of our courts for a clear and satisfactory definition of the phrase citizen of the United States. I find no such definition, no authoritative establishment of the meaning of the phrase, neither by course of judicial decision in our courts nor by the continued and consentaneous action of the different branches of our political government. For aught I see to the contrary, the subject is now as little understood in its details and elements, and the question as open to argument and to speculative criticism as it was at the beginning of the government. Eighty years of practical enjoyment of citizenship, under the Constitution, have not sufficed to teach us either the exact meaning of the word or the constituent elements of the thing we prize so highly.[42]

Of course, there was a simple reason for this fundamental ambiguity baked into the core of antebellum American citizenship law. That is, despite the aspirations or pretensions to national equality voiced in formal political documents like the Declaration of Independence or the constitutional penumbras of privileges and immunities, early American states and localities were in the constant habit of using their local police powers to pass discriminatory laws differentiating their populations along nearly every conceivable social status: religion, ethnicity, race, gender, age, disability, domicile, and poverty. These laws determined who was included and who was excluded, who was welcomed and who was removed, who received privileges and properties and whose lives were marked for expropriation and subordination.

Inequality, Race, and the Limits of Antebellum Police Power

Much history and theory treats the concept of citizenship as the dominant on-off test of modern liberty and inclusion—a unified, universal, and unidirectional marker of the line between freedom and unfreedom. But a fundamentally different understanding pervaded early American public life, where a regime of extraordinary particularity, differentiation, and discrimination predominated. In place of the clear, top-down constitutional enumeration of the rights and responsibilities of citizens in a nation-state, early American law was instead replete with an ambiguous, bottom-up amalgam of state, local, group, and common-law rules, practices, and bylaws that treated early Americans with anything but an undifferentiated or generalized egalitarianism. In *The People's Welfare,* I dubbed this antebellum regime a "well-regulated society"—a society oriented primarily around the concrete practices of local and associational self-governance at the expense of the kind of universal abstract rights near the core of the modern citizenship concept.[43] Here, in place of citizenship rights, social, economic, and political liberty still had much in common with Benjamin Constant's conception of "the liberty of the ancients": featuring (a) the "subjection of the individual to the will of the community," (b) "private actions submitted to a severe surveillance," and (c) "hardly anything that the laws did not regulate."[44]

In place of modern citizenship rights, three alternative features of this early American legal regime were particularly salient: status, membership, and local police power. The web of relations, identities, and issues that converged around early American practices of status, membership, and police power formed a dense and variegated legal history in which questions of rights and powers and issues of inclusion (entry) and exclusion (exit) were constantly debated and decided. Together, status, membership, and local police power determined much about who was inside and who was outside in early American law—who exercised power and whom power was exercised upon; who enjoyed legal immunities and rights and who was legally exposed to a world of "no-law" where violence and coercion remained peculiarly sovereign. The power and persistence of this antebellum regime formed an important backdrop for understanding the reconstruction of modern citizenship in the postbellum period. And it legally underwrote the racial, gender, class, and other status hierarchies that would ultimately inspire future constitutional amendments, social movements, and democratic reforms.

Despite Henry Maine's famous prognostication about a single transformative shift from status to contract, personal status remained an important barometer of rights and obligations in early American law.[45] Though both William Blackstone and James Kent began their commentaries on English and American law with abstract encomiums to the "absolute rights of persons," the vast majority of their tracts was devoted to articulating the rights and duties of persons as they stood in "civil and domestic" relation to one another.[46] Here, the status of citizen, native, alien, or denizen was merely one status among many, and a person's actual bundle of rights, privileges, and immunities was dependent on a host of divergent social positions, political offices, legal jurisdictions, and civic identities as well as differentiated patterns of residence, jurisdiction, service, association, family, age, gender, race, and capacity. Chancellor Kent organized his understanding of the legal "rights of persons" around classic status relationships: husband and wife, parent and child, guardian and ward, master and servant, infants, and corporations. One can get a preliminary idea of the severe differentiation of this hierarchical system by simply comparing the privileges of masters (service) or parents (discipline) to the disabilities of wives (coverture) or servants (bondage). The legal status of slave, Kent's first subdivision of servants, rendered one virtually rightless. In Kent's words: "In contemplation of their laws, slaves are considered . . . as things or property, rather than persons, and are vendible as personal estate. They cannot take property by descent or purchase, and all they find, and all they hold, belongs to the master. They cannot make lawful contracts, and they are deprived of civil rights." At the other end of the spectrum, the legal status of a corporation as an artificial person brought such extraordinary privileges as the right

1. to have perpetual succession;
2. to sue and be sued, and to grant and to receive by their corporate name;
3. to purchase and hold lands and chattels;
4. to have a common seal;
5. to make bylaws for the government of the corporation; and
6. to remove members.

Kent's short list of primary statuses provided but a sampling of the range of rights deprivation possible at the extreme ends of the legal status spectrum. Other nineteenth-century legal treatises highlighted a wide range of legal statuses of dependency and disability from Florien Giauque's *Ohio Manual for Guardians and Trustees of Minors, Insane Persons, Imbeciles, Drunkards* to Carl Knapp's *Treatise on the Laws of the State of New York Relative to the Poor, Insane, Idiots, and Habitual Drunkards* (which also covered the treatment of paupers, tramps, vagrants, abandoned children, lunatics, the blind, and deaf mutes).[47] In contrast to the idea of national citizenship rights determining personal status in early America, such categories suggest that the relationship worked the other way around—that legal status was still a principal determiner of early American legal rights and duties.[48] As a myriad of sociolegal histories on labor, slavery, race, marriage, gender relations, and the poor law have now corroborated, social status remained the key marker of individual possibility and penalty in early America, irrespective of formal citizenship concerns.[49]

The law of personal status was fundamentally about membership, describing the relational rights and duties of persons as members of the multiple constituent subdivisions of local self-governing communities— membership in a public office, a church, a household, a family, an association, or a corporation. Early American law doled out legal privileges and immunities in accordance with membership in a dizzying array of lesser subgroups and affiliations, from the law of agency, partnership, and contract to the laws governing membership in voluntary associations, churches, unions, and corporations to the laws governing participation in towns, municipalities, and political parties.[50] Legal membership in and exclusion from such a range of differentiated self-governing associations determined one's bundle of privileges, obligations, and immunities much more than the abstract and underdeveloped constitutional category of national citizenship.[51] One effect of this distributed and particularized regime of local and associational membership and self-governance was to make the issue of a person's actual bundle of rights and duties the product of a complicated and varied tally of the rules, regulations, and bylaws of the host of differentiated associations to which one belonged. Such local self-governance through intermediary associations frequently involved extensive delegations of public regulatory power to such subsidiary institutions and organizations. And all too frequently, it included the power for localities and associations to discriminate and exclude as well as to inequitably police substantive rights and privileges. Indeed, a crucial ingredient in the persistence of the law of personal status and membership—and a key indicator of the historic limits of early American citizenship—was the discriminatory exercise of local and state police power.

Police power involved the rather far-reaching power of the body politic to regulate liberty, property, status, and numerous other capacities and interests in the pursuit of public safety, health, morals, comfort, and welfare. Notably in antebellum America, such omnibus power was vested in the states rather than the national government and was frequently delegated to further local and subsidiary bodies. Early American iterations of police power thus involved a wide, discretionary authority that controlled a great deal of the actual "working and paying and living and dying" in early American communities.[52] The history of antebellum police power was highly particularized and often discriminatory. Indeed, one of the key characteristics of early American police regulation was the way it assembled or segregated, included or excluded, emancipated or bonded the relevant public or demos. Examples were legion, from the way in which discrete economic inequalities shaped the administration of the poor law to the way in which religion factored into Sunday laws and blasphemy prosecutions to the way gender and sexuality continuously inflected the policing of morality to the way in which race and ethnicity permeated the early development of public health regulation. Indeed, just such particularities of religion, class, gender, ethnicity, and race found their way into the very foundation of the police power regime, as indictments for violating local police regulations frequently hinged on the particular delineation of just such categories: "old and young, male and female, black and white, by night and day."[53]

It would take a separate volume to fully address the complicated relationship of local police power to the general problem of social inequality in early America, from the operation of the local poor law to "the coercive structure of American slave law."[54] For current purposes, three paradigmatic cases must suffice to illustrate the intertwined roles of status, membership, and police power in reproducing the distinctly limited nature of citizenship rights in early American democracy. In *Barron v. Baltimore* (1833), Chief Justice John Marshall upheld the public works powers of the city of Baltimore to regulate harbors and streets for the health of the community even though they diverted water from John Barron's wharf, leaving it essentially unusable. Barron made a fundamental rights claim, arguing that "the liberty of the citizen" was protected against such governmental intervention by the Constitution's Fifth Amendment, prohibiting "the taking of private property for public use, without just compensation." Despite his reputed solicitousness for national power as well as rights of property and contract, Marshall made short order of this national rights claim. "The Constitution was ordained and established by the people of the United States for themselves," he argued, "and not for the government of the individual states." Consequently, the Fifth Amendment applied "solely as a limitation on the exercise of power by the government of the United States, and [was] not applicable to the legislation of the States."[55] Before the Civil War, the protections of the Bill of Rights simply did not apply to the states and thus did not inhibit the power of the states to pass local discriminatory police power regulations. *Barron v. Baltimore* reflected the jurisdictional, divided, and bottom-up nature of early American rights—a world that still separated the spheres of national and state and local governmental power and that understood "citizenship" as quite dependent on local determinations of status, membership, rights, and disabilities.

Another example of the powers of local associations to deny persons rights by excluding them from membership or denying them community resources involved cases concerning the early administration of American poor relief. In early Massachusetts and Maine, a claim to public relief, support, and decent burial was contingent on "settlement" in a particular town, and neither state nor national citizenship trumped the power of these local associations to police their membership and determine basic rights of mobility, association, belonging, and support.[56] To the contrary, town overseers of the poor were vested with extraordinary discretionary administrative authority over the rights of poor people, whether citizens or not. In Maine, any two overseers in any town had authority to commit to the workhouse "all persons of able body to work and not having estate or means otherwise to maintain themselves, who refuse or neglect so to do; live a dissolute vagrant life, and exercise no ordinary calling or lawful business, sufficient to gain an honest livelihood." When Adeline G. Nott complained that Portland's summary practice of rounding up the poor violated her right to a trial and hearing before a judge, Maine's Supreme Court defended the town's "parental" right to have her "removed from temptation, and compelled to cultivate habits of industry." Such local police regulation recognized few constitutional limitations based on claims of either citizenship or due process of law.[57] As Nott's case illustrated, economic and gender discriminations could come together in particularly dangerous ways at the intersection of local poor law and state police power. Unattached poor women, in particular, found little protection in citizenship rights. In 1853, Betsey Brown and her daughter, Almedia—abandoned by husband and father—were summarily thrown into a Portland, Maine, workhouse without any legal process whatsoever by town overseers for "living a dissolute, vagrant life." Almedia Brown died there within the year at age twenty-two.[58]

Three years before *Dred Scott*, the California case of *People v. Hall* (1854) captured the even more hazardous combination of race and discriminatory state police powers.[59] George W. Hall, a "free white citizen" of California, was convicted of murdering a Chinese miner on the testimony of Chinese witnesses. Hall appealed his conviction to the California Supreme Court, claiming that as a white man, he was protected against such Chinese testimony by virtue of state civil and criminal procedure statutes that explicitly excluded witnesses by race. While neither statute mentioned Chinese testimony, the criminal exclusionary rule held that "no Black or Mulatto person, or Indian" should be allowed to give evidence for or against a "white man." Notably, neither statute was framed in terms of citizenship—all whites were protected from all Indian, Black, and Mulatto testimony regardless of claims to citizenship. Race not citizenship was the key determinant of this threshold right of inclusion and exclusion and the basic protection of due process of law.

Hugh C. Murray, California's third and youngest chief justice, had already penned an opinion returning three African Americans (who had been in California before statehood) to slavery as alleged fugitives, citing Roger Taney's opinion in *United States v. Skiddy.*[60] In *People v. Hall,* Murray extended the discussion of race and citizenship beyond the slavery question per se. In one of the more remarkable feats of statutory interpretation in the antebellum period, the chief justice overturned George Hall's murder conviction and upheld his basic right to be protected from Chinese testimony because he interpreted the Chinese as already falling within the explicit statutory exclusion of "Indian" testimony. Drawing on the Naturalization Act of 1790, which restricted naturalization to "free white" persons, Murray held that it was the obvious intent of the California legislature "to exclude every one who is not of white blood" so as "to protect the white person from the influence of all testimony other than that of persons of the same caste."[61]

People v. Hall revealed much about race and the peculiar orientation and limited nature of antebellum citizenship. Like Chief Justice Marshall in *Barron,* Chief Justice Murray did invoke the language of citizen and rights: "The evident intention of the Act was to throw around the *citizen* a protection for life and property, which could only be secured by removing him above the corrupting influences of the degraded castes." But citizenship as invoked by Murray was predicated on exclusion and substantively defined by race. All whites in California were presumed citizens, and Murray envisioned their rights as secure only to the extent that nonwhites (irrespective of their own citizenship claims) were aggressively barred from even the most basic rights. The chief justice concluded with a vicious testament to the racial boundaries of citizenship in antebellum California:

The anomalous spectacle of a distinct people, living in our community, recognizing no laws of this State, except through necessity, bringing with them their prejudices and national feuds, in which they indulge in open violation of law; whose mendacity is proverbial; a race of people whom nature has marked as inferior, and who are incapable of progress or intellectual development beyond a certain point, as their history has shown; differing in language, opinions, color, and physical conformation; between whom and ourselves nature has placed an impassable difference, is now presented, and for them is claimed, not only the right to swear away the life of a citizen, but the further privilege of participating with us in administering the affairs of our Government.

Extending to the Chinese even the fundamental right of testimony, Murray argued, would "admit them to all the equal rights of citizenship, and we might soon see them at the polls, in the jury box, upon the bench, and in our legislative halls."[62]

The exclusions and discriminations of the New England poor law and California criminal procedure were just two examples of the extreme limits of antebellum American citizenship. Citizenship here was not what Hamilton or Bancroft had in mind when they foresaw new possibilities for inclusion, equal rights, and union in the privileges and immunities clause. To the contrary, like poor law administration, Murray's conception of citizen and rights was distinctly inegalitarian—exclusive—policing the boundaries of the imagined self-governing body politic and protecting a racial majority against the public participation and rights claims of minority castes. Here the ideal parameters of formal national citizenship did not factor as the major determiner of substantive rights and duties or inclusion and exclusion. Rather, a myriad of more local, sectionalized, and particularized factors, such as status, class, gender, race, age, and capacity, as well as diverse other prejudices, determined membership in self-governing communities and associations only too eager to flex discriminatory policing powers. In this way, the actual practices of early American democracy came to betray something of its original aspiration.

Free People of Color and the Making
of Modern Citizenship

The constitutional commentaries, treatises, and cases examined thus far should make it clear that a modern conception of American citizenship simply did not function in the antebellum United States the way many have come to expect. Indeed, general national citizenship rights were elusive, ambiguous, inconclusive, and precarious. Explicitly discriminatory state police power laws proliferated with impunity, covering everything from witness testimony and poor law administration to quarantine and the right to travel. Boston segregated its schools, marriage restrictions policed the family, Sunday laws patrolled the Sabbath, liquor controls targeted new immigrants, and free persons of color endured a raft of regulations covering everything from the right to own a dog to the right to own a gun. Of course, most extensive in its discriminating and dehumanizing differentiation, Southern states expounded elaborate special slave codes that created a legislatively imposed form of "civil death" on a significant portion of their population.

But this woeful record of antebellum rights deprivation did not mean that national citizenship and its attendant rights did not matter *at all* in early America. To the contrary, citizenship was still a concept under construction. By the time of the Civil War and the passage of the Reconstruction Amendments, national citizenship did, in fact, emerge as a defining category in modern American constitutionalism. Typically, the story of the making of modern constitutional citizenship has been told through the lens of the struggle over slavery, *Dred Scott,* and the crucible of Civil War. And, no doubt, those epic battles over the slave question per se greatly influenced the rise of modern American citizenship law. But just as significant was another determinative but comparatively understated historical contest—the long nineteenth-century fight of free Black people for "the practical enjoyment of citizenship."[63] Here were the cases of trouble and the harbingers of constitutional change—cases where the uncertain passivity of the formal law of national citizenship was confronted by the real claims and demands of people on the ground. In the antebellum period, the cases that really plumbed the depths of the problem of national citizenship—the cases that anticipated in great detail the very issues to be formally hammered out in the Civil Rights Act of 1866 and the Fourteenth Amendment—involved the equal citizenship claims of free persons of color.

As Martha Jones and Kate Masur have now convincingly demonstrated, free African Americans fought fiercely for their rights, and they did so wielding an explicit and inclusive language of citizenship.[64] Their opponents—most notably Roger Taney (as well as his brother Octavius)—fought equally hard in the opposite direction, pushing the explicit framework of citizenship to an exclusionary extreme. Indeed, the basic terms of debate were already joined at the Articles of Confederation with South Carolina's unsuccessful attempt to insert the word "white" after "free" and before "citizens" in article 4. While South Carolina was unsuccessful on the national level, state citizenship and state comity was, of course, another matter. In Virginia as early as 1779, Thomas Jefferson's "Bill Declaring Who Shall be Deemed Citizens of the Commonwealth," succeeded in inserting the word "white," both as a precondition of Virginia state citizenship as well as a comity condition for receiving equal rights, privileges, and immunities in Virginia: "The free white inhabitants of every of the states, parties to the American confederation, paupers, vagabonds and fugitives from justice excepted, shall be intitled to all rights, privileges, and immunities of free citizens of this commonwealth."[65]

Virginia also produced one of the most extensive early treatise discussions of race, rights, and citizenship in the form of St. George Tucker's edition of *Blackstone's Commentaries* (1803).[66] Compared to his northern, free-state contemporaries, Tucker was obsessed with the citizenship question—and for all the wrong reasons. Four of his six appended "Notes" to Blackstone's "Rights of Persons" (drawn from Tucker's "Lectures on Law and Police" at William and Mary) hinged on citizenship concerns. His "Note H: On the State of Slavery in Virginia" made clear his exclusionary vision of the citizenship question. As Tucker put it, "The absolute rights of the citizens of united America" must not "be understood as if those rights were equally and universally the privilege of all the inhabitants of the United States, or even of all those, who may challenge this land of freedom as their native country." For while America "hath been the land of promise to Europeans, and their descendants, it hath been the vale of death to millions of the wretched sons of Africa."[67] In short, St. George Tucker was not deploying the framework of rights, national citizenship, and race so as to advance an agenda of inclusion and equality. To the contrary, he was promoting a racially restrictive conception of citizenship as part of his plan to use gradual emancipation and the forceful denial of Black citizenship as a legal platform for future emigration, transplantation, and colonization. As early as 1796, the conscious denial of Black citizenship rights was being advocated as a strategic prerequisite for eventual resettlement. As Tucker concluded explicitly, "I wish not to encourage their future residence among us. By denying them the most valuable privileges which civil government affords, I wished to render it their inclination and their interest to seek those privileges in some other climate." Tucker looked to "the immense territory of Louisiana" and "the two Floridas" as affording "a ready asylum for such as might choose to become Spanish subjects."[68]

Thus as early as 1796, Tucker illuminated the enormous stakes of the entire nineteenth-century citizenship struggle. Citizenship alone brought one very little; most substantive early American rights and duties were allocated according to older measures of status, membership, and police. But citizenship did seem to grant one purchase on an important threshold issue—the right to be present or, in the negative, the right not to be so easily removed. At bottom, that is what basic membership through citizenship in a nation provided—a right to a jurisdiction, a claim to a space or place. That might not sound like much substantively, but in an era replete with aggressive traditions of immigration, emigration, travel bans, "warning out," quarantine, forcible enslavement, Indian removal, colonization, and even banishment, this baseline citizenship right proved worth the fight.[69] Though many today view citizenship in primarily aspirational terms as some kind of quest for civic belonging or cultural identity or consensual allegiance or associational community, the stakes in nineteenth-century America were much more stark. Citizenship was about people freed or enslaved, staying or going, appearing or disappearing.[70]

As if to acknowledge exactly these kinds of stakes, a persistent movement grew up in the early nineteenth century specifically around the cause of articulating and defending the rights of free people of color as American citizens. The movement was wide-ranging and disparate in impact—from the local courthouse to the regional customs house to the Congress of the United States, from local advocacy to treatise writing to political action. Substantive issues ranged from local travel permits to military service to the right to vote in New York State to Seaman's Protection Certificates and passports to freedom suits to the fight to defend Prudence Crandall's education of African American girls at her Connecticut boarding school.[71] This was exactly the context for the production of one of the more remarkable of early American legal treatises, William Yates's *Rights of Colored Men* (1838). There, Yates meticulously prepared a set of materials that challenged attempts to deny the citizenship claims of free people of color. Yates began with the spirit, if not the blood, of the American Revolution—"when the services and sufferings of men of color were fresh in the memory." After the revolution, Yates contended, "these men returned to their respective States and homes; and who would have said to them, on their returning to civil life, after having shed their blood in common with the whites, for the liberties of the country—'You are not to participate in the rights or liberty for which you have been fighting?'" Yates lamented the "successive disfranchisements" and "legal disabilit[ies]" of early nineteenth-century law: "the exclusion of colored men from militia service, from naturalization, or the basis of representation; denying them rights of citizenship or suffrage, or the benefit of the public schools; and rendering them incompetent to hold real estate, or to give testimony in court." Of all such deprivations of rights, Yates was most concerned with citizenship: "Deny a man this, and his personal rights are not safe. He may be hindered from going into a State—or, if he enters it, he may be expelled, or treated as an alien." Like St. George Tucker—but from the opposite legal and moral perspective—Yates understood perfectly the stakes of the antebellum citizenship debates.[72]

Yates started with a discussion of one of the most important battles over race and national citizenship before *Dred Scott*—the fight over Missouri's 1820 state constitutional attempt "to prevent free negroes and mulattoes from coming into and settling in the State."[73] Here was the kind of case that seemed to directly implicate claims of a truly national citizenship. Here was a seemingly direct affront to the US Constitution's proviso that "Citizens of each State shall be entitled to all Privileges and Immunities of Citizens in the several States." This was the clause that Alexander Hamilton claimed in *Federalist* no. 80 guaranteed "the inviolable maintenance of that equality of privileges and immunities to which the *citizens of the union* will be entitled."[74] What kind of union was this, and what kind of "citizens of the union" were these if a state could prohibit other states' citizens from ever crossing into its borders?

As a product of the deep divisiveness that spawned the first Missouri Compromise, Missouri's proposed 1820 constitution included several extraordinary and controversial provisions. Article 3, section 26 constitutionally denied the state legislature the "the power to pass laws for the emancipation of slaves without the consent of their owners" and also barred the legislature from preventing "bona-fide immigrants" or "actual settlers" from bringing slaves into the state. Then, as if to negatively mirror those provisions guaranteeing slavery and the movement of slaves into Missouri, the constitution mandated that the state legislature pass laws "to prevent free negroes and mulattoes from coming to and settling in the State, under any pretext whatsoever."[75] In short, in a classic example of the perverse state constitutionalism produced by the slavery controversy, slaves and slave owners were ever "free" to come to the newest state in the Union, while free persons or citizens of color were absolutely prohibited. Here was an early premonition of Abraham Lincoln's constitutional nightmare: "We shall lie down pleasantly dreaming that the people of Missouri are on the verge of making their State free, and we shall awake to the reality instead that" constitutional law "has made Illinois a slave State."[76]

Missouri could not be officially admitted to the Union until its state constitution was presented to and accepted by both houses of Congress. Missouri presented its constitution at the opening of the second session of the Sixteenth Congress, which reassembled on November 14, 1820. And while the legal treatises and formal constitutional commentary might have been comparatively quiescent on issues of national citizenship until the crisis precipitated by *Dred Scott*, the halls of the Sixteenth Congress were anything but. Indeed, the detailed arguments in Congress reflected the rise of a boisterous popular and public debate concerning race, constitutionalism, and national citizenship rights. As the historian Glover Moore noted, "Congressmen became accustomed to dining by candlelight, as the debates over Missouri often lasted from morning to night."[77] Hundreds of pages of the *Annals of Congress* were filled with discussion of the exact question so difficult to find adequately addressed in treatises or court opinions: What were the rights that flowed from citizenship in the United States, and to whom exactly did they belong? Even more significantly, contrary to repeated attempts to deny free persons of color their claims to citizenship, state after state and legislator after legislator rose in 1820 and 1821 to argue exactly the opposite—at great length and with surprising passion and authority.

By the second day of the session, state legislatures in both New York and Vermont had passed resolutions taking issue with Missouri's unusual constitutional mandates.[78] Vermont claimed that Missouri's ban on the immigration of "citizens of the United States" and "freemen of the United States" solely "on account of their origin, color, or features" was "anti-republican, and repugnant to the Constitution of the United States" in direct conflict with the comity clause.[79] Senator Burrill of Rhode Island concurred: "We have colored soldiers and sailors, and good ones, too," but "even if soldiers of the United States" and even if "citizens of other States, enjoying all the privileges of such," "people of this proscribed class cannot enter Missouri." Burrill himself had no difficulty defining what "constituted a citizen" for purposes of article 4, section 2: "If a person was not a slave or a foreigner—but born in the United States, and a free man—going into Missouri, he has the same rights as if born in Missouri." And he analogized Missouri's interstate hostility to other states' citizens to an international "declaration of war."[80]

Senator Otis of Massachusetts bolstered Burrill's arguments against opponents who argued in "bold denial of the fact that free persons of color may be citizens." He spoke at length about "the circumstances which would give to a man the right of citizenship in Massachusetts; for if a man of color could be a citizen there, he would carry his privilege elsewhere." And in Massachusetts, Otis contended, "many persons of color existed in this relation to the State. . . . Persons of this description had received grants of land for serving in your army, and had been reclaimed among your impressed seamen." Against the litany of racially discriminatory state statutes cited by Missouri's defenders, Otis argued that particular disqualifications from office holding or voting did not imply that such persons were not citizens, citing the easy cases of women and minors. "An unjust Government may create many odious distinctions between its privileged orders and other citizens," he observed, "and yet leave the excluded or restricted class in the condition of citizens." But though citizens could be discriminated against in multiple ways, there were certain baseline benefits to citizenship, for as he noted at one point in argument "if a colored man may become a free citizen, *he cannot be sent away.*"[81]

"Cannot be sent away" was one of the central concerns of the entire citizenship fight, trying to establish an outer limit on the power of states and groups and associations to formally exclude, which could also provide a legal basis and precedent for subsequent removal. Immediately on the heels of the citizenship battle in Missouri, a second national contest flared up concerning South Carolina's attempts to do just that. Again debate began with a prohibition on the movement of free Black people—this time into an existing state of the Union. In 1820, the South Carolina legislature passed "An Act to Restrain the Emancipation of Slaves and to Prevent Free Persons of Colour from Entering into this State."[82] The legislature bemoaned "the great and rapid increase of free negroes and mulattoes . . . by migration and emancipation" and put in place a series of stringent provisions to reduce its free Black population. Once again, a major nineteenth-century battle over the contours and implications of citizenship turned not on such things as voting or office holding or jury service (yet alone property or contract rights), but on the more fundamental and baseline (and perhaps life-and-death) issue of a formal governmental attempt to rid itself of a population.

Now, of course, South Carolina was neither the first state nor the last to attempt to limit and remove an unwelcome population. As early as 1793, in fact, Virginia passed two acts aimed at controlling its free Black population. The first sounded like a general police ordinance—an act for "Regulating the Police of Towns"—but here Virginia focused its police authority particularly on "the Practice of Negroes going at Large." The new statute required "every free negro or mulatto" to be "registered and numbered in a book" and provided with an annual certificate specifying "age, name, colour and stature" and, notably, whether such "negro or mullato" was "born free."[83] Upon securing this administrative accounting of its own free Black population, Virginia passed a subsequent statute "To Prevent the Migration of Free Negroes and Mulattoes" into the state. The law subjected free persons of color coming into Virginia to immediate apprehension "by any citizen" and removal from the state by a justice of the peace.[84] Maryland, Delaware, Georgia, and a host of other states soon followed suit in something of a parade of horribles that culminated in the pre–Civil War constitutional debates over such bans in midwestern states like Illinois and Indiana (fearing, as one Indiana conventioneer put it, that Indiana would "become the Liberia of the Southern States").[85]

South Carolina certainly had much company in its attempt to inhibit or reduce its free Black population. But South Carolina's particularly aggressive use of race-based state immigration restriction and local police regulation provoked another vociferous citizenship controversy. At the heart of

South Carolina's regime was an escalating series of draconian punishments for free Black persons in the state. If free Black persons remained in South Carolina for more than fifteen days after a removal order, they were subject to a fine of twenty dollars. If that fine remained unpaid, they could be sold for a term of time not exceeding five years. If such free persons were convicted of circulating "any written or printed paper with intent to disturb the peace or security of the [state] in relation to the slaves of the people of this state," they were subject to a fine up to one thousand dollars for a first offence and fifty lashes and banishment for a second. If free persons of color returned to South Carolina after banishment, they were subject to "suffer death, without the benefit of clergy."[86]

The logic of South Carolina's regime—as well as the very real stakes of the citizenship struggle—was clear in the punitive progression from restriction to removal to sale into slavery to banishment to death. And though South Carolina at first carved out exceptions for "natives" of the state as well as for "seamen" on board a departing vessel, those were not long lasting. By 1822, the state began to construct incentives and penalties to force the removal of its entire free Black population. And it simultaneously clamped down as well on the rights of Black sailors in the infamous restrictions known as the Negro Seamen Act.[87]

Section 3 of South Carolina's new act for "The Better Regulation . . . of Free Negroes and Persons of Colour" provided that "any free negroes or persons of colour" on "any vessel" that should "come into any port or harbour of this state" were "liable to be seized and confined in gaol" until the ship's departure. Upon departure, the captain of the vessel was required to "carry away the said free negro" as well as "pay the expenses of his detention." If the captain refused or abandoned the sailor, such "free negroes or persons of colour" would then be "taken as absolute slaves and sold." South Carolina thus opened a new front in the nineteenth-century citizenship struggle. After all, it was one thing constitutionally for a state to deny its own free Black population a claim to United States citizenship; and indeed, in the case of seamen, Attorney General William Wirt had already issued an opinion in 1821 that "no person is included in the description of a citizen of the United States who has not the full rights of a citizen in the State of his residence."[88] It was also one thing for states like Missouri and South Carolina to attempt to deny free Black citizens of another state equal privileges and immunities under the comity principle of the Constitution's article 4, section 2. But since at least 1803, free Black sailors had been carrying congressionally authorized custom house certificates officially declaring them to be "Citizens of the United States of America."[89] South Carolina was not only denying such free sailor-citizens entry or equal privileges and immunities; it was reserving the power to imprison them and sell them into slavery.

Reaction was fast and furious. And in many ways, it exceeded the special outrage directed at Missouri in 1820. Opposition was international in scope (including a formal remonstrance on the part of Great Britain), and it extended to the middle of the century. Indeed, the Negro Seamen Act formed a backdrop to the discussion of citizenship and the powers of national versus state governments from *Gibbons v. Ogden* straight through to *Dred Scott*.[90] One of the most penetrating commentaries came in the form of a congressional report titled *Free Colored Seamen* (1843). By 1843, a report organized by more than 150 citizens of Boston (including many seamen and owners of vessels) claimed that the violations of rights in ports, which now included Savannah, Mobile, and New Orleans, as well as Charleston, were "of too frequent and too notorious occurrence to admit of any denial or doubt" and in clear violation of the Constitution's article 4, section 2. In Massachusetts, the report made clear, "Their citizens are all free; their freemen all citizens. . . . The colored man has enjoyed the full and equal privileges of citizenship since the last remnant of slavery was abolished within her borders by the constitution of 1780, nine years before the adoption of the Constitution of the United States." And the committee utterly denied that such Negro Seamen Acts were constitutionally legitimate state police power regulations. "It may be difficult, perhaps to assign the precise limits to which this police power of the State may extend," they argued, but there was one limit "about which the committee can conceive there can be no question." Here they homed in on the crucial constitutional limitation on which the antebellum citizenship debates turned: "The police power of the States can never be permitted to abrogate the constitutional privileges of a whole class of citizens, upon grounds, not of any temporary moral or physical condition, but of distinctions which originate in their birth, and which are as permanent as their being."[91] State police powers were not to be construed so broadly as to allow states to discriminate against "a whole class of citizens" on the basis of distinctions originating in birth or being.

Such an argument, of course, about birth, race, discrimination, the limits of state police power, and the power of national citizenship previewed the central issues that would be more fully vetted in *Dred Scott,* Lincoln-Douglas, and the framing of the Fourteenth Amendment. Indeed, one of the more important accompaniments of the Negro Seamen Act controversy was the unpublished 1832 attorney general opinion of none other than Roger B. Taney. After two previous and conflicting attorney general opinions by William Wirt and John Berrien, Taney weighed in on the Black citizenship question with an opinion that presaged his more infamous opinion as chief justice in *Dred Scott:*

1. "The African race in the United States, even when free, are every where a degraded class—& exercise no political influence."
2. "They were never regarded as a constituent portion of the sovereignty of any state."
3. "They were not looked upon as citizens by the contracting parties who formed the Constitution. They were evidently not supposed to be included by the term citizens."[92]

One of the reasons frequently given for the passage of South Carolina's first restrictive seamen act was the alleged involvement of seamen and shipyard slaves in the Denmark Vesey affair in 1822. The Nat Turner rebellion of 1831 similarly served as the backdrop to Taney's stark unpublished opinion. Indeed, in the immediate wake of Turner's revolt, Roger Taney's brother Octavius C. Taney proposed legislation in the Maryland senate to seek federal funds for the deportation of Maryland's free Black population to Africa. As Taney viewed it, "Recent occurrences in this State, as well as in other States of our Union, have impressed more deeply upon our minds the necessity of devising some means, by which we may facilitate the removal of the free persons of color from our state, and from the United States."[93]

The threat of removal, resettlement, and colonization was the deeper context for the important citizenship debates of the early nineteenth century. Indeed, one of the last cases in Yates's alternative treatise on citizenship involved Prudence Crandall's commitment to the education of African American girls. In consequence, Crandall's boarding school was met with every conceivable local police tactic—from informal intimidation to town meeting censure to the attempted warning out of Black girls to the invocation of Connecticut's pauper and vagrancy act. Finally, on May 24, 1833, opponents pushed through the Connecticut general assembly a new anti-Black law: "An Act for the Admission and Settlement of Inhabitants of Towns." Seemingly patterned on the restrictive practices of the historic New England poor laws, this particular measure was aimed directly at recent attempts "to establish literary institutions in this State for the instruction of colored persons belonging to other states and countries, which would tend to the great increase of the colored population of the State, and thereby to the injury of the people."[94] The statute made it a crime to establish such institutions, and Prudence Crandall was promptly prosecuted and jailed. The statute also provided for the removal of Crandall's out-of-state "colored" students. Subsequent litigation received a thorough airing in the abolitionist press, and the question of national citizenship rights and the background threat of the removal of persons of color pervaded the entire discussion. According to William Jay, Crandall's main antagonist throughout the controversy was the New Haven Committee of Correspondence of the American Colonization Society—a movement that Jay portrayed as thoroughly committed to the "compulsory emigration" of African Americans. Jay drove the point home—in a larger text, portions of which were incorporated into Yates's treatise on citizenship—by quoting a Virginia advocate of colonization, William Henry Brodnax: "It is idle to talk about not resorting to force. Every body must look to the introduction of force of some kind or other. If the free negroes are willing to go, they will go; if not willing, they must be compelled to go."[95]

The antebellum fight for the citizenship rights of free people of color was an attempt to blunt that basic oppositional force—to assert a right to stay and not to go—an attempt to stave off the omnipresent threat of removal. A half century of struggle against just such immodest proposals from St. George Tucker to Octavius C. Taney established the main framework of debate for the postwar remaking of modern American citizenship. Of course, slavery was an essential part of that discussion as well. But, from the Missouri question to the Negro Seamen Acts to Prudence Crandall, the rights of free African Americans and the limits of local and state police regulation framed the national citizenship question in the starkest and most unavoidable terms. As William Goodell put it, "The Free People of Color, though not in a condition of Chattelhood, are constantly exposed to it, and at best enjoy only a portion of their rights." Beyond the slavery question per se was the question of "the liberties of the free people of color" as citizens of the United States of America.[96] "Almost the first work the American Anti-Slavery Society asked me to do," Frederick Douglass recalled in a New York City address in 1865, was "to wage a most unrelenting war against what was called the 'Dorr Constitution' [of Rhode Island], because that Constitution contained the odious word 'white' in it. . . . We succeeded in defeating that Dorr Constitution, and secured the adoption of a Constitution in which the word 'white' did not appear. We thought that was a grand *anti-slavery* triumph, and it was; it was good *anti-slavery* work."[97] The long campaign against discriminatory state laws and constitutions—the rules that used "white" to bestow privilege and police exclusion—was an important prelude to the attempt to rewrite national laws and constitutions without "the odious word 'white'" as a foundation. The Fourteenth Amendment to the US Constitution was one direct consequence of this long struggle over antebellum equal citizenship rights.

Constitutional Nationalism and
the New American Citizen

The struggle over citizenship, the crisis over slavery, the battle over states' rights, and the crucible of Civil War forever transformed the public law world of antebellum America. The Thirteenth, Fourteenth, and Fifteenth Amendments constitutionalized the reconstruction of national power and national rights along the lines anticipated in Lincoln's Emancipation Proclamation. The added constitutional clauses "involuntary servitude," "privileges or immunities," "due process of law," "equal protection of the laws," and, for the first time, "citizens of the United States" were no mere textual revisions. Rather, they embodied a wholly new American political and legal philosophy. A new conception of the rights of citizens and persons in a nation-state increasingly supplanted the antebellum understanding of associative citizenship in a locally policed and confederated republic. Such new national rights were not opposed to the general powers of nation-state building. To the contrary, they integrated individuals into the national socioeconomic ambitions and policies of a modern American state.

One of the clearest indicators of this greater transformation concerned national citizenship. Before the Civil War, formal treatise-like considerations of the nature and content of American national citizenship were comparatively hard to find. That changed after the Civil War. Indeed, as early as 1862, Attorney General Bates charted the new course with his celebrated and widely distributed opinion on citizenship holding that "a free man of color . . . if born in the United States, is a citizen of the United States."[98] In 1865, Francis Lieber proposed his series of "Amendments of the Constitution," with Amendment G declaring: "The free inhabitants of each of the states, territories, districts, or places within the limits of the United States, either born free within the same or born in slavery within the same and since made or declared free . . . shall be deemed citizens of the United States, and without any exception of color, race, or origin, shall be entitled to the privileges of citizens." As Lieber noted, "We live in a time of necessary and searching reform. . . . Things have already changed. . . . Let every one contribute his share to the reconstruction."[99] Difficult to find in antebellum constitutional discourse, national citizenship became a ubiquitous topic in postbellum jurisprudence—impossible to miss. Thomas Cooley had to revise Joseph Story's famous *Commentaries on the Constitution* with a new addendum on the emancipation of the slaves, the Fourteenth Amendment, and the idea of citizens of the United States.[100] Similarly James Bradley

Thayer's influential late nineteenth-century casebook on American constitutional law had to prioritize the discussion of citizenship. After an introductory section in which Thayer took up formative issues of constitution making, departments of government, and jurisdiction of the United States, he began his substantive discussion of American constitutional law with a chapter entitled "Citizenship.—Fundamental Civil and Political Rights.—The Later Amendments to the Constitution of the United States."[101] Treatises, articles, cases, and case notes centering on the topic of citizenship law proliferated as never before.[102] And as early as 1875, Theophilus Parsons attempted to synthesize all of American public law around this new constitutional ideal in *The Political, Personal, and Property Rights of a Citizen of the United States.*[103]

The historic work of the Thirty-Ninth Congress—the Reconstruction Congress[104]—including the Freedmen's Bureau Bill of 1866, the Civil Rights Act of 1866, and the Fourteenth Amendment to the US Constitution must be read in this context as something of the constitutional culmination of the great citizenship battles that ultimately precipitated *Dred Scott* and the Civil War. And it is hard to view the legal and legislative achievements of that extraordinary legislative session as anything short of transformative. It produced a new legal and constitutional foundation for what Eric Foner has called "the second founding," wherein "a new definition of American citizenship, incorporating equal rights regardless of race, was written into the Constitution."[105] The Thirty-Ninth Congress was explicitly preoccupied with remedying the problem of discriminatory state police power laws—especially those based on race—that violated the equal citizenship and civil rights claims of Americans qua Americans. Indeed, a fairly consistent logic and set of principles can be tracked throughout this historic legislation concerning the need to legally and constitutionally limit state police powers that discriminated against groups, especially anti-Black laws.

The demands of nondiscrimination and equal citizenship implicated a major reconfiguration in the basic relation of individuals to the American nation-state. As Frederick Douglass appealed to the Reconstruction Congress in 1866: "No republic is safe that tolerates a privileged class, or denies to any of its citizens equal rights and equal means to maintain them." Douglass prophesied that "the Civil Rights Bill and the Freedmen's Bureau Bill and the proposed constitutional amendments" would not reach the fundamental problem without requisite governmental "power to control even the municipal regulations of States," where citizenship could be defined and regulated in locally discriminatory ways. As long as there remained "the right of each State to control its own local affairs," Douglass contended that "no general assertion of human rights can be of any practical value."[106]

The Reconstruction Congress inaugurated a revolution in what W. E. B. Du Bois called "abolition democracy,"[107] fundamentally altering prevailing American configurations of the intimate relationship between public power, private right, and the equal protection of the laws.

The Thirty-Ninth Congress assembled on December 4, 1865. In one of the first pieces of business that day, Charles Sumner submitted a declaratory resolution preemptively announcing the adoption of the Thirteenth Amendment of the US Constitution, abolishing slavery (though formal adoption would await ratification by the state of Georgia two days later). With the tone thus set, Sumner proceeded to introduce resolutions on the conditions for returning remaining rebellious states to normal relations with the Union. His second condition channeled directly abolition democracy as well as the historic aspirations of equal citizenship: "The complete suppression of all oligarchical pretensions, and the complete enfranchisement of all citizens, so that there shall be no denial of rights on account of color or race; but justice shall be impartial; and shall be equal before the law."[108] The Second Freedmen's Bureau Bill, Senate Bill 60, similarly attempted to make good on the promise of a more radically substantive conception of equal democratic and national citizenship. One of the first bills introduced in the Thirty-Ninth Congress, the bill sought to extend and "enlarge the powers" of the 1865 Bureau of Refugees, Freedmen, and Abandoned Lands with its broad administrative mandate for the socioeconomic provisioning of newly freed men and women. The new bill expanded upon the already innovative administrative commissioner and social provisioning measures of the original Freedmen's Bureau with its famous commitment to equitable land distribution—whereby "every male citizen, whether refugee or freedmen . . . shall be assigned not more than forty acres."[109] The 1866 bill—uniquely positioned between the Thirteenth Amendment and the Civil Rights Act of 1866—empowered the secretary of war to direct the issue of "provisions, clothing, fuel, and other supplies, including medical stores and transportation, and afford such aid, medical or otherwise, as he may deem needful for the immediate and temporary shelter and supply of destitute and suffering refugees and freedmen, their wives and children." An additional three million acres of public lands in Florida, Mississippi, and Arkansas were designated for redistribution, and lands were also to be used for the construction of "schools and asylums" for refugees and freedmen.

But especially significant in the context of the long struggle over equal legal citizenship, the Second Freedmen's Bureau Bill also took direct aim at anti-Black laws—the racially discriminatory state police power measures that so preoccupied antebellum activists. In language that anticipated the equal rights provisions of the future Civil Rights Act and Fourteenth Amendment, the proposed bill held that whenever, "in consequence of any State or local law, ordinance, police, or other regulation, custom, or prejudice, any of the civil rights or immunities belonging to white persons are refused or denied to negroes, mulattoes, freedmen, refugees, or any other persons, on account of race, color, or any previous condition of slavery or involuntary servitude, . . . or wherein they or any of them are subjected to any other or different punishment, pains, or penalties, for the commission of any act or offense, than are prescribed for white persons," it became the "duty" of the president through the commissioner to extend military protection and jurisdiction over all such discriminatory cases. The bill further subjected persons enforcing such racially discriminatory local police regulations to a misdemeanor with a fine up to one thousand dollars and/or imprisonment for up to one year.[110] The expansive legislative program of the Second Freedmen's Bureau Bill—combining national substantive socioeconomic provisioning with aggressive federal and administrative policing of local racially discriminatory laws and practices—would have, in the words of one historian, enabled "former slaves to transition into full and equal citizens of a constitutional democracy."[111]

Andrew Johnson, however, had different plans and vetoed the bill in February. The actual extension of the Freedmen's Bureau thus awaited passage of a revised bill later that summer only after the Fourteenth Amendment was already sent to the states for ratification. The vetoed bill, however, was a harbinger of the power and substance of the equal citizenship cause early on in the Reconstruction Congress. Indeed, the Thirty-Ninth Congress continuously advanced the cause against discriminatory laws. Nine days into the historic session, Massachusetts senator Henry Wilson took notice of the fact that although "the slave codes and the laws of these States with regard to persons of color" supposedly "fell with slavery," discriminatory laws were still being executed—"some of them in the most merciless manner." In fact, in several of the Southern states, "new laws" were being framed "containing provisions wholly inconsistent with the freedom of the freedmen." Wilson was referencing, of course, the notorious laws now called Black Codes through which Southern governments replaced slave codes with a series of highly discriminatory, racially specific statutory provisions involving apprenticeship, vagrancy, peonage, and penality. Wilson noted that a pending South Carolina master-servant bill made "the colored people of South Carolina serfs, a degraded class, the slaves of society." The Mississippi legislature had already passed what Wilson called an "arbitrary and inhuman act" directly aimed at the employment of "any freedman, free negro, or mulatto" so as to recreate laboring conditions that one commentator described as "worse off in most respects than when they were held as slaves"—"the old overseers are in power again." Still arguing in the context of insurrection, rebellion, and under the legal authority of the president's Emancipation Proclamation of July 1, 1862, Wilson introduced Senate Bill 9 for the "protection of freedmen." Wilson's bill proposed that all "laws, statutes, acts, ordinances, rules, and regulations" of the rebellious states "whereby or wherein any inequality of civil rights and immunities among the inhabitants" was authorized "by reason or in consequence of any distinction or differences of color, race, or descent, or by reason or in consequence of a previous condition or status of slavery or involuntary servitude" should be declared "null and void" and unlawful.[112] Of course, these were early intimations of Senate Bill 61 "to protect all persons in the United States in their civil rights, and furnish the means of their vindication"—what would eventually become the Civil Rights Act of 1866.

Secretary of State William Henry Seward formally certified the ratification of the Thirteenth Amendment on December 18, 1865, and on January 5, 1866, Illinois senator Lyman Trumbull introduced the new civil rights bill—"the most important measure under [Senate] consideration since the adoption of the constitutional amendment abolishing slavery." Trumbull understood the civil rights bill as "intended to give effect to that declaration and secure to all persons within the United States practical freedom." For what effect "will it now be that the Constitution of the United States has declared that slavery shall not exist, if in the late slaveholding States laws are to be enacted and enforced depriving persons of African descent of privileges which are essential to freemen?" Trumbull took explicit aim at the recently passed laws of the insurrectionary states "relating to the freedmen" that "have *discriminated* against them," denying them certain rights, subjecting them to severe penalties, and imposing on them the very restrictions "which were imposed upon them in consequence of the existence of slavery." The purpose of the present civil rights bill, Trumbull argued, was to "destroy all these discriminations" so as to give effect to the Thirteenth Amendment. The first section of the civil rights bill as amended—the "basis of the whole bill" according to Trumbull—began with citizenship, declaring that "all persons of African descent shall be citizens of the United States" and that "there shall be no discrimination in civil rights or immunities" on account of "race, color, or previous condition of slavery." "Any statute which is not equal to all and which deprives any citizen of civil rights which are secured to other citizens," Trumbull argued, was "an unjust encroachment upon his liberty"—"in fact, a badge of servitude which, by the Constitution, is prohibited." Like Frederick Douglass, Trumbull understood the Thirteenth Amendment and antislavery as also bound up in the larger struggle for full and equal American citizenship. Citing Joseph Story's *Commentaries* as well as *Corfield v. Coryell* on the "privileges and immunities" of citizens,[113] Trumbull declared "persons of African descent, born in the United States, are as much citizens as white persons who are born in the country." Much of the current trouble was rooted in the fact that the former slaveholding states "have not regarded the colored race as citizens, and on that principle many of their laws making discriminations between the whites and the colored people are based." It was now time for Congress to finally declare, under the Constitution, who were citizens of the United States so as to equally protect their "great fundamental rights."[114] The Civil Rights Act passed the Senate on February 2, 1866, and the House on March 13. It too was vetoed by President Andrew Johnson but quickly overridden and made law by both chambers on April 9, 1866. By June, the Thirty-Ninth Congress had also passed the Fourteenth Amendment to the US Constitution so as to constitutionally protect the present and future powers of Congress to fight discrimination and to guarantee the equal enjoyment of substantive rights in the United States of America.

The Fourteenth Amendment reshaped the legal-constitutional landscape of the United States, beginning with a redefinition of national citizenship and the rights entailed thereby. In direct opposition to the myriad of antebellum attempts to limit the citizenship status of all Black Americans (free as well as slave) and to limit national citizenship rights to those rights emanating originally from the states, the Fourteenth Amendment opened with a bold declaration of national membership: "All persons born or naturalized in the United States, and subject to the jurisdiction thereof, are citizens of the United States, and of the State wherein they reside." In contrast to the sectionalized, particularized, and differentiated laws of status, association, and police that dominated the early nineteenth century, the opening clause of the Fourteenth Amendment established one supreme membership in the body politic of the United States that stood above all others. And as the amendment went on to make clear, this was a national citizenship status of consequence—a national citizenship accompanied by constitutional protections against the kind of lesser jurisdictional police laws that contravened the claims of national belonging. As the second clause of the Fourteenth Amendment spelled out the new express provisions of that reconstructed compact: "No state shall make or enforce any law which shall abridge the privileges and immunities of citizens of the United States; nor shall any State deprive any person of life, liberty, or property, without due process of law; nor deny to any person within its jurisdiction the equal protection of the laws." Significantly, the fifth section of the amendment gave the national legislature authority to enforce it through appropriate legislation. Though the constitutional effect of these important clauses would be the subject of the next hundred years of rights debate in the United States, what was clear from the beginning was the establishment of a new preeminent legal status in national citizenship, a distinct shift in public power to the national government at the expense of the states and lesser jurisdictions, and a new cross-jurisdictional concern with the privileges and immunities, due process rights, and equal protection of the laws for all Americans.

As early as 1849, in his argument on the "Unconstitutionality of Separate Colored Schools in Massachusetts" in *Roberts v. City of Boston,* Charles Sumner best articulated such a broad vision of "Equality Before the Law" rooted in an expansive and inclusive ideal of birthright citizenship. At the time, Sumner had to rely on the Massachusetts Bill of Rights provision that "all men are *born* free and equal":

> Within the sphere of their influence no person can be *created*, no person can be *born*, with civil or political privileges not enjoyed equally by all his fellow-citizens; nor can any institution be established recognizing distinction of birth. Here is the great charter of every human being drawing vital breath upon this soil, whatever may be his condition and whoever may be his parents. He may be poor, weak, humble, or black,—he may be of Caucasian, Jewish, Indian, or Ethiopian race,—he may be of French, German, English, or Irish extraction; but before the Constitution all these distinctions disappear. . . . He is a MAN, the equal of all his fellow-men. He is one of the children of the State, which, like an impartial parent, regards all of its offspring with an equal care. . . . The State, imitating the divine justice, is no respecter of persons. Here nobility cannot exist, because it is a privilege from birth. But the same anathema which smites and banishes nobility must also smite and banish every form of discrimination founded on birth.[115]

Sumner's meditation evoked a new and modern understanding of equal citizenship in the United States. And his biting critique of nobility and all discriminations based on birth prefigured a new democratic ethos—an expansive and more generalized conception of exactly who it was that constituted the body politic. Here, a new democratic state was bound to its citizenry without regard to distinction through the creation and protection of equal rights of citizenship. In the Fourteenth Amendment of Sumner's radical Reconstruction, the long antebellum struggle for citizenship found a new national constitutional repository for its broadest ambitions.

In consequence, much of the antebellum legal worldview that pervaded the cases of John Barron, Adeline Nott, George Hall, and so many others began to constitutionally unravel after the Civil War. With the passage of the Fourteenth Amendment, much as its principal author John Bingham hoped, an increased array of national constitutional protections began to slowly but steadily apply to the states. In contrast to John Marshall's defense of a traditional dual federalism in *Barron v. Baltimore,* where the Bill of Rights did not apply to the states, John Bingham argued that the privileges and immunities clause of the Fourteenth Amendment incorporated "the first eight amendments to the Constitution," transforming them into "an express prohibition upon every State of the Union."[116] In *People v. Washington* (1869), the California Supreme Court reversed the appalling reasoning of *People v. Hall* (1856) and declared "null and void" (so far as it "discriminates against persons, on the score of race or color, born within the United States") California's racially discriminatory criminal procedure statute barring witness testimony from any "Indian," "Mongolian," or "Chinese" in favor or against "any white person." The court relied primarily on the Civil Rights Act of 1866, noting: "Certain rights are secured to those who are declared to be citizens of the United States," including the right "to give evidence" and "to full and equal benefit of all laws and proceedings for the security of persons and property as is enjoyed by white citizens."[117] With similar effect, the Maine Supreme Court declared the Portland pauper police law at issue in Adeline Nott's case unconstitutional—in violation of the newly minted Fourteenth Amendment to the US Constitution. As Justice Walton put it, "That article declares that no state shall deprive any person of life, liberty, or property, without due process of law; . . . it needs no argument to prove that an *ex parte* determination of two overseers of the poor is not such a process." Moreover, Walton reflected on the larger ramifications of a legal and racial world that prohibited slavery, servitude, and their badges and incidences: "If white men and women may be thus summarily disposed of at the north, of course black ones may be disposed of in the same way at the south; and thus the very evil which it was particularly the object of the fourteenth amendment to eradicate will still exist."[118] From Maine to California, the Reconstruction Amendments had direct effects on the way courts thought about citizenship, rights, legal process, discriminatory laws, and the relationship of state and federal powers.

But, of course, rather tragically, there were also obvious limits to the constitutional revolution initiated after Appomattox, as meticulously documented in history after history of the legal-constitutional rollback of radical Reconstruction.[119] Charles Sumner seemed to be channeling Frederick Douglass when he proposed simply removing the "odious" word *white* from the Naturalization Act of 1790 so as to create a naturalized American citizenship not based on race distinction. Instead, the Naturalization Act of 1870 added "aliens of African nativity" and "persons of African descent," while continuing to limit and police the citizenship status of other groups, most notoriously the Chinese and Native Americans.[120] Into the twentieth century, the United States Supreme Court would continue to indulge racially and ethnologically charged feats of statutory construction akin to those in *People v. Hall* in efforts to limit immigration and citizenship claims.[121] Indeed, some of the partialness and reluctance of this constitutional revolution was captured within *People v. Washington* itself. Behind the California Supreme Court's broad invocations of citizenship, the Thirteenth Amendment, the Civil Rights Act of 1866, and the Fourteenth Amendment, there remained an explicitly racialized and exclusionary vision of equality before the law. Justice Rhodes's specific holding involved a quite limited vision of the scope of the constitutional antidiscrimination principle: "A law which, while it would not permit a class of persons deemed unworthy to testify against a white person in a matter where such white person's personal liberty is concerned, would yet allow them to testify against a black person in a similar case, would discriminate against the personal liberty of the latter."[122] In other words, this discriminatory statute was unconstitutional for not providing Black persons the same protection *against* Chinese testimony as white persons—a pyrrhic victory for the cause of racial equality to say the least.

When the US Supreme Court had its first opportunity to interpret the Fourteenth Amendment, it fared little better; and the handiwork of the Reconstruction Congress endured the first of many momentous constitutional contractions. It was not Louisiana's Black Code of 1865 that was before the court but a Louisiana statute regulating butchers and slaughterhouses in New Orleans.[123] In the *Slaughter-House Cases,* Justice Miller— almost amnesiac with respect to the long citizenship struggles that precipitated the Reconstruction Amendments—settled on a forced and constrained interpretation of the privileges or immunities of citizens clause of the Fourteenth Amendment that all but eviscerated its potential as the entering constitutional wedge of a broader equal rights revolution in the United States. Miller basically reinscribed the dual tradition of contending state and federal citizenship that many thought the source of the antebellum citizenship problem in the first place. Miller insisted that the Fourteenth Amendment recognized and established "a citizenship of the United States, and a citizenship of a State, which are distinct from each other, and which depend upon different characteristics or circumstances." More importantly, only the privileges and immunities of citizens of the United States were "placed by this clause under the protection of the Federal Constitution." As Miller asked rhetorically, "Was it the purpose of the fourteenth amendment, by the simple declaration that no State should make or enforce any law which shall abridge the privileges and immunities of citizens of the United States, to transfer the security and protection of *all* the civil rights . . . from the States to the Federal Government?"[124] Miller's answer for a 5–4 court was a resounding no. And so the great content of the equal rights of citizens of the United States as championed by the likes of Yates, Sumner, and Douglass was reduced by the US Supreme Court to include things like coming "to the seat of government" or demanding "the care and protection of the federal government" when "on the high seas" or abroad.[125]

From *Slaughter-House* to *Cruikshank,* the *Civil Rights Cases,* and *Plessy v. Ferguson,* things only got bleaker as explicit racially discriminatory police laws and vigilante police actions came before the United States Supreme Court. As James Blaine complained, "By decisions of the Supreme Court, the Fourteenth Amendment has been deprived in part of the power which Congress no doubt intended to impart to it. Under its provisions, as construed by the Court, little, if anything, can be done by Congress to correct the evils or avert the injurious consequences arising" from the abuse of the suffrage and the "numerous flagrant cases" of "unrestrained violence and unlimited wrong."[126] Justice John Marshall Harlan also understood the substantive constitutional reversal that had transpired by 1896. He hailed the new "era introduced by the recent amendments of the supreme law, which established universal civil freedom, gave citizenship to all born or naturalized in the United States and residing here, obliterated the race line from our systems of governments, National and State, and place our institutions upon the broad and sure foundation of the equality of all men before the law." But Harlan viewed *Plessy* as a return to an earlier "mischievous" situation where, though slavery had formally disappeared, "there would remain a power in the States, by sinister legislation, to interfere with the full enjoyment of the blessings of freedom to regulate civil rights common to all citizens, upon the basis of race, and to place in a condition of legal inferiority a large body of American citizens."[127] In dissent, Harlan channeled both the high possibilities anticipated by the Reconstruction Congress and the Jim Crow realities sanctioned by the US Supreme Court.

In the end, John Bingham's dream of the incorporation of the Bill of Rights as national protections against all forms of state discrimination and rights violation remained elusive even after decades of grueling legal development.[128] The due process rights of the poor, the indigent, the vagrant, and the laborer remained remarkably underdeveloped even as Fourteenth

Amendment protections were being expanded to protect corporations and entrepreneurial liberty.[129] And the legal status of emancipated and free African Americans in the United States, while formally transformed, became the site for one of the most ruinous constitutional counterrevolutions in American history. "A century and a half after the end of slavery," as Eric Foner put it, "the project of equal citizenship remains unfinished."[130] And yet, that unfinished constitutional and government revolution was at least begun. The Reconstruction Amendments inaugurated enormous changes in American law, policy, and statecraft, some anticipated, some unforeseen and largely unforeseeable. And there was no turning back. Despite extraordinary resistance and reaction, the American state and American citizenship were now placed on a new national and constitutional foundation with significant ramifications for the future.

THE citizenship struggles of the early nineteenth century culminated in a new vision of citizenship, constitution, and nation. The Fourteenth Amendment established a new status of consequence. Indeed, a new constitutional nationalism pervaded the post–Civil War period—aimed powerfully and precisely *against* the slaveholder's constitution. Where Roger Taney in *Dred Scott* was set to finally define American citizenship in fundamentally racial, exclusionary, and divided terms, constitutional nationalism was directed at making sure that Taney's musings would not remain the law of the land. In 1873, Thomas M. Cooley revised Joseph Story's *Commentaries on the Constitution* and put the nails in the coffin of St. George Tucker's and John C. Calhoun's defenses of sectionalism, slavery, and states' rights: "Finally the people of the country . . . have resisted this doctrine with the utmost expenditure of military force, and at an immense sacrifice of life and treasure have overthrown its adherents. In the courts, therefore, in the Cabinet, in the halls of legislation, and in the arbitrament of arms, *the national view has invariably prevailed.*"[131] John C. Hurd too penned his *Theory of Our National Existence* as a direct complement to his studies on the question in the *Law of Freedom and Bondage,* linking a new vision of the nation to the expansion of citizenship, rights, and equality in an emancipated society. For Francis Lieber, a key characteristic of "the national polity" was "the general endeavor to define more clearly, and to extend more widely, Human Rights and Civil Liberty."[132] Charles Sumner and Frederick Douglass especially exemplified the degree to which postwar nationalism could embrace and promote a distinctly inclusive, egalitarian, and emancipatory vision of civic belonging.[133]

Such constitutional nationalism was an extraordinarily effective vehicle for the construction of generality—for the creation of a much wider conception of the relevant American public, a broader aspiration to democratic equality, and larger scope for the exercise of public power. The amended Constitution now put at its center "citizens of the United States"—opening a decidedly new and generalized field for contemplating the rights of people and the obligations of government in the United States. It implicated nothing less than a new kind of state and the invention of a new juridical subject—a modern rights-bearing citizen. The constitutional reconstruction of the nation—and its instantiation in a new legal framework for governance—brought extraordinary new powers of promotion, protection, and police to the American nation-state. And it rendered problematic older antebellum conventions regarding status, association, and local police regulation. After the Civil War, constitutional law itself emerged as the crucial site for the renegotiation of the relationship of citizens to a more modern American state. As Francis Lieber observed, "At no time has the very character and essence of the American Constitution been so much discussed as in ours."[134] Harold Hyman dubbed this more powerful and prolific national constitutionalism "the Adequate Constitution." Inspired by an 1862 essay by Timothy Farrar, the theory of the Adequate Constitution took direct aim at the limited, compromised, and backward settlement promulgated by Southern ideologues in defense of the slaveholders' constitution. As Hyman put it, "Obeisance to southern dictates by Congressmen and jurists until 1861 had obscured the fact that the Constitution also imposed duties upon the national government, to act positively, as an instrument, to realize purposes that had inspired the creation of the nation. These essential purposes included the nation's duty to preserve itself as the base for the more perfect union, to guarantee to every state a republican form of government, . . . and to provide for the general welfare."[135] The adequacy theorists breathed a new vitality and a new dynamism into the very heart of America's public law.

As early as 1868, the outlines of this new and active vision of public law were already decipherable in John Norton Pomeroy's *Introduction to the Constitutional Law of the United States.* He noted that prior to the just-completed Civil War, a school of thought that included such diverse statesmen as Mason, Jefferson, Jackson, Calhoun, and Taney actively denied that the United States ever was a nation in "any true sense of the term," preferring to view the Constitution as but a compact or treaty binding consociational states.[136] With "the events of the last six years," however, this sectionalist states-rights perspective was overthrown by a more nationalist view emphasizing the people and the public law of a powerful nation-state. With early adherents like Hamilton, Jay, Marshall, Story, and Webster, this theory regarded "the United States as a nation, and its Constitution as . . .

the work of the People of the United States as a whole, as a political unit."[137] It was this conception of the national unity of the people of the United States as a whole and as a generality that triumphed after the Civil War. The citizenship struggles of the early nineteenth century culminated in a new vision of the people, the nation, and the Constitution. The power of that new dispensation would in turn underwrite a vast expansion of the capacities of the modern American state. That process began with a reconsideration of the nature of state police power and a transformation in American public law.

PARADOX
14th
Amendment

2

POLICE POWER

The State and the Transformation of American Public Law

——

The Transformation of the state is also the
transformation of its Law.
—LÉON DUGUIT

The reconstruction of the US Constitution around modern conceptions of the nation and the citizen placed the polity on a new foundation with immense ramifications for social and economic life. But formal constitutional amendment was just the beginning of the revolution in governance that created a modern democratic state in America. Simultaneous with the efforts of legislators and jurists to craft a new and modern constitutionalism, another group of intellectuals, lawmakers, and reformers began to rethink and rebuild the very infrastructure of American government. The major actors, ideas, and institutions involved in this second act of governmental reconstruction are not as well known as those behind the Thirteenth, Fourteenth, and Fifteenth Amendments. But their legacy was also significant and lasting. Their work was less the product of immediate responses to the urgent problems of slavery, Civil War, and reunion than a conscious and more long-term effort to reconstruct a modern American state.

Though it is now common to acknowledge the important state-making initiatives that accompanied the American Revolution and the original establishment of an independent national economy and society,[1] American governance before the Civil War remained highly dispersed and remarkably decentralized. Surely, fiscal, military, and political-economic imperatives spurred significant state development and generated a sophisticated central state policy-making apparatus quite early in American history.[2] But the great mass of substantive antebellum governing authority—the police power—concerning a wide range of the most important issues of the day (health, safety, morals, poverty, welfare, economy, family, labor, slavery) still remained in the hands of individual states and a plethora of relatively autonomous local jurisdictional subdivisions: counties, towns, cities, villages, districts, municipalities, and officers. Early American governance was still profoundly associative, grounded in a multiplicity of local self-governing institutions, corporations, boards, legislatures, and councils.[3]

The early American legal system too reflected the primacy of a more diffuse, locally controlled, case-by-case approach to law and policy making. Despite the admittedly significant inroads made in the direction of codification, general legislation, and a national constitutionalism, the dominant rule of law at the time of the Civil War still remained the jurisdictional, customary, and controversy-based rule of judge-made common law. As Morton Horwitz influentially argued, "Judicial promulgation and enforcement of common law rules constituted an infinitely more typical pattern of the use of law throughout most of the 19th century."[4] As late as 1881, Oliver Wendell Holmes's magisterial researches into Kent's *Commentaries* and American common law portrayed a world in which there continued to be rules "which can only be understood by reference to the infancy of procedure among the German tribes, or to the social condition of Rome under the Decemvirs."[5] The antebellum American state, in short, continued to function in modes still vaguely recognizable within ancient traditions of local self-government as well as early modern Anglo-American practices of common-law rule.[6]

That antebellum regime was forever upended by the revolution in government that forged a distinctly modern state in the United States in the decades after the Civil War. That revolution consisted of several interrelated components that are the subjects of this chapter: new nationalism, new liberalism, legal positivism, antiformalism, and, ultimately, a more robust conception of police power—the power of a state to regulate in the interest of public health, safety, and welfare. This transformation of American public law yielded a polity far more rationalized, centralized, legislated, regulated, and administered than any anticipated by the founders or experienced in the antebellum period. And it marked the emergence of a distinctly modern form of statecraft in the United States that reflected, at least roughly, some of the characteristics of Max Weber's ideal-typical vision of a modern state: a rationalized and generalized legal and administrative order amenable to legislative change; a bureaucratic apparatus of officers conducting official business with reference to an impersonal order of administrative regulations; the power to bind—to rule and regulate—persons and actions within its official jurisdiction via its laws; and the legitimate authority to use force, violence, and coercion within the territory as prescribed by the duly constituted government.[7]

But as anticipated in the introduction to this book, it would be a mistake to evaluate this governmental revolution solely through the prism of the latest state modernization theory. For as this chapter makes clear, democracy also played a crucial role in this governmental transformation. This chapter highlights those elements of critique, reform, public service, public good, and social welfare that were at the heart this era's battles with corruption, plutocracy, and socioeconomic inequality. It is impossible to understand modern transformations of state, law, legislation, regulation, and administration in isolation from the substantive aspirations of modern democratic politics. The radical expansion of police power described in this chapter demonstrates the degree to which this modern American revolution in government was worked out against background conditions of a crisis in democracy and a radical interventionism in socioeconomic policy making.

The more general causes of this legal-political transformation were as complex as the dramatic changes reshaping modern American life more generally at the turn of the twentieth century: a reorganized industrial and corporate economy; an ascendant American labor movement; an increasingly interlocked and interdependent society; rapid advances in science and technology; a growing, diversified, and increasingly mobile national and urban population; and an expanding geopolitical role for the United States in world affairs. Such factors transformed the demands made on government and set in motion political and legal developments that changed the nature of the American state. But the momentous changes inaugurated by this revolution in government are not explicable solely as predictable responses to external social and economic stimuli. Rather, the rise of a modern American state was also the consequence of a concerted and conscious effort at legal reinvention, political re-creation, and democratic reform. The creation of a modern American state involved conscious changes to public law—a creative reworking of the structures, institutions, doctrines, and underlying rationales of American government. Such changes were distinctive rather than formulaic, contingent rather than determined, and historical rather than predictable or inevitable. Modern American state building involved at its core what David Mayhew dubbed "a cognitive enterprise" and what John Dewey talked about as the application of "creative intelligence."[8] This second American revolution in government sought to make lawmaking, state building, and policy making more rational, reasonable, instrumental, efficacious, and democratic—more amenable to human will and changing human needs. The adoption of a more active, creative, and inventive approach to law and statecraft in turn unleashed an endless series of particular policy initiatives (from public utility to social service administration to antimonopoly) through which the modern state extended its reach into nearly every corner of American society and economy. Though it is a commonplace to start inquiries into political modernity with discussions of capital, industrialization, and social class, there are equally good reasons to begin with transformations in the ideas and practices governing the modern democratic state itself.

Imagining a Modern State

Theorists of American political order first began rethinking the nature of the American state during the Civil War as part of the reconception of citizenship, nation, and constitution. The reconstitution of the nation was a distinct catalyst for a more general reconsideration (and reassertion) of governmental authority in the United States. Indeed, it is difficult to separate out the development of new ideas of the state from the general growth of nationalism in this period. It was, after all, a modern nation-state that was coming into being. As Francis Lieber put it in his prescient fragment on "nationalism" dedicated to President Grant on his election in 1868, "The national polity is the normal type of modern government."[9]

With roots in the nationalist oratory of Webster and Lincoln, the immediate post–Civil War period was flooded with treatises advocating constitutional defenses of the Union and strong nationalist theories of the polity. Sidney George Fisher, John Alexander Jameson, Orestes Brownson, John C. Hurd, Elisha Mulford, and others downplayed the original significance of compact, contract, and states' rights in the creation of governmental authority and defended the overriding prerogatives of nation, union, and national government.[10] The impact of this nationalist discourse on ideas of the American state was twofold. First, it clearly articulated an aspiration toward a more powerful, unified, central government in the United States—a testament to and a guarantor of the Union's victory in war. Second, it reflected a more realistic and positivistic assessment of the powers of government to forge a new nation and realize national ambitions. It acknowledged the role of force, coercion, and violence in modern governance and the relationship of necessity to national existence and self-preservation. As Fisher wrote in the heat of battle, "If the Union and the government cannot be saved out of this terrible shock of war constitutionally, a Union and a government must be saved unconstitutionally." As Charles Merriam summarized, "In the new national school, the tendency was to disregard the doctrine of the social contract, and to emphasize strongly the instinctive forces whose action and interaction produces a state."[11] Such lessons were not solely the product of political and legal theory. They were also embodied—made manifest—in the unprecedented national state-building practices of the wartime presidency of Abraham Lincoln and the radical Reconstruction efforts of the postwar Congress.[12] From the suspension of habeas corpus to the military occupation of the South to the far-reaching governmental experiments of the Freedmen's Bureau, late nineteenth-century reformers had plenty of practices as well as theories on which to base a reconstruction of the American state.[13]

Out of these more general considerations of union and nation—and these ambitious new practices of government—there emerged a more focused and systematic reconcepualization of the American state. This new set of political and legal ideas was no longer as preoccupied with past problems of sectionalism and Civil War. Rather, a new generation of theorists and activists seized the reins from the nationalist school and steered directly toward the future, exploring the relationship of the new state to the imperatives of a new program of national social and economic development. These theorists were also more overtly international and cosmopolitan in their influences and vision, drawing on such important intellectual movements as the rise of analytical jurisprudence in England under the leadership of John Austin (inspired by Bentham) and advances in state theory in Germany under the direction of Johann Kaspar Bluntschli (inspired by Hegel).[14] The result was an impressive new set of legitimations and justifications for the expansion, centralization, and rationalization of state power in the United States. These theories provided a template for governmental transformation—an intellectual basis for the myriad of more particular reforms and changes that would dominate American politics and law from 1866 to 1932. Vernon Parrington provocatively dubbed this cooperative nexus of state theory and state action "the conscription of political theory."[15]

The late nineteenth century witnessed the fast development of a more systematic and scientific study of politics. Out of new professional associations like the American Social Science Association and the American Academy of Political and Social Science and new graduate programs at places like Columbia University, Johns Hopkins University, and the University of Chicago, a new generation of students of American politics transformed the way government was conceived and practiced.[16] The new generation built on the foundation bequeathed by the pioneering work of Francis Lieber's *Manual of Political Ethics* (1838) and Theodore Woolsey's more modern-sounding *Political Science or The State Theoretically and Practically Considered* (1878). Lieber and his disciple Woolsey contributed an important American skepticism toward state-of-nature and social-contract theories of social and governmental formation. Like Montesquieu, they favored more sociological, institutional, and historical explanations.[17] In contrast to what they termed the abstract "juristic fictions" of Hobbes, Locke, and Rousseau, they emphasized instead the social and political nature of man, the historic tendency to form communities and institutions, the practical virtues of local self-government, and the reciprocal relationship of individual rights and public duties.[18] But in the end, despite their useful skepticism and their historical defense of positive government, Lieber's and Woolsey's political ethics were still rooted in early nineteenth-century conditions. As Parrington crisply put it, "The need for a coercive state in harmony with a centralizing industrialism was not likely to be realized by a man whose eyes were turned back fondly to a simple village life."[19]

A new generation of modern political science scholarship came of age with the appearance of three texts that more clearly delineated the nature, power, and functions of a modern American state: John W. Burgess's *Political Science and Comparative Constitutional Law* (1890), Woodrow Wilson's *The State: Elements of Historical and Practical Politics* (1890), and Westel Woodbury Willoughby's *An Examination of the Nature of the State* (1896).[20] The culmination of decades of study and reconsideration, these texts together moved American conceptions of state, sovereignty, and public law beyond the classic nineteenth-century understandings of Tocqueville, Lieber, and Woolsey.[21] Rather than orient their inquiries around concepts of local authority, self-government, and civil liberty, Burgess, Wilson, and Willoughby explicitly emphasized the centrality of the modern nation-state and its encompassing political and legal powers. This distinctly modern theory of the American state involved innovation along two theoretical lines: a reconsideration of the nature of the state itself as a legal and political entity and a more positivist, functionalist account of the nature of American state power. In turn, these state theories would greatly affect American conceptions of liberalism and general welfare, legislation and police power, and administration and public service. All of these developments involved fairly long and technical political and jurisprudential analyses. But perhaps the most abstruse and abstract was the attempt to generate a clear and coherent idea of what, in fact, the modern state was itself as an entity. Late nineteenth- and early twentieth-century political and social thought was overrun with a fascinating and important discussion concerning the nature and character of groups—what they were, whether and how they "acted," and what was the source of their influence in the world. The collective identity, legal personality, and peculiar power of groups became one of the key questions of the day; and the subject preoccupied the very best legal and political minds: Otto von Gierke, Frederic William Maitland, Harold Laski, and John Dewey.[22] As the state was viewed as the highest form of group association and collective action, it became the focus of special scholarly attention. Indeed, arguably not since the late seventeenth and early eighteenth centuries had the question of the origin and nature of the state sustained such intense and rigorous scrutiny. It is not hard to understand why. Increasing modern awareness that large collectivities—corporations, cooperatives, unions, and especially states— were exerting unprecedented force in social, political, and economic affairs begged for better explanations. The individualistic theories of the past—social contract, natural rights, and classical economics—no longer adequately explained the present.

Out of these new discussions and new needs emerged a proliferation of contending theories of the nature of the state as an entity in itself. The intellectual roots of these theories were a curious blend. Burgess began with Hegel and the German "idea of the state" (*Staatsidee*) as an abstract ethical entity—a rational unity that acts and knows and wills as "the spirit which is present in the world and which *consciously* realizes itself therein." But it was perhaps Bluntschli, once characterized as attempting to do for the modern European state what "Aristotle accomplished for the Hellenic," who exerted even more influence on American political science through his more grounded conception of the state as an organism or person.[23] In trying to further delineate their conception of the modern state as an entity, American theorists also drew on the evolutionary social organicism of Auguste Comte and Herbert Spencer and the analytical jurisprudential categories of John Austin and Thomas Erskine Holland. Willoughby consciously embraced just such an eclecticism, defending the need to approach the nature of the state as an entity from "a number of viewpoints." In addition to classical conceptions of the "civitas" and Hegelian conceptions of a substantive "being" or spirit, Willoughby devoted special attention to the "central concept of juristic political thinking"—that is, the "envisagement of the State as a legal person"[24]

In the end, the intellectual effort to specifically define the existential character or juristic personality of this thing called "the state" came in for some fairly harsh criticism, as in Morris Cohen's devastating attack on the "communal ghosts" of legal and political philosophy.[25] But it would be a mistake to underestimate the general force of this reconceptualization of the state as an entity in itself with a juristic personality and agency, ready to accept and wield an ambitious new set of governing powers and rationales. For the collective result of this disparate effort was a reimagining of the American state similar to the reimagining of the American nation. This new vision opened the door for an understanding of the state as something more than a simple agglomeration of individuals or groups, more than a jurisdiction or territory, more than a governing council or a representative legislature. These theories yielded an idea of the state as intensely related to and the product of society, country, and government—a whole greater than the sum of its parts. By envisioning the state as an entity itself, these theorists helped to establish and to legitimate an idea of the state not as a passive political reflection of primary social and economic forces but as a powerful prime mover and shaker in its own right with its own ends, objectives, and functions.

While fascination with formal juristic theories of state personality proved short-lived, a more historical, empirical, and functional account of the origins of the state met with longer-term success. Woodrow Wilson's *The State* began with an explicit critique of theological, social-contract, and natural-law theories of the state. Wilson introduced a more realistic vision: "The probable origin of government is a question of fact, to be settled, not by conjecture, but by history." Building on Lieber and Woolsey and the anthropological idea of the sociability of man, Wilson and others developed a more relational and instrumental account of the rise of government and statecraft. Rather than root the state in an ancient act of divine will or some eternally binding primordial compact between ruler and ruled, they emphasized the concrete and contingent human origins of the state in a historical "search after convenience." State and governmental institutions were historically constructed, owing "their existence and development to deliberate human effort."[26] Rather than see the state as a somewhat static entity ever bound by some sort of higher law, this simple historicist move liberated theorists and reformers to think about the state as a dynamic agent for larger human ends, purposes, and objectives—an instrument of social change and development. Willoughby ended his diverse discussion of theories of state by quoting Lester Frank Ward: "Government is becoming more and more the organ of social consciousness, and more and more the servant of Social Will."[27] These were the beginnings of a more sociological conception of the state as a new form of modern organized power rooted in a complex set of social, political, and institutional relationships

Together these new ideas of the state as a dynamic historical actor and a new organizational configuration of power augured important changes in the nature of the American polity from 1866 to 1932. Some of the general implications are already visible in these theorists' express conclusions about the new ends and aims of the modern state. Bluntschli drew on old Roman law ideas of res publica and salus publica in articulating "the public welfare" as "the indispensable object of policy" and "the chief duty of the State." But he distinctly modernized such traditional concepts in his definition of "the true end of the State" as "the development of national capacities, the perfecting of the national life."[28] Wilson also concluded his treatise with a discussion of the active objects of the state as a "beneficent and indispensable organ of society" pursuing "every means, therefore, by which society may be perfected through the instrumentality of government."[29] Willoughby was even more direct about the ultimate objective of the state to "promote the *General Welfare,* either economically, intellectually, or morally." Such a modern perspective, he concluded, pointed "to an inevitable extension of the State's activities far beyond those at present exercised."[30]

Such state ideas were important antecedents to the development of a full-blown pragmatic and progressive conception of statecraft. By 1927, John Dewey's *The Public and Its Problems* consolidated and transformed many of these original modernist intuitions. He began by exorcising the old metaphysics of "the State"—the "unbridled generalizing and fixating tendency" that "produced a magnified idealization of the State . . . beyond criticism." Dewey recommended instead a more pragmatic, antiformalist focus on "the public and its problems"—"a consistently empirical or historical treatment of the changes in political forms and arrangements, free from any overriding conceptual domination such as is inevitable when a 'true' state is postulated." Holding that "the formation of states must be an experimental process," Dewey embraced the full implications of a modern democratic state as a practical public sphere of social cooperation and collective problem-solving.[31] As he put it in *Liberalism and Social Action,* this was a "new liberal" conception of a "state that has the responsibility for creating institutions under which individuals can effectively realize the potentialities that are theirs."[32]

Together, these interventions amounted to a vastly increased self-consciousness about the nature and possibility of the modern state. Stripped of the metaphysics of theology and the majesty of absolutism, the pragmatic rediscovery of the state as a practical and historical problem freed the state to become a more spontaneous instrument of democratic self-governance. Regal notions of raison d'état were displaced by a more democratic and functional raison d'être rooted in the provision of public services in the interest of the public welfare. The concept of the state was disenchanted, historicized, and reappropriated to the modern political tasks of problem-solving and public policy making. The state, power, and rule were no longer formally viewed as ends in themselves but more pragmatically as modern institutional means to the accomplishment of important public ends. Such an instrumental and pragmatic approach to the state opened the door to a vast array of new political, social, and economic possibilities. And in the end, the multitude of problems and objectives embraced by the new conception of the statecraft precipitated a general reworking of both American liberalism and American democracy.

New Liberalism, Positive Liberty, and the Common Good

Armed with new theories of a modern nation-state, American theorists also famously reenvisioned the nature of liberalism in this period. Patterned after a similar effort underway in Great Britain visible in the influential work of T. H. Green, L. T. Hobhouse, and Graham Wallas, American thinkers consciously crafted a "new liberalism" for modern times.[33] In one of the most creative and prolific periods in American political thought since the founding, a plethora of theorists and publicists led by Lester Frank Ward, Walter Weyl, Walter Lippmann, Herbert Croly, and John Dewey reworked the foundational tenets of American liberal and democratic thought amid rapidly changing social and economic conditions. Their self-styled "new" liberalism consisted of three basic positions: first, a devastating critique of "old" or classical liberalism as a political and philosophical anachronism; second, a distinctly positive rather than negative conception of liberty and freedom; and third, a reconstruction of the idea of the public good and the common welfare.

One of the most common features of late nineteenth- and early twentieth-century American thought was a wide-ranging critique of some traditional ways of thinking about society, polity, and economy as well as law. As Walter Lippmann put it in "Some Necessary Iconoclasm," in his precocious *A Preface to Politics*, "If only men can keep their minds freed from formalism, idol worship, fixed ideas, and exalted abstractions," they could attain the more active, instrumental, and inventive statecraft that he felt this revolutionary period required.[34] The idols, abstractions, and formalisms most under fire were a set of old liberal ideas concerning the nature of liberty and the relationship of individuals to the state. In a relentless series of spirited critiques, progressive writers excoriated earlier philosophies of natural right, individualism, and laissez-faire. As they saw it, by the late nineteenth century, the complex and multilayered theories of John Locke, Adam Smith, Jeremy Bentham, and John Stuart Mill were being radically distorted through the double impact of the social Darwinist philosophies of Herbert Spencer and William Graham Sumner and a rapidly industrializing, profoundly inegalitarian economy. What were originally liberating ideas honed in historic battles with despotic and aristocratic regimes were distorting into a caricature of liberty and freedom as something like the bleak obligation to be left alone amid a fiercely competitive social and economic struggle for "the survival of the fittest."

Herbert Spencer had argued in his *Social Statics* and again in *The Man Versus the State* that human development was best achieved by avoiding the "slavery" and "sins" of legislators. Instead of democratic legislative reform, Spencer endorsed the harsh, natural, and "severe discipline to which the animate creation at large is subject: a discipline which is pitiless in the working out of good." The result was an especially brutal and noninterventionist take on the "partial and temporary suffering" that so frequently afflicted humanity. For Spencer, "the poverty of the incapable, the distresses that come upon the imprudent, the starvation of the idle, and those shoulderings aside of the weak by the strong, which leave so many 'in shallows and in miseries,'" were simply "the decrees of a large, far-seeing benevolence."[35] Forsaking its crusading origins in emancipatory revolutions against political authoritarianism, religious coercion, slavery, privation, and monopoly privilege, liberalism in a Spencerian mode was fast transmogrifying into a reactionary and merciless form of laissez-faire apologetics.

Outraged at how liberal ideas could be used to justify inequality, deprivation, selfishness, austerity, and inaction, American reformers began an important and lasting intellectual reconstruction. Their critique of laissez-faire was unyielding. Lester Frank Ward led the way. He eviscerated Spencer's chief American disciple William Graham Sumner's book *What Social Classes Owe to Each Other,* wherein "all attempts at social reform are unsparingly condemned, and reformers of every kind are lashed and goaded in a merciless manner." Ward detected in Sumner's excessively aggressive tone a personally "unhappy victim" as well as a religious-like creed in its last throes. He suggested that Sumner, far from winning any new converts to an "old" philosophy, instead only showed "that the laissez faire doctrine, if it could be carried to a logical conclusion, would be nihilistic and suicidal."[36] Frank J. Goodnow and J. Allen Smith added convincing indictments of laissez-faire's eighteenth-century outdatedness. The "absolute and universal application" of the "political and economic theory known as *laissez faire,*" Goodnow argued in *Social Reform and the Constitution,* "makes social reform impossible . . . and regards political and economic conditions as static rather than progressive in character. The result of its universal application will be to fix upon the country for all time institutions . . . established in the eighteenth century." Smith added, "The doctrine of laissez faire no longer expresses the generally accepted view of state functions, but merely the selfish view of that relatively small class, which though it controls the industrial system, feels the reins of political control

PARADOX

slipping out of its hands. The limitation of governmental functions which was the rallying-cry of the liberals a century ago has thus become the motto of the present-day conservative."[37] In "Individualism, Old and New," John Dewey had no trouble pulling together these and other critical arguments for his devastating portrait of the sclerotic ideas passing for liberalism in the old regime. Dewey charged that old liberalism had grown (a) too static, failing to account for dramatic changes in socioeconomic context; (b) too negative, emphasizing a formal, legalistic liberty from the state instead of a substantive, positive commitment to human freedom; (c) too economistic, defining freedom in almost exclusively monetary terms and ignoring the importance of cultural expression: science, art, intellect, aesthetics, romance; and (d) too individualistic, failing to recognize human beings as fundamentally changing and growing, associative and relational creatures.[38] He called for a new, renascent liberalism to positively meet the challenges of the twentieth century.

Out of this sweeping and multidimensional critique of classical liberalism and laissez-faire, there emerged a new conception of positive liberty—a conception that intersected with simultaneous calls for a more positive law and a more positive state. At the center of this new idea of positive liberty was a critique of classical liberal notion of liberty as a purely negative phenomenon. The locus classicus of that negative definition was John Stuart Mill's influential proclamation in *On Liberty* that "the sole end for which mankind are warranted, individually or collectively, in interfering with the liberty of action of any of their number, is self-protection. . . . The only purpose for which power can be rightly exercised over any members of a civilised community, against his will, is to prevent harm to others."[39] Mill's harm principle captured the essence of a negative liberty perspective— emphasizing individual liberty as freedom *from* outside coercions or interventions by others or by the government. One was most free to the extent that others were individually and collectively limited from interfering with one's own prerogatives. Negative liberty thus placed a first priority on restraining outside power, especially governmental power. Particularly troublesome for new liberals was the way in which Mill's theory transmuted the common-law maxim "sic utere tuo ut alienum non laedas" (use your own so as not to injure another) from a traditional limitation on private property rights into a new formal limitation on governmental action.

The new liberal critique of negative liberty took several forms. First, critics built on A. V. Dicey's observation in *Law and Public Opinion* that the world had changed remarkably since Mill penned his simple negative principle separating private freedom from public coercion. In an urbanizing and industrializing world of complex business and social transactions, private and public interest appeared increasingly intertwined and interdependent. As Dicey put it, "Since 1859 almost every event which has happened has directed public attention to the extreme difficulty, not to say the impossibility, of drawing a rigid distinction between actions which merely concern a man himself and actions which also concern society. . . . Human knowledge has intensified the general conviction that even the apparently innocent action of an individual may injuriously affect the welfare of a whole community."[40] Oliver Wendell Holmes's famous dissent in *Lochner v. New York* (1905) aimed not only at Spencer's *Social Statics* but at Mill's harm principle in precisely this way: "The liberty of the citizen to do as he likes so long as he does not interfere with the liberty of others to do the same, which has been a shibboleth for some well-known writers, is interfered with by school laws, by the Post Office, by every state or municipal institution which takes his money for purposes thought desirable or not, whether he likes it or not." Times had changed so significantly by the late nineteenth and early twentieth century, and social and economic life had grown so interconnected, that even fairly conservative writers and jurists acknowledged the unworkability of Mill's simple bifurcation of private and public, individual and social, negative liberty and positive compulsion As Supreme Court Justice David Brewer noted in *Budd v. New York* (1892), "There is scarcely any property in whose use the public has no interest. No man liveth unto himself alone, and no man's property is beyond the touch of another's welfare."[41] Despite the ever irresistible urge for simple and absolute rules, the complex society and economy emerging in the late nineteenth century made negative liberty, like laissez-faire, a seeming anachronism.[42]

The second more substantive inroad the new liberals made on negative liberty was the idea that formal liberty from outside public intervention did not seem like actual freedom at all, especially when examined in concrete, real-world situations. That was the gist of Roscoe Pound's famous jurisprudential critique of "liberty of contract." Pound began his argument with a genealogy of old liberalism: "It began as a doctrine of political economy, as a phase of Adam Smith's doctrine which we commonly call *laisser-faire*. It was propounded as a utilitarian principle of politics and legislation by Mill. Spencer derived it from his formula of justice. In this way it became a chief article in the creed of those who sought to minimize the functions of the state." But in minimizing the role of the state in modern labor disputes, the formal and negative liberty of the worker to be "free" to contract for sub-subsistence wages, long hours, and poor working conditions seemed to be turning freedom into its opposite. As Pound noted, true liberty did not include the right to contract oneself into slavery. Yet the formal, mechanical, and juristic conceptions of classical legal thought seemed to be doing just that to "the weak and necessitous" in the name of a "negative liberty" of contract.[43] Pound excoriated this overly "individualistic conception of justice, which exaggerates the importance of property and contract, promotes private right at the expense of public right, and is hostile to legislation, taking a minimum of law-making to be the ideal." He advocated instead a more positive, active conception of liberty *in fact*—not formal freedom *from* interference as an end in itself but substantive freedom *toward* the more positive development of human capacities and the establishment of social justice.[44]

In his *Lectures on Jurisprudence,* Pound placed his own contribution "Freedom of Industry and Contract" after T. H. Green's *Principles of Political Obligation.*[45] Green's influential theory of positive liberty resonated all too perfectly with American reform efforts. Green presented the substantive idea so clearly in his lecture "Liberal Legislation and Freedom of Contract" in 1881, that it is worth quoting at length:

> We shall probably all agree that freedom, rightly understood, is the greatest of blessings; that its attainment is the true end of all our effort as citizens. . . . But when we thus speak of freedom, we should consider carefully what we mean by it. We do not mean freedom from restraint or compulsion. We do not mean merely freedom to do as we like irrespective of what it is that we like. We do not mean a freedom that can be enjoyed by one man at a cost of a loss of freedom to others. When we speak of freedom as something to be so highly prized, we mean a positive power or capacity of doing or enjoying something worth doing or enjoying, and that, too, something that we do or enjoy in common with others. We mean by it a power which each man exercises through the help or security given him by his fellow-men, and which he in turn helps to secure for them. When we measure the progress of a society by its growth in freedom, we measure it by the increasing development and exercise on the whole of those powers contributing to social good with which we believe the members of the society to be endowed; in short, by the greater power on the part of the citizens as a body to make the most and best of themselves.[46]

In this way, Green shifted attention away from formal legal conceptions of freedom and liberty as protection from outside compulsion to more social and positive measures of liberty as the power and ability to actually achieve something—to improve and to develop. Analogous to the move already underway concerning the positive state, Green viewed positive liberty as "the liberation of the powers of all men equally for contributions to a common good."[47] Individual liberty and the common good were thus understood as mutually reinforcing rather than opposing forces, and freedom was viewed as having social as well as individual attributes.[48]

American progressive thinkers built directly on this more idealist and positive notion of liberty in reconstructing their notions of the public good. Though ideas of common good and people's welfare had deep roots in American political and legal thought, new theories of positive liberty and positive statecraft brought renewed attention and further development.[49] The locus classicus for the progressive rehabilitation of the public good was John Dewey and James Tufts's *Ethics*. *Ethics* was a revolutionary text combining (a) a comprehensive and critical survey of philosophical ethics from Aristotle to Kant and beyond; (b) a classic statement of the new American social philosophy of positive liberty and the public good; and (c) a practical discussion of a series of contemporary social problems demanding social action, from corporations and unions to prison reform and public administration. In "The Two Senses of Freedom," Dewey and Tufts, like Green, distinguished negative and formal "freedom *from* subjection to the will and control of others" from what they termed "effective freedom" requiring "positive control of the resources necessary to carry purposes into effect, possession of the means to satisfy desires, and mental equipment with the trained powers of initiative and reflection."[50] In "Happiness and Social Ends," Dewey and Tufts went on to articulate a revised utilitarian conception of the true good as positive, inclusive, expanding, and common: "In substance, the only end which fulfills these conditions is the social good." Rejecting the hedonistic, selfish calculus at the heart of traditional utilitarianism, Dewey and Tufts reached for an idea of the common good and the importance of the welfare of others rooted in a more social conception of human beings with inherent social ties finding their own good in common with others.[51] They advocated a new measure for evaluating public laws and policies in terms of their ability to set free "individual capacities in such a way as to make them available for the development of the general happiness or the common good." As they concluded, "The test is whether the general, the public, organization and order are promoted in such a way as to equalize opportunity for all."[52]

Ethics was but one of the more comprehensive statements of the new public philosophy. Dewey went on to develop these germinal ideas much further in a steady stream of articles and books like *The Public and Its Problems*. Lippmann and Croly incorporated elements of positive liberty and the public good in their manifestos *Drift and Mastery* and *The Promise of American Life*. Jane Addams detected "a new conscience"—a "new moral consciousness." Walter Weyl dubbed it a "new social spirit," suggesting, "It involves common action and a common lot. It emphasizes social rather than private ethics, social rather than individual responsibility."[53] In *The Ethical Principle and Its Application in State Relations,* Marietta Kies, a student of Dewey and Henry Carter Adams, even associated this new public spirit with "grace" or "self-sacrifice" as crucial to the progressive development of the state and the nation.[54]

Such testaments to positive liberty and the public good were ubiquitous in the Progressive Era. And the links between new positive theories of statecraft and new theories of liberalism created a potent intellectual environment for action, change, and reform. Indeed, armed with these new substantive conceptions of the nature of modern state power—positive freedom, common good—progressives embarked on an equally ambitious rethinking of the foundations of American public law.

From Legal Positivism to Legal Realism

As Léon Duguit noted, the transformation of the state moved hand in hand with the transformation of law.[55] The making of the modern American state was accompanied by new theories of law that provided new instrumentalities and legitimations of active government. As Roscoe Pound noted, "The changed order of things has been felt in legal science."[56] This transformation of modern American law and jurisprudence took many forms. And legal historians have deployed a dizzying array of names for the basic movement, such as antiformalism, legal pragmatism, sociological jurisprudence, and legal realism.[57] This proliferation of categories sometimes obscures the underlying commonalities linking political, social, economic, and legal thought as well as the more general international convergence of modern legal theories in this period. One such commonality concerns the original contribution of legal positivism to the development of a modern and critical American jurisprudence.

Legal positivism in its simplest sense refers to an understanding of law as humanly posited—that is, law not as established by theological gods but by historical human beings and communities. Positive law is man-made law rooted in empirical social facts—an artifact of historical conventions and contingent social needs. Legal positivism, in short, is a quintessentially modern, disenchanted, antimetaphysical way of looking at the origins and nature of law, rejecting earlier theories of law's links to nature and to the divine. The roots of legal positivism, obviously, are diverse and extensive, stretching all the way back to the general emergence of a more humanistic, skeptical, and scientific outlook on the world.[58] But two sources were more proximate for the American reception of legal positivism. The first was the influential positive sociology of Auguste Comte, articulating the need for the systematic and scientific study of human society liberated from theology and metaphysics.[59] The second was the more concrete legal impact of John Austin's philosophy of law. Austin's *The Province of Jurisprudence Determined* and his posthumously published *Lectures on Jurisprudence* revived interest in the reformist legal ideas of Jeremy Bentham and provided a classic English statement of a positivist approach to law that was rapidly spreading throughout Europe.[60] Approached as a starting point—as an opening argument in a great legal debate—rather than as a final analytical jurisprudence of formal legal categories, legal positivism had a transformative impact on American jurisprudence. It was an opening salvo in legal rationalization in the United States, precipitating a whole range of later critical and functionalist accounts of the relationship between law and politics.

Austin's analytical jurisprudence itself found many adherents and advocates in the United States, including John Chipman Gray, Henry T. Terry, Albert Kocourek, and Wesley Newcomb Hohfeld. For Gray, it was Austin that led jurisprudence out of the bramble bush of theological and moral abstraction and toward a more scientific approach.[61] Austin, following Bentham's original critique of Blackstone, insisted on a harsh analytical separation of law from morality—of the Is from the Ought, so as to cleanse jurisprudence of the myth and magic of some medieval and common-law thinking. Morris Cohen weighed this contribution thus: "Just as Machiavelli separated the science of politics from that of ethics and Grotius made the theory of law independent of theology, so Austin made jurisprudence a distinct science by sharply distinguishing between the legal and the moral."[62] Austin was interested in "positive law"—law as it was made and deployed by officials, law as an expression of force and power and as a tool or instrument of authority.[63]

The modern critical potential of this more objective and instrumental formulation of law as command was not missed by the architects of American sociological jurisprudence and legal realism. Roscoe Pound began his own work crafting a new sociological jurisprudence by drawing explicitly on the inheritance of analytical jurisprudence, especially (1) the idea of law "as something made consciously by lawgivers," (2) the role of "force and constraint behind legal rules," (3) the new emphasis on statute law, and (4) the social consequentialist perspective of utilitarian philosophy.[64] Felix Cohen later rooted the broad intellectual trend toward "functionalism" in philosophy and law in analytical jurisprudence: "If you want to understand something, observe it in action. Applied within the field of law itself, this approach leads to a definition of legal concepts, rules, and institutions in terms of judicial decisions or other acts of state-force. Whatever cannot be so translated is functionally meaningless."[65] Ultimately, American legal pragmatists offered pointed criticisms of analytical jurisprudence as a final formal theory and quickly moved on to more sociological and empirical investigations of lawmaking and state force.[66] But in the end, American theorists all acknowledged the original contribution of positivism to a critical and progressive theory of law. As Julius Stone put it, it was the Austinians who first "washed the law in cynical acid" and established a basis for a more modern, realistic, and pragmatic jurisprudence.[67]

Ultimately, however, the revolution in modern American legal thought pushed past legal positivism in search of a more skeptical cutting edge. Theorists found it in a tradition of antiformalism and critical realism that launched a profusion of new critical perspectives in American jurisprudence from historical and sociological jurisprudence to the more radical reconstructions of legal pragmatism and legal realism proper. The roots of this critical tradition ran deep. Both Perry Miller and David Brion Davis drew connections back to an original revolutionary and radical strain in American religious and political thought.[68] In law, this vernacular antiformalism was reinforced by trends in historical jurisprudence as well as an interest in legal evolution that stretched back to the Scottish Enlightenment. The rise of a more professional and empirical American social science brought another layer of sophistication to the critical historical-sociological analysis of law. Roscoe Pound's sociological jurisprudence was an important jurisprudential synthesis of many of these tendencies, culminating in his more instrumental and policy-oriented vision of modern legal action.[69] Together, these influences began moving modern American jurisprudence out of the shadow of legal positivism toward the more radical formulations of an emergent legal realism.

The long progressive battle against the conservative legal formalisms of the Gilded Age only sharpened the critique.[70] Charles Beard threw down the gauntlet in his critical economic interpretation of American constitutionalism: "In the absence of a critical analysis of legal evolution, all sorts of vague abstractions dominate most of the thinking that is done in the field of law." Following Rudolf von Jhering's instrumental assertion that "law does not 'grow,' but is, in fact, 'made,'" Beard excoriated the unrealistic, "juristic view" of a Constitution above party conflict: "Separated from the social and economic fabric by which it is, in part, conditioned and which, in turn, it helps condition, it has no reality."[71] A host of early twentieth-century reformist law writers joined Beard's attack on the detached, moralistic, and absolute rights formulations of formal jurisprudence. Critical realism emphasized instead the actual politics and everyday economics of legal development: the contingency, the contestedness, and the controversialness of law at particular places and times. In a powerful attempt to demythologize the rule of law, these theorists attacked the notion of law as divinely inspired, as moral imperative, or as formally deductive logic. They suggested instead that law and rights were distinctly social and political products—deeply implicated in the economic and class struggles of a modernizing society and economy.

Of course, this more thoroughgoing legal skepticism was illustrated most eloquently by the high priest of American legal realism, Oliver Wendell Holmes Jr., who in "The Path of the Law" (1897) argued that the law that he was interested in knowing had nothing to do with morals or ethical standards or rightness or "ought-ness."[72] Rather, in a wonderfully subversive move, Holmes took the perspective of the "bad man"—the outlaw. And as he provocatively put it, the bad man did not care two straws for axioms or deductions or the moral roots of law. For Holmes and the bad man, "prophecies of what the courts will do in fact, and nothing more pretentious," were the essence of law. Holmes was not interested in the idealistic aspirations of legalism and rights. He was interested in their real-world consequences: the real power that was exercised by courts in the name of law, the real pain and suffering inflicted—the takings and redistributions and renegotiation of economic and political interests—that ultimately were the effects of "breaking the law" or of "violating a right." No rose-colored glasses here about what went on in courts. Holmes endorsed a harsh analytical separation of law and morality—of the Is and the Ought in law—that remains an important part of American critical legal thought to the present.

As Philip Wiener, Bruce Kuklick, and James Kloppenberg have established, Holmes's realist perspective was very much a part of the distinctive and important American intellectual tradition known as pragmatism.[73] Pragmatism was a tradition with formal philosophical insights honed in the treatises of Charles Peirce, William James, and John Dewey and with perspectives on the relationship of power and knowledge, political economy and statecraft that formed a critical foundation for an emergent American social science. At the center of pragmatism was a deep skepticism about formal and metaphysical debates about the nature of truth and knowledge and a comfortable embrace of a more consequentialist, instrumental, realistic—in a word, pragmatic—assessment of the nature of truth claims. As James once put it, "Truth is something that happens to an idea": the "cash-value" of an idea, to be weighed and evaluated by a knowledge-based community according to the consequences it produces—the work the idea does in the actual historical world. In James's words, truth was nothing more or less than "an idea that will carry us prosperously from any one part of our experience to any other part, linking things satisfactorily, working securely, simplifying, saving labor, it is true for just so much, true instrumentally."[74] By challenging, and in many cases jettisoning, ancient legal and philosophical abstractions like natural law, natural man, liberty of contract, and the like, pragmatists created room for more sociological investigations of the actual impact of those abstractions on social and economic life as it was lived by real human beings and, consequently, opened the door to change—to legislation, regulation, administration, and much-needed political and socioeconomic reform.

If Oliver Wendell Holmes Jr. was the most eloquent and early of legal realists, John Dewey was its most capacious and conscientious theorist.[75] Like his early hero Emerson, Dewey did not write that much directly about law, but in a short essay entitled "My Philosophy of Law," he made all the important connections to his larger pragmatic theory.[76] There he argued that the philosophical dimension in law was concerned primarily with "the principles which can be employed to justify and/or criticize existing legal rules and practices." Historically, he noted, the overarching tendency was to look for that standard outside of time and human history—the will or reason of God or the ultimate and intrinsic law of nature, forging a "distinction between what happens to exist at a given time and what might and should be," or the Ought versus the Is. "What lies back of this identification of source with end and standard," Dewey contended, "is the belief that unless a higher and more fixed source than experience can be found, there is no sure ground for any genuinely philosophic valuation of law as it actually exists." But for Dewey, of course, this metaphysical quest was hopeless—beyond the capabilities of man, reason, or philosophy. Rather, for Dewey (who was a keen student of Hegel), social and historical human experience was the ground—the only possible ground—we have to go on. He argued that experience permeated the philosophy of law as it in fact came down to us: "As a matter of fact [all] legal philosophies have reflected and are sure to continue to reflect movements of the period in which they are produced, and hence cannot be separated from what these movements stand for." Dewey's move, the pragmatic move, was to embrace rather than to try to flee this grounding in human, historical experience. What was required was a historically self-conscious, disenchanted, thoroughly modern legal philosophy that recognized this experiential component (contingent, changing, fallible, human as it was) as the only possible grounding for law. As one of Dewey's more recent disciples, Richard Rorty, put it: "To accept the contingency of starting-points is to accept our inheritance from, and our conversation with, our fellow-humans as our only source of guidance. . . . Our glory is in our participation in fallible and transitory human projects, not in our obedience to permanent nonhuman constraints."[77]

Dewey's philosophy of law was "a program for action to be tested in action," not "something that can be judged (except beyond assertions of fact and matters of logical consistency) on a purely intellectual basis." Law was "through and through a social phenomenon; social in origin, in purpose or end, and in application." It could not be talked about in isolation from society or history but could "be discussed only in terms of the social conditions in which it arises and of what it concretely does there." Echoing James's conception of truth, Dewey argued, "A given legal arrangement is what it does, and what it does lies in the field of modifying and/or maintaining human activities as going concerns." He concluded that, without this emphasis on social activity and social application, "there are scraps of paper or voices in the air but nothing that can be called law."[78]

A host of legal realists followed in Holmes's and Dewey's pragmatic path, advancing a growing skepticism about the usefulness of higher law theories in the development of law and society. Such theories for them were frequently portrayed as simple rationalizations hiding biases, prejudice, and just plain legal uncertainty. The realist goal was to strip courts and laws of what Karl Llewellyn called the "myth, folderol, and claptrap" of theoretical rights talk and to look at law plainly in terms of who was doing what to whom and what were the socioeconomic consequences. Realists were interested in law in action rather than law in theory. Law was nothing more than what happened in fact—what actually, empirically happened or changed in the name of law wherever practiced by legal officers high and low. Llewellen echoed Holmes in the *Bramble Bush:* "The doing of something about disputes is the business of law. And the people who have the doing in charge, whether they be judges or sheriffs or clerks or jailers or lawyers, are officials of the law. What these officials do about disputes is to my mind, the law itself. And rules through all of this are important so far as they help you see or predict what officials will do. That is all their importance, except as pretty playthings."[79]

Morton White best characterized this critical-realist turn in modern American social and legal theory as a "revolt against formalism"—a revolt against false ideals with a goal of exposing underlying actualities. In a strain of critical thought that he traced from John Dewey back to Hegel, White documented the keen skepticism towards abstract formalities and high concepts that distorted social reality in philosophical, political, economic, social, and legal thinking at the time. Not the ideal of freedom but effective freedom—actual freedom—was the objective of modern inquiry: not shadow democracy but real democracy; not abstract equality or formal liberty of contract but real social equality and actual human liberty; not mechanical jurisprudence but a modern, realistic, and sociologically attuned jurisprudence.

It is hard to overestimate the influence and impact of this transformation in modern American legal thought on legal, economic, and social policy. Realist analysis focused directly on who was doing what to whom through the actual instrumentalities of law beneath the glittering generalities, concepts, theories, and justifications. A more realistic vision of law thus had immediate implications for thinking about the existing imbalance of power in modern political democracy as well as the maldistribution of wealth in modern political economy. The lasting contribution of American antiformalism was a thorough demonstration of the distortions and injustices that flowed from a narrow legal conception of the aspirations of individuals, the moral basis of rule, and the public/private compartmentalization of power and right. Realists and antiformalists were committed to illuminating the real-world mobilization of social, economic, and political power often masked by formalities of the rule of law.[80] Most importantly, the antiformalist critique of law was a crucial prerequisite to rethinking the reach and scope of modern social legislation and police regulation in the United States. Critical realism spurred legal development away from the perceived absurdities, irrationalities, and inefficiencies of common-law decision-making and toward a more systematic and rationalized vision of law as a tool of modern governance and policy making—an instrument of a democratic people and a modern state that could be used to accomplish necessary social ends.[81] Indeed, the historicism, realism, and pragmatism at the center of the new American legal thinking meshed perfectly with the simultaneous effort of legal reformers to rethink the nature and extent of modern state police power.

Police Power and the Modern Legislative State

Legal positivism, new liberalism, and antiformalism provided an effective foundation for a transition to a new age of social legislation and police regulation in the United States. And legions of legal and social theorists have cut their teeth describing and diagnosing this great legal transformation— what Franz Neumann referred to as "the change in the function of law in modern society." For Jürgen Habermas, the modern "materialization of law" led to the rise of the "'service administration' of the regulatory state, which assumes tasks of providing basic services and infrastructure, planning and risk prevention."[82] For Paul Vinogradoff, "a new constructive point of view" was developing in modern law in response to "great social crisis": "the individualistic order of society . . . giving way before the impact of an inexorable process of socialization."[83] Harold Laski and Roscoe Pound also pointed to the "socialization of law" as key to modern socio-legal change. As Laski put it, "The great society has outgrown the mould to which the nineteenth century would have fashioned it."[84] Pound highlighted "social control in the service state": "In the nineteenth century, treatises on the science of law were taken up with the nature of law [and] the relation of law and morals. . . . Today we do not ask so much what law is as what it does."[85]

In *Law and Social Order in the United States,* Willard Hurst added important legal flesh to the bare bones of socialization and modernization theories by identifying an all-important shift in emphasis from common law to statute law—from particular, ex post adjudication to general, ex ante legislation—at the heart of this modern legal transformation. Hurst introduced the topic with a simple chart:

SUBJECT MATTER OF LAW

Common Law	*Statute Law*
Contract	Government organization
Tort	Schools
Property	Roads
Mortgage and other security	Taxation
Domestic relations	Public health
Basic crimes against person	Corporate organization
	Public utilities
	Antitrust law
	Securities regulation
	Collective bargaining
	Insurance regulation

Hurst's understanding of the basic transformation was not one-dimensional or unidirectional. The complex interpenetration of common law and statute law—private law and public law—remained characteristic of American legality throughout the twentieth century. But Hurst's chart underscored a significant historical shift in the emphases, technologies, and legitimations of law as the United States moved increasingly away from particularist litigation and one-on-one, small-group relations toward the more general public policy focus of modern legislation and regulation. Citing John Maurice Clark as well as Ernst Freund, Hurst argued that statute law consisted "largely of subject matter" where "everyone—or so many everyones as to constitute big, amorphous groups—is affected in some measure by the character of government organization": "A smoky factory might pollute the air of a whole city; a poor road might cripple whole markets along its extent; inadequate schooling could deprive the general economy of skilled labor and the polity of a literate body of voters." Hurst concluded, "Such problems were too broad" to be resolved by the governing apparatus of judge-centered, private, common-law, case-to-case adjudication. They required instead a decisive turn in the direction of modern legislation and administration.[86]

One of the most unmistakable indicators of this transformation in American public law was the veritable explosion of legislation in the United States at both the state and federal levels between 1866 and 1932. At the first meeting of the American Law Institute in 1923, Elihu Root added to a frenzy of concern about the "flood of laws" when he reported that some 62,000 statutes had been added to the US and state legislative record in the five-year period before 1914.[87] Charles Merriam counted 18,243 legislative acts and resolutions for the biennium 1899–1900 and 23,403 for 1929–1930. Well before the heightened legislative activity of the New Deal, Congress was passing between 1,700 and 2,000 legislative acts per session, and larger states like New York, adding approximately 1,000 statutes to their books every two years.[88] By quantitative standards, statute law—the positively enacted law of the duly constituted popular legislature—was becoming the dominant instrument of American legal development.

But quantitative measures can be deceiving (especially given the number of private acts, internal administrative measures, and simple statutory amendments). Even more significant than the number of statutes being passed in this period was the radical character of some of this legislation—what some commentators started to call "the new social legislation" or "industrial legislation." For many of these statutes involved wholesale revisions of American common law and far-reaching social and economic reforms. From price-fixing regulation and corporate antitrust laws to worker compensation and state and national prohibition laws, this was an era of unprecedented statutory innovation.[89]

The best place to witness the actual operationalization of this transformation of public law and the concomitant rise of statutes and legislation is in the modern development of the legal doctrine of state police power. The peculiar language and terminology of "police power" no longer fully resonates today, as the idea has been incorporated (and rendered less visible) in widespread modern acceptance of general legislative lawmaking power. But in the late nineteenth and early twentieth century, discussion of police power was pervasive. Economists, politicians, social reformers, jurists, and journalists were all too aware of its overweening significance for modern socioeconomic policy making.

State police power was the crucial legal site for the expansion of public authority beyond the ancient bounds and jurisdictions of local and municipal self-governance toward a more capacious, centralized, and generalized conception of state regulatory and governing power. Simultaneously, state police power was the preeminent legal-political technology that powered pubic authority well past older common-law conceptions of the legitimate range of public action. Police power thus marked the crucial inflection point for the transition from primarily juridical to increased legislative and ultimately administrative discretion and authority. Finally, this same police power provided the working template for subsequent attempts to shift the site of a more open-ended legislative, regulatory, and administrative power from the state to the national level. While technically the idea of a "federal" or "national" police power in American law was constitutionally impossible, the steady expansion of state police power was the model for the development of a national plenary power over immigration as well as the subsequent growth and transformation of national taxing, spending, postal, and commerce powers (which some commentators explicitly discussed in terms of de facto federal police power). The story of the seemingly unstoppable growth of state police power offers an inside look into the actual legal workings underwriting the development of the modern America state.

So what was state police power? Basically, "police power" was the name that nineteenth-century American jurists ultimately gave to the powers of a state legislature to pass laws that regulated private interests, properties, and liberties in the more general interest of public safety, health, comfort, order, morals and welfare. Notably, early American states were exercising such powers long before jurists and treatise writers decided on this particular legal nomenclature. Police power was a vibrant and vital political practice long before it was instantiated as a jurisprudential or legal category. Indeed, in its first years of constitutional being during 1781–1801, the state legislature of New York passed police regulations concerning everything from public economy (e.g., lotteries, usury, hawkers and peddlers, frauds, rents and leases, ferries, apprentices and servants, the inspection of flour and meal, etc.) to public morals (e.g., playing on Sunday, cursing and swearing, drunkenness, gaming, strong liquors, inns and taverns, etc.) to public health and safety (e.g., firing woods, ship quarantine, the practice of physic and surgery, etc.) to public order and welfare (e.g., the firing of guns, beggars and disorderly persons, bastards and lunatics, dogs, poor relief, etc.).[90] Such regulatory powers were seen as necessary and integral parts of the development of general lawmaking authority in a crucial democratic moment as powers once derived from royal prerogative or the High Court of Parliament devolved on newly established (and more democratically aligned) American state legislatures.

The police power thus resembled other kinds of governmental power routinely discussed in terms of formal legal categories, for example, the taxing power or the eminent domain power. But what made the police power more distinct, more problematic, and of more interest to discussions of modern state power was its open-ended, almost unbounded quality. This feature of police power was a constant topic of jurisprudential discussion and commentary for well over a century. Massachusetts Chief Justice Lemuel Shaw inaugurated that tradition when he argued classically in *Commonwealth v. Alger* (1851) that "it is much easier to perceive and realize the existence of [police] power than to mark its boundaries or to prescribe limits to its exercise." New York's Justice Andrews concurred in *People v. Budd* (1889), "The generality of the terms employed by jurists and publicists in defining this power, while they show the breadth and universality of its presence, nevertheless leave its boundaries and limitations indefinite." Andrews went on to warn against circumscription: "The moment the police power is destroyed or curbed by fixed and rigid rules, a danger is introduced in our system."[91] For Collins Denny, the police power encompassed "one of the most difficult phases of our law to understand, and it is even more difficult to define it within any bounds." And Lewis Hockheimer simply analogized police power to the "inherent plenary power of a State."[92] In the late nineteenth century, US Supreme Court Justice McKenna described police power as "the most essential of powers—at times, the most insistent, and always one of the least limitable powers of government." Throughout the nineteenth and into the early twentieth century, police power was discussed as an inherent and irreducible attribute of governance and statecraft. New York Justice Woodworth summed things up in one of the other founding police power cases *Vanderbilt v. Adams* (1827): "The powers rest on the implied right and duty of the supreme power to protect all by statutory regulations, so that, on the whole, the benefit of all is promoted. . . . Such a power is incident to every well regulated society, and without which it could not well exist."[93]

This relationship of police power to a capacious and almost unmoored conception of necessitous governance has been the subject of many commentaries on the nature of modern states.[94] And for many commentators, the breadth of police power was tied up with more general European notions of police or *Polizei*. As Marc Raeff, among others, has demonstrated, the Continental *Polizeiwissenschaft* celebrated the broad and positive ambitions of statecraft and governance well beyond the traditional public tasks of mere order maintenance and the administration of justice. Police embraced the more capacious and inherently open-ended task of actively fostering all of "the productive energies of society."[95] As Michel Foucault put it, "The police includes everything."[96] Maurice Block's *Dictionnaire de l'administration française* (1856) captured something of the vastness of police administration in a list of varieties of police: "morals and religion, sanitary police, police relating to public security, rural and forestry police, police of substance—embracing control over butchers, fairs, markets, prices—industrial and commercial police, police control over carriers, and finally judiciary police, or that pertaining to the administration of justice." Robert von Mohl's *Polizei-Wissenschaft* emphasized three overarching objects of police power relating to "the care of the physical, intellectual and moral needs of the public" with chapters devoted to "the care of the State for population, health, aid to the needy, agriculture, trade, education, and religion."[97] For Foucault, the eleven categories of police in Nicolas Delamare's *Traite de la police* (1722) constituted "the great charter of police functions" with three great aims: "economic regulation (the circulation of commodities, manufacturing processes, the obligations of tradespeople both to one another and to their clientele), measures of public order (surveillance of dangerous individuals, expulsion of vagabonds, and, if necessary, beggars and the pursuit of criminals), and general rules of hygiene (checks on the quality of foodstuffs sold, the water supply and the cleanliness of the streets)."[98]

While this European police tradition was an important formative influence, state police power was also a distinctly American legal invention.[99] Indeed, the original phrase "police power" came from none other than the Chief Justice of the US Supreme Court, John Marshall, much as the idea was most fully worked out by Massachusetts Chief Justice Lemuel Shaw.[100] American state police power built on early legal conceptions of *salus populi*, overruling necessity, and a common-law vision of a well-regulated society.[101] The common welfare and safety of society were the highest law. When the public good was at stake, lesser rules and private interests gave way to legislative regulation. In such cases, injury to the individual was *damnum absque injuria* (an injury without a remedy) under the reasoning that "a private mischief shall be endured, rather than a public inconvenience."[102] New York's Justice Hubbard synthesized these police power fundamentals in *Wynehamer v. People*:

> The sovereign power of the state in all matters pertaining to the public good, the health, good order and morals of the people, is omnipotent. Laws intended to promote the welfare of society are within legislative discretion. . . . The police power is, of necessity, despotic in its character, commensurate with the sovereignty of the state . . . and in emergencies, it may be exercised to the destruction of property, without compensation to the owner. . . . It is upon this principle that health and quarantine laws are established; that a building is blown up to arrest a conflagration in a populous town; that the public market is purged of infectious articles; that merchandise on ship board, infested with pestilence, is cast into the deep, and public nuisances are abated. It is the public exigency which demands the summary destruction, upon the maxim that the safety of the society is the paramount law. It is the application of the personal right or principle of self preservation to the body politic.[103]

The proliferation of police laws across almost every conceivable aspect of early American life was testament to the deep roots of police in American law. By 1894, W. P. Prentice could already trace the development of legislative police laws and statutes through a host of permutations: metropolitan and market laws; sanitary regulations; laws relative to game, to intoxicating liquors and oleomargarine; health and quarantine laws; protection of purity in water, in food, and against danger from inflammable oils and explosive substances; vital statistics; offensive trades and nuisances; building laws, tenement and lodging houses; licenses and regulations for occupations; and urban administration. And that was but a sampling. Prentice concluded by noting the ever-larger expanse "for the necessary exercise of police powers . . . as new occasions and new demands arise" in a polity where "the object of government and law is the welfare of the people."[104]

By 1894, that "ever-larger expanse" had arrived. Indeed, the reason that talk of "police power" was so ubiquitous in turn-of-the-century jurisprudence was that it was undergoing something of a transformation. That transformation was twofold. First, the police power increasingly became a more positive public law doctrine that defined modern legislative regulatory power. Second, somewhat less conspicuously, the police power was going national.

One of the chief architects of the transformation in modern police power was Ernst Freund. Freund was one of the great, relatively anonymous revolutionaries in American political and legal history. With German university training, a background in political science, and a long career at the University of Chicago Law School, Freund was well positioned to contribute to the redefinition of legislative, administrative, and regulatory powers underway in the late nineteenth and early twentieth century. He accomplished this through a range of national, state, and local reform activities, numerous scholarly articles, and four influential treatises on the key legal issues surrounding the creation of the modern American state: *Police Power, Standards of American Legislation, Administrative Powers,* and *Legislative Regulation.*[105] Like many of his Progressive Era contemporaries, Freund was aware that he was living in a "new age of legislation," and his legal work can be seen as an attempt to create a new science of modern legislation, regulation, and statecraft. Freund's approach was unmistakably pragmatic, realist, and functionalist. For Freund, modern socioeconomic change, particularly "the growing power, scope, and complexity of private industrial and social action," brought an increasing demand for positive state action in the public interest.[106] That action appropriately took the form of written, legislative enactments in areas of police, revenue, and administration that were increasingly positive and public rather than declaratory and private. These regulatory statutes were the hallmarks of a modern legislative state—a direct consequence of the "increasing complexity of the social and industrial structure" and the expansion of "the functions of government" in pursuit of "the public welfare" and "the public interest."[107]

At the center of this expansion of legislative regulation and the multiplication of the social and economic functions of government stood the substantive legal transformation that Willard Hurst highlighted as a shift from common law to statute law. Together with a bevy of other commentaries, Freund's *Police Power* helped to finally free conceptions of police power from the particular and limiting antecedents of the common law of nuisance so as to establish a new and modern public law foundation for a more general legislative regulatory authority.[108] Freund dubbed nuisance law "the common law of the police power, potentially striking at all gross violations of health, safety, order, and morals." Early English and American law reports were replete with cases of police offenses (e.g., morals offenses, offensive trades, unwholesome provisions, highway obstructions) proceeded against as public nuisances under common-law maxims like "sic utere tuo."[109] But though this case-by-case adjudicatory approach to regulation might have proved useful and effective in simpler, preindustrial times, Freund made clear that "the law of nuisance" was now "inadequate for modern police regulation." Indeed, Freund took pains to explicitly spell out "the shortcomings of the common law as a system of public policy."

Freund's "summary of defects" highlighted common law's particularity rather than generality as well as its ex post rather than ex ante approach to harms. The law of nuisance took "cognizance of practices only when danger passes into actual mischief." Consequently, it did little in advance to prevent broader social harms from occurring in the first place—a significant concern in a world of modern factories, railroads, tenement houses, and modern methods of production and distribution. The common law's penchant for adjusting "purely private interests" in one-off, case-by-case, court-based, and highly particularized fact-based scenarios was simply out of sync with "modern social needs and interests." Moreover, its "individualistic attitude" and assumptions about "equal" adversaries in essentially private conflicts "failed to keep pace with advancing or changing ideas." Private common-law adjudication was "expensive and dilatory"— inaccessible to the general public, owing to the profound advantage it ascribed to pecuniary resources and professional lawyering skills. "For many of the modern conditions requiring control or relief," Freund concluded, "not even the very elastic and comprehensive law of nuisance affords an adequate or appropriate remedy, and we are forced to the conclusion that the common law of torts and crimes does not furnish the protection called for by present needs."[110]

In this way, a general legislative authority wrested its freedom from the constraining peculiarities of common-law regulation. The police power traded in its ancient common-law roots in rather murky ideas like overruling necessity and Blackstonian notions of "offences against public police" and became a formal and positive category of the public law of a modern state. Freund began his treatise by noting two original objects of government: (1) the maintenance of national existence (the law of overruling necessity) and (2) the maintenance of justice (the redress of right and wrong via the administration of civil and criminal justice). To these more traditional, defensive and protective functions of government (which reflected a more negative conception of liberty and a limited role for government), Freund added a third as increasingly characteristic of modern states, namely, the positive promotion of public welfare through "internal public policy." As Freund put it, "the care of the public welfare, or internal public policy, has for its object the improvement of social and economic conditions affecting the community at large and collectively, with a view to bringing about 'the greatest good of the greatest number.'" It was here that an expanded conception of police power did its work, no longer primarily preoccupied with negative common-law protections or the simple maintenance of civil and criminal justice but reconstituted as an instrument for the positive promotion of public welfare and the satisfaction of public needs and necessities. Freund summarized, "No community confines its care of the public welfare to the enforcement of the principles of the common law. The state places its . . . resources at the disposal of the public by the establishment of improvements and services of different kinds; *and it exercises compulsory powers for the prevention and anticipation of wrong by narrowing common law rights through conventional restraints and positive regulations which are not confined to the prohibition of wrongful acts. It is this latter kind of state control which constitutes the essence of the police power.*"[111]

In this way, Ernst Freund helped to transform the police power from a more limited doctrine of community self-defense and protection hemmed in by traditional common-law maxims and local and customary legal procedures into a more positive and affirmative authority to legislate broadly on behalf of the general welfare. Modern legislation and regulation needed to be instrumentally responsive to direct public policy needs rather than constrained by traditional common-law routines. Reinvented as the legislative "power of promoting the public welfare by restraining and regulating the use of liberty and property," the modern police power created a new and powerful public law foundation for the modern legislative state. Innumerable other commentators reinforced Freund's positivist conception of police power. Lewis Hockheimer proclaimed, "The police power is the inherent plenary power of a State . . . to prescribe regulations to preserve and promote the public safety, health, and morals, and to prohibit all things hurtful to the comfort and welfare of society."[112] And judges and courts also followed suit, linking the police power more directly to the promotion of public welfare. Citing a host of cases upholding modern police power regulation, Justice McKenna argued in *Bacon v. Walker* (1907) that the police power "is not confined, as we have said, to the suppression of what is offensive, disorderly or unsanitary. It extends to so dealing with the conditions which exist in the State as to bring out of them the greatest welfare of its people."[113]

By linking the police power with the general promotion of public welfare in a positive legislative state, jurists and law writers paved the way for the explosive growth of police power regulation in the Progressive Era. Regulatory statute books swelled, case numbers rose exponentially, and expositions on police power proliferated. A new forcefulness and resourcefulness crept into discussions as progressives expanded the scale and scope of American legislative power, calling for the police power to be "more freely exercised and private property more freely controlled to meet the needs of the changed conditions of society." Some progressives saw in the police power "almost unlimited opportunities for adopting whatever legislation the augmenting demands of social pioneers may require."[114] As Freund noted, the modern police power encompassed the whole range of public and governmental regulatory interests from the primary social interests of "safety, order, and morals" to the regulation of economic interests in the guise of burgeoning industrial legislation to the nonmaterial or ideal interests in the "cultivation of moral, intellectual and aesthetic forces" to the political interests secured via the increased regulation of the governmental machinery itself. Under these general categories, Freund arranged his eight-hundred-page encyclopedic survey of America's new legislative regulatory state.

But legislative police power not only dramatically expanded its scale and scope in this period; it also began a slow and steady ascent up the levels of American government. As historians have frequently noted, the period between 1866 and 1932 witnessed a thoroughgoing nationalization and systematization of American social and economic life necessitating a distinctive upward shift in decision-making power.[115] Leonard D. White surveyed the extent of state centralization even before the onset of the New Deal: the evidence "demonstrates a steady accretion of power and influence by the state governments over the administrative powers of local officials especially in the fields of public finance, education, health and highways, as well as a steady extension of federal influence over the states, particularly in the regulation of commerce." In 1923, Leonard Thompson identified a similar trend toward "federal centralization": "Since the Civil War there has been a marked tendency for the federal government to increase its activities."[116] Indeed, one of the more important aspects of this transformation in public power was the construction of a de facto (if not de jure) nationalization of police power.

In *United States v. Dewitt* (1870), the United States Supreme Court adopted the clear antebellum constitutional consensus that the police power was explicitly a state and local rather than a federal power. Echoing Chief Justice Marshall's analysis in *Barron v. Baltimore,* refusing to apply the Bill of Rights to the states, Chief Justice Chase held that though Congress clearly had the authority to regulate interstate commerce, it did not have a general national power to pass regulations of internal state police in the interests of public health, safety, and welfare. The police power remained with the individual states and localities, and the national government wielded nothing analogous to the general plenary authority of state legislatures to regulate liberty and property in the public interest.[117] But, of course, one of the great stories of the period after 1866 was that Congress increasingly secured the power to do precisely that—crafting an increasing national legislative power to police society and economy through the creative exercise of commerce, taxing, spending, and even postal powers. As Charles Evans Hughes told the American Bar Association in 1918, the most significant decisions of the recent Supreme Court involved three aspects of such federal expansion: (1) "the extended application of the doctrine that federal rules governing interstate commerce may have the quality of police regulations"; (2) "the approval of the cooperation of nation and states"; and (3) "the recognition of the sweeping authority of Congress over the relations between interstate common carriers and their employees."[118] In the areas of business, labor, transportation, morals, health, safety, immigration, and education, powers and issues that were once the exclusive domain of state and local governments moved up into the purview of the national government in one of the most significant aggregations of political power in American history. And as Ernst Freund argued in 1920, the role of law and the judiciary in that transformation was pivotal: "The consolidation of our own nation has proved our allotment of federal powers to be increasingly inadequate; and had it not been aided by liberal judicial construction, our situation would be unbearable."[119]

One of the most important advocates of such an expansive legal construction of federal legislative power was Robert E. Cushman. Cushman would eventually go on to write one of the most important treatises on the emergence of independent regulatory commissions on the national level.[120] But first he took up the conundrum of federal police power. In a series of influential articles in the *Minnesota Law Review,* Cushman noted, "The enumeration of the congressional powers in the Constitution does not include any general grant of authority to pass laws for the protection of the health, morals, or general welfare of the nation. It follows, then, that if Congress is to exercise a police power at all, it must do so by a process something akin to indirection." Cushman argued that if Congress wanted to elevate state police powers to the national level, it would have to "cloak its good works under its authority to tax, or to regulate commerce, or to control the mails, or the like, and say, 'By this authority we pass this law in the interest of the public welfare.'"[121] As will be seen in subsequent chapters, that is exactly what Congress did in passing such important national health, safety, economic, and morals regulations as the Pure Food and Drug Act (1906), the Harrison Narcotics Tax Act (1914), the Child Labor Tax Act (1919), and the National Prohibition Act (1919). Through spending power and federal grants in aid to the individual states, Congress was able to wield even more national regulatory authority through the incentive power of the public purse.[122] Consequently, the United States achieved a centralization of national legislative police power authority even before the

Supreme Court accepted an expansive interpretation of the interstate commerce clause at the height of the New Deal. Indeed, many of the central components of an increasingly national legislative state were well established in the United States by the time Franklin Delano Roosevelt won election to the presidency in the fall of 1932.

Examples of the nationalization of legislative and policing prerogatives formerly thought to belong primarily to states and localities made up a veritable history of turn-of-the-century public policy making. The nationalization of citizenship had important implications for the subsequent federalization of immigration law in the United States. A whole slate of local and state port laws, pilot laws, poor laws, and passenger regulations at issue in such important antebellum police power cases as *Miln v. New York* (1827) and the *Passenger Cases* (1849) was increasingly displaced by the nationalization of immigration policy underway at least since *Henderson v. New York* (1875).[123] The Chinese Exclusion Act (1882) coupled with the articulation of a the national "plenary power doctrine" by Justice Stephen Field in *Chae Chan Ping v. United States* (1889) increasingly redefined immigration regulation and the power to exclude foreigners as "an incident of sovereignty belonging to the government of the United States."[124] Morals regulation underwent a similar nationalization from the Comstock Act of 1873 to the White-Slave Traffic Act of 1910 straight through to the national experiment with Prohibition.[125] In the field of public health regulation and quarantine—long thought to be an exclusive purview of states and localities—authorities similarly pushed for greater federal coordination and control in search of a more coherent national strategy to combat epidemic disease. By 1870, early marine hospitals morphed into the Marine Hospital Service—direct progenitor of the US Public Health Service. As Surgeon General Walter Wyman made the case for national quarantine in 1898: "No effort will be spared to prevent our commerce being hampered by disease, for this is modern quarantine, to strip commerce of disease, both for its own good and for public safety."[126]

Something of an early peak in this nationalization of police power was reached during World War I when the Woodrow Wilson administration launched another extraordinary program of legislative and central state action that included such expansive initiatives as conscription, espionage and sedition, national prohibition, and an extraordinary experiment in domestic price control known as the Lever Act, or the Food and Fuel Control Act of 1917. As one contemporary critic put it, "The power demanded is greater than has ever been exercised by any king or potentate of earth; it is broader than that which is exercised by the Kaiser of the Germans. It is a power such as no Caesar ever employed over a conquered province in the bloodiest days of Rome's bloody despotism."[127] In 1918, J. Reuben Clark Jr. was charged by Wilson and the attorney general of the United States with compiling a compendium of American "emergency legislation" dealing especially with regulations "for the public use, benefit, or welfare." Clark began by listing the major wartime congressional acts, including the National Defense Act, Naval Appropriation Act, Council of National Defense Act, Shipping Board Act, Naval Emergency Fund Act, War Resolution, German Boat Resolution, Car Service Act, Emergency Shipping Fund Act, Espionage Act, Land Condemnation Act, Aviation Act, River and Harbor Act, Priority Shipment Act, Agricultural Act, Food Control Act, Air Station Act, Urgent Deficiencies Act, Explosives Act, Patents Act, and the Trading with the Enemy Act. Here war powers and emergency legislation blended rather seamlessly with an expanded conception of police power to generate a striking example of the reach and significance of the modern transformation of American public law.[128]

Police Power and the Myth of Lochner

Unfortunately for conventional historical understanding, the most famous police power case in American law remains *Lochner v. New York* (1905). Whether referred to in terms of the *Lochner* court, the *Lochner* era, Lochnerism, or just plain old vanilla *Lochner,* Rufus Peckham's majority opinion striking down an 1895 New York police statute known as the Bakeshop Act continues to loom large not only over constitutional history but over contemporary jurisprudence and politics as well. The New York Bakeshop Act was a quintessential state police power regulation and progressive reform aimed at ameliorating sanitary and health conditions in fetid bakeries and establishing maximum hours for laborers at a ten-hour day and sixty-hour workweek. Peckham held that the regulatory statute interfered with the substantive "right of contract between the employer and employees," which was "part of the liberty of the individual" protected by the due process clause of the "Fourteenth Amendment of the Federal Constitution."[129] Substantive due process and liberty of contract thus began their long-term careers overshadowing the actual history of police power in American constitutional memory.

Indeed, so famous (or infamous) was *Lochner* as a canonical (or anticanonical) case, that the "Lochner era" came to stand for and define the entire legal-historical period. In a way, the exception swallowed the rule. The complex, substantive history of the development of legislative police power was subsumed beneath ever more accounts of the same set of particularized and rarified Supreme Court doctrinal pronouncements. Instead of the legal history of police power, histories of the *judicial review* of police power predominated. Instead of empirical accounts of the growth of legislation and regulation, treatises and casebooks devoted almost exclusive attention to the more negative or naysaying question of the limits on power and the judicial review of legislative and administrative action. The history of judicial review is surely important as is the history of constitutional limitations, but they represent only a small (and not necessarily representative) slice of the actual history of law in America.

With respect to the history of police power, the mythology surrounding *Lochner* has so skewed historical attention as to create the legal fiction known as "laissez-faire constitutionalism." Curiously, this idea originated in a pointed progressive critique of a certain kind of judicial activism. Charles Beard was a chief instigator in this critical tradition. In a chapter entitled "Writing Laissez-Faire into the Constitution," Beard described the rise of a rearguard action in late nineteenth-century law that exalted private property rights and vigorously opposed the efforts of reform-minded state legislatures to regulate property, franchises, and corporate privilege in the larger public interest. According to Beard, conservative jurists strived for a new jurisprudence—"some juristic process for translating laissez-faire into a real restraining force." In the Fourteenth Amendment, substantive due process, and liberty of contract, they found potent weapons to secure "federal judicial supremacy for the defense of corporations and business enterprises everywhere."[130] As evidence for his thesis, Beard devised an oft-cited litany of the malevolent cases through which laissez-faire was written into the Constitution by a probusiness, antiregulatory Supreme Court. Beard reached the constitutional pinnacle of this era, *Lochner v. New York* (1905), with the same conclusion intimated by Justice Holmes in dissent—American courts were guilty of deciding cases upon a social theory and economic interests out of sync with the democratic majority and the people's welfare. Thus an original instantiation of the idea of *Lochner*—of the invention of laissez-faire constitutionalism by an activist, economically interested Supreme Court bolstering the conservative status quo against regulatory police power intervention—received one of its classic early statements.

Charles Beard was not alone in propagating this progressive criticism of antidemocratic judicial overreach.[131] Beard was joined in his crusade by such critics as Louis Boudin, J. Allen Smith, Edward Corwin, Frank Goodnow, and Gustavus Myers, whose book titles reflected the main lines of the progressive critique of the politics of law: *Government by Judiciary, The Growth and Decadence of Constitutional Government, Court over Constitution, Social Reform and the Constitution.*[132] Frank

Goodnow opened his investigation with a straightforward statement of progressive purpose: "To ascertain, from an examination of the decisions of our courts, . . . to what extent the Constitution of the United States in its present form is a bar to the adoption of the most important social reform measures which have been made parts of the reform program of the most progressive peoples of the present day." J. Allen Smith more aggressively attacked the immanent "reactionary" spirit of US constitutional law—"its inherent opposition to democracy, the obstacles which it has placed in the way of majority rule." Louis Boudin began his exposé in *Government by Judiciary* succinctly: "We are ruled by *dead Men* . . . generations of dead judges."[133] Vernon Parrington captured the main thrust of the progressive attack: "Discovering when it attempted to regulate business that its hands were tied by judicial decrees, the democracy began to question the reasons for the bonds that constrained its will."[134] For many, that was the heart of the critique of law: the socioeconomic inequities of industrialization galvanized a mass of popular democratic reform legislation that was in turn frustrated by a countermajoritarian judicial obstructionism. The turn-of-the century Supreme Court became in Max Lerner's words "one of the great American ogres, part of the demonology of liberal and radical thought."[135] And *Lochner v. New York* was the bête noire.

In short, much of what eventually became the myth of *Lochner* originated in a normatively charged and sometimes polemical progressive critique of a particular set of judicial doctrines, rulings, and behaviors. The progressive critique of the court and a certain style of judicial activism was the critical and negative counterpoint to their new vision of modern American public law. The original progressive critique of *Lochner*, in other words, was neither a critique of law in toto nor intended as an empirical description of the general role of law in America life. By midcentury, however, the specificity of the original progressive critique was increasingly overtaken by a more totalizing vision.[136] Somewhat ironically, the particular progressive critique was conflated with more general legal-historical experience. What began as a focused attack on a certain form of judicial review morphed into a more general assessment of an American constitutional tradition inherently hostile to regulation, redistribution, and reform. The idea of *Lochner* as an accurate reflection or depiction of a larger legal-historical reality took hold. And other important aspects of legal change and innovation—including much of the positive record of progressive legislative and regulatory accomplishment—were rendered less historically apparent.

Lochner's legacy today is as powerful as ever in a mainstream constitutional history organized around constitutional moments like 1787, 1868, and 1937 and themes of judicial review, constitutional rights, Lochnerism, and its New Deal repudiation.[137] In the field of labor law and history, themes of Lochnerian and laissez-faire obstructionism continue to prevail.[138] And the specter of *Lochner* continues to haunt recent histories of the troubled rise of a modern American administrative and social-welfare state.[139] In consequence, Lochnerism perhaps exudes more real force today on legal and historical interpretation than it ever laid claim to in its own distant past.[140] American interpretations of law remain strangely entranced by *Lochner*-era notions of government by injunction, government by judiciary, laissez-faire constitutionalism, classical legal thought, substantive due process, liberty of contract, the revival of natural law theory, Holmes and Brandeis dissenting, and the constitutional revolution of 1937.

In the middle of the so-called *Lochner* era itself, however, doubts had already surfaced about the actual representativeness or concrete efficacy of the *Lochner* decision. In 1913, Charles Warren undertook a fairly comprehensive survey of the constitutional fate of state regulatory legislation in the US Supreme Court between 1887 and 1911. Organizing his findings according to constitutional objection—due process, obligation of contracts, and commerce clause—Warren found that of 560 Fourteenth Amendment cases, only three state laws relating to social justice were overturned (including *Lochner*). Of 302 cases decided on the more established grounds of contract and interstate commerce, only thirty-six general state social and economic regulations were declared unconstitutional. Overwhelmingly, the vast majority of state regulatory laws in Warren's catalog were upheld by the Supreme Court: "anti-lottery laws; anti-trust and corporate monopoly laws; liquor laws; food, game, oleomargarine and other inspection laws; regulation of banks, telegraph and insurance companies; cattle, health and quarantine laws; regulation of business and property of water, gas, electric light, railroad (other than interstate trains) and other public service corporations; negro-segregation laws; labor laws; laws as to navigation, marine liens, ferries, bridges, etc., pilots, harbors and immigration."[141]

Warren's list reflected an important, immutable fact about public law at the turn of the twentieth century—that this was an era of unprecedented expansion rather than limitation of legislative police power. As Ernst Freund himself recognized at the time, decisions in the *Lochner* mode did not "stop the onward course of the type of legislation which it checked only slightly."[142] *Lochner* was, of course, followed three years later by *Muller v. Oregon* (1908), which upheld legislation limiting women's hours of labor.[143] And by 1917 in *Bunting v. Oregon,* the US Supreme Court upheld the constitutionality of another Oregon statute providing that "no person shall be employed in any mill, factory, or manufacturing establishment in this state more than ten hours in any one day" (with certain exceptions).

Citing statistics from most Western countries, the court took judicial notice of "the well-known fact that the custom of our industries does not sanction a longer service than 10 hours per day" in reaching the decision that "it is enough for our decision if the legislation under review was passed in the exercise of an admitted power of government"—that is, the police power.[144] In the field of labor legislation and labor administration, John R. Commons was simultaneously charting the continued onslaught of legislation and administrative regulation governing employment and unemployment, wages and hours, safety and health, social insurance, and collective bargaining.[145] The new social and economic regulatory legislation flowed fast and furiously. Reams of statutory and administrative and regulatory materials inaugurated the modern legal era. And the overwhelming mass of new laws, ordinances, rules, regulations, and administrative adjudications testified to the direction of modern legal change in this period. Behind the highly visible, negative critiques of *Lochner,* legal writers, reformers, and activists were busy reworking the foundations of social legislation and state police power.[146] These positive reformulations of law were far more central to the actual "change in the function of law in modern society" than anything resembling Lochnerism or laissez-faire constitutionalism.

In his synthetic *History of American Law,* Lawrence Friedman summarized the basic position of laissez-faire constitutionalism by quoting from Edward Corwin's classic text *The Twilight of the Supreme Court* and noting the five key cases that "annex[ed] the principles of laissez-faire capitalism to the Constitution and put them beyond the reach of state legislative power."[147] The five cases are wholly familiar to students of constitutional history: *Wynehamer v. New York* (N.Y. 1856); *In Re Jacobs* (N.Y. 1885); *Godcharles v. Wigeman* (Pa. 1886); *Ritchie v. People* (Ill. 1895); and *Lochner v. New York* (U.S. 1905).[148] In drawing conclusions about the basic relationship of law and political economy in this volatile and voluble period, it is worth thinking about the economic representativeness of these canonical laissez-faire constitutional cases: liquor prohibition (*Wynehamer*), cigar rolling in tenements (*Jacobs*), a nail mill (*Godcharles*), clothing manufactories (*Ritchie*); and the hours of bakers (*Lochner*). Notably, Rufus Peckham closed his majority opinion in *Lochner* with an extended discussion of three appellate cases concerning the licensing and regulation of horseshoers.

What was not included or represented by such cases? Nothing less than the dominant sectors of the late nineteenth- and early twentieth-century American economy: (1) transportation and shipping (railroads, highways, grain elevators, ports, streetcars); (2) communications (telegraph and telephone); (3) energy (electricity, water, coal, and petroleum); (4) agriculture and horticulture; and (5) money and banking. And what do we know about these areas of economic activity? They were anything but reflective of a political economy of laissez-faire. These were the preeminent areas of industrial and corporate consolidation and expansion in this period as well as the economic activities that attracted the most intense governmental interest and intervention. Indeed, these were precisely the major sectors of the American economy that lawyers, economists, reformers, and legislators were busily redefining as increasingly public in nature—public utilities and public service corporations—subject to interventions ranging from enhanced police powers to direct rate regulation to outright public ownership. The so-called *Lochner* era, in short, might more constructively and accurately be referred to as the era of police power and public utility.

Common Law

3
_____

PUBLIC UTILITY
The Origins of Modern Business Regulation
——

Public utility is the sole origin of justice.
—DAVID HUME

This chapter concerns one of the more remarkable innovations in the history of democratic attempts to control the corporation and, in turn, the larger American economy. In the late nineteenth and early twentieth century—after important antecedent changes in corporation law—lawyers, economists, legislators, and democratic reformers pieced together a new regime of modern business regulation. At the very center of that project was the idea of public utility, or what was referred to at the time as the "public service corporation."

While most historical accounts of the rise of modern economic regulation in this period trumpet the significance of antitrust or antimonopoly policy, the legal invention of the public service corporation and the public utility was even more significant for the future relationship of American polity and economy.[1] For in many ways, the modern American administrative and regulatory state was built directly upon the legal foundation laid by the expanding conception of the essentially public services provided by corporations in emergent sectors of the modern American economy: transportation, communications, energy supply, water supply, and the shipping and storage of agricultural products. In law, the original architects of the administrative state and the founders of the very first casebooks and classes on administrative and regulatory law—people such as Bruce Wyman, Felix Frankfurter, and ultimately James Landis—basically began their work on the legal, political, and economic problems posed by public service corporations and public utilities. The public utility, the public corporation, and the modern American administrative and regulatory state, in other words, grew up together.[2]

In the end, the public utility idea and the public service corporation became the central vehicles through which progressive policy makers pioneered a more capacious notion of "public interest" in politics and economics and a more comprehensive conception of the "social control of American capitalism."[3] Much as original notions of utility fueled an earlier era of governmental reform in England, modern concepts of public utility and public service propelled new democratic conceptions of economic and social justice.[4] Some of the most important manifestos of the era noted the close link between the public utility idea and the more expansive agenda of progressive economic regulation and reform. Henry Carter Adams turned first to Granger laws to challenge the laissez-faire presumptions of Herbert Spencer's *Social Statics*. John Commons began his influential *Legal Foundations of Capitalism* with a prolonged analysis of *Munn v. Illinois* and business "affected with a public interest." In *Other People's Money*, Louis Brandeis proposed "banks as public-service corporations" as a solution to the era's banking problems.[5] Richard T. Ely's famous statement to the opening meeting of the American Economic Association mentioned both western water supply and midwestern rate discrimination as exemplary places to begin thinking in essentially public rather than private terms: "We hold that there are certain spheres of activity which do not belong to the individual, certain functions which the great co-operative society, called the state—must perform. . . . In looking over the field of economic life, . . . there are things which individuals ought not to perform because the functions concerned are public; and in certain places the wastes of private competition are too enormous."[6] This centrality of the public utility idea to the modern project of economic regulation did not escape the attention of the period's best legal historian. Willard Hurst noted increased late nineteenth-century discontent with the legitimacy of the market on grounds of utility: "The market simply did not prove sufficiently serviceable to allow it the central place as a resource allocator which public policy was prepared to give it between 1750 and 1890. Our prime symbol of this changed judgment was the growth of the law of public utilities."[7]

But the public utility idea was not just a legal doctrine, an intellectual program, or a reform ambition. Rather, the power and historical significance of public utility comes from the way in which it burrowed its way to the very core of the American legal and political-economic system. This was an idea quickly transformed into concrete political-economic reality with momentous consequences for the future configuration of American democracy and capitalism. Simply put, public utility took over turn-of-the-century statute books, commission reports, and court records. And it dominated the period's legal output: legislative, administrative, and judicial. It was the cutting-edge and the avant-garde. Indeed, the public utility idea was the key legal site for the steady expansion of state regulatory power, pushing traditional conceptions of police power beyond the constraints of the common-law and constitutional limitations and growing an impressive progressive policy-making toolkit that ultimately included things like comprehensive price and rate controls, ongoing administrative and bureaucratic supervision, municipal ownership, and public works. It culminated in unprecedented interventions, such as World War I's Food Administration (initially justified by the idea that in times of war all businesses were "affected with a public interest") and the New Deal's Tennessee Valley Authority. To this day it continues to hold sway in some important sectors of the economy governed by a distinctive law of "regulated" or "network" or "utility" industries.[8]

The concept itself expanded relentlessly beyond initial initiatives in special areas like transportation, communications, energy, and water supply to the regulation of things like hotels, warehouses, stockyards, ice plants, insurance, and milk, to name just a few. Railroad commission and public utility reports proliferated. They consisted of complaints, investigations, rules, cases, holdings, findings, and deliberations that usurped huge swaths of law library space, sometimes dwarfing other legislative and judicial materials. From the Civil War to the New Deal, the problem of public utilities preoccupied if not consumed the very best economists, lawyers, and policy makers. In railroading—the original and paradigm case—state commissioners had organized themselves into the National Association of Railroad Commissioners by 1889. And by 1929, the Interstate Commerce Commission had its own practitioners bar association with almost two thousand members and a formal registry of practitioners that totaled over eight thousand. Kenneth Culp Davis has estimated that the extraordinary number of activities and personnel involved in railroad administration alone in this period dwarfed the personnel and output of the entire federal court system itself.[9]

A quick but more concrete sense of this massive scale and scope of the public service corporation project is suggested by Bruce Wyman's two-volume, 1,500-page, five-thousand-case treatise, *The Special Law Governing Public Service Corporations,* published in 1911—at the height of progressive activism concerning the relationship between business and American democracy. Building on earlier texts by Harvard Law School colleague Joseph Henry Beale and anticipating Felix Frankfurter's very influential work on public utilities and interstate commerce, Wyman consolidated and summarized two generations of legal-economic regulation in response to the emergence of the large-scale business corporation in the late nineteenth century. Through the public service concept, he brought together three important and overlapping areas of legal-economic development in this period: the early law of public callings and public carriers; the emerging law of public utilities; and new developments in the law of public works, public employment, and public contracting. "Twenty-five years ago," Wyman noted, "the public services which were recognized were still few and the law as to them imperfectly realized." But his massive treatise was now a testament to a "present state of the public service law" in which there was now "almost general assent to State control of the public service companies."[10]

And how extensive were such public utilities and public service companies by 1911? In just the first three chapters of his treatise, Wyman covered the following types of businesses: ferries, bridges, bonded warehouses, log driving, tramways, railways, pipelines, transmission lines, elevated conveyors, lumber flumes, mining tunnels, gristmills, sawmills, drainage, sewerage, cemeteries, hospitals, booms, sluices, turnpikes, street railways, subways, wire conduits, pole lines, waterworks, irrigation systems, natural gas, water powers, grain elevators, cotton presses, stockyards, freight sheds, docks, basins, dry docks, innkeepers, hackmen, messenger service, call boxes, gasworks, fuel gas, electric plants, electric power, steam heat, refrigeration, canals, channels, railroads, railway terminals, railway bridges, car ferries, railway tunnels, union railways, belt lines, signal service, telegraph lines, wireless telegraph, submarine cables, telephone systems, ticker service, associated press, public stores, grain storage, tobacco warehouses, cold storage, safe deposit vaults, marketplaces, stock exchanges, port lighters, floating elevators, tugboats, switching engines, parlor cars, sleeping cars, refrigerator cars, and tank cars.[11]

So we arrive at a historical conundrum. For here we have this big, powerful, proliferating thing at the very center of American law and political economy—what Felix Frankfurter called "perhaps the most significant political tendency at the turn of the century."[12] And yet for all intents and purposes, today, it has been eclipsed from view and erased from all but the most specialized legal-historical memory. What was once at the forefront of law, economics, and public policy discussion has been relegated to a backbench concerning fewer and fewer things, such as municipal electricity, gas, and water. What happened?

Keeping in mind the possibility that reports of the death of public utility have been greatly exaggerated, two answers to this question require at least preliminary mention.[13] The first answer involves something of a success story. For the most part, lawyers, economists, and reformers who promoted the public utility idea essentially won. The overarching goal of the public utility idea was an enlarged police power—an expansive conception of state (and ultimately, federal) regulatory power over the economy. By the time of the US Supreme Court's landmark decision in *Nebbia v. New York* in 1934 (concerning the state price regulation of milk during the Great Depression), the conception of state police power was so thoroughly expanded through the infusion of the public utility concept that the court no longer found it necessary to designate a specific kind of business specially "affected with a public interest" to justify almost any kind of economic regulatory regime seen as in the "public interest" generally.[14] The public utility idea had done its main work. Through a volatile era, its unique conception of public interests in distinctly public services fended off attempts to constitutionally limit or cabin state police power and, in fact, greatly reinvigorated and expanded the range and reach of the original police power idea. Frank Goodnow was well aware of the important work done in this regard by 1916 when he summed up this transformation: "The first change in ideas . . . was made in the class of activities which are often spoken of generically as 'public utilities.' On the theory that the public interest was peculiarly concerned in those cases . . . the conception of regulation in the public interest came finally to be held."[15]

But if the legal and constitutional story by the time of *Nebbia* was something of a victory for the proponents of an expanded notion of public interest, soon thereafter in political economy, the public utility idea began a slow retreat. Indeed, the last half century or so has witnessed a sustained effort on the part of law and economics commentary to undermine and undo the public utility idea. Perhaps aware of the intimate connection between public utilities and the rise of the regulatory state, two generations of critics of regulation have taken direct aim at almost every aspect of the progressive public utility paradigm.[16]

Because of this mixed record, a full reckoning with the public utility idea first requires an exercise in historical recovery. To that end, this chapter attempts to exhume something of a world we have lost—the lost world of public utility law—a world in which conceptions of public interest, public service, public goods, and public utilities were anything but marginal. Bracketing common wisdom, the rest of this chapter attempts to recapture the original genesis of the public service corporation at the turn of the twentieth century. It explores an initial emergence of a legal idea of public service and public utility that was innovative, capacious, and extraordinarily efficacious and reinforces Willard Hurst's intuition that the law of public utilities was the "prime symbol" of changing conceptions of the market and regulation in this period. The public service corporation was one of the major progressive responses to the emerging power of big business in the twentieth century, and it yielded a new understanding of the relationship of the corporation, business, and democracy in modern America with important policy implications for regulation, administration, legislation, and adjudication to this very day.

A World We Have Lost?
Nineteenth-Century Antecedents

A clear picture of the emergence of the law of public utilities first requires an examination of its historical antecedents. The public service corporation and public utilities regulation emerged at the nexus of important developments in three separate areas of law: an age-old area of English common law pertaining to "public callings"; the rise of state legislative police power; and the early nineteenth-century American regime of corporation regulation through the state legislative charter. The way these areas of law converged through the nineteenth century established a promising channel for the emergence of a modern and synthetic understanding of public service corporations and public utilities.

The Common Law of Public Callings. Long before the advent of the regulation of business through statutes and corporate charters, the common law developed ample provisions for the public control of certain kinds of economic trades, callings, occupations, and enterprises. With legal and policy roots in English jurisprudence as deep as the medieval guild system and as complex as the history of assumpsit, judges in the earliest law reports fairly consistently singled out a set of essentially "public" or "common" callings and trades for special legal treatment. The common surgeon, tailor, blacksmith, victualler, baker, miller, innkeeper, and, perhaps most importantly, the common carrier were held to different public legal standards in the performance of their tasks than more ordinary private interactions.[17] And they were subject to a special class of common-law restrictions and duties, such as a duty to provide a service once undertaken and a duty to serve all comers.[18] While the individual cases are as numerous as the case law is diverse, something of the spirit of the early common-law understanding is suggested by Blackstone's summary in his *Commentaries:* "There is also in law always an implied contract with a common inn-keeper, to secure his guest's goods in his inn; with a common carrier or bargemaster, to be answerable for the goods he carries; with a common farrier, that he shoes a horse well, without laming him; with a common taylor, or other workman, that he performs his business in a workmanlike manner. . . . Also if an inn-keeper, or other victualer, hangs out a sign and opens his house for travellers, it is an implied engagement to entertain all persons who travel that way."[19]

Other English jurists invoked larger legal ideas of "public trust," "public rights," "public good," and "public employment" when discussing public callings. Once a person removed economic activity from the local and private world of household and neighborly interaction and held themselves out generally to do business with "the public," special public legal obligations followed. Lord Chief Justice John Holt described this in 1701: "Wherever any subject takes upon himself a public trust for the benefit of the rest of his fellow-subjects, he is *eo ipso* bound to serve the subject in all things that are within the reach and comprehension of such an office"[20]

Of special significance for the development of modern public utility law was Matthew Hale's discussion of the public calling of wharfingers in his influential treatise *De Portibus Maris*—what Bruce Wyman called "the most famous paragraph in the whole law relating to public service."[21] Legal historians Harry Scheiber and Molly Selvin have detailed how Hale exerted great influence over the subsequent development of the American law of public ways: highways, waterways, rivers, ports, bridges, and roads.[22] And he most clearly articulated the notion of juris publici—rights belonging to the public at large—in certain kinds of public spaces, throughways, and even activities. It was regarding the wharfinger that Hale first elaborated the notion of economic activities "affected with a public interest," which would become so significant after the US Supreme Court's decision in *Munn v. Illinois* (1877):

> If the king or subject have a public wharf, unto which all persons that come to that port must come and unlade or lade their goods . . . because they are the wharfs only licensed by the queen . . . or because there is no other wharf in that port, . . . in that case there cannot be taken arbitrary and excessive duties for cranage, wharfage, pesage, etc., neither can they be inhanced to an immoderate rate, but the duties must be reasonable and moderate, though settled by the king's license or charter. For now the wharf and crane and other conveniences are affected with a publick interest, and they cease to be *juris privati* only; as if a man set out a street in new building on his own land, it is now no longer private interest, but is affected with a publick interest.[23]

The American reception of these English common-law doctrines concerning public spaces and public callings was swift and certain. Securing public rights in highways, rivers, ports, and public squares through the use of such precedents was a major preoccupation of antebellum American jurists.[24] And from the earliest days of the republic, certain occupations and businesses continued to be governed by special common-law rules owing to their status as common or public callings. Indeed, large bodies of case law rapidly grew up around two of the most important public callings in early American law: the law of innkeepers and the law of common carriers. Harbingers of the commercial expansion and increasing cosmopolitanism of the nation and its traveling and shipping public, common carriage and innkeeping quickly drew the attention of leading American jurists. Joseph Angell and Isaac Redfield both contributed elaborate treatises on the law of common carriers.[25] And none other than Joseph Beale added a 638-page tome, *The Law of Innkeepers and Hotels: Including other Public Houses, Theatres, Sleeping Cars*.[26] For Beale, this exploration of the law of public callings directly complemented his work on public carriers, public utilities, and ultimately railroad rate regulation more generally. As he acknowledged, "The law of innkeepers was the earliest developed and is the simplest and clearest of those topics of law which are concerned with the various public-service callings."[27] Such works quickly charted the path from the ancient legal notion of common callings to the most modern forms of public utility rate regulation. Even before the rise of the state regulation of business through statute and corporate charters, the common law provided surprisingly robust technologies for securing public rights against private forms of economic encroachment.

State Police Power and the Corporate Charters. The regulation of economic activity affected with a public interest did not remain within the exclusive purview of the common law for very long. Much as case-by-case, ex post remedies of the common law of nuisance quickly took on the more systematic, ex ante form of legislative regulation under the state police power, the common law of public callings likewise was supplemented and superseded by municipal ordinances and state statutes. Two very different types of legislation simultaneously entered the regulatory mix: general state police power regulations and the more specialized statutes known as state charters of incorporation. The shifting relationship between these two very different types of legislation is central to the most important developments in nineteenth-century business and economic regulation. Indeed, the modern law of public utilities was born at the intersection of the laws of police power and corporation.

The development of nineteenth-century legislative police power regulation of economic activities formerly controlled by the judicial administration of the common law is a topic both enormous and complex. For current purposes, the most important development concerns the way that in area

after area of the economy—from ports to wharves to inns to common carriers to warehouses to urban marketplaces and beyond—American localities and states began rapidly drafting ordinances and regulatory statutes
that built on the economic reasoning of common-law precedent but also
pushed toward a much more comprehensive, rational, and codified
system of economic regulation.[28] The overarching legal and political justification for this expansion of police power remained an awareness of the
public rights and public interests implicated in certain kinds of economic
activity as anticipated in the common law of public callings. The protection
of the public in a flourishing market, corporate, commercial, and ultimately
industrial economy demanded more expansive, predictable, and prospective measures.

Nowhere was this shift to statute more carefully analyzed and ultimately
rationalized than in the classic police power opinion of Massachusetts Chief
Justice Lemuel Shaw in *Commonwealth v. Alger* (1851). Upholding the legislature's right to establish a wharf line in Boston harbor beyond which no
private structures should encroach, Shaw's reasoned defense of the public
interest moved deftly from common law to codification, from nuisance to
police power, from public calling to public utility, and from the ancient
wharfinger to modern land-use regulation. He first defended the authority
of the legislature to pass regulatory statutes with broad implications for the
entire economy: "Wherever there is a general right on the part of the public,
and a general duty on the part of a land-owner or any other person to respect such right, we think it is competent for the legislature, by a specific
enactment, to prescribe a precise, practical rule for declaring, establishing,
and securing such right, and enforcing respect for it." Shaw argued, "The
power we allude to is the police power—the power vested in the legislature
by the constitution to make, ordain, and establish all manner of wholesome and reasonable laws, statutes, and ordinances . . . as they shall judge
to be for the good and welfare of the Commonwealth."[29]

Similar legislative and judicial reasoning accompanied the slew of ordinances and statutes that paced an expanding American economy: regulations of lotteries, hawkers and peddlers, rents and leases, mines, ferries, apprentices and servants, attorneys and solicitors, the exportation of flaxseed
and other goods, the inspection of lumber, staves and heading, public auctions, fisheries, flour and meal, the practice of physic and surgery, beef and
pork, sole leather, inns and taverns, shipping, and common carriers.[30] Rather
than leave the regulation of a growing economy to common-law judges or
laissez-faire theorists, states and localities codified the rights and responsibilities of key economic actors and activities. Thus, states like Massachusetts
supplemented the common law of common carriers with many additional

statutory provisions. In the 1840 Act Concerning Passenger Carriers, for example, the legislature specified penalties when the life of any passenger was lost through the "negligence or carelessness" of the proprietors of railroads, steamboats, stagecoaches, or other common carriers. And in 1851, it added a more elaborate statute concerning passengers' personal effects—trunks, carpetbags, valises, parcels, and the like.[31] Cities like Boston promptly passed ordinances and granted licenses for the governance of inns, common victuallers, and other licensed houses in the city.[32] Examples could be multiplied a thousandfold across the various legislative jurisdictions of early nineteenth-century America. And one of the persistent features of this legislative intervention from the beginning was explicit, sometimes quite detailed, price administration or rate setting: from the regulation of the ancient assize of bread to the early mill acts to the precise setting of prices for ferriage and cartage to the even more explicit rate setting practiced during the canal and early railroad eras.[33] Common-law origins were still decipherable in such statutes, but a new and far more capacious regulatory state was methodically supplanting traditional legal and economic frameworks. In *Standards of American Legislation,* Ernst Freund captured the essence of this transition from legal to legislative and common law to police power with an epigraph from Edmund Burke: "Nothing in progression can rest on its original plan. . . . Legislators ought to do what lawyers cannot." Freund outlined the vast "shortcomings of the common law as a system of public policy" and called for a more affirmative use of legislative police power and general regulatory statutes "to define vague restraints or prohibitions, to strike at antisocial condition . . . and to give effect to altered concepts of right and wrong and of the public good."[34]

The second important element in the construction of modern American business regulation was the development and proliferation of a different kind of legislative statute, not general but special: the state charter of incorporation. The American practice of economic promotion and regulation through state corporate chartering did not develop in a legal vacuum. Indeed, it is only through acknowledging the wider context of both the common law of public callings and a new explosion of state police power legislation that we can properly assess what the increased use of corporate charters added to the American economic regulatory environment. And it is only by keeping in mind all three modes of nineteenth-century economic regulation—the common law, state police power, and corporate chartering— that one can get a full picture of the interrelationship of the corporation, economy, law, and democracy.

Before general incorporation statutes became predominant in the United States around 1875, most corporations came into being through a special charter secured directly from the state legislature.[35] After 1800, the appetite for chartering (not only business corporations but municipal corporations, charitable associations, churches, academies, etc.) in legislative sessions almost matched the legislative appetite for general police power statutes. Between 1789 and 1865, for example, Connecticut passed roughly three thousand special acts incorporating every conceivable kind of social and economic organization, filling five thick volumes under forty-six separate titles.[36] Two characteristics of this early special charter regime had important implications for an emerging law of public utilities.[37] First, the special charter was a legal tool through which the legislature extracted what Ernst Freund dubbed an enhanced or "enlarged police power."[38] In exchange for a host of special corporate privileges—for instance, monopoly power, eminent domain power, tax exemption, property grant, public financing, or rights to collect tolls—legislatures carved out expanded public powers of oversight and regulation.[39] Second, this enlarged police power seemed to support the conclusion of early histories that these original specially chartered corporations were essentially seen as public callings or public franchises.[40] That was exactly Willard Hurst's conclusion: "From the 1780s well into the mid-nineteenth century the most frequent and conspicuous use of the business corporation—especially under special charters— was for one particular type of enterprise, that which we later call public utility and put under particular regulation because of its special impact in the community."[41] State governments initiated, directed, and were fully invested in state railroad development.[42]

A growing case law only reinforced this original understanding of the public interest, public service, and public utility character of early chartered corporations. Courts uniformly rejected an overly strict contract theory of the charter that some corporations argued exempted or inoculated them from further regulatory or legislative control. The definitive discussion of this issue arose in an early railroad regulation case, *Thorpe v. Rutland and Burlington Railroad Company* (1855). There, Vermont Chief Justice Isaac Redfield (a leading legal authority on common carriers) rejected a railroad corporation's argument that its original 1843 charter immunized it from costly subsequent police power regulations that required railroads to fence their lines and maintain cattle guards at crossings. Citing Roger Taney in *Charles River Bridge* as well as John Marshall in *Dartmouth College*, Redfield insisted that corporate charters be strictly construed "in favor of the public" so as not to interfere with general legislative police power to regulate persons and property in the public interest.[43] Redfield contended that "there would be no end of illustrations upon this subject," listing just some of the "thousand things" that the legislature regulated on all railroads, in-

cluding "the supervision of the track, tending switches, running upon the
time of other trains, running a road with a single track, using improper rails,
not using proper precaution by way of safety beams in case of the breaking
of axle-trees, the number of brakemen on a train with reference to the
number of cars, employing intemperate or incompetent engineers and servants, running beyond a given rate of speed." He closed with a series of
citations—essentially a field guide to the early American doctrine of police
power—"by which persons and property are subjected to all kinds of restraints and burdens, in order to secure the general comfort, health, and
prosperity of the state." And he justified the imposition of legislative regulation on corporations of all sorts: "Slaughter-houses, powder-mills, or
houses for keeping powder, unhealthy manufactories . . . have always been
regarded as under the control of the legislature. It seems incredible how
any doubt should have arisen upon the point now before the court."[44]

As Chief Justice Redfield was defending the reach of the police power to
corporations in Vermont, Chief Justice Shaw in Massachusetts was carving
out a specially "enlarged" or enhanced police power in the case of corporations perceived to have especially important duties to the public. According to Joseph Henry Beale, the case of *Lumbard v. Stearns* (1849)
"profoundly influenced" the development of one of "the most modern and
most important branches of the law"—that is, "that which regulates and
controls public-service companies."[45] Drawing on his extensive experience
with legislation, adjudication, and regulation concerning Massachusetts's
extensive network of mills and public infrastructure, Shaw was well positioned to assess the considerations of public policy, public interest, and
public utility that accompanied industrialization: "That the improvement
of the navigation of a river is done for the public use, has been too frequently decided and acted upon, to require authorities. And so to create a
wholly artificial navigation by canals." Even the establishment of a great
mill for manufacturing purposes was a legitimate object of great public interest "since manufacturing has come to be one of the great public industrial pursuits of the commonwealth."[46] In *Lumbard,* Shaw argued that the
Massachusetts Act to Incorporate the Springfield Aqueduct Company
essentially created a public service company subject to the higher obligations and regulations of a public utility.[47] The corporate charter was replete with special legislative provisos, including eminent domain power,
an obligation to provide water to fight fires, special penalties for corrupting
water, and, perhaps most significantly, a vesting of "superintending powers"
in the board of health and the county commissioners. Shaw had little trouble
detecting an overarching "public use" in the entire statute—in its title,
enacting clause, and entire purview: "The supply of a large number of

inhabitants with pure water is a public purpose. . . . By accepting the act of incorporation, they undertake to do all the public duties required by it."[48]

The constitutional historian Leonard Levy—like Joseph Henry Beale—located the historical origins of the law of public service corporations and the state regulation of "businesses affected with a public interest" precisely in Shaw's jurisprudence and these early Massachusetts decisions that upheld the regulation of "turnpike, bridge, canal, mill, and railroad companies." As Levy put it, "Although privately financed and operated for private gain, these enterprises were all characterized by Shaw as 'public works' because they were established by public authority on consideration that the public would benefit from them."[49]

The Emergence of a Modern Public Utility Idea. The modern public utility idea drew directly on these legal-intellectual precedents. From the ancient common law of public callings, it derived the idea of the special duties and obligations of individuals and properties holding themselves out as doing business with the general public. From the antebellum police power, it inherited a well-established tradition of prospective legislative and regulatory action as well as the ancient legal principle of the subservience of private interest to the public good—salus populi supreme lex est (the people's welfare is the supreme law). And from the experience of legislative corporate chartering, the public utility idea acquired the long-established American practice of viewing business corporations (as well as other forms of incorporated associations) as artificial and formal creatures of the state subject to enlarged regulatory and administrative supervision. Out of these early roots and traditions, there emerged a distinctively more modern and expansive concept of regulation in the public interest at the turn of the century. Three new elements in the transformation of public law made public utility the entering wedge of modern economic regulation in the United States.

First, the public utility idea drew directly on the positive conception of statecraft and the public duties of a modern polity discussed in Chapter 2, particularly as they concerned the provision of public services. Though this idea claimed many different forms at the turn of the century, the most penetrating analysis came by way of Léon Duguit's influential essay "Law and the Modern State."[50] There Duguit pioneered his thesis that the idea of public service was rapidly "replacing the old theory of sovereignty as the basis of public law." Drawing on recent trends in sociological jurisprudence and an ever more functionalist and pragmatic conception of law, Duguit rooted his distinctively modern theory of state in social functions, public duties, and public service. Like Ernst Freund, Duguit argued that modern governance was rapidly moving beyond traditional functions of defense and order, obliging the state to provide for the public welfare and improved socioeconomic conditions through the public provision of public services.[51]

Public utility was very much at the core of this new, pragmatic understanding of the public service functions of the state. Moving beyond older conceptions of the state rooted in contract, sovereignty, or fiscal-military imperative, John Dewey outlined a more modern and pragmatic quest for a "democratic state" dedicated to "the utilization of government as the genuine instrumentality of an inclusive and fraternally associated public." For Dewey, the growing awareness that more and more businesses were "affected with a public interest" was a step forward in the development of that functionalist, democratic, and service-oriented state.[52] Felix Frankfurter concurred, arguing in "Public Services and the Public" that no task was more profound for modern government than its role "in securing for society those essential services which are furnished by public utilities."[53] Elementary examples of this trend toward public services included the evolution of education and charity from private to public affairs and the development of "the postal and telegraph system" into "public service[s] of primary importance."[54] To these basic examples of the public service idea, Duguit added public lighting and "the necessity of organizing transportation into a public service." Duguit concluded in perfect sync with the architects of public utility law in the United States: "Any activity that has to be governmentally regulated and controlled because it is indispensable to the realisation and development of social solidarity is a public service so long as it is of such a nature that it cannot be assured save by governmental intervention."[55]

Second, the modern public utility regime embodied the maturation of the police power and administrative regulation. Of course, as made clear in earlier chapters, police power and administrative regulation had been features of American governance since the founding of the republic. But with the rise of public utility regulation, these established practices took on a distinctly new, enlarged, and purposeful form. A new self-consciousness and inventiveness propelled discussions of police power and administrative law as the first systematic treatises and analyses of scholars like Freund, Goodnow, and Rexford Tugwell synthesized, reorganized, and in the end transformed the fields of inquiry, usually around the topic of public utility.[56]

The modern police power came of age in the public utility era, and the contemporaneous treatises of Ernst Freund bore explicit witness to this auspicious convergence. For Freund, the Granger cases, the law of public service corporations, public use, and public utility harbingered the growth and maturity of modern police power. The increased power to regulate businesses, the corporation, and the economy through public utility was an essential part of the long process through which the police power moved beyond older common-law and constitutional limitations and traditional concerns of order maintenance so as to embrace the more ambitious and prospective mission of securing the public welfare and making internal public policy. Noting the almost limitless expansion of public utility in the early twentieth century (beyond natural monopolies, railroads, common carriers, inns, grain elevators, banking, insurance, and others), Freund concluded: "If a business is affected with a public interest its charges are subject to reasonable regulation . . . , it may be required to render services without discrimination, and the amount and manner of service may be regulated in the interest of public convenience. . . . A great expansion of the police power may be expected by further development and application of this doctrine."[57] Rexford Tugwell saw in precisely this confluence of legal-regulatory events and concepts a new public interest in the economy—"the right of the government to interfere in business affairs. Under its aegis public utilities arise and the police powers are brought to bear in the field of industry."[58]

Administration and administrative law likewise grew and expanded as they interacted with public utility. Felix Frankfurter identified the "general recognition" and "self-conscious direction" of administrative law as a consequence largely of the public utility revolution.[59] Public utility put the "public" in American public administration. The pioneering administrative law casebooks and treatises of Joseph Henry Beale, Bruce Wyman, and Frankfurter reflected this.[60] Beale, Wyman, and Frankfurter seamlessly and simultaneously advanced the ideas of public service, public interest, regulation, and administration as they promoted and expanded the range of acceptable administrative action. Beale's *Cases on Carriers* (1898), Wyman's *Principles of Administrative Law* (1903) and *Public Service Corporations* (1911), and Frankfurter's *Cases under the Interstate Commerce Act* (1915) connected public callings, common carriers, public utilities, an enlarged state police power, and the new kind of administrative power ultimately nationalized in the Interstate Commerce Act. For William Howard Taft, the Interstate Commerce Commission inaugurated nothing short of an administrative revolution in governance: "The inevitable progress and exigencies of government" brought a recognition of this "new field of administrative law which needed a knowledge of government and an experienced understanding of our institutions safely to define and declare."[61] Public utility law incubated just such a modern concept of administration.[62]

From just such broadened conceptions of public service, police power, and administration there emerged the final, culminating piece of the public utility idea—that is, a more generalized and autonomous conception of the public interest.[63] Key was the all-important idea of generality—moving older ideas of salus populi, people's welfare, and res publica beyond the particular confines of customary, common-law, and ancient constitutional categories toward a broader and more modern conception of general regulation in the public interest. There was no clearer text on this transformation than Rexford Tugwell's dissertation at the University of Pennsylvania, *The Economic Basis of Public Interest* (1922). Tugwell charted the rise of a more general doctrine of public interest as it moved from legislative police power through public utility to the wider notion of "the relationship the business bears to the welfare of the public."[64] As Tugwell summarized: "The definition of police power in all the recent cases brings it into the broad field of public interest, so that the regulation of business in its economic aspects, its prices and its standards of service, flows from the general interest of the public just as does the right of regulation of business to secure the health, morals and safety of the community."[65]

Significantly, this new construct of economic regulation in the public interest was not specially limited to the problems of monopolies either natural or unnatural. Though monopoly was a problem for which public utility provided a response, monopoly was just one of many important factors that could justify a public utility.[66] Tugwell began with the monopoly question but quickly articulated a much larger set of public interest justifications. Imposition, oppression, necessity, unreasonable charges, harmful prices, or harmful standards of service were all justifiable regulatory concerns when dealing with public utilities.[67] The public utility idea grew capaciously beyond the so-called natural monopoly question to embrace a potentially unlimited number of economic activities where the law imposed a duty to be reasonable in dealing with the public. As legal scholar Nicholas Bagley has argued, "An extraordinary range of market features— the costs of shopping around, bargaining inequalities, informational disadvantage, rampant fraud, collusive pricing, emergency conditions, and more—could all frustrate competition and . . . warrant state intervention" via the enlarged law of public callings and public utilities.[68] Conditions such as necessity, exorbitant charges, arbitrary control, and consumer harm could all now trigger new affirmative legal obligations in the public interest. "All must be served," Bruce Wyman observed, "adequate facilities must be provided, reasonable rates must be charged, and no discriminations must be made."[69] Access, sufficient service and supply, cost reasonableness, and nondiscrimination worked together in the law of public utility to generate a novel concept of government's obligation to regulate for the public welfare.

This was the modern concept of public utility—the cutting edge of a more general idea of economic regulation in the public interest. As Oliver Wendell

Holmes argued in *The Common Law*, one of the creative elements in modern law was its capacity for generality. Concerning private law, Holmes's great achievement in 1881 was charting the emergence of a modern, "general theory of liability, civil and criminal," out of the morass of earlier common-law particularities.[70] In American public law, the public utility idea had the same effect. As Felix Frankfurter concluded: "Suffice it to say that through its regulation of those tremendous human and financial interests which we call public utilities, the government may in large measure determine the whole socio-economic direction of the future."[71]

Utilities, Railroads, and State Regulatory Commissions

As the preceding discussion demonstrates, there was no single, definitive point of historical departure from which to date the exact birth of the public utility idea. From ancient English common-law precedents on common carriers to some of the first private companies and first public regulations established in the Americas,[72] the older historical roots of public utilities were as variegated as they were widespread. Even the more particular mechanism of administrative regulation through various kinds of boards, commissions, and agencies had broad and diverse legal-historical roots.[73] Highway commissioners, canal commissioners, bank commissioners, water commissioners, poor law commissioners, boards of health, and various other administrative entities had long exercised the power to supervise, administer, and regulate callings, associations, businesses, and corporations deemed important to the people's welfare. Indeed, as early as 1832, Connecticut was in the habit of establishing a special "board of commissioners" in the charter of each and every railroad it incorporated.[74]

Although a single point of historical departure is elusive, it is still possible to detect within this complex mesh of laws and institutions certain historical trajectories or trends that are central to explaining the dramatic emergence of modern public utilities law at the turn of the twentieth century. In the historical developments just outlined, one can detect a general trend from highly particularized (and retrospective) common-law adjudications on public callings to more generalized (and prospective) legislative police power statutes (frequently coupled with ad hoc administrative delegations of supervisory authority) to the regulation of particular franchises through special provisions included in state charters. By the middle of the nineteenth century, there was not so much a systematic law of public utilities as a wide proliferation of regulatory devices and measures—from sporadic court judgments enforcing common-law understandings to various state and local police power statutes and ordinances to the host of highly differentiated and individualized provisions of special franchise charters. By 1869, Massachusetts had passed more than a thousand general and special statutes attempting to pin down the legal status of its railroad companies.[75]

Two things transformed and modernized this old regime. First, with respect to business corporations in particular, the regulatory control afforded through the state charter regime grew more attenuated owing to vast changes in state corporation laws combined with the increased nationalization and internationalization of commerce and business that quickly outpaced or preempted many state and local regulatory initiatives. The special, local, and state-by-state initiatives that characterized antebellum public policy making concerning public utilities soon gave way to a centralization and rationalization of administrative regulation at both state and national levels. Felix Frankfurter captured this confluence of events as follows: "The modern system of state utility regulation thus coincid[ed] with the efforts . . . to arm the federal government with powers adequate to assure interstate public services."[76]

Second, one particularly important and highly visible form of common carrier and public service corporation—the railroad—burst onto the American scene with an economic ferocity unmatched by any historical force short of war. As Alfred Chandler argued, railroads remade the American economy. They were "the nation's first big business," and they marked the beginnings of modern corporate finance, modern corporate management, modern labor relations, and thus, not surprisingly, the "modern governmental regulation of business."[77] Just as the scale and scope of railroads transformed the American economy, the scale and scope of railroad administration changed the face of American regulation. As Frankfurter noted, "Railroad regulation was the precursor of the far-flung system of utility control today."[78] Railroads were not the first transportation companies in the United States, and railroad commissions were not the first administrative agencies. But the size and extent of this infrastructural and regulatory intervention forever altered the relationship of the modern American economy and the administrative and regulatory state. The railroads ushered in modern public utility regulation on a scale and with a national impact that was simply unprecedented.

Something of the magnitude of "the railroad problem" was broadcast to the nation in 1869 when Charles Francis Adams opened his history of the Erie Railway in the *North American Review* with a comparison to the Barbary pirates and then closed it with an allusion to the fall of Rome. Adams talked about the railroad problem not in terms of market failure or

imperfect competition but as nothing less than a national "emergency."
Allusions to war and plunder and banditry infused Adams's narrative of
endemic economic and political corruption: "The freebooters have only
transferred their operations to the land, and the commerce of the world is
now more severely . . . taxed through the machinery of rings and tariffs,
selfish money combinations at business centres, and the unprincipled corporate control of great lines of railway, than it ever was by depredations
outside of the law."[79] From E. L. Godkin, B. O. Flower, and Frank Norris
to William Jennings Bryan, Robert La Follette, and Theodore Roosevelt, a
steady drumbeat of rhetorical and political criticism followed Adams's
original railroad exposé providing a consistent prod to governmental action well into the twentieth century.

But even more significant for the subsequent history of regulation than
the muckraking zeal that greeted the Gilded Age was a rising chorus of organized democratic political discontent with railroad policy making. As
Arthur T. Hadley put it in *Railroad Transportation*, things were "dangerously near the point where revolutions begin."[80] Across the nation, but especially in agrarian and midwestern states like Illinois, Iowa, Wisconsin,
and Minnesota, voluminous complaints about extortionate and discriminatory railroad pricing (between long hauls and short hauls and between
competitive and monopolistic routes) produced intense political pressure
for more aggressive state action. This pressure culminated in a proliferation of new comprehensive state regulations of railroads, warehouses, and
grain elevators—organizations and corporations that many felt dispropor-
tionately controlled the price of agricultural and other products across wide
swaths of the country.[81] Given the increasing complexity and scope of this
new economic problem, states turned to a much more powerful mechanism
of regulatory oversight and enforcement—the state administrative regulatory commission.

The modern state railroad commission movement launched in Massachusetts. "Neither competition nor legislation have proved themselves effective agents for the regulation of the railroad system," Adams argued in
"The Government and the Railroad Corporations," so "what other and
more effective [instrument was] there within the reach of the American
people?"[82] The Massachusetts Board of Railroad Commissioners (1869)
was the modern regulatory response. To be sure, the use of commissions,
officers, and boards was anything but unprecedented in early American
state governance. With respect to utilities, Massachusetts had already uti-
lized state commissions for banking as early as 1838 and for insurance in
1854. With respect to railroads, New Hampshire and Connecticut pioneered state commissions in the 1840s and 1850s to report on railroad

conditions and public safety (on the model of English precedent).[83] But the Massachusetts board brought a new level of general supervisory authority as well as a more permanent administrative regulation. The legislature granted the commissioners "general supervision of all railroads in the Commonwealth" with a special charge to ensure "compliance of the several railroad corporations with the provisions of their charters and the laws of the Commonwealth." The board essentially received plenary authority to investigate and make recommendations to all railroads in the state as to repairs, stock, stations, rates of fares for passengers and freight, and, for that matter, any other "change in the mode of operating its road or conducting its business." They were empowered to investigate, inspect, and gather information on nearly all aspects of Massachusetts railroading, from material conditions (track and accidents) to financial management (inspecting books, accounts, receipts, and profits).[84] More importantly from the perspective of public service and democratic access—that is, serving the people directly in their dealing with the railroad corporations—the board was charged with *hearing complaints* and *receiving petitions*. Before the establishment of the commission, citizens seeking remedies for corporate or railroad economic harms were left to rely on the more ponderous and less effective processes of courts (where in individual cases they were frequently outmatched by railroad counsel) or the state legislature (where general access was difficult and not always egalitarian).[85] As state legislatures moved away from so-called private bills in the early nineteenth century, the administrative complaint and petition became a renewed point of open and democratic access addressing citizen needs and grievances.[86]

The *Annual Reports of the Massachusetts Board of Railroad Commissioners* were comprehensive and state-of-the-art compendiums of information and recommendations on railroading and governance that prefigured the modern bureaucratic ethos.[87] Beyond common-law adjudication, police power legislation, and special charter provisions, the board now allowed for a consistent, ongoing, and systematic supervision of the railroad enterprise throughout the state. The concentration of oversight authority in a single agency was a vast improvement over the somewhat haphazard and sporadic coordination possible through the earlier panoply of statutory provisions, charter stipulations, and common-law adjudications. And indeed, the board was so successful that the Massachusetts legislature did not feel compelled to alter its basic structure and mission until 1913 when the Massachusetts Public Service Commission replaced the board. Nor did the Massachusetts Supreme Judicial Court see fit to challenge its existence or its basic regulatory authority. In 1869, the court commented on such administrative powers almost nonchalantly: "The powers and duties in question belong to that class not strictly judicial, but partaking both of the judicial and the executive character, . . . the exercise and control of which may be vested by the legislature at its discretion . . . in commissioners or other officers."[88]

The Massachusetts railroad commission has been sometimes mischaracterized as a "weak," "voluntary," or "advisory" form of administrative regulation, owing to its lack of direct authority to set and enforce actual railroad rates and prices. The board was authorized to recommend rates and hear complaints about unfair or discriminatory fares, but it had no direct coercive or enforcement powers beyond the threat of proposing legislation to that effect. But it would be a mistake to underestimate the commissioners' actual regulatory power, as they induced railroad reform by continuously bargaining in the shadow of possible future legislation and regulation—up to and including the threat of state ownership. And future legislation and regulation were forever coming.[89] In 1892, the board boasted its effectiveness in consistently reducing rates in Massachusetts despite the lack of direct enforcement power.[90] As one observer commended commission results around the same time: "It has held the railroads in close obedience to the laws; it has corrected abuses, settled grievances, secured the passage of wise laws and prevented those that seemed unwise. It has secured uniformity in accounts and reports of the roads and has established confidence and a friendly feeling between the people and the railroads as common carriers."[91] On account of this success, fifteen states established railroad commissions on the Massachusetts model by the time the national Interstate Commerce Commission was formed in 1887.[92]

The Massachusetts commission's lack of direct administrative rate-making and enforcement power only underscored the historical significance of the great change inaugurated when the Illinois legislature passed An Act to Establish a Board of Railroad and Warehouse Commissioners in 1871.[93] Notably, Illinois's state railroad commission emerged directly out of a wave of popular protest that put railroad reform at the very center of the state constitutional convention of 1869–1870. Indeed, much of the 1871 legislation was explicitly mandated by new constitutional directives insisting that railroads be placed under strict public-utility-type controls. Constitutionally, Illinois railways were declared "public highways"— equally "free to all persons for the transportation of their persons and their property." Further, the constitutional revision directed the state general assembly to establish price controls—"reasonable maximum rates of charges" for "passengers and freight on the different railroads in this state." And finally, as if to underscore popular democratic concern with corporate corruption and economic impropriety, the constitutional convention

also charged the assembly with passing laws "to correct abuses and prevent unjust discrimination and extortion" in railroad pricing across all the
roads in Illinois.[94]

The Illinois Railroad and Warehouse Commission Act was thus no ordinary piece of legislation. In addition to responding to explicit constitutional
mandates, the commission legislation was but one piece in a packet of detailed statutes on warehouses and railroads passed in March and April, including a revision of Illinois's general railroad incorporation act, an act
concerning railroad injuries, an act prohibiting unjust rate discriminations
and extortions, an act regulating the transportation of grain by railroad
corporations, an act setting maximum rates for charges on passengers, and
an act for the construction of railroad stations and depots.[95] In short, from
its constitutional convention forward, Illinois (like many other midwestern
states) demanded a detailed and thoroughgoing account and regulation of
railroad corporations and warehouse companies and established a new
permanent commission to oversee and enforce this heightened regulatory
response (to investigate, prosecute, and in some cases directly penalize violations of Illinois law). Like Massachusetts, Illinois began with comprehensive
reporting and data gathering (along some forty-plus legislatively specified
dimensions) to ensure that "railroad companies and warehouses, their officers, directors, managers, lessees, agents, and employees" were complying
with "the laws of the state now in force."[96] But in 1873, the legislature
added a final piece of modern administrative machinery in authorizing the
commission itself to develop a schedule of maximum rates for the transportation of passengers and freight on all railroad corporations doing
business in the state that would be deemed prima facie "reasonable" in all
Illinois courts.[97] In pioneering the development of a state board that could
establish reasonable maximum rates and institute proceedings to enforce
them, Illinois established something new and produced immediate precedent for regulation of the national railway system. Iowa, Wisconsin, Minnesota, Georgia, and California soon followed Illinois's lead. And by the
time the Interstate Commerce Commission was founded, ten states had implemented the Illinois model.[98]

Despite sharing a certain lineage with the common carriers and public
callings as well as earlier state and local commission experience, this was a
new kind of regulatory regime. Arguably for the first time, regulatory policy
displayed almost all of the characteristics that continue to define modern
administrative regulation: fact-finding, data gathering, reporting, publication, inspection, investigation, prosecution, delegation, price setting, adjudication, rule making, and regulatory enforcement. Much as antebellum
police power regulations attempted to improve on the ad hoc and ex post

litigation of violations of common-law rules, here legislatures pushed forward a new kind of comprehensive regulatory apparatus to enforce formidable new state regulations of railroads, warehouses, and grain elevators. The strong midwestern state regulatory commission was a direct result of the effort to move beyond the limitations of common-law and statutory modes of regulation—to self-consciously create a more modern and comprehensive regulatory administration.

No aspect of this new regulatory regime was more important than the way it attempted to alter the existing balance of power between corporations and citizens. Declaring railroads to be "public highways" with open and equal access to all citizens was a foundational public and democratic principle. That was supplemented by a public utility commitment to reasonable rates and nondiscrimination in service. Central to the actual implementation of such public-interest principles was the invention of the administrative commission itself as a new site of open democratic access for receiving citizens' petitions, complaints, and grievances. "Many complaints have been received," the commission noted in its first report. Though many railroad regulations were on the books, statutes were being violated and were difficult to enforce through conventional legal processes.[99] Citizen suits against out-of-compliance or discriminating and extorting railroads went nowhere given the expense of litigation and the deep pockets of the nation's largest corporations. One Minnesota railroad commissioner complained to the US Senate, "As a general rule, or invariably, the citizen concluded that he could not afford to litigate with the railroad company."[100] Accordingly, section 11 of the Illinois commission statute authorized the commission "whenever it shall come to their knowledge, either upon complaint or otherwise, or they shall have reason to believe that any such law or laws have been or are being violated, they shall prosecute or cause to be prosecuted all corporations or persons guilty of such violation."[101] The commission thus began pursuing more direct enforcement measures either via its own powers or those of a state's attorney to protect the public's interests against wayward railroad corporations.

Almost immediately, the Illinois commission began aggressively exercising its new legislatively derived powers of investigation, regulation, administration, and even prosecution. In its first year of existence, upon receiving satisfactory evidence of "unjust discrimination and extortion" of the rates on the Chicago and Alton Railroad, it instructed J. H. Rowell—the state's attorney for McLean County—to file an information in the nature of a quo warranto to "declare the charter of that company forfeited" in violation of the new Illinois railroad regulation. It added that "the prosecution will be pressed with vigor."[102] Given open violations of existing laws regarding warehouses and grain elevators, the board again instructed the state's attorney—this time for Cook County—"to institute proceedings against said delinquent owner or manager of warehouses." After a delay forced by the Great Chicago Fire, these latter proceedings ultimately formed the basis of the litigation that would culminate in *Munn v. Illinois*.[103] Finally, after joint conferences with railroad commissioners from Minnesota and Wisconsin, the board moved to more comprehensively deal with the problem of unjust, extortionate, and discriminatory rates, reasoning that it was "the duty of every government to protect its citizens against all forms of injustice and oppression" and that this was especially the case when "offenses [were] committed by railroad corporations in this State."[104]

Following the legislature's directive in 1873, the commission prepared a schedule of maximum railroad rates that were held to be prima facie evidence of reasonableness in Illinois courts. The details of this extraordinary exercise of authority in many ways exemplify a new form of modern regulatory and administrative power that reached something of a peak of development in the early twentieth century. The commission began with a meticulous and formal classification of every conceivable kind of freight—anything that one could possibly take on a train. The list below reproduces only classified freight beginning with the letters *Ca:*[105]

Cabbage, in small lots, crates or hhds	2
Cabbage, car loads, same as potatoes	
Cabinet ware	See furniture
Cabinet organs	1
Caissons	2
Cable chain	4
Camphene, in wood	1 ½
Candles	2
Candles, 2,000 lbs. or more	4
Canvass	1
Canvass, roofing	2
Canes	1
Cane mills	2
Cannon	2
Cannon, on wheels, or if flat car required	Class A
Candy	1
Canned goods	2
Canned goods, 100 boxes or over	3
Caps, in boxes, strapped	1
Caps, in boxes, not strapped	1 ½

Caps, in trunks	1 ½
Capstans	2
Carboys and contents	D 1
Carboys, empty	1
Carboys, empty, car loads	Class A
Cards	1
Card board	2
Carpets and Carpeting	1
Carpet, hemp	1
Carpet lining	1
Carpenters' tools	1
Carriages and sleighs, not boxed	1 ½
Carriages, well boxed	D 1
Carriage springs, boxes and axles	2
Car springs, rubber	2
Car springs, volute, boxed	4
Car wheels and axles	4
Car wheels and axles, car loads	Class D
Carts in pieces	1
Casks, large, empty	1 ½
Cassia	1
Cast-iron grain mills	2
Castor oil, in glass	1
Castor oil, in wood	3
Cauldron kettles	2

Here, the numbers 1 through 4 stood for first through fourth class; 1 ½, for one and a half first class; and D1, for double first class.

The commission then reproduced seventeen separate schedules for these newly classified freights—first through fourth and A through D, with additional schedules for flour and meal; salt, cement, plaster, and stucco; all grain and mill stuffs (except wheat); wheat; lumber; horses and mules; cattle and hogs; and sheep. The schedules listed the commission's rates by both miles and per one hundred pounds and listed the existing comparative rates of *each and every major railroad in the state.* Table 3.1 presents a sampling for just two Illinois railroad lines.

Welcome to the world of modern administrative regulation. This kind of detailed exercise in direct rate making and price setting would become the cornerstone of modern public utility regulation, and it would remain the paradigm of the modern administrative state in action for the next one hundred years (eclipsed more recently by the equally complex administra-

Table 3.1. Two Illinois Railroad Freight Schedules

Miles	Commissioners' Rates	Rockford, Rock Island, St. Louis	Peoria, Pekin, and Jacksonville
1	13.20	13.20	
5	15.40	15.40	13.00
10	17.60	17.60	15.00
15	19.80	19.80	16.00
20	22.00	22.00	18.50
25	23.65	23.65	19.50
30	25.30	25.30	21.00
35	26.40	26.40	23.00
40	27.50	27.50	25.00
45	28.60	28.60	27.00
50	29.70	29.70	29.00
60	31.90	31.90	32.00
70	34.10	34.10	34.00
80	36.30	36.30	38.00
90	38.50	38.50	
100	40.70	40.50	
125	46.20	46.00	
150	51.15	51.00	
175	55.27	55.25	
200	59.40	57.30	
225	63.52	60.60	

Source: "Schedule No. 1—Merchandise—First Class—in cents, per 100 pounds," in *Fourth Annual Report of the Railroad and Warehouse Commission of the State of Illinois* (Springfield, IL: State Journal Steam Print, 1874), 378–394.

tive process of notice-and-comment rulemaking). Into the early twentieth century, this particular activity—rate making—would preoccupy countless regulators, businessmen, practitioners, judges, economists, social scientists, legal scholars, and popular commentators. Millions of pages of ink would be consumed debating such extraordinarily complex things as the best means of calculating a rate of return, the nature of a "reasonable" versus an "unreasonable" rate, and the comparative interests of corporations, shareholders, and the public at large. And from the very beginning, there was an acute awareness of the enormity of the economic regulatory task at hand. The Illinois commission quoted from the very first issue of the *Journal of the Railway Association of America:* "So complicated does the subject become, upon even a slight examination, that railway managers are

loath to commit themselves to positive statements as to the cost of particular portions of their traffic; and much of the reticence . . . is no doubt due
to an unwillingness to put themselves on record concerning many points
which are by no means clear even to themselves."[106] More than a century
after such early concerns about the complexity of calculating things like
investment, cost, return, and rates in railroading, Stephen G. Breyer began
his own inquiry into the difficulties and problems inherent to modern regulation with detailed examinations of cost-of-service rate making and historically based price regulation.[107]

Systematic administrative and regulatory rate making of the kind
launched by the Illinois Railroad and Warehouse Commission was a new
thing under the sun. Accordingly, commissions coupled their new exertions
of regulatory authority with the self-conscious development of a legal-
political framework with which to justify their new administrative forays.
From the beginning, state commissions proactively defended and extended
their new powers with extraordinarily detailed (and largely accurate) legal
histories of both the law of common carriers as well as state legislative police power.[108] The briefs they developed along with state's attorneys were
some of the most comprehensive and well-informed statements concerning
the law of regulation in the United States—anticipating future state and US
Supreme Court doctrine. And they supplemented legal precedents concerning state regulatory power with bold political-philosophical arguments about public utility, public service, and the public good:

> We consider that nothing can justly be called an "innovation," in its of-
> fensive sense, that the public good requires. Railroads themselves are an
> innovation upon the modes of travel and transportation of fifty years ago,
> and it would be strange if the duty of the state was limited to granting
> them privileges without inquiring whether those privileges were abused.
> We conceive it to be the duty of the state to do for its citizens all that is
> necessary for the public good, and which it in the nature of things can do
> better than the private individual, as expressed by John Stuart Mill: "The
> ends of government are as comprehensive as the social system, and con-
> sist of all the good and all the immunity from evil which the existence of
> government can be made directly or indirectly to bestow."[109]

Given the broad expansion of state and regulatory power inherent in the
state administrative rate-making process, it was perhaps inevitable that this
new wave of activity by aggressive midwestern state railroad commissions
would soon yield two classic constitutional questions. First, what was the
relationship between the police powers now wielded by state railroad com-

missioners and the constitutional power of the federal government to regulate interstate commerce? Second was the extensive regulatory power of
these new state administrative authorities to set and police rates and prices
constitutional? These questions would be answered in short order by the
establishment of the Interstate Commerce Commission and the momentous
opinion of the United States Supreme Court in *Munn v. Illinois* (1877).

Interstate Commerce and the Road from Munn

State railroad commissions continued to proliferate and expand their
powers over intrastate railroads, warehouses, and grain elevators throughout
the late nineteenth century. By the early twentieth century, they were joined
by even more powerful state public utility and corporation commissions
that presided over a growing array of public utilities and public service corporations in industries like telecommunications, electricity, gas, lighting,
and water. The commission system was fast becoming the default mode of
administrative regulation and a permanent feature of American democratic
governance. But a major constitutional concern lurked beneath the surface.
State common carrier and public utility regulation was legally rooted in
state police power—the power to regulate the internal police of a state for
the public health, safety, and welfare. Since the early decisions of the Marshall Court, the US Supreme Court had struggled to demarcate matters of
state internal police from interstate commerce.[110] The rapid rise of interstate and transcontinental railroading made inevitable a regulatory and jurisdictional clash between state police power and federal commerce power.

As state railroad commissions policed rates that affected interstate routes,
the battle was joined. At first, the US Supreme Court was deferential, citing
the dormant commerce clause doctrine whereby states were free to internally regulate aspects of railroading that touched on interstate commerce
so long as Congress had not itself preemptively legislated in the area. Chief
Justice Waite articulated the doctrine in *Peik v. Chicago and Northwestern
Railway*: "Until Congress undertakes to legislate for those who are without
the State, [the State] may provide for those within, even though it may indi-
rectly affect those without."[111] By 1886, however, as the increasingly interstate character of railroad transportation became more apparent, the court
reversed course. In *Wabash, St. Louis and Pacific Railway v. Illinois*, Justice
Miller reached back to Chief Justice Marshall and *Gibbons v. Ogden* and
held Illinois's attempt to regulate "transportation which includes Illinois in
a long carriage through several States" to be an unconstitutional state regulation of interstate commerce "among the states." Miller concluded that the

proper power of regulation in this case belonged to Congress, "whose enlarged view of the interests of all the States, and of the railroads concerned, better fits it to establish just and equitable rules."[112]

The *Wabash* case thus threw back to Congress the crucial question of the regulation of genuinely interstate railroads. As Robert Cushman put it, "The Supreme Court decided with bluntness and finality that the states could not regulate interstate railroad traffic within their own limits even in the absence of Congressional regulation." With this new constitutional directive, the 150 or so federal legislative proposals that had been introduced in Congress for regulating interstate railroading for the past twenty years received renewed attention and urgency.[113] Within months, Congress passed the Interstate Commerce Act of 1887, establishing the first independent federal regulatory agency in the United States.

It is difficult to overstate the significance of the Interstate Commerce Commission (ICC) in the history of regulation in the United States. As I. L. Sharfman put it, "It is well-nigh universally recognized that the Interstate Commerce Commission is not only the oldest but the most powerful" of the federal agencies that exercise "authoritative control of economic conduct." Charged by a congressional charter with "protecting and promoting the public interest," the ICC was "the outstanding agency of economic control in our governmental establishment."[114] The Act to Regulate Commerce (1887) created the prototype federal regulatory agency consisting of five commissioners appointed to an original term of six years at a salary larger than any federal judge except those on the Supreme Court. The act placed interstate railroads and common carriers under an unprecedented degree of federal supervision and control. It mandated that charges be "reasonable and just" and that rates and facilities be equal and nondiscriminatory. It prohibited special rates, rebates, drawbacks, and any other "undue or unreasonable preference or advantage." And it pulled back the corporate veil of secrecy in requiring railroads to print, post, and file rate schedules while granting the commission broad powers of inquiry and investigation into books, papers, tariffs, contracts, agreements, and all other aspects of business management.[115]

The Interstate Commerce Act was based primarily on a Senate bill circulating since 1883 that culminated in the famous Cullom Report.[116] Senator Shelby Cullom's Senate Committee on Interstate Commerce made clear the extent of the railroad problem in the United States and the broad democratic concern with objectionable business practices. Indeed, the report began with an eighteen-point bill of indictment against industrial excess entitled "Causes of Complaint against the Railroad System." Among the concerns: "unreasonably high" local rates; rates bearing little relation to "cost of service"; "unjustifiable" and "improper" and "unreasonable" discriminations; an elaborate system of "secret special rates, rebates, drawbacks, and concessions, to foster monopoly, to enrich favored shippers and to prevent free competition"; "favoritism and secrecy"; speculation; "dishonest agents"; extortion; the making of a "privileged class"; overcapitalization and watered stock; and "extravagant and wasteful" railroad business management. The report early illuminated the interconnections between common carrier law, public utility law, unfair competition, and increasing concern with the noxious practices of "industrial monopoly."[117]

In addition to these widespread corporate and economic abuses, the Cullom Report also made clear the overriding concern for democratic access and public accountability. The thirteenth complaint noted that "the common law fails to afford a remedy for such grievances." House and Senate debate thoroughly ventilated this frustration with the common-law status quo. "Courts can be corrupt," Congressman Hepburn reminded his colleagues: The aggrieved "stands there alone, weak and poor and ignorant . . . with a ten-dollar case or a one-hundred dollar case. He must make his own case against a wealthy corporation." Robert La Follette referred to the federal commission idea as "the poor man's court." "Few indeed dare enter into litigation with railways," LaFollette contended, and the creation of a commission remedied this problem: "Every citizen of the United States is given the right to present his grievances and have his case tried without the attendant cost which now practically closes the courts to him."[118] The Interstate Commerce Act ultimately provided that "any person, firm, corporation, or association" or "any body politic" could now complain by petition directly to the Interstate Commerce Commission for investigation, recording, notice, and potential court proceedings undertaken by the commission itself in a summary way.[119]

In a final push to coordinate federal and state railroad commission regulation, the first chair of the Interstate Commerce Commission, Thomas M. Cooley, invited representatives of the state railroad commissions to Washington, DC, for a series of influential general conferences "with a view of perfecting uniform legislation and regulation concerning the supervision of the railroads."[120] The resultant National Association of Railroad and Utilities Commissioners would continue to influence policy making on public utilities into the New Deal and beyond.[121] A key presence at these early conferences was the chief statistician of the ICC, Henry Carter Adams. Adams would become one of the central innovators in modern institutional economics as the movement for regulation moved beyond utilities per se to the social control of American business writ large. As Adams put it, "Men are coming to realize the disastrous consequences likely to emerge from the continued sway of irresponsible corporate power. They see that an extension of governmental agency alone can retain for them the fruits of an advanced industrial civilization."[122]

Beyond issues of federalism and state versus interstate regulation, questions remained about the actual extent of a commission's constitutional regulatory authority. The formative cases on that issue were decided together by the US Supreme Court in 1877 in litigation commonly (if misleadingly) referred to as the Granger cases.[123] Chief Justice Morrison R. Waite's majority opinions in *Munn v. Illinois* (together with companion cases regarding railroad rate regulation in Iowa, Minnesota, and Wisconsin) provided an early and authoritative discussion of the fundamentals of police power and public utility regulation.[124] Hereafter, *Munn* and its progeny would become the new starting point for most legal and economic discussion of public utilities and the administrative regulatory state.[125]

Waite provided his most comprehensive discussion of the underlying principles of public utility regulation in the Illinois case involving Munn & Scott—the managers and lessees of a public warehouse known as the "North-western" grain elevator in Chicago. So, notably, the Munn & Scott elevator was not a railroad and not incorporated. Here was the more difficult case, then, to establish a more general state police power to set rates for public utilities—without the same long and dense set of precedents concerning common carriers and without the additional state claim of control through the corporate charter. And so it was the Illinois legislature's power to set a maximum grain storage rate rather than the commission's power to establish a schedule of maximum rates for railroad corporations that was the direct issue in *Munn*. The companion case *Chicago, Burlington, and Quincy Railroad v. Iowa* then decided the railroad rate-making question on the basis of the principles outlined in *Munn*.

Chief Justice Waite's opinion in *Munn v. Illinois* is famous for a reason. Like Hale in *De Portibus Maris* or Shaw in *Commonwealth v. Alger* or Redfield in *Thorpe v. Rutland*, Waite synthesized a mass of previous material and precedents and adapted them for a new age. By the time of *Munn*, the arguments and precedents that accumulated in favor of state police power regulation, rate setting, and even basic commission oversight of railroads, warehouses, and grain elevators—the first modern public service businesses—were extensive and formidable. Waite reached back into this rich tradition of established doctrines regarding highways, public callings, legislative power, state police power, the regulation of corporations, and the special obligations of public services and boldly advanced them past claims that the due process clause of the Fourteenth Amendment rendered such regulation constitutionally problematic. Despite the force of the still quite new constitutional amendments, Waite was able to easily sustain the

broad legislative and regulatory powers in their entirety. In doing so, he
provided a fresh and firm constitutional foundation for the new and rapidly developing law of public utilities.

Fittingly, given its canonical status, Waite began his opinion in *Munn*
with some general principles that he deemed as old as the idea of "civilized
government": "A body politic . . . is a social compact by which the whole
people covenants with each citizen, and each citizen with the whole people,
that all shall be governed by certain laws for the common good. . . . This
is the very essence of government."[126] From this source, Waite derived the
police powers: "nothing more or less than powers of government inherent
in every sovereignty"—"the power to govern men and things." Through
the police powers, "the government regulates the conduct of its citizens one
towards another, and the manner in which each shall use his own property, when such regulation becomes necessary for the public good."[127] Since
colonization, Waite noted, states had regulated "ferries, common carriers,
hackmen, bakers, millers, wharfingers, innkeepers, etc., and in doing so
[fixed] a maximum charge to be made for services rendered, accommoda-
tions furnished, and articles sold." To the question of the effect of the due
process clause of the Fourteenth Amendment upon the constitutionality of
such regulations, Waite responded simply that with the Fifth Amendment's
due process clause duly in force, Congress conferred power upon the city
of Washington to regulate "the rates of wharfage at private wharves," rates
and fees for "the sweeping of chimneys," "the weight and quality of bread,"
rates for "hackney carriages," "rates of hauling by cartmen, waggoners,
carmen, and draymen," and "rates and commission of auctioneers." In
short, Waite implied, nothing in the Fourteenth Amendment "supposed
that statutes regulating the use, or even the price of the use, of private
property necessarily deprived an owner of his property without due process of law."[128]

At this point in his opinion, Waite might have chosen to stop—content
with this well-established argument about police power and legislative authority to set rates and prices in the public interest.[129] Instead, Waite pushed
forward toward a clearer articulation of what he called "the principles upon
which this power of regulation rests." Waite reached back further to the
common law—"from whence came the right which the Constitution
protects"—to Lord Chief Justice Matthew Hale and *De Portibus Maris*
and the ancient price regulation of ferries, wharfingers, and warehouses to
justify what Ernst Freund would later dub that "enlarged police power" in
areas of distinctive public interest and public service. "When private property is 'affected with a public interest,'" Waite famously noted, quoting
Hale, 'it ceases to be *juris privati* only.'" Property becomes "clothed with
a public interest when used in a manner to make it of public consequence,

and affect the community at large. When, therefore, one devotes his property to a use in which the public has an interest, he, in effect, grants to the public an interest in that use, and must submit to be controlled by the public for the common good."[130] Business "affected with a public interest," thus entered the legal-economic lexicon for the first time as a constitutional test for determining which economic activities were public utilities subject to special and extensive state regulatory controls.

For Waite, Chicago's grain elevators certainly belonged in just such a category—as businesses "of public interest and use," the elevators stood "in the very 'gateway of commerce.'" They took toll from all who pass— "every bushel of grain for its passage 'pays a toll, which is a common charge'"—and should thus "conform to such regulations as might be established by the proper authorities for the common good."[131] If grain elevators were public utilities, railroads posed an even easier case, and Waite took only around fifty words to dispose of that issue: "Railroad companies are carriers for hire. They are incorporated as such, and given extraordinary powers, in order that they may the better serve the public in that capacity. They are, therefore, engaged in a public employment affecting the public interest, and, under the decision in *Munn v. Illinois* . . . subject to legislative control as to their rates of fare and freight."[132]

The Supreme Court decisions in *Munn* and its companion cases thus provided a sweeping, unapologetic, and foundational defense of the new powers of a rapidly emerging administrative regulatory state. The prolific activities of the state railroad commissions—particularly their new departures in rate making and law enforcement—changed the face of regulation in America. And despite new arguments from dissenters and defendants about the Fourteenth Amendment, due process rights, and the special sanctity of corporate charters, the US Supreme Court had little difficulty sustaining the new regulatory regime in its entirety—across four key states, from legislature to commission, from warehouses to railroads. Surveying some three hundred years in the history of common-law and state regulation of economic activity, Waite penned another field guide to the common law of public rights and common carriers, the state police power, and an emerging law of public service corporations. The work of the Illinois Railroad and Warehouse Commission, *Munn,* and Chief Justice Waite thus nicely set the stage for the explosive emergence of what might be called the public utility era. As Bruce Wyman concluded, "Any discussion of the foundations of our industrial relations must begin with that decision. . . . Upon the right understanding of this accommodation of private rights to public duties depends the true conception of our general theory of the function of state regulation."[133]

Given the robust consensus about *Munn*'s status as a canonical case on governmental regulation of the economy (and given the extraordinary amount of academic commentary originally focused on this particular set of decisions), it is worrisome that the prevailing legal-historical wisdom on *Munn* remains somewhat problematic. The heart of the problem is a persistent interpretive tendency to see *Munn* as a constitutional endpoint rather than a new beginning. While the road *to Munn* is reasonably well understood, the road *from Munn* is comparatively neglected—obscured beneath an obsessive concern with the supposed rise of laissez-faire constitutionalism. There is a tendency to see *Munn* as akin to the climax of an essentially early nineteenth-century story—a story still under the influence of figures like Lord Hale, Lemuel Shaw, and Roger Taney and archaic-sounding concerns such as common carriers, juris privati, sic utere tuo, and ferries and wharfingers. That is a mistake. For though Waite and the state railroad commissioners were well aware of the importance of precedent and the long history of Anglo-American economic regulation, they are better understood as paving the way for the likes of Felix Frankfurter and James Landis and more modern-sounding concerns like public utility, administrative rule making, and even securities regulation. *Munn* and the Illinois Railroad and Warehouse Commission were not the backward-looking last gasps of the well-regulated society; they were the forward-looking harbingers of a new democratic state.

Especially problematic is a common myopic reading of *Munn* and Waite's designation of businesses "affected with a public interest" as yet another example of the development of constitutional limitations in a Gilded Age. In depicting the ultimate triumph of laissez-faire in law, Max Lerner held that *Munn v. Illinois* along with the *Slaughter-House Cases* (1873) stood out "in melancholy solitude as part of the 'road not taken' when two paths diverged for the Supreme Court in the constitutional wood."[134] Charles Fairman also noted that the key "phrase whose currency sprang from that memorable opinion"—that is, business "affected with a public interest"— "came presently to denote a rigid category that closed against various newer measures of public control." "It took the Great Depression," *Nebbia,* and the New Deal, Fairman noted, continuing the familiar line of argument, to finally get the Supreme Court back on track.[135] Even Harry Scheiber, who did as much as anyone to illuminate the public regulatory power of the legal doctrines underlying Waite's opinion in *Munn,* in the end concluded that the public interest doctrine proved to be as much a restraint on the power of the state as an enabling doctrine: "The *Munn* doctrine was fated to become, in the hands of an increasingly conservative Supreme Court, an equally effective shield against public regulation for business the court deemed strictly private."[136] A similar interpretive tendency has relegated even the Interstate Commerce Commission to an uneven history of missed opportunity.[137]

This narrow reading of *Munn,* together with a relative neglect of subsequent developments in public utility law more generally, skews our reading of the legal history of regulation in America. Far from being a "road not taken," *Munn* was the very superhighway down which reformers drove a truckload of far-reaching experiments in the state regulation of new economic activity. And the ramifications went well beyond economic matters alone. The very next time the phrase "affected with a public interest" was used in the Supreme Court, it was uttered by dissenting Justice John Marshall Harlan in an unsuccessful attempt to widen the constitutional arena for civil rights regulation in the *Civil Rights Cases* (1883):

> The doctrines of *Munn v. Illinois* have never been modified by this court, and I am justified, upon the authority of that case, in saying that places of public amusement, conducted under the authority of the law, are clothed with a public interest, because used in a manner to make them of public consequence and to affect the community at large. The law may therefore regulate, to some extent, the mode in which they shall be conducted, and, consequently, the public have rights in respect of such places, which may be vindicated by the law. It is consequently not a matter purely of private concern.[138]

Over the next fifty years, the Supreme Court with few exceptions used the phrase "affected with a public interest" to uphold a wide variety of extensive economic regulations. In *Western Turf Association v. Greenberg* (1907), the court used the language to sustain a California statute regulating admission policies at "any opera house, theatre, melodeon, museum, circus, caravan, race-course, fair, or other place of public amusement or entertainment."[139] State appellate courts used *Munn* to even greater regulatory effect.[140] Moreover, the court made perfectly clear that the fact that a business or industry was not found to be legally "affected with a public interest" did not insulate that activity from ordinary police power regulations. In *Schmidinger v. Chicago* (1913) and *Holden v. Hardy* (1898), the court upheld a detailed regulation of the sale of bread in Chicago and an eight-hour day for Utah workers in mines and smelters without ever taking up counsel's contention that those police power regulations required a special finding of business "affected with a public interest."[141]

Contrary to some well-established interpretations regarding the relationship of law and economic regulation in the late nineteenth and early twentieth centuries, *Munn v. Illinois* did not mark the beginnings of an era of constitutional limitations or classical legal thought or laissez-faire political economy. On the contrary, *Munn* inaugurated an extraordinary era of innovation in the social control of business, industry, and the market. It set in motion a panoply of new ideas like public utilities, rate regulation, price discrimination, fair rate of return, valuation, just price, and economic planning that dominated the legal and economic treatises of the era. It propelled an agenda of economic regulation and controls that culminated in some of the more far-reaching experiments in public and government ownership of economic enterprises in United States history.[142] Felix Frankfurter, from his perspective as one of the central legal advocates for the increased social control of business in the early twentieth century, understood exactly the implications of *Munn* and early public utilities law for the economic state-building project of progressivism. In an extraordinary essay titled "Rate Regulation" that he wrote with Henry Hart for the original *Encyclopaedia of the Social Sciences*, Frankfurter summed up the accomplishment:

> The resultant contemporary separation of industry into businesses that are "public" and hence susceptible to manifold forms of control, of which price supervision is one aspect, and all other businesses, which are private, is thus a break with history. But it has built itself into the structure of American thought and law; and while the line of division is a shifting one and incapable of withstanding the stress of economic dislocation, its existence in the last half century has made possible, within a selected field, a degree of experimentation in governmental direction of economic activity of vast import and beyond any historical parallel.[143]

The public interest doctrine of *Munn* did not insulate private business from regulation. Rather, it created a new legal field of important economic activity that could be subjected to unprecedented state control from direct price regulation to outright public ownership.

In *The Economic Basis of Public Interest*, Rexford Tugwell provided a short list of the economic activities that he could envision as essentially public services by 1922.[144] He enumerated fourteen public classifications that covered a vast portion of American economic life:

1. Railways and other common carriers including express services, oil and gas pipe lines and cab and jitney lines.
2. Municipal Utilities, so called, such as water, gas, electric light and power companies and street railways.

3. Turnpikes, irrigation ditches, canals, waterways and booms.
4. Hotels.
5. Telephone, telegraph and wireless lines.
6. Bridges, wharves, docks and ferries.
7. Stockyards, abattoirs and grain elevators.
8. Market places and stock exchanges.
9. Creameries.
10. Services for the distribution of news.
11. Fire Insurance businesses.
12. The business of renting houses.
13. Banking.
14. Businesses of preparing for market and dealing in food, clothing, and fuel.

Tugwell's list of public interest services suggests that progressives viewed the law of public utilities as a vibrant and expansive arena for experimenting with unprecedented governmental control over business, industry, and the market. While today many would restrict the idea of public utility to a couple of closely circumscribed industries (such as water, electricity, gas), in the early twentieth century, the utility idea encompassed urban transportation, railroads, motor bus and truck, telecommunications, radio, pipelines, warehouses, stockyards, ice plants, banking, insurance, milk, fuel, and packing.[145] As Bruce Wyman commented on the future elasticity of the public utility idea, "What branches of industry will eventually be of such public importance as to be included in the category . . . it would be rash to predict."[146] For progressive legal and economic reformers, this capacious and open-ended legal concept of public utility was capable of justifying state economic controls ranging from statutory police regulation to administrative rate setting to outright public ownership of the means of production. Moreover, after *Munn* it was possible to consider a whole range of reforms appended to the basic idea of the public service corporation—from Mary Barron's notion of the "state regulation of the securities of railroads and public service companies" to Florence Kelley's advocacy of "the public regulation of wages, hours, and conditions of labor of the employees of public service corporations."[147] Indeed, the public utility idea was so capable of further growth as to ultimately produce one of the most ambitious administrative and regional planning initiatives of the New Deal—the Tennessee Valley Authority.

One of the main reasons for the conventional misreading of *Munn* is the tendency to focus almost exclusively on high court opinions and to overemphasize the judicial review of administrative action. This traditional con-

stitutional approach overstates the negative, naysaying function of the judiciary and radically underplays the myriad of positive, everyday political
and governmental actions that steadily constituted the public utility era—
actions cataloged in literally thousands of volumes of public utility reports
that dominated the period. So while there is no question that important
judicial pronouncements like *Wabash, St. Louis & Pacific Railway Company
v. Illinois* (1886) or *Chicago, Milwaukee & St. Paul Railway Company v.
Minnesota* (1890; 134 U.S. 418) or *Smyth v. Ames* (1898; 169 U.S. 466)
greatly affected and sometimes inflected the public utility movement, they
did not fundamentally inhibit it.[148] Instead, the main story line of legal-
political development is precisely the one outlined so well by Frankfurter
and Tugwell—the story of the creation of a public utility policy and jurisprudence that would grow to dominate economic policy making and business regulation into the New Deal and beyond. The public utility idea was
one of the most important innovations in the progressive effort to extend
democratic control over the American business corporation. And when it
merged with new ideas of the social and social democracy, it provided a
robust foundation for the development of a modern law of regulated industries and an even broader movement for the social control of American
capitalism.

4

SOCIAL LEGISLATION

From Social Welfare to Social Police

———

There has been a social revolution.

—Edith Abbott

The new conceptions of citizenship, police power, and public utility out-lined in the previous chapters transformed traditional understandings of the reach and responsibilities of government and established a new public law foundation for the modern American legislative and regulatory state. But as this chapter aims to make clear, that new state was not created for its own sake—the project of a special class of "state builders" responding to relatively autonomous political, bureaucratic imperatives. Rather, the modern American state was born in a time of intense socioeconomic trans-formation, unrest, and uncertainty—a period of almost continual social crisis that put unrelenting new demands on existing technologies of gov-ernment. A mood and language of profound social conflict and economic disorder pervaded this period. The sociologist E. A. Ross was hardly alone when he worried in 1901 that "the grand crash may yet come."[1] Brooks Adams offered one of the characteristically bleaker assessments when he introduced his brother Henry's *The Degradation of the Democratic Dogma* in 1919: "Our country is as much in the midst of a social war now as she was when Lincoln died." Louis Adamic captured something of the fierce and often violent spirit of the age when he entitled his 1931 best-seller *Dynamite*.[2]

The modern American state was thus created simultaneously with a re-consideration of its social objects. The internal legal-political changes bound up in populism, progressivism, and reform were inextricably linked to fun-damental transformations in modern social and economic life.[3] Oliver Wendell Holmes Jr. produced an aphorism for the ages when he summed up this basic critical-realist insight into the nature of modern legal-political change in 1881: "The life of the law has not been logic: it has been experience." The "felt necessities of the time" determined "the rules by which men should be governed."[4] From 1866 to 1932, those felt necessities could not have been more acute. In consequence, society and economy became explicit products of state policies to an unprecedented degree as diverse constituencies buffeted government at all levels (local, state, and national) with demands for solutions to pressing public problems. One cannot understand the dramatic transformations in American life in the late nineteenth and early twentieth centuries without reckoning with this mutually constitutive interrelationship of law and society at the center of a new democracy.[5]

In economic policy making, the idea of public utility allowed progressive reformers to pioneer an unprecedented expansion of state control over turn-of-the-century economic activity. In social policy making, public utility had an analog in what this chapter introduces as the idea of "the social." Of all of the important arenas of policy making in turn-of-the-century America, social regulation was a site of early and intense innovation. The reconstruction of society, the social sphere, and social life as appropriate objects of legal and governmental supervision was a chief focus of the governmental revolution that gave rise to the modern American state. Using the new knowledges of modern "social science," new ideas of "social welfare" and "social control," and new techniques of social regulation, reformers pioneered an array of new methods for provisioning and policing the social in a modern age.[6] Many of those methods were simultaneously being applied to economic life in a parallel attempt to socially control business, capitalism, and the market.[7] The result was a multiplicity of new initiatives, programs, and powers that, on the one hand, laid the foundation for the development of a modern social welfare state in the United States, including fundamental revisions of poor law and labor law as well as the invention of social work, social insurance, and social security. On the other hand, the very same tendencies vastly expanded the range and reach of a modern American police and penal state, featuring new modes of morals and sex regulation, a new criminology, the policing of families, and even the practice of eugenics.

Because of the sharply divergent normative implications of social welfare and social police, many scholarly analyses separate out the two developments as discrete and contending impulses, as in, humanitarian reform versus social control or social bonds versus social engineering or the welfare state versus the carceral state.[8] But a clean separation of the history of social provision from the history of social police is not possible. They were bundled together in the larger historical development of modern social regulation involving both a social justice and welfare function as well as a social control and policing function.[9] Modern social regulation involved an overarching *socialization* process that François Ewald described as a new way of conceiving of social obligations and legal-political relations, "where the link between one individual and another is always mediated through the society they form, with the latter playing a regulatory, mediatory, and redistributive role."[10]

The story of the emergence of this modern American tradition of social regulation and social governance begins when new and expansive conceptions of police power and public utility met with an equally new and expansive conception of the social. This chapter thus foregrounds the legal and political nature of modern social reproduction—the degree to which modern social life is thoroughly implicated in reconfigurations of legal and state power. It begins with a general account of the new intellectual and legal efforts to study and map society and to bring about a more efficient and modern social control through law. From the reconceptualization of the idea of social ordering and provisioning to the reconsideration of the social bases and social imperatives of law and governance, fin-de-siecle America witnessed a thoroughgoing resocialization.

Alexis de Tocqueville was the first social theorist to recognize that democratic revolution affected much more than formal politics—that is, that it involved matters of "social form" or "social state." For that penetrating insight, John Stuart Mill deemed Tocqueville's *Democracy in America* "the first philosophical book ever written on Democracy [and] the first analytical inquiry into the influence of Democracy."[11] Modern democracy involved densely interconnected processes of both governmental and social transformation yielding more generalized modes of social regulation. At the center of that project was a socialization and generalization of police power. As Michel Foucault put it, "Police power must bear 'over everything.' . . . It is the dust of events, actions, behavior, opinions—'everything that happens'; the police are concerned with 'those things of every moment.'"[12] The socialization of modern American democracy worked a veritable revolution in governance as techniques of social regulation, police, and discipline extended in unprecedented ways across the social body and social space. The modern American "birth of the social" implicated at its core new forms of legislative, administrative, and, ultimately, police power.

The American Birth of the Social

Of course, commentary on social life is as old as civilization itself. And a certain sophisticated self-consciousness about society as a site for analysis and political action dates back at least to the Enlightenment and the important revolutions through 1848 that assembled modernity against the old regime. But there was something distinctive and significant about the way the social as an object of knowledge, law, and statecraft burst on the modern American scene in the post–Civil War era. The concept of the social simply seized the day, becoming the lingua franca of an ascendant social science and a veritable obsession of progressive activism and reform. *The Encyclopaedia of the Social Sciences* (1935)—something of a monument to the intellectual and policy achievements of this crucial period—was replete with the language of the social, from social change and social conflict to social welfare and social work.[13] And lest one think that the social was but an intellectual preoccupation disconnected from political and legal action on the ground, the equally monumental *New Encyclopedia of Social Reform* (1908) testified to the vast proliferation of organizations, movements, and substantive policies dedicated to the reconfiguration of modern social provision and social order.[14]

Reasons for this modern rise of the social are not difficult to discern. Modern social theory, from the Scottish Enlightenment to the classics of Marx, Weber, and Durkheim, originated in the problem of a modern social life cut loose from the moorings of localism, hierarchy, and tradition. The massive shifts that Henry Maine and Ferdinand Tönnies characterized in terms of "status to contract" and "Gemeinschaft to Gesellschaft" captured the social rupture of modern changes in scale, generality, class conflict, rationalization, and the division of labor.[15] In the United States, social Darwinism infused existing modernization and development theories with a new energy and "scientific" status, as society "envisaged as an organism" propelled new explorations and explanations of social evolution, social processes, and social change.[16] The simultaneous advance of the capitalist industrial marketplace, the intensification of the communications and transportation revolution, and the disorienting force of mass immigration and urbanization only reinforced the general sense that social life had irretrievably changed and that traditional forms of social regulation, social order, and social control no longer sufficed. A pervasive sense of new material conditions—of great change in the fundamentals of socioeconomic organization and the arrival of a new mass society and economy—permeated the period. Modern American social science reorganized around new models of social interdependence, social explanation, and social policy making.[17] And legal theorists mapped a corresponding transformation in the "socialization of law."[18] Notice of a great change in modern social conditions suffused the more general texts of the era. "We have arrived at a new time," announced Winston Churchill in 1909. "And with that new time, strange methods, huge forces, larger combinations—a Titanic world—have sprung up around us."[19] Five years later, Graham Wallas famously posited a "Great Society" that joined "Great Industry" and changed the social world: "During the last hundred years the external conditions of civilized life have been transformed by a series of inventions which have abolished the old limits to the creation of mechanical force, the carriage of men and goods, and communication by written and spoken words. One effect of this transformation is a general change of social scale."[20]

The birth of the social in late nineteenth- and early twentieth-century America is thus hardly news. But beneath these more commonly noted expressions of the ascendancy of social language and social knowledge, a larger and more significant social revolution was underway in basic ways of thinking about the construction of thought itself, the nature of the individual, the objects of democratic self-governance, and the technologies of law and policy making. Together, this constellation of new modes of social thought and social action—new categories and classifications as well as new legal tools and legislative-administrative techniques—undergirded an entirely new approach to social governance and social regulation, from social provision and social welfare to social police and social control.

The starting point for this social revolution in governance was an increased recognition of the sociality of reason itself—a socialization of ideas. William James's social psychology, John Dewey's social intelligence, and George Herbert Mead's concept of the social self provided a new intellectual foundation for an emergent American social science as well as progressive social reform. In his prescient dissertation, "Pragmatism and Sociology," C. Wright Mills identified the crucial interconnection of epistemology, sociology, and policy in this period: "It is precisely the importance of the accomplishment of Dewey, and in this connection even more so of G. H. Mead, that the social angle is intrinsically knit to the rational: the answer to the tension is a social theory of mind." Mills correctly identified the emergence of what he termed a kind of "sociological rationality" at the center of the progressive and pragmatic projects—as a bold alternative to both "biological determinism" as well as "a laissez-faire type of calculating individualism."[21]

As Richard Rorty, Robert Pippin, and Terry Pinkard have argued at some length, this embrace of the basic sociality of reason itself had a formal philosophical pedigree in what Pippin dubbed "the Kantian aftermath." Hegel's substantive revision of Kant's notion of the autonomy or spontaneity of reason insisted on the irreducibly social and historical nature of reason, wherein, famously, philosophy came to be understood not as "a mirror of nature" but as "its time held in thought." As Pippin summed up

Hegel's radicalization of Kant on modern reason, "In accounting for the fundamental elements of a conceptual scheme, there is and can be no decisive or certifying appeal to any basic 'facts of the matter,' foundational experiences, logical forms, constitutive 'interests,' 'prejudices,' or guiding 'intuitions,' to begin or end such account. We can appeal only to what we have come to regard as a basic fact or secure method or initial, ordering intuition."[22] "What we have come to regard" was, of course, an irretrievably social and historical question just as consciousness itself was socially and historically mediated. From this perspective, "the justification of our most authoritative claims to knowledge" was social and historical rather than individual, logical, or formal. As Rorty captured this pivotal move in the history of modern philosophy, we have to "stop thinking of Hegel as a metaphysician who believed in spooky immaterial causes, and to start thinking of him as the first thinker fully to appreciate the *social* character of knowledge—the first to have realized that Descartes' individualism steered philosophy onto the wrong track."[23]

This underlying position on the basic social nature of reason, thought, knowledge, and psychology suffused the entire pragmatic and progressive program. Despite divergent approaches, both Mead and Dewey paid tribute to James's *Principles of Psychology* for its breakthrough notions of "habit," "stream of consciousness," and the "social self."[24] As Dewey argued in "From Absolutism to Experimentalism," the more abstract sciences (e.g., mathematics and physics) divorced traditional philosophic thinking from existence and experience. In welcome contrast, in thinking about thinking, "Jamesian psychology led straight to the perception of the importance of distinctive social categories, especially communication and participation," recognizing what is distinctively human and social in thought as well as action.[25] In "The Need for Social Psychology," Dewey reached the seemingly inevitable conclusion that "mind" represented "something acquired"—"a reorganization of original activities through their operation in a given environment," in short, "a formation, not a datum; a product, and a cause only after it has been produced." Mind was social, "an offspring of the life of association, intercourse, transmission, and accumulation" and the product of the "objects of attention and affection which the specific social conditions supply." This basic sociality of mind was the cornerstone for Dewey's more extensive reflections on social intelligence, intelligence firmly bound up within community: "Intelligence is a social asset and is clothed with a function as public as its origin, in the concrete, in social cooperation."[26] And it also had direct implications for democracy, wherein "the socialization of intelligence" was *the* modern democratic social method: "Every autocratic and authoritarian scheme of social action rests on a belief that the needed intelligence is confined to a superior few, who because of inherent gifts are endowed with the ability and the right to control the conduct of others. . . . It is the Democratic Faith that [intelligence] is sufficiently general so that each individual has something to contribute."[27] Central to the entire pragmatic project was the basic recognition that truth was a social, relational, and associational product—something that "happens to an idea" in William James's famous rendering—and not some kind of inherent "stagnant property" or final, formal metaphysical essence.[28]

It was a short step from this conception of social psychology and social intelligence to a pragmatic understanding of the essentially social nature of the self and personality and ethics. In place of what they called the Kantian "theory of moral individualism," Dewey and Tufts's *Ethics* insisted on a thorough modernization of the ancient Aristotelian ideal of the social nature of man.[29] Here, T. H. Green (whom Edward Caird described as "democrat of the democrats" and Dewey dubbed "the prophet of our times") and British idealism were again important harbingers of this reorientation of modern social thought. As early as 1889, Dewey distilled from "the philosophy of Thomas Hill Green" his basic conclusion that "without society, and the conditions afforded by it, there can be no individual, no person."[30] By 1908, when Dewey and Tufts published their pathbreaking *Ethics*, their conception of a thoroughly social individual was the linchpin of their moral and political philosophy: "Apart from the social medium, the individual would never 'know himself'; he would never become acquainted with his own needs and capacities. He would live the life of a brute animal."[31] These were the lineaments of "the social self" more fully developed by Dewey's Michigan colleagues Charles Horton Cooley and George Herbert Mead. Following James's and Cooley's notions of consciousness as "necessarily social," Mead suggested, "The self is no longer a Cartesian presupposition. . . . Its development is wholly dependent upon another or others who are necessarily as immediate as the self."[32] In his book-length introduction to social psychology *Human Nature and Conduct,* Dewey concluded, "Connections with our fellows furnish both the opportunities for action and the instrumentalities by which we take advantage of opportunity. All of the actions of an individual bear the stamp of his community as assuredly as does the language he speaks."[33] In contrast, the "non-social individual" was simply "an abstraction arrived at by imagining what man would be if all his human qualities were taken away."[34]

It is difficult to overstate the general influence of this modern idea of a fundamentally social individual in turn-of-the-century American thought and policy. It underwrote an intellectual revolution in American social science, as sociology moved from humble beginnings in Comte, Simmel, and Ward to the new emphases on social process, group life, and human association that challenged abstract reflections on a priori human nature or an imagined social contract. In contrast to "the individualistic view of history," Albion Small declared, "The subject matter of sociology is the process of human association. . . . To the sociologist, every type of individual, every combination of activities, every institution, whether economic, political, scientific, or religious, is of interest, not for its separate self, but so far as it can shed or reflect light about the articulations and the motivations of the process as a whole."[35] The social self was also a rallying cry for a broad spectrum of reform as Jane Addams announced "a new social consciousness"; Scott Nearing, a new "social sanity"; and Walter Weyl, "a new social spirit." Central to Weyl's "new democracy" was a "new spirit" distinctly social: "Its base was broad. It involves common action and a common lot. It emphasizes social rather than private ethics, social rather than individual responsibility."[36] This sociality of reason and self soon made its effects felt in a contemporaneous socialization of law and policy. From the beginning, in fact, the American birth of the social was intimately bound up with social law and social legislation.

From Common Law to Social Legislation

The birth of the modern social in the United States was no mere paper revolution. To the contrary, the major changes in intellectual perspective wrought by the sociality of reason, the socialization of consciousness, and the social self were ultimately geared toward action—public action and legal action. In addition to T. H. Green and British idealism, the other early progenitor of this transformation in social thought was the philosophic radicalism of utilitarianism. From his earliest work on ethics to his later clarion calls for a "new" and "renascent" liberalism, John Dewey consistently acknowledged his debt to the precocious antiformalism, consequentialism, and active social reformism of Jeremy Bentham—"the first great muck-raker in the field of law" and "an inventor in law and administration."[37] Bentham's concern with social ends, social consequences, social purpose, and social good, Dewey noted, brought an important new emphasis on "legislation," on "social economic arrangements," and, ultimately, on social reform: "The existing legal system was intimately bound up with a political system based upon the predominance of the great landed proprietors through the rotten borough system. The operation of the new industrial forces in both production and exchange was checked and deflected at almost every point by a mass of customs that formed the core of the common law. Bentham approached this situation not from the standpoint of individual liberty, but from the standpoint of the effect of these restrictions upon the happiness enjoyed by individuals."[38]

In the end, Dewey took exception to a certain irreducible individualism in the utilitarian calculus, incorporating the social into his own vision of new democracy: "We cannot think of ourselves save to some extent *social* beings. Hence we cannot separate the idea of ourselves and of our own good from our idea of others and of their good." The active and free cooperation of all alike in the common pursuit of genuinely "common" ends, Dewey contended, was "the root principle of the morals of democracy."[39] This more social conception of common ends and public happiness could bring "radical social changes," provided "it combined capacity for bold and comprehensive social intervention with detailed study of particulars and with courage in action."[40]

Bold and comprehensive social intervention was exactly the end result of this social shift in American thought. Much as utilitarianism underwrote the famous "nineteenth-century revolution in government" in Britain, the American birth of the social ultimately manifested itself in another great wave of legal, legislative, and governmental change.[41] This change in ideas wrought a change in instrumentalities of public law. Once society itself was established as the seemingly boundless object of efficacious lawmaking, it vastly expanded the social imaginary in terms of the kinds of legislation, regulation, and administration that could be envisioned and undertaken. Indeed, the birth of the social launched one of the most important developments in the history of American social policy making—the rise of a modern concept (and practice) of *social legislation*. This revolution in social governance was prefigured by two important developments—the rise of a new conception of a distinctly social law and a complementary new vision of social rights.

The socialization of law took many forms in this period. As noted earlier, a rich tradition of American antiformalism ultimately yielded more modern forms of legal positivism, legal pragmatism, and legal realism that fueled the great expansion of state police power at the turn of the twentieth century. Integrating the concept of the social into this more positive, popular, and instrumental conception of law was central to finally breaking down some of the formalist encumbrances within both natural law and common law traditions, propelling an important shift to social legislation and democratic administration as crucial sites for modern problem-solving and policy making. In England, A. V. Dicey himself acknowledged this important shift in law's basic orientation from "the natural individualism of the common law" to the "trend of collectivist legislation."[42] In Germany, the so-called social utilitarianism of Rudolf von Jhering "placed jurisprudence upon the basis of a sound realism" through its "fundamental proposition that legal conceptions exist for men . . . whose weal and woe is so largely conditioned by administration of law."[43] Paul Vinogradoff similarly discerned "a new *constructive* point of view" emerging out of "the great social crisis" that provoked both Eugen Ehrlich's sociology of law as well as the French tradition of Durkheim and Duguit: "The individualistic order of society is giving way before the impact of an inexorable process of socialization." A new "social solidarity" was quickly replacing older individual and juridical concepts of law and state with new "public services and the duties corresponding to it."[44]

In the United States, Roscoe Pound's "sociological jurisprudence" most fully explicated the significance of this social turn for American law. Pound too began by noting the vast socioeconomic transformations that created a new "relationally organized society" in a "new social age."[45] In meticulously surveying the consequent advances in modern legal thought from analytical jurisprudence to historical jurisprudence to social science, Pound highlighted the tragic anachronism of "American jurists working out the applications of common law individualism after the individualist philosophy and economics have lost their momentum, . . . insisting upon views of liberty of contract . . . and of the fellow-servant rule which are out of all relation to actual life."[46] Following Dewey, Mead, and Weyl, Pound recognized the basic social nature of and social interests in the modern self as well as the new public interests and social needs that were the appropriate objects of modern law and governance:

> A whole lecture might be given up to a catalogue of social interests. . . .
> This includes claims to peace and order, the first social interest to get legal recognition, the general safety long recognized in the maxim that the public safety is the highest law, the general health, the security of acquisitions, and the security of transactions. . . . Closely related and hardly less important is the social interest in the security of social institutions, domestic, religious, political, and economic. . . . Recent legislation is full of examples of the necessity of reconciling the security of economic institutions with the individual life. Some other social interests, namely, in the general morals, in the use and conservation of social resources, and in general progress, social, political, economic, and cultural, can only be mentioned in passing. But finally, and by no means least, there is the social interest in the individual life—the claim or demand asserted in title of social life in civilized society that each individual be secure in his freedom, have

secured to him opportunities, political, social, and economic, and be able
to live at least a reasonably minimum human life in society.[47]

Such a thoroughly social perspective required a more positive, "social
law," which, as Michael Willrich put it, "meant law that purposefully reshaped society by directly addressing concrete problems of social life, such
as legislation regulating the hours and wages of industrial workers, regulatory measures to inspect housing and police the milk supply, and social insurance systems." Sociological jurisprudence thus attempted to "force
judges to explicitly consider the 'social facts' and 'social interests'—the
actual contexts and consequences of their decisions."[48] Pound summed up
the key commitments of sociological jurists:

1. They look more to the *[social] working* of the law than to its
   abstract content.
2. They regard law as a *social institution* which may be improved by
   intelligent human effort, and hold it their duty to discover the best
   means of furthering and directing that effort.
3. They lay stress upon the *social purposes* which law subserves rather
   than upon sanction.
4. They urge that legal precepts are regarded more as guides to results
   which are *socially just*.
5. From the *sociological school*, they await "the development of the
   pragmatic movement for systematic and detailed applications of
   pragmatic conceptions and methods to specific problems."[49]

All these developments were evidence of a great modern shift away from
an individualist common law and toward social legislation and social administration, or, as Pound put it, "from the standard of so-called legal justice to that of social justice." And "in all cases of divergence between the
standard of the common law" and this new standard of public opinion and
social law, Pound was confident that "the latter will prevail in the end."
"A Bench and Bar trained in individualist theories," he concluded, "cannot
prevent progress to the newer standard recognized by the sociologist."[50]

An important accompaniment of this socialization of law was a more
modern understanding of the social nature of rights. Now, of course, the
general idea that freedom and rights had some irreducibly social dimensions had an ancient pedigree.[51] But modern social transformation brought
a fundamental advance in perspective. As Robert Pippin translated the key
move, freedom became "not just a question of free will but the freedom of

*I nocphAse
FReelun
yes*

persons in relation to other persons—freedom as a form of social life." Axel
Honneth elaborated: "What this means is that public life would have to be
regarded not as the result of the mutual restriction of private spheres of
liberty, but rather the other way around, namely, as the opportunity for
the fulfilment of every single individual's freedom."[52] What T. H. Marshall
famously dubbed modern "social rights" were a direct consequence: "By the
social element I mean the whole range from the right to a modicum of economic welfare and security to the right to share to the full in the social
heritage and to live the life of a civilized being according to the standards
prevailing in the society. The institutions most closely connected with it are
the educational system and the social services."[53]

In the United States at the turn of the twentieth century, this new orientation toward distinctly social rights consumed American legal-political
thought and action. For Walter Weyl, a social conception of rights was a
foundation for the vast practical reform project of *The New Democracy*:
"It is this social interpretation of rights which characterizes the democracy
coming into being, and makes it different in kind from the so-called individualistic democracy." "The inner soul of our new democracy is not the
unalienable rights, negatively and individualistically interpreted," Weyl contended, "but those same rights, 'life, liberty, and the pursuit of happiness,'
extended and given a social interpretation."[54] John Dewey similarly held
that a new social and "effective freedom" needed to replace "formal"
and "empty" conceptions of negative rights as the raison d'être of a truly
socialized and activist ethics. Rights and obligations were "strictly cor-
relative" in an irreducibly social individuality. Dewey argued, "Absolute
rights, if we mean by absolute those not relative to any social order and
hence exempt from any social restriction, there are none." To regard rights
as "private monopolies" was to ignore their fundamental "social origin
and intent."[55]

This increased recognition of the social nature of rights in modern societies implicated social action as well as social thought. Traditional conceptions of rights were simply not up to the task of meeting the increased social demands of modern societies and economies. Rights of habeas corpus,
free speech, and free press, Walter Weyl pointed out, could not "secure a
job" for the elderly or protect against "low wages or high prices" or save
someone from jail for "having no visible means of support." Social rights
and social democracy involved a program of action to be tested in action.
Weyl's vision of an explicitly "socialized democracy" culminated in a new
"industrial program," "political program," and "social program."[56] Dewey
and Tufts's new social ethics similarly concluded with Henry Seager's

detailed program of action outlined for the American Association for Labor Legislation:

I. Measures to protect prevailing standards of living.
- i)   worker's compensation laws
- ii) compulsory illness insurance
- iii) invalidity and old age insurance
- iv) insurance against premature death
- v)   provision against losses due to unemployment, including public employment bureaus

II. Measures to elevate standards of living.
- i)   postal savings bank
- ii) child labor laws
- iii) maximum hour laws
- iv) sanitation and safety legislation and the special regulation of dangerous trades
- v)   free public education and special industrial training.[57]

These were but samples of the revolution in American social policy launched by the new social legislation.

Modern social legislation was indeed the culmination of the transformation in conceptions of social thought, social self, social law, and social rights documented thus far. Legislation and regulation were the ineluctable result of these basic changes in ideas of law and rights. As Emile Durkheim noted, "Genuine liberty . . . is itself the product of regulation. . . . Only social rules can prevent abuses of power."[58] Scott Nearing's "Philosophy of Social Legislation" deemed it a "social necessity" that in a modern heterogeneous community such social regulations and social rules increasingly take the form of legislation—social legislation.[59] Roscoe Pound followed up his important interventions on sociological jurisprudence by advocating a more modern approach to legislation "as a social function"—"to compel law-making to take more account and more intelligent account of the social facts upon which law must proceed." Pushing beyond the limits of earlier utilitarian conceptions of social utility, Pound argued that the "socialization of law" involved a new "stage of legislation" positively attuned to the satisfaction of "human wants," "human demands," and the securing of vital "social interests."[60]

But while the new social legislation was the product of literally thousands of important citizens, activists, reformers, and legislators, it was Ernst Freund who most carefully illuminated the exact nature of this important social transformation in "standards of American legislation."[61] Just as the

general public utility concept developed out of a set of sophisticated extensions of and departures from earlier common-law and charter precedents,
Freund charted the path from common-law and police-power regulation
to the arrival of a new kind of distinctly modern social legislation. Freund's
interpretive work essentially freed the police power from its common-law
roots so as to establish it as an independent basis for social legislation in
the general interest. "The care of the public welfare, or internal public
policy, has for its object the improvement of social and economic conditions affecting the community at large and collectively," Freund contended,
and social legislation shifted the "idea of public good from security of the
state . . . to the welfare of the mass of people."[62]

In her extraordinary treatise *Principles of Social Legislation*, Mary Callcott highlighted the importance of Freund's critique of the common law in
making room for new kinds of statutes: "The labor problem, the housing
situation, sanitary regulations, these were some of the things that the
Common Law could not reach." Callcott reprised Freund's indictment of
the major shortcomings of the common law in a modern society: its failure
"to keep pace with advancing of changing ideals"; its "neglect of nonmaterial human rights"; its "abstract and undifferentiated" conception of
rights and obligations; its lack of recognition of "the fundamental social
and economic changes brought about by the industrial revolution"; its
limited vision of "social security"; its vague "concept of public injury"; and
its general ineffectiveness in guarding "against practices injurious to the
weaker elements of society."[63] The degree to which such common-law limitations continued to control police legislation into the late nineteenth
century highlighted the seismic shift entailed by the rise of the social. Once
the concept of the social was allowed to permeate the safety, health, and
morals parameters of nineteenth-century legislative police power, a new
modern state power was born. Freund introduced the modern "growth of
social legislation" thus: "The possibility of embarking upon new policies
seems to be foreshadowed by the growing insistence of what is called the
new social conscience."[64] Helen Clarke's treatise *Social Legislation* captured
this general extension of legislative power under the heading "The Police
Power and the Social Service State." Here, the pivotal move was again the
expansion of police power beyond the strictures of common-law harm and
traditional measures of safety, health, and morals so as to generate a more
robust and comprehensive legislative power to regulate in the public interest
and on behalf of the general welfare. "Although there were benevolent and
humanitarian persons in all western countries who sought during the nineteenth century to remedy many of the ills which were inevitable in a new
economic society," Clarke contended, their efforts were largely delayed and

forestalled by reigning common-law limitations. With the birth of the so-cial, "American philosophy" was infused with a new belief in the social value "of every personality, by a concern for the welfare of the people generally, and by governmental participation in the achievement of rea-sonable happiness here and now for all." In public law, the new social philosophy received expression in the vast expansion of police power legis-lation, requiring "the state not only to prevent unfortunate occurrences but to compel positive action for the general welfare."[65]

These were the roots of a modern conception of social legislation. In their epic treatise *Principles of Labor Legislation,* John Commons and John An-drews embraced just such a capacious vision of social police power: "Hereafter, for our purposes, in speaking of the police power, we shall use the term in this broad sense, to imply all the powers of government, whether state or federal, whether of police, taxation, or interstate commerce, in so far as they are used to justify that indefinite extension of power to abridge liberty or property without compensation for some newly recognized public purpose."[66] Clarke agreed, "The police power in reality includes all those powers, not otherwise defined, which have for their purpose the protec-tion of the public rather than private interests." She viewed this enlarge-ment of general legislative power "to act for the protection of the public welfare" as nothing short of the foundation of a new "Social Service State." "The twentieth century has seen such a great expansion in the exercise of the police power," she noted, "that we can safely say that we now have a state one of the primary purposes of which is to render social service." "Jus-tified on the theory that the welfare of the people is the supreme law of the land," Clarke concluded that "the Social Service State" was now "partially realized."[67]

A new social service state wielding a new social legislation was more than an intellectual accomplishment. The social legislation treatises of Callcott and Clarke (like the compendiums of Freund and Commons) brimmed with explicit examples of new social policy legislation: poor law revision, child welfare legislation, mothers' pension laws, housing and city planning leg-islation, public health laws, public education reform, public recreation laws, liquor legislation, vice laws, labor legislation, maximum hours and min-imum wages, laws for the regulation of worker health and safety, social insurance, health insurance, old age and invalidity insurance, widows' and orphans' benefits, child protection legislation, unemployment relief, and so-cial security.[68] These were the beginnings of a new state focused more intently on issues of social welfare as well as social police with massive implications for the future of American social policy making.

The Roots of Modern American Social Police

But social provision and social welfare were only half of the story of turn-of-the-century American social policy making. For just as poverty and labor came into view as pressing social questions demanding radically new social legislation and administration, another range of issues—discussed under the category of social problems—came to be similarly understood and acted on. Here, the policy consequences were just as momentous, but they cut in a more troubling direction. While new techniques of social provision created the foundation for an expansive modern social-welfare state, this other side of the force launched an equally expansive agenda of social policing, crime control, and penality—the beginnings of a new American police state.

While poverty, inequality, and economic domination were indeed chief social concerns of this era, reformers and policy makers turned equal attention and energy to social questions of a different sort—questions of morality, sexuality, and criminality. Indeed, the general concern with the social question that accompanied the rise of the social in modern America soon spawned a host of alternative social tracts and treatises devoted to a litany of so-called social problems, social disorders, and even social pathologies: John Henry Crooker, *Problems in American Society: Some Social Studies* (1889); Samuel George Smith, *Social Pathology* (1911); Charles A. Ellwood, *The Social Problem: A Reconstructive Analysis* (1919); Lyman P. Powell, *The Social Unrest* (1919); Grove Samuel Dow and Edgar B. Wesley, *Social Problems of Today* (1920); James Ford, *Social Problems and Social Policy* (1923); Ezra Thayer Towne, *Social Problems: A Study of Present-Day Social Conditions* (1924); Stuart Alfred Queen and Delbert Martin Mann, *Social Pathology* (1925); Henry S. Spalding, *Social Problems and Agencies* (1925); and Mabel A. Elliott and Francis E. Merrill, *Social Disorganization* (1934).[69]

The general trend in thinking about the social question was clear as author after author pivoted directly from discussions of poverty, economic inequality, and social provision to a different set of social concerns and social issues like immorality, defectiveness, and criminality. Ezra Thayer Towne's *Social Problems* (1916) was typical, beginning with social welfare chapters on immigration, child labor, women in industry, the sweating system, and labor and unemployment but then shifting seamlessly to new social priorities like the blind and the deaf, the feebleminded and the insane, crime and punishment, marriage and divorce, the liquor problem, prostitution, and venereal disease.[70] James Ford's *Social Problems and*

Social Policy (1923) began with classic general excerpts on social purpose, social ethics, and social legislation by the likes of Dewey, Pound, and Freund but then quickly turned to the social problems of "defectiveness" (feeble-mindedness, insanity, epilepsy, blindness, deaf-mutism, deformity, disability) and "criminality" (eugenics, immigration and crime, the city and crime, the modern prison, and juvenile delinquency).[71] Queen and Mann's *Social Pathology* (1925) was more specific, transitioning from typical social reform concerns like child saving, child labor, and child support to the further underlying problems of the "unmarried mother," the "illegitimate child," "sex irregularity," "prostitution," and "syphilis and gonorrhea." The latter concerns mirrored Samuel Smith's idea of a turn from "pathologies of condition" like poverty to "pathologies of conduct," triggering not so much techniques of social welfare as a new criminology and social "therapeutics," implicating such things as social "sanitation," social statistics, inspection, public health, and eugenics.[72]

Now, of course, many of these supposedly "new" social problems and pathologies had long been objects of American law and policy making. Indeed, soon after independence, early American courts and legislators resuscitated age-old common-law and statutory traditions of policing and punishing ill-defined groups of supposed social outcasts, dependents, and vagrants variously defined as "rogues, vagabonds, common beggars, and other idle, disorderly and lewd persons."[73] As the earlier discussion of citizenship made clear, a long list of deficiencies and disabilities based on status, class, race, ethnicity, nationality, gender, religion, morality, sexuality, ability, and paternity (as well as a wide array of other specific habits, conduct, and characteristics) rendered various groups and individuals continually subject to ostracism, exclusion, and sanction. By the end of the nineteenth century, a law of dependency, delinquency, and disability had become increasingly codified and systematized in official treatises and digests.[74]

But while the unequal and punitive treatment of the poor, the different, and the allegedly criminal had a progeny and legal history older than scripture, something unique and significant was implicated in the modern reorganization of such ancient categories into the new socio-politico-scientific matrix of social problems and social pathologies. The modern socialization of dependency, disability, and delinquency transformed concerns that had once been thought of as occasional, exceptional, and anomalous into more of an ongoing, normalized, and everyday feature of modern social, legal, and political life. Here, the formal policing of the exception steadily gave way to a more generalized policing of the social norm, rendering the police power ever more continuous, efficacious, and expansive—capable of traversing the entire extent of the social body. As Michel Foucault once

observed, here the power of social police no longer depended "on the innumerable, discontinuous, sometimes contradictory privileges of sovereignty, but on the continuously distributed effects of public power."[75]

This functional generalizability of modern social police had important
intellectual as well as organizational dimensions. The final edition of Stuart
Queen's *Social Pathology* acknowledged the direct influence of some twenty-
five or so professional periodicals and an additional fifty or so social
organizations, as social police became scientized and medicalized via publications like the *American Journal of Hygiene, Psychiatric Quarterly,* and
Public Health Reports, while being simultaneously institutionalized and op-
erationalized through associations like the American Association of Social
Workers, the National Conference for Mental Hygiene, and the YWCA.[76]
Texts and associations like these trumpeted the broad social ambition of a
new "scientific" and "organizational" approach to social problems that jet-
tisoned preoccupation with individual "character defects" and charitable
fascination with "down-and-outs" and "slum-dwellers." A solution to the
problems of social pathology, Stuart contended, required a "thorough reorganization of the social order through an economic program, a health program, a mental hygiene program, an educational program, and a program
for the making of public opinion."[77] Scott Nearing similarly endorsed solutions to what he called "social maladjustment" through "careful inquiry,
thorough publicity, and sane social action," culminating in broad social
programs aimed at "efficient education plus wise remedial legislation."[78]
And indeed, two of the major consequences of this intellectual and organizational revolution were, first, a vast expansion of the array of characteristics, conditions, and conduct deemed socially problematic or pathological; and second, an equally expansive transformation in the underlying
legal techniques of social regulation and police. In consequence, social
policing itself moved further away from early roots and rationales in social provision and social welfare and toward increasing emphasis on new
social strategies of penality and punishment.

There are many policy arenas in which to view this steady enlargement
of problems, pathologies, and offenses deemed subject to modern social policing. But one of the best places to witness the modern socialization and
generalization of police power is the regulation of morality and sexuality.
For though American morals regulation was as old as the republic, the long
Progressive Era obsession with immorality, vice, obscenity, sexuality, temperance, prohibition, and prostitution featured a double movement at the
heart of the modern socialization of police—a revolutionary broadening
of social offenses and an equally expansive invention of new techniques of
legal regulation and crime control.[79]

For a significant segment of the reform community, the more general problem of social crisis and the social question discussed above in terms of social welfare also involved fundamental questions of social morality. E. A. Ross, for example—one of the foremost innovators in the new sociology of social control, social psychology, and social evolution—moved consistently in this direction. He followed up his classic 1901 discussion in *Social Control* concerning modern industrial societies with his *Sin and Society* (1907), decrying a new iniquity in modern societies revolving around the "moral insensibility" of the new "criminaloid." By 1922, Ross had moved on to full-scale moral jeremiad in *The Social Trend,* a book bemoaning the general decline of higher "religion, education, family morals, and community spirit," that resulted in such things as "The Menace of Migrating Peoples," "The Menace of Race Suicide," "Opium-Smoking as a Gangrene," and "Alcohol as the Vice of the Occident."[80] Ross was neither alone nor the most moralistic or polemical. Harold Begbie's *The Crisis of Morals* (1914) decried turn-of-the-century moral decline: "our pompous novels about adulterous wives, our comic plays about martyrdom and murder, our dirty minded advertisements, our prurient pictures and photographs, . . . our hideous architecture, our insanitary slums, our soul-killing and brutalizing competition."[81] Austin Phelps compiled a volume of late nineteenth-century pamphlets that explicitly linked such general themes of American moral failure and spiritual-religious crisis to specific policing prescriptions with respect to immigration, alcohol, and tobacco, from Josiah Strong's racialist "Our Country" to Rev. Wilbur Fisk Crafts's "In Regard to Intemperance and Other Social Problems of the Anglo-Saxon Nations" to Simpson Ely's "Ten Chapters Against Tobacco."[82]

But beyond such ubiquitous calls for moral regeneration (whether of Anglo-Saxon, social gospel, or Christian socialist varieties), the new social police drew stronger inspiration from a series of more explicitly sociolegal reflections. When timeless concerns about public morality merged with the rise of the modern American social, a new template for social thought and social control was born. James Hayden Tufts's *America's Social Morality* (1933) traveled a well-worn path from social ethics and social science to a more dogmatic focus on social morality. Writing for the American Social Science Series and relying on the Chicago-school sociology of Robert Park, Ernest Burgess, and Roderick McKenzie, Tufts argued that the great modern social transformation from rural to urban industrial life raised distinctly "moral problems": "The massing of population, combined with the great mobility of modern city dwellers, destroys the neighborhood group that was so effective in both social control and mutual helpfulness." Consequently, "home life" became "a more difficult proposition": "Boys' gangs flourish, supervision of the recreation of young people disappears, entertainments from movies to night clubs and dance halls are commercialized, temptations to gambling, intemperance, and illicit sex relations are frequent." Increasingly confident in the use of "moral statistics" on recent social trends (abortions, suicide, marriage, divorce rates, criminal records), Tufts recommended an increased sociolegal interrogation under such headings as "The Mores of Sex, Marriage, and Family," the "Young Delinquent and Professional Criminal," "Temperance and the Vices," "Gambling," "Prostitution," and the "Unsolved Problem of Intoxicants."[83] In a brief essay titled "Public Recreation and Social Morality," Jane Addams also made the case for investments "in the advance of a higher social morality" so as to combat the modern lures of "unnatural vice," "petty crime," saloons, and even the playing of "craps in a foul and stuffy alley."[84]

But it was in the area of sex and sexuality, of course, that the new social sciences surrounding social control, social pathology, and social morality came together with spectacular force, insistently broadening the horizon of social police and expanding extant conceptions of "offense" and even "criminality." Charles Margold's *Sex Freedom and Social Control* (1926) was dedicated to the proposition of viewing sex as a distinctly "social problem." Edward Devine introduced this pioneering text: "The sex relation is of social concern. . . . Rational social co-operation in promoting a sounder and more adequate sex morality is essential." Margold began this sociological work on sex and sexuality under the direction of Charles Horton Cooley; thus, it was a small leap for Margold to integrate sex, society, and social control: "Matters of sex conduct, marriage, procreation, love, are of course, necessarily included in the social nature of man's life. . . . No man lives his human life, sexual or other, altogether for himself, without giving and receiving suggestions, corrections, encouragements, and controls. All men and women are socii, living an inescapable social life, knowingly and unknowingly communicating, stimulating, determining, conditioning each other. This fact gives social control an inherent and invariable place in every individual's living." Margold concluded that this invariably social and public nature of sex legitimated, indeed necessitated, greater social, legal, and public controls: "It will be maintained in this study that conduct of this sort, as of all sorts, must become subject to social control of some kind in so far as society achieves any moral organization at all."[85] Margold was hardly alone in this preoccupation with sex, society, and social control.[86]

This steady socialization of sex and sexuality expanded opportunities for social policing across an ever-increasing set of moral concerns: illegitimacy, the unmarried mother, the unadjusted girl, the individual delinquent, and, ultimately, "sex irregularity." Stuart Queen relied on William Healy's *Individual Delinquent* and W. I. Thomas's *Unadjusted Girl* to enlarge jurisdiction for the policing of sexual morality, noting that delinquency in girls was also bound up in "amusement, adventure, pretty clothes, favorable notice, distinction, freedom in the larger world."[87] Such texts routinely moved on as well to the policing of mental and physical disabilities, feeblemindedness, "nervous and mental diseases," and "alcoholism and drug addiction," as well as syphilis, gonorrhea, and prostitution. In turn, each of those newly socialized categories of problem, pathology, offense, crime, disease, or disability only created further opportunities for expansion. Elliott and Merrill's *Social Disorganization,* for example, bore down on an age-old "sex offense" rendered anew under the socialized heading "Social Control of Prostitution." In the process, the social construction of the "crime" of prostitution underwent a not-so-subtle revision. What was before a matter of relatively discrete individual acts or concrete offenses, now morphed into eleven ambiguous categories of various kinds of "loose women":

> (1) "juvenile" prostitutes, girls from ten to fifteen who often appear in Juvenile Court on sex charges; (2) "potential" prostitutes, who are willing to accept money for sex relations which, however, may also be on a voluntarily free basis; (3) "amateur" prostitutes, who sell themselves occasionally but who continue to live at home; (4) "young professional" prostitutes, who have recently entered the regular life of a wanton; (5) "old professional" prostitutes, established residents of houses of prostitution; (6) "field workers," streetwalkers, who take men to their cheap rooms or to hotels; (7) "bats," superannuated prostitutes, rendered unattractive by drink and drugs to all but the least particular among the bums and homeless men; (8) "gold-diggers," called "boulevard" women, who may supplement their income from their regular patron by mercenary relations with other men; (10) "loose" married women, who deceive their husbands and receive pay; (11) "call girls," who receive remuneration from relations with men arranged by telephone calls from disorderly hotel keepers and the like.

Elliott and Merrill also took notice of the roles of "ignorance," "feeblemindedness," "venereal disease," "organized vice," and "lonely and unattached young men living apart from their homes and families." And they simultaneously expanded the sites for social surveillance from parlor houses, brothels, flats, disorderly hotels, and tenements to "soft-drink parlors, poolrooms, lady-barber shops, manicure parlors catering to men, cabarets, night clubs, speakeasies, and the ubiquitous roadhouse."[88] Stuart Queen similarly joined increasing behaviors to more public spaces as fitting objects of an expanding social and morals police, noting "for many young people sex irregularities may be traced pretty directly to unsupervised dance halls, amusement parks, low grade theaters, cabarets and excursion steamers."[89] This expansive and expanding discourse of morals, social, and sexual policing was greatly amplified by an even broader and concurrent transformation in the nature of modern American criminal justice.

Criminal Justice, Social Hygiene, and the Injunction and Abatement Acts

Central to the new forms of American social police that emerged in the early twentieth century was the way in which changing conceptions of gender and sexuality closely intersected with changing technologies of law, governance, and statecraft. New sociocultural relations and new forms of state power were both transformed at the busy intersection of law and society. The collision of new legal practices and changing sociocultural exigencies yielded a powerful new template for social policing and launched a long American war on crime. Important changes in the nature, definition, and locus of morals and sex transgression were joined to a dramatic expansion of basic American standards of criminal liability and public offense.

Francis Allen dubbed this legal transformation "nothing less than a revolution in public conceptions of the nature of crime and the criminal, and in public attitudes toward the proper treatment of the . . . offender."[90] For Bill Stuntz, this revolution was the pivot point for what he talked about as "the collapse of American criminal justice"—the decline of an earlier local and comparatively "lenient" regime featuring "low crime rates, frequent acquittals, and a small prison population" and the rise of a "more centralized, more legalized, more bureaucratized" American police and carceral state.[91] At the core of this criminal justice revolution was a tremendous explosion of new penal regulations that vastly expanded the range of behaviors, identities, and activities subject to criminal or penal sanction. Roscoe Pound captured the impact of this extraordinary development on the ground: "Of the one hundred thousand persons arrested in Chicago in 1912, more than one half were held for violation of legal precepts which did not exist twenty-five years before."[92] Notably, the key growth sector for this accelerated accumulation of new burdens placed on criminal justice and police involved morality and sexuality. As Stuntz put it, "Between the late 1870s and 1933, America's criminal justice system fought a series of cultural battles in which criminal law . . . was a key weapon: against polygamy, state lotteries, prostitution, various forms of opium, and, last but definitely not least, alcoholic drink. Taken together, these legal battles constituted a two-generation culture war [that] transformed both the law and politics of crime."[93]

At the center of this revolution in conceptions of criminality and offense was the intersection of the social and heightened concerns about immorality and crime. Again, Roscoe Pound—the American progenitor of sociological jurisprudence—most clearly articulated the basic move and its implications for modern criminal liability. From his very first commentaries on criminal jurisprudence, Pound attacked the overweening individualism of nineteenth-century categories, which he viewed as out of place in an increasingly complex, interdependent, urban, and industrial society: "Our criminal law is a growing cause of popular discontent with the legal system, [and] the difficulty here again is exaggerated respect for the individual." Pound maintained that individual interests should only partly concern modern law, increasingly counterbalanced by the competing "public interests" and "social interests" profitably advanced by emerging social-welfare states.[94] Pound's social interests—collective claims, "which are involved in the maintenance, the activity, and the functioning of society"—hewed closely to the contours of modern state police power: security, safety, conservation, health, peace, public order, and general welfare. For Pound, modern criminal law had "for its province the securing of social interests." In place of the traditional view of criminal law as retributive ex post punishment for past individual misdeeds and "vicious will," Pound endorsed a mobilization of legal institutions and police agencies protecting modern social interests via the establishment of a more preventative criminal administration: "what goes on before the commission of an offense, with the conditions that generate offenders and insure a steady grist to the mill of criminal justice." "What goes on before and leads up to the crime," Pound contended, "often much more surely and inevitably than the committed crime leads to conviction and the appointed penal treatment."[95] For Markus Dubber, Pound's new social approach basically removed "the person" from criminal law, replacing it "with a new, amorphous victim, 'society,' whose 'social interests' are protected against 'anti-social conduct.'"[96]

Pound's excavation of the implications of the social—social self, social interests, social legislation—for modern criminal administration mirrored the way his contemporary Ernst Freund saw modern law moving from an essentially common-law basis of "civil and criminal justice" concerned with the "maintenance of right and the redress of wrong" to a modern police power concerned with "public welfare or internal public policy" and "the primary social interests of safety, order, and morals." In modern states, police power and social welfare were not confined to the prohibition of individual harms; rather, the state "exercises its compulsory powers for the prevention and anticipation of wrong by narrowing common law rights through conventional restraints and positive regulations which are not confined to the prohibition of wrongful acts."[97] Francis Sayre's "Public Welfare Offenses" more fully elaborated this momentous shift in criminal law and morals policing away from traditional preoccupation with individual responsibility, free will, concrete harm, mens rea, and retribution. Sayre documented the overarching shift in legal administration and criminology from a nineteenth-century orientation concerned with the protection of "individual interest" to a twentieth-century focus on "collective" and "social and public interests," wherein "correctional treatment should change from the barren aim of punishing human beings to the fruitful one of protecting social interests."[98] Sayre's appendix detailed a case-annotated list of the ever-expanding genre of such public-welfare offenses no longer requiring mens rea:

1. Illegal Sales of Intoxicating Liquor
    a. Sales of prohibited beverage
    b. Sales to minors
    c. Sales to habitual drunkards
    d. Sales to Indians
    e. Sales by methods prohibited by law
2. Sales of Impure or Adulterated Food
    a. Sales of adulterated or impure milk
    b. Sales of adulterated butter or oleomargarine
3. Sales of Misbranded Articles
4. Violations of Anti-Narcotic Acts
5. Criminal Nuisances
    a. Annoyances or injuries to the public health, repose, or comfort
    b. Obstructions to highways
6. Violation of Traffic Regulations
7. Violations of Motor-Vehicle Laws
8. Violations of General Police Regulations, Passed for the Safety, Health, or Well-Being of the Community.[99]

According to Markus Dubber, Sayre provided a "blueprint for the twentieth century depersonalization of American criminal law and its transformation into a state regulatory scheme." This was nothing short of the beginnings of modern criminal administration and the twentieth-century American war on crime.[100]

Some of the controversial import of this dramatic social transformation of modern American criminal, police, and regulatory law was suggested by legal realist Karl Llewellyn's quip that "when you take 'the legal' out, you also take out the 'crime.'" Llewellyn's point was that the shift away from traditional concepts of legal criminality to modern social and administrative policing involved an attenuation of the centrality of criminal acts per se and an increased focus on the policing of a broader array of social transgressions. Modern criminal law became increasingly "strategic," ceasing "to define the conduct and intent that prosecutors actually sought to punish, and instead treated crime definition as a means of facilitating arrests, prosecutions, and convictions."[101]

This strategic expansion of criminality, penality, and offense was particularly acute in the early twentieth-century policing of morality and sex. Indeed, something of the culmination of the push for the enhanced social policing of morality and sexuality in this period was the American social hygiene movement. Though a great number of other individual reforms and causes embraced this new criminal justice orientation toward social prophylaxis, prevention, deterrence, treatment, and psychology, the American Social Hygiene Association (ASHA) epitomized three especially important developments: (1) the steady broadening of the definition of crime or offense toward social infractions, (2) the development and transformation of specific legal and legislative techniques and practices, and (3) the increased medicalization of offense and crime through the deployment of the apparatus of public health. In the merging of new conceptions of the social, criminal administration, and public health and hygiene, a thoroughly modern social police was born.

Officially established in 1913, the American Social Hygiene Association built upon a late nineteenth-century tradition that historians have traditionally discussed in terms of a "purity crusade."[102] But while moral reform had diverse roots in this period of American history from Comstockery and antipornography to ubiquitous temperance organizations and vice committees, what distinguished the social hygiene movement was its broad and bold program of direct legal action. As early as 1905, for example, Prince Morrow's American Society for Sanitary and Moral Prophylaxis, endorsed an extensive program of "sanitary, moral, and legislative" action against "the spread of diseases which ha[d] their origin in the Social Evil"—that is, prostitution.[103] Harvard president emeritus Charles W. Eliot opened the first meeting of the ASHA with an ambitious call to social action and legislation against "vice diseases" as grave dangers to family, society, and "civilization." Taking note of the "remarkable progress of medicine, and especially of preventative medicine," Eliot invoked the analog of war in outlining the "new duties and responsibilities" imposed on society: "In dealing with such portentous evils, society can no longer place first considerations concerning innocency, delicacy, and reticence, any more than in dealing with war. The attack on them must be public and frank."[104] Eliot's address—and indeed, the entire first volume of the association's journal, *Social Hygiene*—was nothing short of a detailed map for the kind of expansive war on vice, crime, and immorality that transformed American criminal justice:

1. *Social surveys:* "The first work of the Association is the work of ascertaining present conditions as regards sexual vice in American cities and towns. These inquiries should be thorough and universal; and the results should be published in the way most likely to inform the leaders of public thought and action."
2. *Legal studies:* "The Association should study the various sorts of police action against vice, and the various statutes intended to regulate vicious resorts." "To exhibit and to publish this record of the total failure of well-meant police measures must be one of the first labors of the new Association."
3. *Legislation and police:* "A third important object of the Association is to devise and advocate effective police procedure and effective legislation with regard to vice. In some American communities improved laws, courts, or police administration have already been secured."
4. *Organization:* "Part of the work of the Association should be contributory to other organizations that advocate suppression of disorderly houses and disreputable hotels, the gratuitous treatment of venereal diseases at public expense to prevent or diminish contagion, the promotion of total abstinence, and the provision of wholesome pleasures, both out-of-doors and in-doors."
5. *Prosecution:* "The Association should always be ready to take part in the prosecution of men or women who make a profit out of obscene publications, indecent shows, immoral plays, and prostitution."
6. *Sex regulation:* "The Association ought to advocate actively the common use of the recognized safeguards against sexual perversions—such as bodily exercises, moderation in eating, abstinence in youth from alcohol, tobacco, hot spices, and all other drugs which impair self-control, even momentarily."

7. *Temperance and tobacco:* "Social hygiene would be effectively promoted by reduction or rejection of the drinking and smoking habits in American communities."

8. *Medical ethics:* "One of the most difficult tasks of the Association . . . is to bring about a serious change in the ethics of the medical profession. . . . It should now be impossible for a conscientious physician to fail to protect from marriage with a man whom he knows to be diseased the woman whom the diseased man is proposing to marry. . . . Recent discoveries in regard to the contagion, duration, and far-transmission of venereal diseases have made it necessary to put limits on the physician's pledge of secrecy, lest he become a silent participant in one of the worst crimes."

9. *Sex education and "educational propaganda":* "The Association proposes to take active part in bringing about certain educational changes which will touch first parents, then teachers, then adolescents, and lastly children."[105]

What made the American social hygiene movement stand out in the crowded field of turn-of-the-century moral reform was the transformative nature of its approach to law reform. In a period already swelling state and federal criminal codes, social hygiene made additional inroads in the fields of morals policing, criminal administration, and sex regulation. Issues of *Social Hygiene* regularly concluded with a detailed "Resume of Legislation upon Matters Relating to Social Hygiene," which canvassed proposed and enacted legislation state by state. In 1914, Kentucky considered bills for a state vice commission; an injunction and abatement act against houses of prostitution; the prohibition of pandering; increasing marriage requirements with respect to "communicable or transmissable" disease; encouraging girls under sixteen to leave home for purpose of marriage; the licensing of employment agencies with respect to females and houses of "bad repute, ill fame, assignation, or amusement kept for immoral purpose"; increasing the age of consent; punishing property owners of places of public prostitution; increasing divorce requirements with respect to "loathsome" disease; use of houses abutting any school or college for females for "unlawful sexual intercourse"; and the censorship of motion picture films.[106] In 1915, the association reported the introduction of over eighty state bills (half of which became law) on sex and sexuality under the subject headings: (1) age of consent and fornication, (2) prostitution, (3) injunction and abatement laws, (4) state reformatories and industrial homes for girls, (5) perversion, (6) venereal diseases, (7) sterilization, (8) children, (9) amusements, and (10) miscellaneous (with further numbered references to adultery, birth control, dance halls, employment agencies, hotels, indecent exposure, marriage, morals court, motion pictures, obscene literature, rape, saloons, and women police).[107] By 1917, forty-four state jurisdictions had introduced some 300 social hygiene measures of which over 160 became law, including 38 measures for commercialized vice (pimping, pandering, white slavery, homes for girls and women); 31 bills regarding sex offenses (adultery, fornication, lasciviousness, age of consent, carnal knowledge, incest, rape, sodomy, and seduction); 36 bills on amusements, pictures, literature, and recreation; and 66 assorted medical measures (venereal diseases, fake-cure advertisements, venereal disease and marriage certificates, quarantine, midwives, unsanitary dwellings, and the sterilization of defectives).[108]

Of special concern to the ASHA legal reform agenda was the crusade against prostitution. Progressive Era antiprostitution campaigns involved an unusually large number of significant cultural and policy innovations, including invocations of "white slavery," public health hysteria over venereal disease, eugenical charges of "defectiveness" and feeblemindedness, and even the pioneering expansion of federal police power in the guise of the Mann Act.[109] The Committee of Social Hygiene conveyed something of the fierce and seemingly unlimited spirit of the crusade when they concluded (following the advice of fourteen vice commissions, seventy-two cities, and intellectuals like Abraham Flexner) that we "must throw down the gauntlet to the whole horrible thing."[110] Of particular concern to reformers was the imperviousness to existing regulation of the segregated "red-light" prostitution districts in most American cities, large and small, from New Orleans's notorious Storyville to the Avenue for Ladies Only in East Grand Forks, Minnesota, to Chicago's Levee district, composed of some two hundred brothels, bucket shops, and gambling houses.[111]

In response, moral and hygiene reformers introduced one legal reform that epitomized the more general trend toward modern social police and criminal administration in this period—what they called "the Fight for a Red Light Abatement Law."[112] The deployment of so-called injunction and abatement acts in the legal crusade against municipal red-light districts displayed the intricate mechanics of modern legal and policy innovation. Passing and enforcing injunction and abatement acts were top priorities (indeed, near obsessions) of the social hygiene movement as well as of municipal vice committees, and they nicely illuminated the legal underpinnings of the new American war on vice and crime.

The injunction and abatement acts were new state police power statutes passed in at least thirty-eight states by 1920.[113] Universally regarded as an effective new weapon in the war on vice, the injunction and abatement acts succeeded in wiping out most municipal red-light districts within the next decade.[114] The acts were part of a much commented on revival of "government by injunction" in this period of which the labor injunction is the best known example.[115] Like the labor injunction, the injunction and abatement acts introduced a new set of extraordinarily powerful law enforcement mechanisms and procedures. With roots in the late nineteenth-century fight against illegal saloons and liquor abatement, the injunction and abatement acts brought several efficacious innovations to the war on vice more generally. First, the acts authorized legal proceedings against property owners rather than those found guilty of certain "immoral" acts or crimes. Indeed, the acts defined certain kinds of uses of property (e.g., upon which lewdness, assignation, or prostitution was conducted) as public nuisances per se, dispensing with elaborate findings of facts establishing nuisance-like conditions. Second, the acts authorized more summary proceedings before a judge in equity, dispensing with a defendant's right to a traditional criminal trial by jury. Third, the legislature vastly expanded the range of public and private persons who could initiate actions against such establishments (ultimately including virtually every citizen in certain counties, cities, or states), breaking with long-held common-law rules regarding the existence of special injury. Fourth, temporary and permanent injunctive remedies made it possible to cease illicit activities at such properties immediately and perhaps permanently. Violations of such injunctions and restraining orders resulted in contempt of court. Finally, orders of abatement provided for buildings to be "closed" and for all property used in the conduct of the public nuisance to be sold. Additional taxes, fines, and jail time rounded out this vast list of new pains, penalties, and punishments.

But key to the success of the injunction and abatement laws was a more general legal transformation of note. For the injunction and abatement acts expanded the reach of state police power in the social and morals arenas, much like the idea of public utility pushed past traditional common-law and constitutional limitations concerning business and industry. The doctrinal story of the road to injunction and abatement is relatively complex. But it built upon several developments already alluded to: the expansion of police power toward the regulation of public morals, a new concern for the public welfare and society at large as objects of legal protection, and a shift from concern with remediation of crime after the fact to prevention of crime to assure future safety. Furthermore, the injunction incorporated techniques from equity law as prelude to more robust and effective criminal administration. This was a revolution in basic technologies of modern governmentality and police.

"The bawd we have always had with us and the bawdyhouse," mused a Kentucky judge in 1898, reflecting on the age-old nature of the problem of houses of prostitution as well as the equally age-old morals fight against them.[116] In the early nineteenth century, the legal weapon of choice against such "disorderly houses" involved the common law of nuisance. Importantly, nuisance law in this period drew a fairly harsh distinction between a private nuisance and a public nuisance. The term "private nuisance" denoted a tortious offense at common law that hurt or harmed another landowner in the enjoyment of private property. As such, it was remediable via an ordinary civil proceeding.[117] In contrast, a public or common nuisance, according to Blackstone, was an inconvenient or troublesome offense to the whole community and not merely to some particular person or property. It was criminally indictable only. Public nuisances were a group of minor crimes and misdemeanors. Disorderly inns, bawdy houses, bothersome hog pens, malarial ponds, and the like ranked among those public nuisances at common law that upon criminal indictment could be suppressed.[118] Public nuisances were not generally subject to a civil suit without proof of some kind of special, individualized injury or damage.

One important distinction between public and private nuisance concerned the availability of equitable remedies—including the injunction. Equity's summary, administrative way of doing justice without the aid of a jury and its arsenal of extraordinary remedies made it a formidable system of jurisprudence. But the crucial fact for the idea of an injunction and abatement act against prostitution is that equity supposedly relinquished its criminal jurisdiction with the abolition of the Court of Star Chamber. If equity had no criminal jurisdiction, how could the injunction be deployed against public nuisances like houses of prostitution?[119]

Two important and somewhat esoteric nineteenth-century exceptions had created an opportunity for legal and regulatory innovation. First, interference with public state property rights—so-called purpresture—affected the "whole community in general" and was criminally indictable as a public nuisance at common law, yet nineteenth-century judges carved out room for an injunction to protect public property.[120] So too in cases where a private individual experienced so-called special damage to private property from a public nuisance.[121] From 1850 to 1900, American jurists built out these exceptions, transforming equitable jurisdiction over nuisance from a remedy protecting individual private property rights into a powerful public policy-making instrument. What was originally a tool designed to mete out justice between particular private parties became a mechanism for regulating more general social and economic behavior viewed as opposed to the public welfare. And though this juridical instrument applied equally to economic, health, and safety nuisances, it experienced particularly robust growth in the area of public morals—radically extending the right to wield the injunction against disorderly houses, illegal saloons, gambling houses, and even prize and bull fights.[122]

Much as the public utility concept pushed beyond common-law categories of common calling and carrier regulation, these legal antecedents pushed morals and criminal policing beyond early common-law origins and limitations. The injunction was an important supplement to indictment, preventively deterring future conduct while also responding to past offense. Equity's summary procedures similarly allowed for the development of a more proactive, comprehensive, and administrative approach to crime and police as opposed to relying on ex post, case-by-case prosecution after the fact. Moreover, the injunction took aim at property as well as person and restricted the uses of property well into the future. By the late nineteenth century, nuisance law as a regulatory tool was no longer impeded by elaborate requirements for the factual establishment of some kind of distinctively public harm, and state attorneys general found themselves increasingly utilizing the injunction and equity's summary proceedings as a first-order crime-fighting tool.[123]

The injunction and abatement acts formally codified these developments and extended the regulatory and police project even further. Iowa was among the first states to experiment with a statutory nuisance injunction and abatement scheme in its long fight against saloons and liquor. In 1884, after increasing penalties and easing evidentiary requirements for keeping "houses of ill-fame," the state legislature turned immediately to the "sale of intoxicating liquor" and implemented a scheme that would soon become a template for future injunction and abatement acts. It featured, first, a general statement declaring as a matter of statutory law that buildings, establishments, or "the ground itself" in or on which the "unlawful manufacture or sale" of intoxicating liquor took place was per se a public nuisance and thus abatable as such with additional fines and prosecutions for the maintenance of said nuisance. Second, by abatement, the legislature meant the closing of the building for such purposes as well as the removal, sale, and/or destruction of the "furniture, fixtures, vessels, and contents" that also made up the public nuisance. Third, Iowa declared that "any citizen" in the county could bring "an action in equity to abate and perpetually enjoin" the nuisance, thus making the entire citizenry private attorneys general. And fourth, violation of such an injunction subjected the offender to a "contempt" proceeding, which brought further fines and punishments.[124] Duplicated by other states in the alcohol context in the late nineteenth century, these powerful and expanding features became the weapon of choice of urban vice committees and the social hygiene movement in the early twentieth-century fight against the red-light district.[125]

With these statutes, it was clear that legislatures and courts throughout the country had broken with the traditional common law of public nuisance. Injunction and abatement acts were a new kind of police legislation, wherein equitable remedies were now clearly embraced so as to shape public policy and regulate public morality according to the dictates of the legislature and public opinion. The overall goal of these statutes was general social police, and they expanded the nature of offense, crime, procedure, and punishment accordingly. And they were upheld by state courts and the US Supreme Court as such. In *Mugler v. Kansas,* Justice Harlan upheld such liquor regulations as straightforward applications of an expanded police power: "the power which the States have of prohibiting such use by individuals of their property as will be prejudicial to the health, the morals, or the safety of the public." "The supervision of the public health and the public morals is a governmental power, 'continuing in its nature,'" Harlan maintained, "to be dealt with as the special exigencies of the moment may require," and for such purposes, "the largest legislative discretion is allowed."[126]

The injunction and abatement acts passed between 1910 and 1920 were even more extensive and included harsher penalties than the predecessor liquor acts of the 1880s. A 1914 Massachusetts antiprostitution law, for example, kept open a large number of punitive options, including criminal and civil forfeiture of property. Upon a decree permanently enjoining the establishment, the sheriff was directed to "sell all furniture, musical instruments, and movable property used in conducting and maintaining the nuisance."[127] Courts were also given the discretion to keep the premises closed and prohibit any other use for considerable time spans. Most statutes included provisions further loosening evidentiary rules so as to expedite the removal of public nuisances. Such extraordinary expansions in state policing authority were uniformly upheld by state courts. Indeed, from Boston to Sacramento, the enjoinment and elimination of brothels was legitimated with powerful defenses of the states' police power to regulate in the public health, safety, welfare, and morals. In *Chase v. Revere House* (1919), the Massachusetts Supreme Judicial Court upheld the state's 1914 statute by claiming a legitimate exertion of the police power included "all necessary measures for the promotion of the good order of the community and the public morals."[128] There was no longer any discussion of the property basis of equitable jurisdiction or the limits of old common-law remedies. Instead, discussion turned exclusively to the reasonableness of direct legislative initiatives to secure public order and morals. As the Illinois Supreme Court declared in *People v. Smith* (1916), "Under the police power the State may interfere whenever the public interest demands it, and a large discretion is vested in the legislature to determine not only what the interests of the public require but what measures are necessary for the protection of such interest."[129] The Illinois court expressed a conception of general public regulatory power that was one of the primary outgrowths of the Progressive Era expansion of social police.

On the ground, the implications were all too clear as the injunction and abatement acts took center stage in the aggressive vice raids that ultimately sealed the fate of many American red-light districts. The *Chicago Tribune* regularly tracked Chicago's version of a "vice war" in terms that drove home the everyday effects of the Illinois Supreme Court's endorsement of broad regulatory powers of social police. On April 4, 1918, the *Tribune* noted, Chicago city officials (health commissioner, police chief and deputy, city prosecutors, state's attorneys, corporation counsel, and, notably, Chief Justice Harry Olson of Chicago's municipal court) met in conference at the University Club to set in motion "all the city's judicial, police and prosecution powers" against prostitution. That evening, an extensive series of police raids on "cabarets, saloons, houses, and flats" led to the arrest of some 205 "immoral" women, who would be subject to medical tests for communicable diseases and imprisoned at the isolation hospital or tried on state vagrancy charges. As the paper noted, "The health department can do this under its police powers." But another key part of this raid involved the exercise of the injunction and abatement act—as police and health officials posted signs warning property owners that "premises are being used for unlawful purposes" and would be subject to abatement. As Chief Justice Olson put it, "It makes no difference whether the cases are found in hotels, apartment buildings, or wherever, the signs will go up and persons found to be a menace will be handled by the health department." The *Tribune* concluded, "The police and other authorities expect to drive out some supposedly strongly entrenched vice spots by this method." Notably, this extraordinary exercise of local police power by municipal and state officials could be traced back to a "request from Washington" noting that the city had "ample power under its police and health department rules to rid the city of the element which is held to be a menace to men in uniform."[130]

In 1918, Josephus Daniels, secretary of the navy and chair of the Interdepartmental Social Hygiene Board charged the Law Enforcement Division of the War and Navy Departments' Commissions on Training Camp Activities to prepare "standard forms of laws" to be transmitted to all state legislatures concerning "the repression of prostitution, the control of venereal disease and for the rehabilitative and curative treatment of sex offenders." Daniels was joined on the Interdepartmental Social Hygiene Board by Secretary of the Treasury William McAdoo, Secretary of War Newton Baker, and Assistant Surgeon General C. C. Pierce, as well as representatives from the various military medical corps and the US Public Health Service. The ensuing *Standard Forms of Laws* included model state laws for "the repression of prostitution," "fornication," "the control of venereal disease," "the establishment and management of reformatories for women and girls," and "the care of the feeble-minded" (which included provisions for "sterilization" and "defective delinquents")—the latter justified under the reasoning of the National Committee of Mental Hygiene that "large numbers of prostitutes are mentally abnormal" and that society needed to be protected "against the menace" of "unrestrained activity" by "sex offenders who are feeble-minded."[131]

The centerpiece of this new military and civilian effort of social policing, however, was "the well-known Injunction and Abatement Act." The model act contained expansive applications to nuisances involving "lewdness, assignation, or prostitution" and targeted a range of potential persons involved. It charged state attorneys general as well as county attorneys or, indeed, "any person who is a citizen of the county" to bring an action in equity seeking a temporary injunction and ex parte restraining order. Trial proceedings allowed "general reputation" as well as other prima facie evidence of nuisance or knowledge thereof, as well as expansive provisions for the "order of abatement," the sale of property, "punishment for contempt," as well as a "tax against property."[132]

The immediate reason for this unusual military interposition into state legislative and regulatory processes was the armed services' experience with venereal disease during World War I.[133] But the foundation for this unprecedented and coordinated attack on sex offenders, prostitutes, the feeble-minded, and other "women and girls" was built over the previous three decades as new conceptions of social problems intersected with potent new technologies of law and policy making to create a fundamental change in the nature and incidence of modern social policing. The repercussions of those changes regarding law, gender, and sexuality would have important ramifications from "the great war" to "the war on crime" and beyond.

5

ANTIMONOPOLY

Regulated Industries and the Social Control of Capitalism

———

To hold the balance between the material and the human
values is the oldest and the newest economic problem.
—WALTON HALE HAMILTON

The emergence of a modern concept of the social was hardly confined
to the sociocultural spheres of American life. To the contrary, new ideas
of social control, social welfare, and social police quickly cascaded into
every corner of turn-of-the-century policy making, especially political
economy. When expansive concepts of the social and socioeconomic rights
combined with new regulatory technologies of police power and public
utility, a new era in American economic regulation and new democratic
control over the economy commenced. The triggering mechanism for this
modern transformation of law and economics was an age-old American
preoccupation—antimonopoly. Amid a wave of unprecedented industrial
consolidation and corporate concentration, antimonopoly returned to gal-
vanize a broader movement for the social control of corporations, trusts,
and American business writ large. The subsequent emergence of regulated
industries law transformed the economy and reshaped the modern American democratic state.

The public utility idea introduced in Chapter 3 was but the tip of the
spear of a more fundamental transformation in the relationship of the state
and economy in turn-of-the-century America. As Felix Frankfurter understood, *Munn v. Illinois* (1877) and the triumph of the idea of business affected with a public interest was only the beginning. Over the next half
century, the invention of the public utility idea was indeed followed by "a
degree of experimentation in governmental direction of economic activity
of vast import and beyond any historical parallel."[1] The achievements of
the public utility movement were real and significant. The movement gen-

eralized concepts of public interest, public necessity, duty to serve, and non-discrimination. And it originally filled the gap in corporate regulation that opened after an initial decline in older common-law and state charter controls. The public utility idea inaugurated a series of bold experiments in corporate and industrial regulation that culminated in comprehensive, commission-based oversight and control. And it is important to remember that public utilities law *was* antimonopoly law. As Alfred Chandler argued, railroads were "the nation's first big business," ushering in a large-scale transformation in corporate organization, finance, and management.[2] In turn, railroad and utility regulation cast the die for the subsequent control of monopolies both natural as well as unnatural.

As popular concern about corporate power, economic coercion, and industrial injustice moved beyond the case of railroads or grain elevators per se, the antimonopoly tradition expanded again to envelop a wider swath of American business, commerce, and industry. When the original innovations of public utility merged with this broadened antimonopoly impulse, a modern law of regulated industries was born. From the state railroad commissions to the Interstate Commerce Commission, from the US Industrial Commission to the Bureau of Corporations, from the Sherman Antitrust Act to the Federal Trade Commission, from state public utility commissions to the Federal Radio Commission and the Federal Power Commission, the period between Reconstruction and the New Deal witnessed the rise of a new political-economic agenda centered on the administrative and regulatory control of an emergent corporate capitalism.

Arthur T. Hadley was among the first to build out from the special case railroads, in his *Railroad Transportation* (1885), to the more general problem of corporate concentration and what he termed "industrial monopoly." Hadley's baseline was the original public, state-created regime of "legal" or "natural" monopolies, including transportation service, postal service, and municipal utilities—all of which generated "most fruitful experiments in legislative control." But by 1886, he noted with alarm the new problem of "*private* monopolies," where "business interests . . . made competition practically impossible." "There is nothing which the average citizen distrusts and fears so much as the power of great corporations," Hadley argued, especially those corporations with "a virtual monopoly in their own line of business" at odds with "our theories of industrial freedom."[3] Hadley's growing concern about new private monopolies was only bolstered by a proliferation of late nineteenth-century antimonopoly exposés, such as John C. Welch's "Standard Oil Company" (1883), Henry Demarest Lloyd's "The Story of a Great Monopoly" (1881) and "Lords of Industry" (1884), and Henry George's writings on land monopoly.[4] In reckoning with such new monopolies and monstrosities, Welch resorted to the image of the devil himself—Monster and Fiend—from Milton's *Paradise Lost:* "Whence and what art thou execrable shape?"[5] Henry Demarest Lloyd and Henry George concentrated on the more secular threat of monopolistic wealth poised against commonwealth and private monopolies threatening public right.[6]

As corporate concentration and combination moved beyond railroads to the economy at large, economic reformers like Hadley advocated extending the public-use and right-to-regulate rationales developed in public utilities law to the new industrial and factory monopolies. Hadley was joined in this quest by one of the more original economic thinkers of the era, Henry Carter Adams. Adams was brought to the Interstate Commerce Commission by its first chairman, Thomas Cooley, to produce important statistical and accounting reports on railways and public utilities. From that formative transportation and utilities experience, Adams generated a comprehensive critique of the "evils" of laissez-faire as well as a commitment to what he termed "industrial responsibility" in a "truly democratic industry." In a classic essay, "The Relation of the State to Industrial Action," Adams zeroed in on the new problem of "private" and "industrial monopoly," which he defined as "a business superior to the regulating control of competition." Like Hadley, Adams acknowledged the deep roots of the American antimonopoly tradition: "The existence of monopolies . . . has always been regarded as an infringement of personal rights, [and] free people have always revolted against the assumption of peculiar privileges" as "odious, grasping, and tyrannous." But while traditional monopolies flowed mainly from royal prerogative and charter privilege, new private and industrial monopolies seemed to be emerging from the very "conditions of modern business activity" itself, especially "the law of increasing return which gives the large producer the advantage." Such modern industrial monopolies now fueled the same popular democratic "distrust." "The public is deprived of its ordinary guarantee of fair treatment," Adams argued, and monopoly privileges are "perverted from their high purpose to serve private ends."[7] Adams's solution—in sync with his hands-on ICC experience—was to restore social harmony by "extending the duties of *the state.*" The question of the era was "whether society shall support an irresponsible, extralegal monopoly" or whether such new agglomerations of private wealth and power would be "managed in the interests of the public."[8]

Of course, Hadley and Adams were only two important voices in the surge of antimonopoly regulatory sentiment that engulfed the late nineteenth century. By 1901, the remarkable Fanny Borden compiled a bibliography in "Monopolies and Trusts in America" containing over five hundred entries covering everything from conferences, legislation, public ownership, and interstate commerce to coal, coffee, flour, milk, mining, nails, newspapers, oil, railways, sugar, telegraph, and tobacco.[9] By 1908, Chicago's John Lewson introduced a digest of over four hundred fifty cases on "monopolies and restraints of trade" with a further listing of over one hundred state constitutional and statutory provisions respecting monopoly and antitrust. As Lewson described this prodigious output, "The investigator of the trust problem finds himself in a maze of Legislation, Case-Law and Trust literature. About thirty states have legislated directly on the subject of monopolies, [and] almost seven hundred authors have made important contributions on various phases of the trust problem."[10] This veritable legal and political obsession with the so-called monopoly problem hastened the case for extending regulation beyond transportation and utilities—beyond state railroad commissions and the ICC—to the whole of American political economy.

Two things are especially noteworthy about this resurgence of regulatory antimonopoly. First, in keeping with the deepest roots of American antimonopoly in revolutionary traditions of antimonarchism and anti-aristocracy, late nineteenth-century antimonopoly resonated with distinctly political and democratic themes. American antimonopoly was first and foremost a question of the democratic distribution of power and authority in a supposedly self-governing republic. Monopolies and new concentrations of private and industrial economic power were seen as potential threats to democracy itself—threats to self-rule and the democratic control over life, liberty, and happiness as exercised by citizens, households, producers, and proprietors.[11] New aggregations of private economic authority in a rapidly industrializing economy were viewed as new sources of private coercion and economic domination—a "new feudalism"—upending the existing balance of socioeconomic power, exacerbating inequality, and distorting and corrupting democratic political processes.[12] Senator John Sherman introduced the Sherman Antitrust Act in 1890 in just these terms as nothing less than a new political "bill of rights" and a democratic "charter of liberty." Alluding to the "monopolies and mortmains of old," Sherman drew attention to the new "inequality of condition, of wealth and opportunity that has grown within a single generation out of the concentration of capital," wherein "these combinations . . . reach out their Briarean arms to every part of the country." Sherman conjured threats of general social disorder and "kingly prerogative": "If we will not endure a king as a political power we should not endure a king over the production, transportation, and sale of any of the necessaries of life. If we would not submit to an emperor we should not submit to an autocrat of trade, with power to prevent competition and to fix the price of any commodity."[13]

This broad political and social-democratic perspective on antitrust continued to drive antimonopoly policy making through the long progressive period. The Sherman Act was a superstatute. "A charter of freedom," Charles Evans Hughes called it, "the act has a generality and adaptability comparable to that found . . . in constitutional provisions."[14] Louis Brandeis continued to advocate for such a broad interpretation even after the Standard Oil and Tobacco cases in 1912: "What does democracy involve? What does liberty involve? Not merely political and civil and religious liberty, but *industrial liberty* also." Brandeis contended that "the will of the American people as expressed in the Sherman Law" was aimed precisely at the antidemocratic character of "private monopoly"—a "power in this country of a few men so great as to be supreme over the law."[15] As Lina Khan has observed, "Brandeis and many of his contemporaries feared that concentration of economic power [aided] the concentration of political power, and that such private power [could] itself undermine and overwhelm public government."[16]

Second, as should be obvious given the direct links with public utility and railroad regulation, this democratic antimonopoly moment was about much more than antitrust enforcement or "break-'em-up" trust-busting.[17] Beyond the economics of monopoly or "the curse of bigness," the progressive antimonopoly tradition involved a broad reform effort to extend democratic regulatory control over a wider stretch of American business, commerce, and industry. This was seen as an especially urgent task given the wavering efficacy of older common-law and state charter controls. Original American antitrust was therefore of a piece with other expanding legal techniques, tools, and technologies: police power, administrative regulation, public utility law, and an emerging law of unfair competition. Indeed, it was the way police power, public utility, unfair competition, and antimonopoly came together that generated the template for a modern law of regulated industries. American antitrust and competition policy, properly construed, was confined neither to negative economic dialectics nor narrow common-law limitations. Rather, it was a crucial component in a larger and more positive public policy agenda—a movement for the public, democratic, and social control of American business. As Edward Adler put it, "The law of railroads, shipping, banking, corporations, partnership, brokerage, trade marks, 'unfair competition,' 'restraint of trade,' 'monopoly,' and related subjects has been much discussed, but little attention has been devoted in this country to a study of the things of which all these particular subjects are commonly but phases,—the doing of business."[18] Fueled by a reenergized American antimonopoly tradition, the economic regulatory agenda of the long Progressive Era was devoted to this more omnibus and encompassing cause—the social control of American business writ large.

The movement for the social control of business and the resulting law of regulated industries had important ramifications for American law and economy. Indeed, they were central components of a reconfiguration in the very nature of modern American capitalism. The vast economic changes of the late nineteenth and early twentieth centuries realigned economic actors and institutions in a market system more industrial, more organized, and more corporate. Regulated industries law ensured that it was also more regulated and controlled. The resultant form of modern American corporate capitalism was decidedly more state and policy centered, shaped and directed by a new legal and administrative regime of rules and regulations that characterize this new era in American economic history.

The social theorist Jürgen Habermas used the term "organized" or "state-regulated" capitalism to capture this structural shift to a new stage in accumulation and governance processes. For Habermas, advanced capitalism featured both increased economic concentration—that is, the rise of large national and multinational corporations and the increased organization of "markets for goods, capital, and labor"—as well as increased state intervention in the market in the form of advanced legal and administrative regulation.[19] Friedrich Pollock used the term "state capitalism" to similarly draw attention to the degree to which state regulation in the late nineteenth and early twentieth centuries fundamentally shifted political-economic control to the legal-administrative state apparatus. For Pollock, "The replacement of economic means by political means as the last guarantee for the reproduction of economic life" changed the "character of the whole historic period" and marked "the transition from a predominantly economic to an essentially political era."[20] The "socially embedded, socially regularized" character of modern capitalism elevated the state to a key role in "structuring, facilitating, and guiding (in short, 'regulating' or, better, 'regularizing') capital accumulation."[21] The institutional economist Walton Hamilton heralded a new American politics in his *Politics of Industry,* wherein "a host of procedures and arrangements—*political in character*—invaded the domain of business." "There has arisen, quite apart from the ordinary operations of state," Hamilton argued, a new "government of industry" with its own "constitution and its statutes" and its own "administrative and judicial processes."[22]

Now, of course, as economic thinkers as diverse as Adam Smith and Karl Polanyi recognized long ago, there never was historically any purely "economic" era of laissez-faire or simple free-market or price-theory control. As Polanyi expressed it best, "Economic history reveals that the emergence of national markets was in no way the result of the gradual and spontaneous emancipation of the economic sphere from governmental control. On the contrary, the market has been the outcome of a conscious and often violent intervention on the part of government."[23] Economic developments have always moved hand in hand with interconnected developments in law and politics as implicated in the very notion of "political economy." "Public economy" and the "well-ordered marketplace," for example, were well-established aspects of early American economic life before the Civil War as a multitude of local and state rules regulated trade, sales, products, establishments, and corporations.[24]

But while state involvement in the economy had deep roots in American history (from state police power regulation of markets and goods to Alexander Hamilton's reports on manufactures and money and banking to the public promotion of internal improvements in Henry Clay's so-called American System), it would be a mistake to underestimate the impact of industrial change. The crises of late nineteenth- and early twentieth-century industrial, corporate capitalism were different from the developmental issues involved in the emerging commercial, maritime, trade, and urban market economies of the antebellum years. The regulatory controls were consequently of a different order. Federal and centralized techniques augmented and often displaced state and local regulations in an effort to address the problems of a consolidated and cartelized national economy. Moreover, those techniques were increasingly administrative—the product of federal independent regulatory commissions newly invented to investigate, police, and direct the interstate market as never before.[25] Finally, and most importantly, the private common-law framework of much early American economic regulation ultimately gave way to a prolific public law jurisprudence generating new statutory and administrative rules and regulations progressively governing more areas of the nation's economy.

This surfeit of rules and regulations marked a new era in government-business relations in the United States and a reconfiguration of the relationship of law and American capitalism—a revolution, if you will, in political economy. The state and regulation assumed prominent new roles in this decidedly mixed and regulated economy.[26] Behind this vast reconfiguration of American economic and corporate life stood the new democratic reform movement. Walter Weyl's *The New Democracy* (1913) surveyed "certain political and economic tendencies in the United States" and made clear the interdependence of a "social program," a "political program," and an "industrial program" in any true, substantive reform of American democracy. Weyl emphasized the democratic goal of a reformed political economy as follows: "It is the attainment by the people of the largest possible industrial control and the largest possible industrial dividend. The democracy seeks to attain these ends through government ownership of industry; through government regulation; through tax reform; through a moralization and reorganization of business in the interest of the industrially weak."[27] John R. Commons and Richard T. Ely similarly viewed their lifelong work in political-economic reform as but subchapters in a new, larger, and more democratic distribution of wealth in America.[28] Together with Henry Carter Adams, Commons and Ely would import substantive democratic commitments like these into the heart of American political economy in the consequential intellectual revolution known as institutional economics.

From Institutional Economics to the Social Control of Business

Of particular importance to the new set of legal, regulatory, and administrative practices bound up in the movement for the social control of capitalism was the emergence of institutional economics. The extraordinary intellectual (as well as political and legal) output of this distinctive generation of economists—from Henry Carter Adams and Thorstein Veblen to Richard Ely and John Commons to Walton Hamilton and Robert Lee Hale—underwrote one of the more fundamental governmental revolutions in modern times.[29] This historical community of economists, thinkers, and reformers self-consciously crafted an ambitious agenda of legal and political intervention— in effect, a legal-intellectual framework for economic regulation. And the language, conceptualizations, and active reform proposals of this group of economists and law writers played a key role in the development of new legal and political controls over the burgeoning national economy and regulated industries.[30]

The intellectual roots of institutional economics were broad and diverse.[31] They ranged from the general emergence of pragmatism, sociology, and modern American social science to the broad influence of the German historical school to the more particular development in American economics of a social and evolutionary counterpoint to classical and neoclassical political economy.[32] Institutional economics built directly on emerging theories of the social, social control, and the increasingly social nature of modern societies discussed in Chapter 4.[33] And institutional economists thoroughly absorbed the critical realism that pervaded turn-of-the-century pragmatism,

jurisprudence, and social science. Indeed, institutionalism involved an unrelenting critical project that struck straight at the heart of orthodox economic thinking.

Of course, critiques of classical political economy were hardly a new
thing under the sun by the turn of the twentieth century. The likes of Marx,
Carlyle, and Ruskin had already built up a formidable case against the
"dismal science": "to live miserable we know not why; to work sore and
yet gain nothing; to be heartworn, weary, yet isolated, unrelated, girt-in
with a cold universal Laissez-faire."[34] But what made the American institutionalists' critiques distinctive was the fact that they developed after the
marginal revolution and internally within the discipline of professional economics. Indeed, the critical institutionalist perspective provided the blueprint that launched the new American Economic Association (AEA) in
1885. Richard T. Ely, Henry Carter Adams, Edwin R. A. Seligman, and
other progressive economists pioneered the AEA precisely to challenge the
scientific pretensions of classical and neoclassical economics so as to put
modern political economy on a more realistic and empirical foundation.
The first official report of the AEA skewered economic orthodoxy: "It made
no endeavor to ascertain how men actually do act; it only undertook to
philosophize respecting the results, provided they acted in a certain assumed
manner."[35] Richard T. Ely found in traditional economics not only a faulty
epistemology but a gospel of wealth and laissez-faire apologetics: "It means
that the laws of economic life are natural laws like those of physics and
chemistry, and that this life must be left to the free play of natural forces."
The result was socially Darwinian: "'This industrial world is governed by
natural laws. . . . These laws are superior to man. Respect this providen-
tial order—let alone the work of God.'"[36]

In place of an unscientific science of pure thought, the economists and
social scientists who founded the AEA promoted a "New Political Economy"
in sync with the critical spirit of modern social science: "pursuing the in-
ductive method, ascertaining how men actually do act, gathering statistical
and historical material, and educing the laws of human action from a wide
observation of phenomena."[37] Just as the antiformalism of the turn of the
century upended conventional notions of literature, philosophy, law, politics, and society, in the hands of the institutionalists, its "cynical acids"
challenged reigning dogmas in economics.[38] Indeed, institutional economics
was bound up with four critical moves: (1) the shift from economic statics
to dynamics, processes, and historical evolution; (2) a move away from atomistic assumptions about homo economicus toward a more realistic conception of social individuals and social psychology; (3) a general turn from
formal, abstract theorizing to the actual investigation of concrete social

organizations and institutions; and (4) a comparative shift in emphasis from the nature of a free market to the reality of the regulatory state.

Much the way Lester Frank Ward answered Herbert Spencer's *Social Statics* with a more developmental and evolutionary account in *Social Dynamics,* the American institutionalists demanded an approach to the economy that could explain change over time. Here the contributions of Thorstein Veblen were particularly significant. "The sciences which are in any peculiar sense modern," Veblen argued, "take as an (unavowed) postulate the fact of consecutive change. Their inquiry always centres upon some manner of process."[39] The problem, as Wesley C. Mitchell later stated it, was that neither the "the theory of value and distribution as worked out by Ricardo, nor the refined form of this theory presented by Veblen's teacher J. B. Clark deals with consecutive change in any sustained fashion." Instead, classical political economy was "limited to what happens in an imaginary 'static state.'" For the institutionalists, this "static" quality relegated orthodox economics "to the 'taxanomic' stage of inquiry represented, say, by the pre-Darwinian botany of Asa Gray."[40] Walton Hamilton dubbed such a method of procedure "economic statics." If economics was to be a fully "modern" rather than "antiquated" discipline, it had to become an evolutionary science attuned to questions of process, change and continuity, and the complex, interconnected development of actual economic institutions over time.[41]

If a more realistic conception of time, change, development, and process was a first-order requirement of a more realistic economics, a close second was a more believable rendering of human nature. Veblen, Mitchell, and Hamilton—indeed most American institutionalists—insisted that "economic theory must be based upon an acceptable theory of human behavior." By the time Walton Hamilton arrived in Ann Arbor in 1910 as an economics graduate student and instructor, the road to a more realistic conception of human nature and psychology had already been paved at the University of Michigan by the pragmatic ethics of John Dewey and James Hayden Tufts as well as the social psychology of George Herbert Mead and Charles Horton Cooley.[42] For Hamilton, Cooley's sociological trilogy *Human Nature and the Social Order* (1902), *Social Organization* (1909), and *Social Process* (1918) was especially important in challenging "common sense notions" of "atomic individualism," which were "inadequate to explain contemporary society."[43] For Hamilton and Cooley, "the complex life of the modern world" was not to be crowded into mechanical and individualistic forms. Rather, for institutionalist economists, a vision of the individual in society—"'individual' and 'society' remaking each other in an endless process of change"—was alone adequate to the task of studying modern "social organization" or formulating a contemporary social and economic program.[44]

Just as William James and George Herbert Mead challenged prevailing notions of the nature of the individual personality and its myriad preferences, wants, desires, interests, and inclinations, modern social psychology rendered problematic homo economicus.[45] Walton Hamilton bemoaned the fact that "the extreme individualism, rationality, and utilitarianism which animated eighteenth century thought still finds expression in neo-classical economics." The thin economic and pecuniary account of individual self-interest struck institutionalists as "nothing more than a blanket formula" that elided all of the "concrete influences" and "conflicting values" that "animated the behavior of individuals." Hamilton argued that such an account "falls short of explanation because self-interest is not a simple thing that can be easily discerned, but a huge bundle of conflicting values wherein the present and the future are at variance. . . . It failed to note that my life and yours is a continuous thing, and that what I do today constrains my acts tomorrow."[46] In their elaborate critiques of individual, rational, and economistic self-interest, the institutionalists anticipated the mature argument of John Dewey in *Individualism, Old and New* that, taken together, the machine, money, and pecuniary culture characteristic of the age obscured and crowded out such things as "the spiritual factor, equal opportunity and free association and intercommunication." In place of the actual, real development of individualities, "there is the perversion of a whole ideal of individualism to conform to the practices of a pecuniary culture. It has become the source and justification of inequalities and oppressions."[47]

Third, beyond the quest for a more realistic account of a more thoroughly modern social self, institutionalists also turned to the larger social surround. In particular, they drew attention to the complex web of "institutions"— "social arrangements capable of change rather than obstinate natural phenomena"—from which the new political economy drew its name. Neither the individual nor the economy could be understood abstracted from the real social and institutional world that gave them meaning and possibility. The links between the evolutionary approach, the critique of a crude theory of individual self-interest, and the importance of "the scheme of institutions under which one lives and must seek his good" was obvious to these thinkers. Hamilton declared boldly that "the proper subject-matter of economic theory is institutions" and that "the institutional approach was the only way to the right sort of theory":

> "Institutional economics" alone meets the demand for a generalized description of the economic order. . . . Such an explanation cannot properly

be answered in formulas explaining the processes through which prices emerge in a market. Its quest must go beyond sale and purchase to the peculiarities of the economic system which allow these things to take place upon particular terms and not upon others. It cannot stop short of a study of the conventions, customs, habits of thinking, and modes of doing which make up the scheme of arrangements we call "the economic order." It must set forth in their relations one to another the institutions which together comprise the organization of modern industrial society.[48]

The road was thus paved for an early series of "historically and institutionally specific studies . . . of market institutions and pricing processes" that culminated in new theories of imperfect and monopolistic competition as well as Gardiner Means's more influential work on "administered prices."[49] The institutional approach to prices in turn spurred the mass of empirical and sociohistorical investigations of pricing in particular industrial and institutional settings that dotted early twentieth-century economic writing.[50] Hamilton stated the overarching ambition thus: "Accounts of how . . . in the abstract prices are made were available in abundance. Yet, with notable exceptions, little was at hand upon the structures of particular industries, their distinctive habits, their unique patterns of control, and the multiplex of arrangements—stretching away from technology to market practice—which give magnitude to their prices."[51] "If learning were a mere search for hypothetical truth," Hamilton wryly concluded, "the principles governing the economic life of cave men, the inhabitants of Mars, or of a Crusoe-infested island might be worth formulating."[52]

Finally, this new focus of the American institutionalists on dynamics rather than statics, the real social economy rather than ideal rational actors, and historical and institutional rather than theoretical and abstract renderings of business, industry, and the market yielded an economics directly concerned with the problem of control—social control—and particularly those mechanisms of control available through law, politics, the state, and new technologies of legislative and administrative regulation. For the institutionalists, the problem of control was not exogenous to the operations of a free market or a second-order question in theorizing the modern economy; rather it was constitutive and foundational. J. B. Clark's son, John Maurice Clark, made that all too clear in *The Social Control of Business*—the most complete and far-reaching attempt to make economic theory relevant to the modern problem of control: "When we speak of the 'social control of business' we must first take some pains to avoid the implication that business exists first and then is controlled. Control is rather an integral part of business, without which it could not be business at all.

The one implies the other, and the two have grown together." Clark distinguished at least three levels of control that are always present in any modern economy: (a) the informal controls that all economic groups developed "out of their own needs and customs"; (b) the common-law controls of courts "in settling disputed cases" and establishing controlling ground rules in areas like property, contract, patent, copyright, bankruptcy, tort, and crime; and (c) the controls "resulting from legislation" and modern administration "which change the rules for the future, with a definite purpose of bringing about some new result."[53] According to the institutionalists, this underlying control aspect of economic order was frequently ignored or theorized away in a classical and neoclassical political economy still too much under the sway of an antimercantilist pedigree.[54]

From the very beginning, the social control theories of the American institutionalists sped away from the laissez-faire inheritance of classical economics. The original platform of the American Economic Association was unambiguous on this point: "We regard the state as an educational and ethical agency whose positive aid is an indispensable condition of human progress. While we recognize the necessity of individual initiative in industrial life, we hold that the doctrine of *laissez-faire* is unsafe in politics and unsound in morals; and that it suggests an inadequate explanation of the relations between the state and the citizens."[55] The first meeting of the AEA featured Henry Carter Adams's famous call to arms "The State and Industrial Action," conceived as the economic rebuttal to Herbert Spencer's "The Man versus the State."[56] Adams began by noting the "long list of acts passed by Parliament pertaining to industrial affairs," which Spencer regarded as "an invasion of the domain of personal liberty" and an "encroachment upon the '*régime* of contract.'" In contrast to Spencer's laissez-faire dream, Adams proffered an alternative relationship of "government and industry" in which "the State" exercised "a controlling and regulating authority over every sphere of social life, including the economic, in order to bring individual action into harmony with the good of the whole." Adams's critique of Spencer was but prelude to his endorsement of a broad positive program for the governmental control of industrial action, from Granger laws, railroad regulation, and public utility to educational reform, factory legislation, and general government enforcement and supervision of competition.[57]

Thus, already in the first volume of a still emerging institutional economics, Henry Carter Adams could offer up a thumbnail policy sketch for the social control of business. And in the end, the new economic ideas of the institutionalists were ideas in action. The pragmatic and realist revolution in modern economic thought was a plan of action to be tested in action. From intellectual roots reconfiguring economic theory around a more realistic and sociohistorical understanding of institutions and social control, there quickly developed a more concrete and expansive legal and legislative policy-making agenda. The ultimate goal was a democratic transformation in the relations of American polity, society, *and* economy. The vehicle for achieving that goal was the construction of a modern regulatory and administrative state.

Antimonopoly, Public Utility, and Unfair Competition

Institutional economics and the movement for the social control of business thus involved a major turn in political economy toward law and the state. For institutionalists, collective control was essential to almost every aspect of economic life, intimately bound up with statecraft, public policy, and the rules of law that preoccupied John Commons's and Richard T. Ely's foundational inquiries in *Legal Foundations of Capitalism* and *Property and Contract in Their Relations to the Distribution of Wealth.*[58] Indeed, here the institutionalist revolution in economics meshed seamlessly with an emergent legal realism that also foregrounded the constitutive force of public power in all matters of supposedly private right and action. Morris Cohen and Robert Lee Hale were the principle architects of a legal realist project devoted to uncovering the ubiquitous role of law and statecraft in the construction of property, contract, and the market. Exploding the fiction of the invisible hand, they implicated the visible state directly in the legal-political structuring of capitalism. In the revealingly entitled article "Property and Sovereignty," Morris Cohen explored the fusion of private right and public power that generated "the character of property as sovereign power compelling service and obedience." Cohen reminded students of property that the ideal of "laissez-faire has never in fact been completely operative." In "Coercion and Distribution in a Supposedly Non-Coercive State," Robert Hale further unmasked the public force behind private power, contending that an overly rigid public-private distinction obscured the formative role of the positive law in constructing the exchanges that determined so much of the distribution of wealth and power in America.[59] By exposing the public underwriting of property, contract, and enterprise in law and politics, the institutional-realist critique related the distribution of wealth directly to the allocation of power in a democratic republic. And as Morris Cohen concluded, "It would be as absurd to argue that the distribution of property must never be modified by law as it would be to argue that the distribution of political power must never be changed."[60]

This more realistic assessment of law's relationship to state and economy provides the proper context for reckoning with the extraordinary wave of antimonopoly sentiment and antitrust policy making that engulfed the United States in the late nineteenth and early twentieth centuries. Casting a bright light on the informal and legal mechanisms of economic control that pervaded the industrial economy, American institutionalists and realists highlighted the problem of organized private coercion—the rapid ascendancy of new forms of private power wielded by massive corporations and trusts. The economic power of business was no longer justified as a natural outcome of the choices of rational individuals, voluntary cooperation, or the laws of supply and demand. Rather, it was interrogated as to its implications for the imbalance and concentration of power and wealth in a democratic republic. Reformers increasingly considered monopoly and the concentration of economic interests as a problem in itself with grave implications for what Willard Hurst called "the balance of power." Hurst understood the balance of power as a first-order principle of American constitutionalism: "Any kind of organized power ought to be measured against criteria of ends and means which are not defined or enforced by the immediate power holders themselves. It is as simple as that: We don't want to trust any group of power holders to be their own judges upon the ends for which they use the power or the ways in which they use it."[61] For Hurst, American antitrust policy provided "an example unique in our legal history for a long-continued, broadly accepted, peacetime attempt to use law direction to affect the balance of power within the community."[62]

By the turn of the twentieth century, an increasing number of legal and economic commentators came to see the growing economic force of monopoly and big business as a constitutional problem in this sense—as an imbalance of power and control in a democracy. In *Freedom through Law: Public Control of Private Governing Power,* Robert Lee Hale argued that the new concentrations of private economic power were slowly taking on many of the attributes formerly thought of as the exclusive prerogative of public sovereignty. Hale held that these new forms of "private government" were just as capable of exercising social force and coercion and destroying liberty as "public government itself."[63] But whereas public power had been the subject of developing constitutional protections since the seventeenth century at least, these new forms of private economic domination were increasingly escaping traditional mechanisms of control (competition, common law, charter, and state statute). The problem of monopoly and private governing power, in the eyes of many realists and institutionalists, demanded new legal, legislative, and administrative restraints—an expansion of police power, public utility, and the law of unfair competition so as to set up a new democratic state as a countervailing regulatory force to the new power of business and corporations in American socioeconomic life.

Despite the analytical power of such critical realist and institutionalist perspectives, however, classic accounts of American antimonopoly and antitrust have unfortunately largely ignored them. Conventional chronicles have continued to emphasize the internal economics of antitrust shorn of sociopolitical context, while isolating antitrust as a discrete and independent arena of policy making.[64] Classic business and economic history accounts of antitrust, for example, have emphasized vertical integration, managerial hierarchy, allocative efficiency, consumer welfare, and a limited and backward-looking American state. For Thomas McCraw, adversarial legalism, "the tiny size of the United States government," and the "illogical," "aesthetic" nature of critiques of "bigness" combined to make modern American antimonopoly something of a misguided political-economic anachronism. McCraw summed up the Brandeisian crusade against bigness as follows: "Brandeis misunderstood the forces underlying the rise of big business and consistently advocated economic policies that were certain to reduce consumer welfare."[65] McCraw's critique closely toed the line of the new antitrust orthodoxy of Robert Bork, who claimed to "conclusively" and "exclusively" establish the original legislative intent of the Sherman Act as "consumer welfare" and the neoclassical economic criteria that value implied—namely, maximization of wealth and allocative efficiency.[66]

As business histories deemphasized and depoliticized the power and effect of the American antimonopoly tradition, conventional political histories tended to cabin and isolate the juristic, common-law underpinnings of antitrust policy making with equally underwhelming assessments. William Letwin's classic history of the Sherman Act rested on the baseline assumption that "American economic policy has always rested on two principles: 1) government should play a fairly confined role in economic life, and 2) private economic activities should be controlled largely by competition."[67] Ellis Hawley's famously "ambivalent" account of antimonopoly policy similarly emphasized America's "libertarian" and "liberal individualistic traditions," wherein "long devotion to a philosophy of laissez-faire, local rights, and individual liberty" made Americans "reluctant to use the federal government as a positive instrument of reform."[68]

On the basis of just such assessments of the inherent limits of American law and economics, historians of corporation law, economic concentration, and antimonopoly have constructed a composite portrait of regulatory failure fit for a Gilded Age. Its common features ranged from the rise of general incorporation laws to the decline of the regulatory "artificial entity" theory and the triumph of corporate personhood in *Santa Clara v. Southern Pacific Railroad* (1886).[69] It gained momentum through the slow but inevitable decline of common-law corporate controls like the ultra vires doctrine as well as a states' ability to regulate "foreign" (i.e., out-of-state) corporations.[70] The conventional narrative reached something of a crescendo in the race-to-the-bottom charter mongering that culminated in New Jersey's corporation act of 1889 and the reincorporation of the Standard Oil Company in that "traitor state." Finally, Delaware's General Corporation Law of 1899 completed the revolution that "turned corporate law inside out." For one hundred years, Joel Seligman argued, the business corporation could "exercise powers or seek capital" only in ways dictated by state and charter. With the New Jersey and Delaware revolution, the "corporation could be a lawmaker itself."[71] The resultant triumph of the corporation as a natural and normal business unit, in the words of Morton Horwitz, worked to "legitimate large-scale enterprise and to destroy any special basis for state regulation of the corporation that derived from its creation by the state."[72]

No doubt, the late nineteenth century did witness an internal transformation of corporate law regarding the general regulatory effects of the original rules that formed a corporation qua corporation in the first place. What is missing from the conventional story, however, is a comparable account of the almost simultaneous creation of brand-new sites and creative new rationales for the continued regulation of corporate power in the United States. For wholly coincident with the corporate rush to New Jersey and Delaware was a concerted effort by reformers to exercise new legal and political controls over corporate capitalism. While not discouraging the formation of many new corporations, progressive reformers built a new regulatory regime aimed precisely at those industries, monopolies, and corporate practices that posed the greatest threats to and problems for democracy. Here, a whole host of factors from the nature of certain industries (dealing with necessities or public provisions) to the characteristics of certain monopolies (in terms of scale, scope, and structure) to a new set of corporate practices and behaviors (like corruption, coercion, and unfair competition) triggered new rounds of regulatory innovation, expansion, and enforcement. This was the road from a revolution in corporate governance law to a revolution in regulated industries law.

A full reckoning with the nature and effects of American antimonopoly and antitrust not only requires a move past some conventional portraits of a "race to the bottom," regulatory failure, and the historic limits of American statecraft. It also requires a more holistic account of the situatedness of antitrust within a panoply of highly interrelated and interdependent regulatory technologies and strategies at the intersection of the laws of police power, public utility, and unfair competition. And one should not underestimate the continued regulatory effectiveness in some states of common-law controls, charter restrictions, general incorporation, ultra vires, the law of foreign corporations, and state antimonopoly enforcement. From remarkably robust common-law doctrines to continued state legislation to general state police powers to the rise of public utility and trade regulation to the construction of de facto federal regulatory and administrative authority, turn-of-the-century American law provided a broad regulatory environment for the further development of antimonopoly and antitrust policy making. Beyond the problem of monopoly or "bigness" per se, it is important to understand the Sherman Act, the Clayton Act, and the creation of the FTC within this larger framework of the expansion of state and federal police power control over corporations, businesses, and economic activities formerly dealt with through common-law and charter restrictions. For as was the case with the development of the public utility regime that culminated in the establishment of the Interstate Commerce Commission, exactly at the point when an earlier regulatory regime built around common-law and state charter controls began to falter, the Sherman Act inaugurated a broad new set of federal initiatives aimed at maintaining and expanding public control over a rapidly transforming American business and industry.

The political economist Myron Watkins thoroughly understood the interconnections between public utility, antitrust, and the emerging law of unfair competition in the omnibus movement for the social control of business. Watkins captured the ultimate regulatory force of the ICC for interstate carriers: "We are regulating you, not one of your functions or part of your actions. . . . Now the interests of national commerce are supreme. Hence, your first allegiance, your primary duty is to the federal regulatory power."[73] Watkins read the ultimate effect of antimonopoly and antitrust in an interrelated context: "It is for the protection of the [general] public interest against the nefarious designs and the unfair practices of this element of the business world that the anti-trust laws are properly maintained." Refusing to see antitrust confined to negative laissez-faire economic or common-law legal principles, Watkins emphasized the long, positive arm of an American policy that launched a "path for the development of sound public policy toward trade, the protection and fostering of honest enterprise, prudent investment and efficient management, [sober industry and fair dealing], and the prohibition and discouragement of every opposite course of business conduct."[74]

It was this broader, interconnected, and more positive aspect of antitrust and antimonopoly policy that generated a more open-ended federal economic regulatory control over American business in the early twentieth century. And it was this longer and more continuous arc of legal-regulatory policy making that was the central concern of a new generation of political economists at the turn of the century. Walton Hamilton was one of the key innovators in this capacious new economic thinking that synthesized the perspectives of economics, law, history, and politics. Pushing quickly beyond older, siloed arguments about monopoly and trust-busting, new institutionalists took stock of much larger, longer regulatory traditions in the United States and created a new intellectual foundation for future regulatory and administrative innovation across the modern economy. For Hamilton, the Sherman Act in isolation was merely "the elementary ordinance." What was important was the longer and larger "pattern of the public control of business" that had grown up around it: "Over the centuries this fabric of control has been woven. Public policy, the common law, the usages of trade, statutes of the realm, opinion popular and unpopular, decrees of judges have all left their impress on it. . . . The law of industry is the cumulative result of countless expediencies shaped to countless occasions, a corpus distilled from myriads of decisions about everyday matters."[75]

In the late nineteenth and early twentieth century, monopoly and competition were not solely economic issues. The whole movement for evolutionary-institutional economics and the social control of business manifested economic questions that were understood as deeply intertwined with the larger social, political, and legal surround. They could not be dealt with as if they involved only "the axioms and corollaries of a book of mathematics."[76] The great conversation about trusts, monopolies, and competition that preoccupied fin de siècle America sounded not in a language of consumer welfare and allocative efficiency. Rather, it resounded with the larger social question of inequality, the perennial political problem of democracy, and a burgeoning ethical discourse about economic justice and social fairness in a democratic republic. Strong ties, in other words, bound antitrust law directly to larger progressive innovations concerning public utility and public goods as well as politico-economic corruption and unfair trade.

Public Utility and Antimonopoly. Richard T. Ely, an early and ardent advocate of institutional economics, first started writing seriously about monopoly and the trust problem in the 1880s. Monopoly was the predominant topic of a series of *Baltimore Sun* articles that he compiled for his

Problems of To-Day: A Discussion of Protective Tariffs, Taxation, and Monopolies (1888). Ely's presentation made clear three key features of the late nineteenth-century American antimonopoly tradition. First, the topic of monopoly was understood as of "tremendous practical importance," or as Ely put it, "No problem of to-day is so pressing." Second, the problem of monopoly was understood not as an isolated, technical problem of law and economics but as a social problem inextricably intertwined with the entirety of American political economy. Ely viewed "the general growth of monopoly," for example, as both "a cause and a consequence" of renewed attention to protectionism as well as the labor question.[77] Finally, antimonopoly was part and parcel of the historic development of the modern public utility idea. Indeed, Ely introduced his examination of monopoly after a discussion of Western Union and the possibility of a "government telegraph" and then elaborated it with further chapters on the gas supply, street railroads, water supply, electric lights, railroad consolidation, and public roads and canals.[78]

Ely's approach to monopoly was firmly rooted in the United States' long antimonopoly tradition. Ely approached the trust question per se—"monopoly in its most concentrated form"—through a rumination on Henry George and land monopoly, that is, "the way in which our public domains and empires of valuable lands have been conferred on private corporations." He endorsed "more vigorous efforts . . . to guard the interests of the public against land plunderers."[79] Here was that age-old theme of the private corruption of the public interest. Ely decried "government by special interests" and the private "lobbies that exist everywhere," concluding, "government is created to promote the general welfare, and when it is used to advance special interests . . . it is perverted from its original purpose."[80]

Within this traditional antimonopoly and anticorruption framework, Ely began to incorporate the insights of institutional economics and especially the continued development in law of the public utility idea. Before deploying the distinction between so-called natural and artificial monopolies, Ely introduced the prior significance and normative implications of the all-important public-private distinction: "The post-office is a public monopoly and is a national blessing. The telegraph is a private monopoly, and the fact that it is so is nothing less than a national calamity. Private monopolies are odious." While Ely viewed public monopolies as key to civilization and "productive of vast benefits," private monopolies were "contrary to the spirit of the common law and of American institutions"—"a perpetual source of annoyance and irritation."[81] Public utility was front and center in Ely's concerns: "A correct course of action" was predicated on that "public spirit that leads people to reflect on the public welfare," considering "measures from the standpoint of the greatest good to the greatest number," wherein "public goods and public property are watched with jealous care" and where "public enemies are exposed."[82] Ely's solutions and remedies to the problem of monopolies both natural and artificial followed the state interventions and public regulations endorsed by institutional economics and the public utility idea. For natural monopolies, Ely recommended government ownership and in some cases government operation. For other monopolies, Ely urged (in addition to the reform of tariff law and patent law) the reform of the law of private corporations and the establishment of state and federal bureaus of corporations. And for the effects of monopoly on the larger distribution of wealth in the United States, Ely proposed the regulation of bequests and inheritances, through taxation and other measures, so that the "vast fortunes may gradually be broken up and wealth more widely diffused."[83]

The close connection between public utility regulation and antimonopoly and antitrust was even more pronounced in some of the distinctly legal texts that addressed the antimonopoly problem at the turn of the century. Two of the great innovators in the American law of public utility were Joseph Henry Beale (whose work on the law of hotels, innkeepers, and railroad rate regulation was formative) and Bruce Wyman (Beale's coauthor and one of the founders of modern American administrative law). In a pioneering article entry titled "Monopolies" in the *Cyclopedia of Law and Procedure*, Beale and Wyman made clear the conceptual and practical continuity between early corporate charter regulation, the public utility idea, and modern antimonopoly and antitrust.[84] After a general introduction on medieval franchises and patents of monopoly, Beale and Wyman divided the modern monopoly problem into two categories: (a) monopolies created by franchises and (b) monopolies created by combinations. Like Ely's original classification of public and private monopolies, Beale and Wyman's first category—monopoly by state or government franchise—reflected the deep historical roots of antimonopoly in an established law of public service corporations and public utilities. Beale and Wyman canvassed about one thousand cases from across US jurisdictions concerning franchise monopolies granted by legislatures or subordinate bodies dealing with public health (e.g., noxious waste removal, slaughterhouses), public safety (e.g., skilled employments, fiduciary businesses, the sale of liquor), public institutions (e.g., schools and public works), and public services (e.g., transportation and public utilities per se). Here again, the point was to emphasize the extensive state regulatory and administrative tradition that prefigured and framed public policy concern about the trust problem and the concentration of industry that riled the late nineteenth century (well beyond common-law precedents on contracts and conspiracies in restraint of trade). Contra conventional wisdom on a weak-state, common-law, or laissez-faire baseline, turn-of-the-century lawyers, judges, and economists were well prepared to evaluate the new kinds of trusts, monopolies, and holding companies rapidly emerging in that period within a broad-based and well-established regulatory tradition regarding corporate efforts to monopolize the market. As Beale and Wyman concluded about monopolies created by private combination rather than public franchise: "Any scheme to corner the market by getting control of the available supply is illegal; and so all contracts made in promotion of such a scheme are unenforceable. Whatever device may be used to get control of supplies, whether by option or by lease may be held to have the taint of monopolization if the intent is to regain control of the market thereby."[85]

While the distinction between natural and artificial (or public and private) monopolies remained crucial to the structure of antimonopoly thinking and policy making, there was also a general movement in the direction of applying public utility models and remedies to the entire range of monopoly and trust problems. Bruce Wyman was again in the avant-garde of this movement. In his important treatise *Control of the Market: A Legal Solution of the Trust Problem* (1911), Wyman made the case for explicitly extending the public utility solution to monopolies and trusts. Favoring the robust regulation of the trusts by law rather than destroying them through disaggregation of capital, Wyman turned to historic examples from the law of public service corporations, public employment, and public utility. "I have come to believe in the control by the State of all businesses which have outgrown the regulation of competition," Wyman argued. "All businesses which have a virtual monopoly . . . are so affected with a public interest as to be within the class of callings which are considered public employments."[86] Wyman accused trusts and monopolies of pursuing predatory competition under cover of a law of private business, while public service corporations had to meet the substantive standards of public utility law: "One must serve all that apply without exclusive conditions, provide adequate facilities to meet all the demands of the consumer, exact only reasonable charges for the services that are rendered, and between customers under similar circumstances make no discriminations." Wyman basically made the case for applying these hard-fought public utility standards of equal access, adequate services, reasonable charges, and nondiscrimination to the problem of the trusts. He advocated "the immediate extension of this coercive law of public employment to cover the industrial trusts," holding that, "if this law be enforced against the trusts, perhaps a solution of the problem would be found."[87]

While Wyman's approach to trusts as wholesale public utilities was never fully adopted, the public utility model remained a powerful weapon in the larger fight against monopoly. The most important manifestation of this influence was the rapid and widespread proliferation of state public utility commissions—which moved well beyond the confines of the original state railroad commissions to more vigorously police so-called natural monopolies. By the beginning of the twentieth century, public utilities—providing cities and individuals with water, gas, electricity, streetcars, railroads, and other services—proliferated across the United States. Building on earlier late nineteenth-century concerns about the discriminatory rates charged and inadequate services provided by railroads, these new utilities came under increasing scrutiny explicitly as potential monopolies placing their own interests above the interests of the public. New advocates of expansive public utility regulation saw these new kinds of economic enterprise as requiring an expansion of the new kind of social control developed for businesses "affected with a public interest"—that is, administrative regulation.

One product of this new set of public utility and antimonopoly concerns was the rapid proliferation of the state public utility commissions. These commissions were vested with considerable administrative and regulatory power. They could hire staff, conduct valuations of utility property, fix rates of service, establish standards for the quality of service, impose uniform accounting standards, require reports from the utilities at regular intervals, issue certificates of convenience and necessity that controlled the construction or expansion of utilities, and investigate unjust and discriminatory rates either on the complaint of the public or on its own initiative. During the heyday of state utility commissions, debates revolved around the best ways of ensuring quality service at reasonable rates, promoting democratic governance, limiting corruption, increasing efficiency, and ensuring investment in future services. Their appearance, expansion, and proliferation was but one powerful example of just how pervasive was the assumption that government needed to be deeply involved in the management of a large segment of the economy—especially in cases of natural monopolies.

By the beginning of the twentieth century, the need to hold utilities accountable and ensure that their actions reflected public preferences and furthered the public interest was unquestioned. Privately owned public utilities, which typically operated under the terms of municipal- or state-granted franchises, were perceived to be the source of two principle evils. First, their insatiable political appetite for advantageous terms in contracts and franchise agreements supported the worst kinds of corrupt party and boss politics. Second, and more importantly, utilities were considered quintessential natural monopolies. With tremendous fixed costs, many were concerned that, like the railroads on which they were modeled, utilities would undermine the public interest by charging exorbitant and discriminatory prices. As one commentator noted in 1906, "No one now, conservative or radical, stands for unregulated monopoly, while all thinkers and writers on the subject recognize public services as necessary and natural monopolies."[88] By 1930, nearly every state established public utility commissions to regulate virtually every aspect of utility businesses. The variety and comprehensiveness of the state utility commission laws was aptly illustrated by something called the Bonbright Utility Regulation Chart, put together in 1928 by Bonbright & Company.[89]

Providing more than forty data points on each public utility commission in the United States, the chart described the structure of each commission—the number of members, whether they were elected or appointed, the length of their tenure, their salaries, how they were removed from office, and the specific courts to which aggrieved parties might appeal decisions of the commission. It identified the specific kinds of utilities under each commission's jurisdiction, listing no less than nine categories (electric light, heat and power, gas, street railway, interurban railway, motor vehicles, water, telephone and telegraph, pipeline, railroad). It evaluated each commission's powers over electric and gas companies on nineteen different criteria, including whether the enacting law spoke to utility property valuation, rate making, discriminatory rates, terminable or indeterminate permits, investigations initiated either by complaint or by the commission itself, certificates of convenience and necessity, accounting, capitalization and securities, and consolidations and mergers. The chart also detailed the specific reporting requirements for electric and gas companies and the commissions' authority over municipal electric plants.

Perhaps the most striking fact about the Bonbright Utility Regulation Chart was its very existence. It was indicative of a political economy consumed by the extension of social control over large capitalistic enterprises. Laws imposing statewide control over at least part of the public utility industry were the product not of a small group of activists operating at a particular moment in a single state but of the considered decisions of nearly every state legislature in the United States over a period of decades. The debate over the need to subject utilities to government regulation and the best means of doing so was had over and over again, and each time the debate ended with the creation of a statewide administrative commission with expansive public regulatory powers.

Unfair Competition and Antimonopoly. The link between the public utility movement and its concern with natural monopoly and the antimonopoly movement's focus on new artificial combinations and concentrations was clear. The public utility idea stood opposed to private monopoly. But the progressive antimonopoly tradition had another important dimension that was crucial in the development of regulated industries law, and that was the law of unfair competition. As early as the original formation of the Interstate Commerce Commission—something of a culmination in the first wave of public utility regulation—there existed a curious mixture of antimonopoly with a newly emergent concern with corporate corruption and unfair trade practices. And as Laura Phillips Sawyer has reminded us, a concern with "fair trade" was at the center of early twentieth-century debates over antimonopoly and antitrust.[90]

Even at the first stages of public utility regulation—with the original invention of state railroad commissions—the idea of railroads as common carriers and publicly regulated utilities was entangled with antimonopoly and unfair trade rhetoric and policy. New York State's Hepburn Committee was formed in 1879 in response to popular agitation ranging from the chamber of commerce to the Anti-Monopoly League to Tammany Hall, who joined forces to attack "alleged abuses in the management of railroads chartered by the state of New York." The "alleged abuses" highlighted not just problems of scale or concentration but a bevy of other complaints concerning corporate practices, including discriminatory rates, special privileges, stock manipulation, secrecy, public injury, and even workers' injuries on New York's public highways.[91] At the national level, the movement for the establishment of the ICC in 1887 began with a similar condemnation of railroad corporate practices that fostered monopoly, enriched favorites, and obstructed free competition from high, discriminatory, and special rates to secrecy, speculation, and watered stock.[92] Corrupt trade practices and unfair competition played key roles in the pioneering development of regulatory and administrative control over America's railroads.

The Sherman Antitrust Act, of course, was passed a mere three years after the Interstate Commerce Act by a nearly unanimous Congress, famously declaring illegal "every contract, combination in the form or trust or otherwise, or conspiracy, in restraint of trade or commerce among the several States." With similar sweep it also imposed penalties on "every person who shall monopolize, or attempt to monopolize, or combine or conspire with any other person or persons, to monopolize any part of the trade or commerce among the several States." And the same intermix of concern with trusts, corruption, inequality, economic concentration, corporate control, public utility, and unfair competition dominated the original discussion of the problem of monopoly and trusts. Senator John Sherman introduced the bill by directly invoking the broad powers of an early American state regulatory regime in which antimonopoly was about much more than the common-law and conventional restraints of trade (let alone business efficiency). Sherman introduced a range of state case law that illustrated the scope of the current problem as well as the feverish efforts of state officials to respond. He cited at length Michigan Supreme Court Chief Justice Champlin Sherwood in a recent case involving the Diamond Match Company. Sherwood deemed the enterprise of Diamond Match in Michigan to be "an unlawful one" and the contract at issue in this case as void "against public policy." But it was Sherwood's broad perspective on antimonopoly that animated Sherman's efforts to now bring to the national level some version of the police powers used by the states to regulate and control the excessive corporate powers of "the cotton trust, the whisky trust, the sugar-refiners' trust, the cotton-bagging trust, the copper trust, the salt trust, and many others":

> Monopoly in trade, or in any kind of business in this country, is odious to our form of government. It is sometimes permitted to aid the Government in carrying on a great public enterprise or public work under governmental control in the interest of the public. The tendency is, however, destructive of free institutions and repugnant to the instincts of a free people, and contrary to the whole scope and spirit of the Federal Constitution, and is not allowed to exist, under express provision in several of our State constitutions. Indeed, it is doubtful if free government can long exist in a country where such enormous amounts of money are allowed to be accumulated in the vaults of corporations, to be used at discretion in controlling the property and business of the country against the interests of the public and that of the people for the personal gain and aggrandizement of a few individuals. . . . It revives and perpetuates one of the great evils which it was the object of the framers of our form of government to eradicate and prevent.[93]

Neither wealth maximization nor an exclusive concern with size or bigness (let alone a singular focus on consumer welfare) controlled the original American debate about trusts and monopolies. Rather, the legal, legislative, and administrative record was replete with worry about politico-economic corruption and a litany of corporate misdeeds that threatened the public. "Corners, rings, patents of monopoly, pools, cartels, trusts, holding companies, 'Gary dinners,' interlocking directorates, 'communities of interest,' 'gentlemen's agreements,' closed shops'"—with just such a motley array of terms, Walton Hamilton introduced the "hydra-headed" monopoly problem—a problem "as old as industrial society and as new as the latest court decision."[94]

While the Sherman Act did not expressly condemn unfair competition, it was clearly aimed at what Milton Handler called "the brutal and oppressive practices" of large enterprises. "The dominant economic position of these combines," Handler noted, "made their methods particularly venomous."[95] The Antitrust Act, together with continued concern about business practices in rapidly consolidating industries, soon generated two additional federal administrative interventions—the US Industrial Commission and the Bureau of Corporations. The Industrial Commission was created by Congress in 1898 to undertake a comprehensive investigation of "the industrial life of the nation" and "the important changes in business methods" so as to diagnose the "economic problems" that were so riling the nation.[96] Of the commission's nineteen volumes, the first two were dedicated to trusts, corporations, and industrial combinations—the consolidating establishments that created so much public "apprehension of monopoly." The commission took note of the recent "progress of legislation aimed to prevent trusts or avert their evils and dangers" as well as the government's desire "to protect the public from all the dangers of conspiracy and extortion."[97] The commission's highly detailed reports on business conduct and industry practice brought renewed attention to the problem of corporate excess, especially with respect to price discrimination, stock watering, promotion profits, and unfair trade practices.[98] In 1903, Congress created the Bureau of Corporations in the Department of Commerce and Labor—a direct forerunner of the Federal Trade Commission—to make further "diligent investigation into the organization, conduct, and management of the business of any corporation, joint stock company or corporate combination engaged in commerce among the several States."[99] The bureau conducted exhaustive investigations into some of the country's most conspicuous monopolies and trusts. The bureau's reports on the petroleum and tobacco industries formed a basis for the Department of Justice's subsequent antitrust prosecutions that famously dissolved Standard Oil and American Tobacco in 1911.[100] The bureau's uncovering of Standard Oil's railroad rebates also played a key role in the passage of the Hepburn Act (1906), extending the ICC's regulatory powers over the interstate transportation industry.[101]

From the Interstate Commerce Commission and Sherman Antitrust Act to the Industrial Commission and Bureau of Corporations, concern about economic concentration and corporate consolidation constantly mixed with overarching worries about unfair modes and methods of competition. Indeed, for many, what made the rise of trusts and monopolies so especially dangerous was the introduction and proliferation of business practices that subsequently came to be seen as unfair, if not illegal, as documented in thousands of pages of subsequent antitrust actions: intimidation by threats of spurious lawsuits or a ruinous price war, the operation of bogus independents, the use of fighting brands, exclusive dealer arrangements, tying contracts and railroad discrimination.[102] The Standard Oil Company was accused of local price cutting, espionage, bogus independents, and preferential rebates. American Tobacco was attacked for utilizing bogus independents, fighting brands, and exclusive dealer arrangements. National Cash Register was cited for a litany of offenses, including espionage, enticement of competitors' employees, shadowing competitors' salesmen, inducing breach of contract, and circulating false reports. International Harvester was accused of exclusive dealing contracts, while American Can cut off competitors' sources of supply.[103] The list of corporate abuses detailed in antitrust litigation went on and on. As the National Industrial Conference Board put it, "The Whiskey Trust, the American Sugar Refining Company, the Eastman Kodak Company, the du Pont de Nemours Powder Company, the Corn Products Refining Company, and numerous others . . . were charged with using one or another of the kinds of competitive practices of the monopolistic type, which are now regarded as unfair."[104] The original federal antitrust prosecutions, in other words, marked the beginning of the development of a more robust law of unfair competition that ultimately formed the basis for the Federal Trade Commission and Clayton Acts.

Beneath this new wave of federal action against unfair monopolistic competition, the common law and state antimonopoly legislation also remained active in policing unfair trade. Common-law case law was chock full of competitive torts: fraud, misrepresentation, misappropriation of trade secrets, inducement of breach of contract, substitution of goods, malicious interference, infringement of trade designation, defamation, attacks on competitors and competitors' goods. As Milton Handler noted, however, the common law "reached only the crudest competitive excesses," and the private, case-by-case regulation of unfair competition via common-law judges was really no match for the expansive new trade practices of Standard Oil, American Tobacco, and National Cash Register.[105] State regulatory legislation quickly tried to make up for common-law limitations. By the time of the Industrial Commission's reports on trusts, corporations, and industrial combinations, twenty-seven states and territories had passed statutes to "prevent the formation of monopolies by fit regulations and penalties," and fifteen added explicit constitutional provisions.[106] And a host of other state police power regulations took aim at unfair and anticompetitive practices in general. These included restraint of trade and price discrimination statutes, false advertising laws, bribery laws, trademark statutes, food and drug legislation, labeling laws, prohibitory laws, chain store laws, statutes prohibiting sales below cost, trading stamps laws, state fair trade acts, acts prohibiting the appropriation of customer lists, advertising regulations, and proration laws.[107]

This mass of legal and legislative regulatory activity concerning monopoly and unfair competition came to a head in the creation of the Federal Trade Commission. Joseph E. Davies was Woodrow Wilson's commissioner of corporations. Hailing from Robert LaFollette's progressive Wisconsin, Davies was steeped in both institutional political economy and the Wisconsin Idea's multiple experiments with commission regulation in the democratic public interest.[108] Under his leadership, the Bureau of Corporations produced one of the first comprehensive analyses of the direct relationship of the antimonopoly movement to the underlying problem of competitive methods—*Trust Laws and Unfair Competition* (1916).[109] More importantly, as commissioner, Davies began to push the Wilson administration toward a strengthening of the Sherman Act, additional legislation on unfair competition, and the development of a powerful independent "Interstate Trade Commission" to now do for American trade, in general, what the Interstate Commerce Commission did for the railroad problem. Davies's "Memorandum of Recommendations as to Trust Legislation" proposed aggressive "administrative control to prevent monopoly from using its most potent weapon, unfair competition."[110] Davies endorsed Justice John Marshall Harlan's broad defense of administrative regulation in *Interstate Commerce Commission v. Brimson*: "Nor can the rules established for the regulation of [interstate] commerce be efficiently enforced, otherwise than through the instrumentality of an administrative body representing the whole country, always watchful of the general interests, and charged with the duty, not only of obtaining the required information, but of compelling, by all lawful methods, obedience to the rules."[111] Davies recommended new federal legislation to regulate noxious trade practices ranging from interlocking directorates, holding companies, and stock watering to price fixing, full-line forcing, special privileges or rebates, espionage, and bogus independents. Davies even cited the New Jersey "Seven Sisters" laws, urging that "holding companies and mergers should be prohibited" and subject to review "by a commission analogous to the Public Utilities Commission." The Bureau of Corporations' "Survey of the Trust Question" thus did much to anticipate the content of the Federal Trade Commission and Clayton Acts and an emerging synthesis of the law of trade regulation.

With the formation of the FTC and the passage of the Clayton Act, the movement for the regulation of trade and competition entered a new phase. In September 1914, the Federal Trade Commission Act declared unlawful "unfair methods of competition in commerce" and empowered the new independent regulatory agency to not only investigate business and corporate practices but to prevent persons and corporations from using such "unfair methods" as "the most important means of preventing the development of monopolies."[112] In October, the Clayton Antitrust Act added a more detailed list of proscribed anticompetitive practices, including price discrimination, tying contracts, holding companies, and interlocking directorates. It also famously exempted certain labor and agricultural organizations and activities from the antitrust laws.[113] In 1935, the FTC took stock of a seemingly ever-growing list of twenty-five unfair methods of competition condemned in its cease and desist orders: (1) false or misleading advertising; (2) misbranding of quality, purity, origin, source; (3) bribing buyers and customers; (4) procuring trade secrets of competitors by espionage or bribery; (5) inducing employees or competitors to violate contracts; (6) making false and disparaging statements about competitors; (7) intimidating suits for patent infringement; (8) trade boycotts or combinations to prevent the procurement of goods; (9) passing off your products as competitors' products; (10) selling old as new; (11) paying excessive prices for supplies so as to buy up all; (12) concealed subsidiaries; (13) merchandising schemes on lot or chance; (14) resale price maintenance agreements; (15) combinations to control price, divide territory, or eliminate competition; (16) misleading techniques, deception; (17) imitating standard containers but with less content; (18) concealing business identity; (19) false claims as to location, size, authorization, and government endorsement; (20) trade associations for uniform prices; (21) entrapment or coercion of customers; (22) misleading names of products; (23) selling below cost; (24) dealing unfairly or dishonestly with foreign purchasers; and (25) monopolistic reciprocal dealing.[114]

By 1938, the FTC had taken under advisement some 27,060 requests for action against unfair competition, including 12,726 complaints. It had also completed well over one hundred studies and investigations into corporate practices ranging from 11 pages on southern livestock prices (1920) to a 101-volume survey of gas and electric utility corporations (1928–1935). FTC investigations led to significant subsequent legislation and administrative regulation as in the passage of the Packers and Stockyards Act of 1921, the establishment of the Federal Oil Conservation Board in 1924, and the Robinson-Patman Act in 1936. The commission's Trade Practice Conferences covered almost two hundred separate industries from the Anti-Hog-Cholera Serum and Virus Industry in 1925 to the Warm Air Furnace

Industry in 1932.[115] By this time, however, the massive regulatory interventions of the progressive movement for the social control of business had begun to mature into a modern law of regulated industries.

Regulated Industries Law

"We are living in the midst of a revolution," John Maurice Clark noted in 1926, "a revolution that is transforming the character of business, the economic life and economic relations of every citizen, the powers and responsibilities of the community toward business and of business toward the community."[116] By the time Clark completed his "Materials for the Study of Business" in the School of Commerce and Administration of the University of Chicago, *The Social Control of Business* had indeed brought tremendous changes to the regulation of corporations, business, and industry. The various strands of economic regulatory innovation—public utility, antimonopoly, and fair competition—had come together to produce a whole more than the sum of its parts. The result was a rather staggering pattern of comprehensive regulation that included common-law, statutory, and administrative supervision of American economic life. Corporation regulation through state charter controls was no longer the center of economic policy making. Rather, an extraordinary range of legislative and administrative regulations was now directed at substantive economic, corporate, and industrial conduct. Clark offered up a suggestive list of legislative and regulatory achievements of the new movement for the social and democratic control of business: control of railroads and of public utilities, land reclamation and flood prevention, radio and aerial navigation laws, the trust movement and antitrust laws, conservation, the Federal Reserve system, labor legislation, social insurance, minimum-wage laws, industrial labor arbitration, pure-food laws, public health regulation, and city planning and zoning. On the frontier, Clark suggested, were health insurance, control of the business cycle and unemployment, control of large fortunes and the distribution of wealth, and what Clark called the "social control of the structure of industry itself," through the "democratization of business" itself.[117]

Clark's list of policy achievements and policy agendas merely hinted at the full scale and scope of the progressive achievement in the regulatory control of business, industry, and the market that culminated in a modern law of regulated industries. By 1937, Milton Handler dedicated his pioneering casebook in trade regulation and competition policy to Louis Brandeis with a reference to the "Sisyphean task" of simply trying to keep

pace with "the accelerated tempo of change" in the field of economic regulation.[118] In grappling with the increasingly unwieldy topic of "the progressive penetration of government in business," Handler began with a quick
tour of the vast range of New York statutes that confronted economic
enterprise in that state. By 1931, *McKinney's Consolidated Laws of New
York* comprised sixty-seven separate volumes with section titles ranging
from Arbitration, Banking, Benevolent Orders, and Business Corporations
to Salt Springs, State Charities, Tenement Houses, and Workmen's Compensation.[119] Even before organizing an economic venture, Handler noted,
one had to consult the statutory provisions regarding "Business Corporations, General Corporation, Stock Corporation, General Associations,
Membership Corporations, and Partnership laws." Beyond such general
regulations for implementing a New York private enterprise in the first
place, Handler noted a host of other more particular statutes concerning
business names, methods of raising capital (blue sky and usury regulations),
zoning restrictions, construction rules and permitting and inspection processes, and equipment standards. As Handler put it, "The entrepreneur
constructing his own plant will find himself in a maze of fire control, illu-
mination, safety, and sanitary requirements."[120] And, of course, an equally
complex and special maze of licensing restrictions guarded certain New
York professions and businesses, including physicians, surgeons, dentists,
optometrists, pharmacists and druggists, nurses, midwives, chiropodists,
veterinarians, certified public accountants, lawyers, architects, engineers
and surveyors, shorthand reporters, master plumbers, undertakers and em-
balmers, real estate brokers, junk dealers, pawnbrokers, ticket agents,
liquor dealers, private detectives, auctioneers, milk dealers, peddlers, master
pilots and steamship engineers, weigh masters, forest guides, motion picture operators, itinerant retailers on boats, employment agencies, commission merchants of farm produce, and manufacturers of foreign desserts,
concentrated feeds, and commercial fertilizers. Factories, canneries, places
of public assembly, laundries, cold storage, shooting galleries, bowling al-
leys, billiard parlors, the storage of explosives, the sale of minnows, the
operation of educational institutions (and motor vehicles), and filling stations all required special licenses.[121] Even these fairly elaborate provisions
paled in comparison to the detailed state regulations impinging on entry
into the business of banking or insurance or the provision of gas, electricity,
or communications—with foreign corporations encountering additional obstacles and restrictions. If one's business required employees, a law library
of labor relations controls affected the operation: laws regarding industrial
accidents, workers' compensation, limits on child labor, maximum hours
that varied according to sex, age, and occupation, and factory and wage

regulations. If one's business involved the production of food, commodities, or household goods, an equal litany of restrictions was triggered, ranging from adulteration, advertising, and trademark restrictions to minimum standards to weights and measures and inspection regimes.

Regarding special industries like railroads and utilities, states like New York developed separate codes with commission oversight and detailed price and production controls. In New York, that was the case with liquor control, and it was also the case with the Milk Control Act of 1933 made famous in *Nebbia v. New York* (1934).[122] The result of an extraordinary set of economic dysfunctions detailed in the *Report of the Joint Legislative Committee to Investigate the Milk Industry* (as well as special investigations by the FTC), the Division of Milk Control of the New York Department of Agriculture and Markets was ultimately charged with regulating the entire statewide milk industry: "production, storage, distribution, manufacture, delivery, and sale of milk and milk products." An elaborate license regime was the gateway to comprehensive administration and regulation. Licensees had to satisfy the commissioner that they were "qualified by character, experience, financial responsibility and equipment to properly conduct the business, that the issuance of the license will not tend to a destructive competition in a market already adequately served, and that the issuance of the license is in the public interest." Licenses were revocable for a whole range of offenses against public health, public welfare, or the public economy of milk. And commissioners were given select powers to fix prices and establish quotas as well as to undertake an advertising campaign on milk consumption, public health, and child nutrition. As Handler noted, "This mandate coupled with the broad rule-making powers of the department permit . . . an almost unlimited degree of control."[123]

But extensive as these regulations appear, they represent but a small fraction of the total of modern business regulation. A much larger backdrop concerned "legislation enacted *before* the New Deal, the regulations of state and federal administrative agencies, the statutes of the forty-eight states, the ordinances of our countless municipalities, and the substantive rules formulated by our courts."[124] The business historian Alfred Chandler highlighted the transformation in business/government relations inaugurated by three pioneering federal interventions alone: the Interstate Commerce Commission (1887), the Sherman Antitrust Act (1890), and the Federal Trade Commission and Clayton Acts (1914). But already by 1917 and 1918, John A. Lapp could compile an ambitious and comprehensive two-volume listing of federal economic regulations (a primitive forerunner to the Federal Register). Contending that "scarcely any business can be done involving shipments across state lines without consulting" the vast number of rules, regulations, and "restrictions in the interest of the common wel-

fare which the federal government has thrown about business," Lapp summarized and reproduced a range of pioneering federal regulatory initiatives, including

1. Federal banking legislation (including the establishment of the
   Federal Reserve System)
2. The Income Tax Act, the Corporation Tax Act, and other federal
   revenue regulations
3. Federal food, drug, meat, and narcotics acts
4. Federal labor regulations, including the Employers' Liability Acts,
   child labor legislation, and assorted public works, safety, and
   inspection acts
5. New trademark, copyright, and bankruptcy legislation
6. Establishment of the Public Health Service
7. Federal regulations of horticulture and agriculture
8. Federal regulations of immoral commerce
9. The Shipping Board Act
10. The Federal Good Roads Act.[125]

As Dexter Merriam Keezer and Stacy May noted in 1930: "The free working
of free private enterprise in a competitive system is an American ideal that
has never existed except in theory." Governmental regulation was "a heritage of common law," and the United States had been adding to the "amount
of such regulation ever since." By 1930, the government touched the economic system at so many points that a list of policies would involve "a
lengthy undertaking":

1. Government "promotion of privately owned business through such
   mechanisms as the tariff, land grants, loans and subsidies, the
   gathering and dissemination of statistics, . . . the promotion and
   protection of foreign trade, and through the . . . patent laws."
2. General exercise of the state police power "to take action necessary
   for the protection of the public health, welfare, safety, and morals."
3. Emergency measures, including "the government operation of
   railways" and "such peace-time measures as the Adamson Act."
4. "Permanent regulatory measures" in specific areas like those
   involving products harmful to public health (e.g., the Pure Food
   and Drug Act) or those bound up in the labor question (e.g.,
   "compulsory social insurance and minimum wage, hours of labor,
   and child labor legislation").
5. Direct federal and state provision of goods and services including the
   activities of federal arsenals, "highway building and maintenance, the

issuing of currency, the postal service, police service, the Coast Guard, Geological Survey, weather bureau," and so on.[126]

These were just some of the policy consequences of the long progressive crusade for the social control of business and the economy. As Milton Handler concluded, "Our legislation thus runs the gamut of our economic problems and a list of all the varied objectives of these laws would encompass most of the aims of our economic order."[127] This modern American regulatory and administrative state left few aspects of economic life untouched through the first half of the twentieth century.

THE movements for antimonopoly, public utility, and unfair competition came together to form a new legal-political architecture for modern American economic regulation at both the state and federal levels. The modern legal, legislative, and administrative tools forged in the epic battles over railroads, monopolies, and corrupt business practices together moved the primary site of regulatory control beyond case-by-case limitations of common-law adjudication and corporate chartering. The regulation of the corporation per se—a corporation qua corporation—through the formal policing of the act of incorporation itself was no longer the singular focus of regulatory policy making. To the contrary, from general incorporation to *Santa Clara* to the revolutions in New Jersey and Delaware corporation law, there was a discernible progression toward what Gerard Henderson dubbed a more "liberal theory," which looked on the corporation "as a normal business unit, and its legal personality as no more than a convenient mechanism of commerce and industry."[128] By the time the Internal Revenue Service started counting such things in the early twentieth century, there were approximately 300,000 business corporations in the United States. And the American penchant for forming corporations of every conceivable size, purpose, and character—including churches and voluntary organizations—continued unabated for the rest of the century.

What the larger movements for the social control of business created, however, was a new site of countervailing state power and a new set of cross-cutting regulatory criteria and technologies. State legislative power continued to police economic activities deemed harmful or prejudicial to public health, safety, and welfare. Public utility law brought heightened scrutiny to businesses specially affected with public interest and held them to higher standards in terms of pricing, service, discrimination, and public convenience and necessity. Antimonopoly contributed an additional overarching concern with corporate structure, concentration, scale, holding companies, interlocking directorates, and the democratic balance of politico-economic power. Finally, unfair competition law greatly expanded administrative jurisdiction concerning unlawful business practices and corruption, from issues of fraud and secrecy to a vast array of new methods for restraining competition. Taken together, these legal, regulatory, and ultimately administrative policy innovations opened a new and expansive horizon for the future democratic control of American capitalism.

Two additional consequences flowed from these legal and political-economic developments. First, a modern law of regulated industries consolidated around the extraordinary array of new legal controls that now policed modern American business. The number of statutes (federal and state) as well as administrative rules and adjudications that now surrounded corporate and economic activity in the United States produced an entirely new field of legal and regulatory investigation, practice, and policy making. From the early efforts of Bruce Wyman and Felix Frankfurter to reckon with emergent modern regulation in public service corporations and the Interstate Commerce Commission, the regulatory field now expanded to include wider and wider swaths of the nation's major trades and industries.[129] The original railroad paradigm of "just, reasonable, and non-discriminatory rates and practices" via "publicly filed tariffs" was applied by Congress to more and more formally regulated industries in the Shipping Act, the Packers and Stockyards Act, the Communications Act, the Motor Carrier Act, the Federal Power Act, the Natural Gas Act, and ultimately the Civil Aeronautics Act.[130] State public utility commissions followed suit. But formal rate and price regulations were but part of the new regulated industries regime. As Willard Hurst pointed out, "By 1940 the Anti-trust Division of the Department of Justice was charged with duties respecting more than 30 acts of Congress, most of which had some direct relation to the allocation of control over the economy."[131] And the Department of Justice was not alone; the successive establishment of the Interstate Commerce Commission, the Federal Reserve Board, the Federal Trade Commission, the US Shipping Board, the Federal Power Commission, and the Federal Radio Commission marked a coming of age of the independent regulatory commission as a principal site of economic regulation and a new national centerpiece of regulated industries law.

The role of government in American business, industry, and commerce expanded so substantially in this period that increasing "government competition with private enterprise" became a matter of public concern. By the early 1930s, Harry Laidler estimated that the "entrance of government into the field of business" resulted in some 7,000 municipalities owning their own waterworks while 1,800 others owned electric lighting or gas plants. The progressive proliferation of public ownership included "municipal markets, beaches, piers, airports, golf courses, fuel yards, heating plants, ice plants, milk distributing agencies, and laundries."[132] And the development of public port, terminal, and transportation authorities brought even more so-called government in business.[133] In May 1932, a special congressional committee was formed to investigate "Government competition with private enterprise," spurred on by complaints about "the Government's usurpation of business functions" by the US Chamber of Commerce, the National Manufacturers' Association, and the Federation of American Business. The committee ultimately cataloged a range of "active and unfair competition" by the government across a staggering array of over three hundred separate industries, from defense manufacturing to lumber and timber.[134] Laidler summarized the policy motives for this turn to public production and ownership in terms that resonated with the broader progressive movement for democratic social control:

> Sometimes the extension of a public service was advocated as a means of providing for improved community health or safety, as in the case of our water supply, hospitals, and public fire departments; of developing better educational, cultural, and recreational facilities for the masses, as in the movement for public schools, playgrounds, museums, libraries, or concerts; or of promoting trade and commerce, as in the construction of public roads and the expansion of postal facilities. At other times its advocates urged it as a means of reducing living costs, of improving quality, of strengthening the nation's defense, of raising labor standards, of decreasing crime, of preventing the destruction of a natural resource, of obtaining governmental revenue, of discouraging the use of certain commodities, such as liquor, or encouraging the use of certain services, such as water, and of promoting, in various ways, the public welfare.[135]

The second important thing produced in the move from public utilities to regulated industries was a ready-made template for subsequent New Deal policy making. Indeed, the regulatory themes of police power, public utility, antimonopoly, and unfair competition came together in some of Franklin D. Roosevelt's most specific and far-reaching campaign proposals. In his famous Portland speech on "public utilities" in September 1932, Roosevelt synthesized multiple aspects of the progressive vision. He began by underscoring the "vast importance of the American utilities in our economic life" and proceeded to outline the first principles that governed his overarching political-economic philosophy. Those first principles were the bedrock of the idea of governmental police power: "The object of Government is the welfare of the people. . . . When the interests of the many are concerned, the interests of the few must yield." Government was to be "of service"—especially when the common public possessions and resources "that belong to all of us—that belong to the Nation" were "at stake." Roosevelt re-counted the legal history of the public utility going all the way back to Lord Hale, noting "the rendering of good service was a necessary and public responsibility." And he noted the degree to which public responsibility for and supervision of these common public goods generalized out from the common law to legislative regulation to administrative commission—the latter of which he called "a Tribune of the people." He then denounced the monopoly—"the Insull monstrosity"—a sprawling billion-dollar holding company built up against the people and sound public policy indulging excessive prices, watered stock, and arbitrary inflation of capital accounts. "These financial monstrosities," Roosevelt noted, indulged methods of "private manipulation" for "selfish greed" not seen since the early days of "railroad wild-catting." Taking note of a recent report by the Federal Trade Commission, Roosevelt called for a "new deal" culminating in regu-lation and control of such holding companies by a powerful independent regulatory agency like the Federal Power Commission. He even floated the possibility of a federal "governmentally owned and operated service" when "reasonable and good service is refused by private capital."

Roosevelt closed his extraordinary address on monopoly, public utility, and governmental regulation of public goods in the public interest by ad-mitting his ideas on the topic were "radical." As he concluded his pithy summation of the progressive agenda for the democratic control of busi-ness and regulated industries, "My policy is as radical as the Constitution of the United States."[136] Roosevelt's speech on public utility, antimonopoly, and unfair competition anticipated some of the most ambitious regulatory and administrative innovations of his mature New Deal. Indeed, the secu-rities and public utility concerns outlined in Portland in 1932 ultimately found their way into the Securities Act of 1933, the Securities Exchange Act of 1934, and the Public Utility Holding Company Act of 1935, marking a national consolidation of sorts for the regulatory and administrative re-forms of the long progressive campaign for a more democratic control of business and industry. And the monopoly, unfair competition, and democ-racy worries expressed in Portland continued to inform the vision of a fun-damental "conflict between dictatorial industrial power and democracy" that guided New Deal antitrust into the late 1930s. Roosevelt described the continued fight against "new dynasties" and "economic royalists" in 1936: "We are waging a great and successful war. It is not alone a war against want and destitution and economic demoralization. . . . It is a war for the survival of democracy."[137]

6

DEMOCRATIC ADMINISTRATION

Public Service and Social Provision

Society constantly gives birth to new needs, and each one of
them is for the government a new source of power.
—ALEXIS DE TOCQUEVILLE

So far we have examined transformations in key building blocks of the
modern American state and a new democracy: citizenship, police power,
public utility, social legislation, and antimonopoly. However, another crucial element in modern American statecraft has been implicated but not yet
thoroughly discussed: modern administration and administrative law.

Bruce Wyman, who along with Frank Goodnow, Ernst Freund, and Felix
Frankfurter has long been considered a founder of the field of administrative law, defined it in 1903 as that "body of rules which defines the authority and the responsibility" of departments of the government and
"regulates the right and duties of officials in their various relations."[1] Departments of the government included everything from officers, agencies,
commissions, and boards to bureaus, authorities, departments, and divisions. Such entities existed at every level of government from the municipal to the national and were surprisingly sprawling and differentiated
given the roughly 100,000 or so separate jurisdictional units and governing
districts that together constituted the United States of America.[2]

From Reconstruction to the start of the New Deal, administration in the
United States underwent an extraordinary expansion. As a consequence, a
distinctly modern concept of administrative law was born. Ernst Freund
gave Frank Goodnow credit for popularizing the term "administrative
law"—"its subject matter being the administration of public affairs, as distinguished from legislation on the one side and from the jurisdiction of the
courts on the other."[3] And the US Supreme Court followed suit, using the
term explicitly (courtesy of Goodnow's *Comparative Administrative Law*)
for the first time in its 1909 *Reports*. Though "administrative law [did] not

come like a thief in the night," Felix Frankfurter accurately noted, "general recognition" and "self-conscious direction" in the legal profession were associated with this founding generation.[4] As Chief Justice Charles Evans Hughes summarized in 1931, "The distinctive development of our era is that the activities of the people are largely controlled by government bureaus in State and Nation. It has been well said that this multiplication of administrative bodies with large powers has raised anew for our law, after three centuries, the problem of 'administrative justice.'"[5] These were the rumblings of a modern administrative revolution.

Something of the substantive policy implications of that revolution were suggested by Felix Frankfurter in his original administrative law casebook: "Governmental regulation of banking, insurance, public utilities, industry, finance, immigration, the professions, health and morals, in short, the inevitable response of government to the needs of modern society, is building up a body of enactments not written by legislatures and of adjudications not made by courts. . . . These powers are lodged in a vast congeries of agencies," the systematic exploration of which was "the concern of Administrative Law." The modern American citizen was now far more likely to be affected in everyday life by administrative processes rather than by direct legislative or judicial action. Kenneth Culp Davis supplemented Frankfurter's original policy listing with significant examples of what administration protected the American public against by the end of this formative era: "excessive prices of electricity, gas, telephone, and other utility services; unreasonableness in rates, schedules, and services of airlines, railroads, street cars, and buses; disregard for the public interest in radio and television and chaotic conditions for broadcasting; unwholesome meat and poultry; adulteration in food; fraud or inadequate disclosure in the sale of securities; physically unsafe locomotives, ships, airplanes, bridges, elevators; unfair labor practices either by employers or unions; false advertising and other unfair or deceptive practices; inadequate safety appliances; uncompensated injuries related to employment; cessation of income during temporary unemployment; subminimum wages; poverty in old age; industrial plants in residential areas; loss of bank deposits."[6] Following Max Weber's lead, Theodore Lowi deemed this expansive application of rationalized social control through administrative law "the *sine qua non* of modernity" itself.[7]

The nature and significance of this turn-of-the-century administrative revolution, of course, have not escaped the notice of historians, social scientists, and legal scholars. Indeed, a cottage industry of academic work has grown up around the rise of the modern American administrative state.[8] But much like conventional wisdom on the nature of the American state itself, orthodox thinking on American administration and administrative law has often obscured the most significant aspects of this modern governmental revolution. The essence of the problem is the degree to which modern administration is still traditionally viewed as a problem of command and control and the rightful power of rule.[9] Here, the formalist vestiges of prerogative, sovereignty, and even lordship continue their reign in an administrative discussion framed primarily around juristic conceptions of delegation, separation of powers, the rule of law, and constitutional limitations. Debate about the modern "problem of bureaucracy" continues to revolve around the coercive and extractive powers of government and the ever-present threat of bureaucratic despotism posed by a distant and removed central authority. Behind this orthodoxy looms the postwar ideological specter (made famous by Friedrich Hayek) of administration as the first step on the road to the totalitarian menace of bureaucratization, planning, and ultimately serfdom.[10]

Of late, however, dissatisfaction with this conventional portrait of the problem of bureaucracy has grown into the beginnings of a substantial revision.[11] In place of administration as antidemocratic threat, emphasis is increasingly placed instead on a much longer history of the crucial role of administration in the actualization of everyday democratic governance. In place of formalistic constructions of top-down rule and coercive command and control, this revision illuminates another side of administration— administrative power as the disposition of things. Here, attention is placed squarely on administration's necessary role in the implementation of substantive public policies: the actual distribution, redistribution, and regulation of public goods and public services.[12] The administrative state was not constructed for the independent benefit of autonomous public administrators. Rather, it was the functional vehicle of the larger socioeconomic policy goal of public provision so as to achieve a more just distribution of power and resources in a democratizing and modernizing society. Here emphasis shifted from means to ends, inputs to outputs, rules to policies, rights to regulations as administration and administrative law were deployed as modern tools and pragmatic technologies for solving everyday public problems pertaining to pressing public needs.[13] By highlighting the substantive socioeconomic dimension of administration, progressive reformers developed a more robust and positive conception of administration as a necessary part of any modern democratic state. Substantive administration was a key component of the new democratic projects concerning citizenship, police power, public utility, social policy, and antimonopoly.

This chapter takes up this new democratic view of progressive public administration. It outlines the extraordinary growth of American administration at the turn of the twentieth century as well as the historic progressive crusade for administrative reform along more democratic and public-service lines. Two kinds of reforms were especially central to progressive administration. First, and most famously, progressives obsessed about *political* administration. They confronted the real public problem of increased political corruption emerging within Gilded Age industrialism—a new feudatory of robber barons, politicos, bosses, patronage, privilege, and private interest. "The rule of the oligarchy," Fred Howe called it, producing an anti-democratic "carnival of legislation for the benefit of the few."[14] With the pervasive sense that existing institutions and spheres of American governance—legislative, executive, and judicial—were now captured by private interests, progressives turned to administrative reform in an effort to resuscitate the democratic ideal of government for distinctly public rather than exclusively private, special, or pecuniary interests. In the city and the reform of municipal administration, progressives launched bold experiments in democratic administrative transformation.

Second, progressives pioneered a more substantive *socioeconomic* administration in the area of public provision. For beyond the problem of political corruption, late nineteenth-century industrial change also exposed, with especially searing effect, the social problem of American material inequality and economic deprivation. From Jacob Riis's evocative photographs of immigrant tenement labor to Edith and Grace Abbott's assault on traditional poor law to John Commons's pioneering work on labor reform, progressives launched a far-reaching policy conversation about economic insecurity, inadequate standards of living, and the unequal distribution of wealth in modern America.[15] Reformers viewed this baseline economic precarity and inequality as nothing short of a failure of substantive American democracy, requiring radical legal, institutional, and policy innovation. In response, they pioneered new administrative approaches to the public problem of social welfare in major reforms of both poor law administration and labor administration. This progressive transformation of American public provision and social service was a centerpiece of this modern administrative revolution.

With the proliferation of new technologies of socioeconomic provision and political reform, the American state—along all of its jurisdictional dimensions (local, state, and federal)—reached an inflection point in modern development. Positive conceptions of statecraft and law yielded a more pragmatic and instrumental vision of government directed toward the resolution of public problems and the satisfaction of social needs. Public administration and administrative law achieved a new self-consciousness and visibility as the principle vehicles for the general delivery of an ever-expanding array of state services. The period from 1866 to 1932 was nothing less than an age of democratic administration.

The Growth of Modern American Administration

The first thing to note about the history and trajectory of administration is that administration is coincident with governance. Far from being a modern invention—or some kind of radical departure from an original political or legal tradition—administration is among the oldest practices of governments.[16] Indeed, it is impossible to conceive of government without administration.[17] Laws need to be enforced, legislation needs to be implemented, collective goods need to be secured. Governance is mostly a pragmatic matter of actions and practices, making administration perhaps the most truly reflective aspect of legal and political culture.

Bernard Bailyn famously found the "origins of American politics" in the formidable and positive administrative tasks of the first colonial legislatures from land distribution to the building of wharves, roads, ferries, public vessels, and civic buildings to the establishment of towns, schools, colleges, and religious institutions. About 60 percent of the laws passed in colonial Virginia, Bailyn noted, were essentially administrative—"pertaining to social and economic problems."[18] Hendrik Hartog followed this trail of administration from colonial legislatures into county courts in eighteenth-century Massachusetts, identifying a "continuum of criminal and administrative action" wherein court responsibilities "were defined less by its formal legal jurisdiction than by the needs of governance"—especially the administration of liquor licensing, poor relief, and road building and repair.[19] By the early nineteenth century, Alexis de Tocqueville deemed this pervasive, popular, and local approach to positive administration something like the essence of democracy in America. Tocqueville was fascinated by the "municipal administration" of New England and the array of local officers—"selectmen," "assessors," "collectors," "surveyors of highways," and "tithing men"—carrying out the administrative policies of "well-regulated" communities, from the "construction of sewers" and the location of "slaughterhouses" to "public health" administration and "licensing."[20] John Stuart Mill, who credited *Democracy in America* with revolutionizing his thought beyond utilitarianism, took special note of those portions of Tocqueville dedicated to American local administrators and the "habit of superintending" local interests and the "proceedings of their government": "tithing-men, listers, haywards, chimney-viewers, fence-viewers. . . . , timber-measurers, and inspectors of weights and measures."[21] Administrative boards, commissions, departments, and offices were the heart of a highly visible and often-commented-upon early American governmental tradition with deep roots in the early republic.

This early original penchant for administration was hardly confined to local, regional, or municipal governance. In England, as John Brewer and Steve Pincus have most effectively argued, the rationalization and centralization of nation-state administration—especially around fiscal and military prerogatives—was an important harbinger of modernity (and revolution) since at least the seventeenth century. For Brewer, "The late seventeenth and eighteenth centuries saw an astonishing transformation in British government, one which put muscle on the bones of the British body politic, increasing its endurance, strength and reach." At the heart of this governmental revolution were the clerks—those "pale and shadowy figures" at "the seat of dullness"—who implemented "the growth of a sizable public administration devoted to organizing the fiscal and military activities of the state." Pincus summed up the broad administrative trend that upended Europe from the Glorious Revolution to the French Revolution as "state modernization": "An effort to centralize and bureaucratize political authority, an initiative to transform the military using the most up-to-date techniques, a program to accelerate economic growth and shape the contours of society using the tools of the state, and the deployment of techniques allowing the state to gather information."[22]

Contravening theories of American exceptionalism, this early modernization of national administration did not bypass the early United States. Jerry Mashaw has now definitively established the long and deep historical origins of American administrative law and a national administrative state. "From the earliest day of the republic," Mashaw demonstrated, "Congress delegated broad authority to administrators, armed them with extrajudicial coercive powers, created systems of administrative adjudication, and specifically authorized administrative rulemaking." Of the fifty-one major federal administrative agencies at the time of the Administrative Procedure Act (1946), eleven traced their origins to statutes passed before the Civil War—and most of those to the extraordinary creation of federal administration in the very first Congress: the US Customs Service, Veterans Pensions, Patent Office, Office of Indian Affairs, Commissioner of Internal Revenue, General Land Office, Bureau of Marine Inspection and Navigation, Passport Division, Office of the Chief Engineers, Office of the Comptroller of the Currency, and Postmaster General.[23] Mashaw described the vital activities (and internal administrative rules and practices) of a wide range of administrative officers from the attorney general and US attorneys to Treasury and customs and postal officials, culminating as early as 1852 in a national steamboat inspection regime that administratively "combined something of the 'New Deal' independent regulatory commission with 'Great Society' health and safety regulation."[24] Nicholas Parrillo has supplemented this rich portrait with an even wider accounting of the army of administrative officials enabled by the comprehensive fee, prize, and bounty systems that proliferated before the modern "salary revolution" in American government: district attorney fees for successful prosecutions, tax "ferret" fees for detecting tax evaders, naval bounties for captured ships, land officer fees for homestead applications, government doctor fees for deciding veteran's benefits, and so on.[25] National administration and a surprisingly sophisticated structure of administrative law were entrenched in the United States for a century *before* the so-called invention of modern administration in the Interstate Commerce Act of 1887.

So we now have a new and long history of administration to contemplate from 1787 to 1887 and beyond. Clearly, administration is not a recent American invention. The question remains, however: What exactly is the relationship between the sprawling early American regime of administration irrefutably cataloged by administrative historians and the changes in administrative regulation that took place at the turn of the twentieth century? Are these regimes of a piece—similar, contiguous, and continuous—reflective of an evolution rather than a revolution? Or are there still some dramatic differences and changes circa 1887 that suggest not a move from absence to presence but perhaps a transformation nonetheless?

Despite deep historical roots in the American governmental tradition, the increased proliferation, professionalization, centralization, and rationalization of administration in the late nineteenth and early twentieth century amounted to a change in kind—a transformation nonetheless. While commentators like Tocqueville long recognized the roots of administration in the practical politics of addressing social problems and meeting collective needs (from poor relief to local infrastructure development), the very nature and conception of those problems and those needs were fundamentally transformed in the era of mass society and mass democracy. The basic direction of change moved distinctly from a political culture of particularity with a wide tolerance of distinction to one of generality with a preference for uniformity. Localized, jurisdictional, and quasi-private rule making and office holding ineluctably gave way to a more centralized, political, and distinctly public vision of administration and administrative law. What Nick Parrillo called "familiar imposition"—an older local form of governance featuring norms imposed with "reference to a single face-to-face community"—steadily transitioned toward a more impersonal, universal, and external administrative regime of "alien imposition" where more professionalized officers administered general rules for governing an expansive nation of strangers.[26] As was the case with the law of police power and public utility, older sets of particularized common-law rules designed for the private adjudication of individualized disputes—in this case, the common law of officers and office holding—ultimately yielded to more public, generalized, and ultimately nationalized administrative authorities. Just as conceptions of national citizenship and constitutional rights grudgingly shed an earlier history of localism, particularity, and an endless series of distinctions and discriminations, the nature of social representation through democratic politics and statecraft moved slowly but surely toward more generalized conceptions of social need and public interest.[27] The political culture of generality involved a new vision of a democratic society responsible for the production of its own collective future as well as a new understanding of positive and purposeful political freedom.[28] Administration was a primary vehicle of this modern vision of state and law—a new public administration and administrative law committed to serving society's needs and meeting a redefined general public interest.

Such new and positive ideas of statecraft, law, and administration quickly moved the American polity beyond traditional concerns with the maintenance of public order and early techniques of local-legal policing and fiscal-military organization. A distinctly modern notion of a *public service state* came into being, self-consciously oriented around the significant new obligations of tackling large-scale public problems and satisfying ever-expanding socioeconomic needs. No one apprehended this functionalist shift from "public authority" to "public service"—potestas to potentia—better than the French legal sociologist and state theorist Léon Duguit. He argued that patrimonial and authoritarian forms of state were in decline amid the rise of new forms of social interdependence and democratic political aspiration. As he observed, "Government and its officials are no longer the masters of men imposing the sovereign will on their subjects. . . . They are simply the managers of the nation's business."[29] Duguit came to the attention of most Americans through the interventions of Harold Laski, who counseled Roscoe Pound that "the most striking change in the political organization of the last half century is the rapidity with which . . . the state has been driven to assume a positive character. . . . We live in a new world, and a new theory of the state is necessary to its adequate operation."[30] Laski's other chief correspondent, Felix Frankfurter, was already building such a new theory of the state around what he called "public services and the public." Beyond the "traditional functions of police and justice," Frankfurter identified a new relationship of "the public and its government" structured around the new "tasks of government, the demands citizens make upon government, [and] the instruments by which these demands are executed."[31] In consequence, modern public law added to its purview an ever-expanding body of rules and institutions for the efficient management, organization, and control of public services and policies. As Duguit concluded, "Public law is thus no longer the body of rules regulating the relation of a sovereign state with its subjects; it is rather the body of rules inherently necessary to the organization and management of certain services."[32]

This was the road to a reimagined administration and administrative law. The modern reorientation of a reorganized state around the provision of public services brought increased attention to the science of public administration and the development of administrative law as scholars like Frank Goodnow, Ernst Freund, Bruce Wyman, Woodrow Wilson, Felix Frankfurter, and James Landis elevated the topics to new heights of analytical scrutiny and self-consciousness. Two generations of political and legal scholars worked tirelessly, as Ernst Freund put it, to make administrative law "more familiar to the public, and especially to the legal profession," turning it into one of the more "recognized branches of public law."[33] Modern administration was becoming a central part of what Woodrow Wilson would call the "new meaning of government." Wilson held that the expansion and rationalization of governmental administration was a necessary product of the increasing functions and demands placed on modern social service states, from conservation to pure food and drugs to labor and price regulation to public health and sanitation: "Nowadays we consider it the duty of statesmen to see that women are not overburdened with work; that children are not dwarfed and stunted by too great a burden of labor; that factories are properly ventilated; that dangerous machinery is properly guarded; that rivers are kept pure and cities clean; that hospitals are provided; that education is put within the reach of everybody, and that the humblest citizen of our country has a full chance to live and thrive."[34] "Administration is everywhere putting its hands to new undertakings," Wilson argued in "The Study of Administration" (1887).[35] In "The Task of Administrative Law," Felix Frankfurter similarly connected the growth of administration and administrative law to new tasks of state: "Profound new forces call for new social inventions. . . . The 'great society,' with its permeating influence of technology, large-scale industry, and progressive urbanization, presses its problems." Leonard D. White defined "public administration" simply as "the management of men and materials in the accomplishment of the purposes of the state"—"the most efficient utilization of the resources at the disposal of officials" and "the most rapid and complete achievement of public purposes."[36]

As Freund, Frankfurter, White, and many others made clear, the turnof-the-century revolution in administration was very much concerned with efficiency, expertise, professionalization, rationalization, centralization, and scientific and technical management and organization. But at its core, they emphasized the degree to which the self-conscious development of modern administration and administrative law turned on a new generalization of social and public interest. The invention of modern American administration was distinctly connected to a positive reform agenda with the progressive idea of the state serving as an efficient mechanism for securing larger social and public purposes. Herbert Croly famously articulated a broad vision of progressive democracy bound to the "expression of a permanent public interest" as "interested in efficient administration as it is in reconstructive legislation."[37] For Felix Frankfurter, public service, public interest, and public trust were at the very heart of the project of administrative law from the first state railroad commissions to the more omnibus state public utility commissions to the national development of the first independent regulatory commissions. The "range and complexity" of these commissions, Frankfurter contended, "constituted new political inventions responsive to the pressure of new economic and social facts." Frankfurter frequently invoked Governor Charles Evans Hughes's famous 1907 defense of administrative regulation: "Domestic commerce must be regulated by the State. . . . There is also need of regulation and strict supervision to ensure adequate service and due regard for the convenience and safety of the public. The most practicable way of attaining these ends is for the Legislature to confer proper power upon a subordinate administrative body."[38] "Commodore Vanderbilt's 'the public be damned' had at last a counterpoise" in what Frankfurter called "the quiet work of public administration"— "solid proof that government could meet needs of society at once the most complicated and fundamental."[39]

With the development of a new and positive conception of law and the state increasingly oriented toward public service, social needs, and general welfare, the American administrative state and administrative law underwent an audacious expansion. This was a governmental revolution secured in action as well as ideas. And there are innumerable sites to see its real-world consequences: from the development of a professional civil service inaugurated with the Pendleton Act of 1883; to the research, bureau, and budget movements; to the periodic efforts for governmental reorganization at federal, state, and municipal levels; to the application of techniques of scientific management to public administration.[40] But perhaps the best quick way to assess the scale and scope of the administrative revolution is to simply take stock of the proliferation of administrative agencies. Frankfurter himself concentrated primarily on the significance of the more-or-less independent national regulatory commissions:

The Interstate Commerce Commission with its tight grip on railroads, telephones, telegraphs, and pipe lines; the Federal Reserve Board created in 1913 to regulate the delicate fiscal mechanism of the country; the Federal

Trade Commission established in 1913; the Federal Tariff Commission of 1916; the Federal Farm Loan Board, the beginning of active measures for the relief of agriculture; the Federal Water Power Commission around which will center some of the basic problems of the years to come; the Federal Radio Commission in 1927 . . . all imply a breadth and depth of governmental activities that make the tasks of government today really different in kind and not merely in degree from those that confronted government a hundred years ago. There are wholly new interactions between citizen and government.[41]

In his compilation "Executive Departments, Bureaus and Independent Establishments of the United States Government," George Cyrus Thorpe estimated that by 1925 some *"two hundred* bureaus and commissions, or similar establishments, whose functions have been accumulating for a century" were now chargeable with the federal government business "in which a citizen may be concerned."[42] Even with a conservative definition of "agency," the growth of national administration was considerable (see Table 6.1).[43]

But though histories of administration and administrative law tend to focus on the national government, it is important to acknowledge strikingly similar developments at the state and local levels as well. Administrative centralization and rationalization was not a one-way street to national consolidation. As Samuel Hays pointed out, an "upward shift" in "decision-making and power" was characteristic of much social and political organization in this period from grassroots and local institutions to municipal government and state administration.[44] Indeed, the basic pattern of agency development in New York State very much mirrored the national story (see Table 6.2). The 1916 listing in *Officers, Boards and Commission of Texas* compiled by the Texas Legislative Reference Division also attested to the prolific establishment of an administrative public service state on the state level.[45]

At the municipal level, the expansion of administration accompanied an equally rapid growth in governmental services. The Brookings Institution compiled a chronological accounting of the introduction of public services in the city of Detroit, which expanded from 23 activities in 1824 to 306 in 1920.[46] Essential services included street paving (1835), sewerage (1836), water supply (1836), elementary school (1842), street lighting (1850), high school (1858), library (1865), organized police patrol (1865), sanitary patrol (1867), organized firefighting (1867), food inspection (1879), outdoor relief (1883), quarantine of contagious diseases (1887), garbage collection (1888), street cleaning (1895), playgrounds (1904), public health

Table 6.1. Federal Agencies, 1860–1932 *Official Register of the United States*

Year Started	Agency	Year Started	Agency	Year Started	Agency
1861	Government Printing Office	1910	Commission of Fine Arts	1923	Personnel Classification Board
1862	Bureau of Equipment and Recruitment	1913	Arlington Memorial Bridge Commission	1924	Board of Tax Appeals
1862	Treasury Department, Bureau of Internal Revenue	1913	Federal Reserve Board	1924	Federal Oil Conservation Board
1862	Department of Agriculture	1913	Department of Labor	1924	George Washington Bicentennial Commission
1864	War Department, Bureau of Military Justice	1914	Federal Trade Commission	1926	Board of Mediation
1865	Bureau of Freedmen, Refugees and Abandoned Lands	1915	National Advisory Committee for Aeronautics	1926	National Capital Park and Planning Commission
1865	National Home for Disabled Volunteer Soldiers	1916	Bureau of Efficiency	1927	Federal Radio Commission
1870	Department of Justice	1916	Tariff Commission	1927	Mount Rushmore National Memorial Commission
1871	Civil Service Commission	1916	United States Shipping Board and Merchant Fleet Corporation	1928	Porto (Puerto) Rican Hurricane Relief Commission
1874	Bureau of Engraving and Printing	1917	Alaska Relief Fund	1928	United States Supreme Court Building Commission
1883	Civil Service Commission	1917	Employees' Compensation Commission	1929	Federal Farm Board
1887	Interstate Commerce Commission	1917	Federal Board for Vocational Education	1929	George Rogers Clark Sesquicentennial Commission

(*continued*)

Table 6.1. *(continued)*

Year Started	Agency	Year Started	Agency	Year Started	Agency
1890	United States Geographic Board	1918	Housing Corporation	1930	Investigation of Enforcement of Prohibition and Other Laws
1894	Bureau of Agricultural Engineering	1919	Bureau of Prohibition	1930	Veteran's Administration
1902	International Bureau of the American Republics	1920	Federal Power Commission	1931	Yorktown Sesquicentennial Commission
1903	Department of Commerce	1921	General Accounting Office		
1904	Isthmian Canal Commission	1923	American Battle Monuments		

Source: Official Register of the United States (Washington, DC: Government Printing Office, 1816–1959).

nurses (1908), traffic control (1909), and technical high school (1912). Public health services alone grew to encompass more than forty-four items, including sanitary patrol (1867), food inspection (1879), general hospital (1883), contagious disease hospital (1885), milk inspection (1887), bacteriology laboratory (1893), medical inspection (1902), tuberculosis hospital (1906), venereal disease clinic school children (1906), school nurses (1908), Pasteur Institute (1915), health education nurses (1920), medical college (1920), maternity hospital (1922), mosquito clinic (1925), and cancer clinic (1928). Educational services swelled to sixty-five categories, including elementary schools (1842), high school (1858), classes for foreigners (1875), teachers' college (1881), truancy police (1883), classes for incorrigibles (1883), free textbooks (1892), kindergarten (1895), classes for the deaf (1899), evening high school (1905), classes for defective speech (1910), mental inspection of cripples and mental defectives schoolchildren (1911), technical high school (1912), classes for the anemic and blind (1912), junior college (1917), parental school (1918), medical college (1920), general college (1925), law college (1927), and radio instruction (1930). Other services included a zoo (1890), an art library (1893), bathing beaches (1894), the inspection of electrical wiring (1896), band concerts (1898), comfort stations (1906), old-age support (1914), family adjustment services

Table 6.2. New York State Agencies, 1860–1932 *Guide to Records in the New York State Archives*

Year Started	Agency	Year Started	Agency	Year Started	Agency
1862	National Guard	1901	Department of Health	1921	Board of Estimate and Control
1867	Board of Charities/Social Welfare	1901	Department of Labor	1921	Automobile Bureau
1868	Fisheries Commission	1902	Water Storage Commission	1922	Water Control Commission
1870	Rinderpest Commission	1904	River Improvement Commission	1922	Veterans' Relief Commission
1872	Temporary State Park Commission	1904	Department of Education	1922	Commission on Pensions
1874	Commission in Lunacy	1905	Water Supply Commission	1923	Housing and Regional Planning Bureau
1876	Office of Superintendent of State Prisons	1905	Commission of Gas and Electricity	1923	Bureau of Relief of Sick and Disabled Veterans
1876	Office of Superintendent of Public Works	1906	New Prison Commission	1923	Department of Public Works
1879	Commissioners of Quarantine	1907	Commission on Probation	1924	Council of Parks
1880	Board of Health	1907	Public Service Commission	1924	Bonus Commission
1882	Board of Railroad Commissioners	1908	Board of Parole for State Prisons	1924	Bureau of Motor Vehicles
1883	Civil Service Commission	1908	Department of Highways	1924	Board of Transportation
1883	Bureau of Labor Statistics	1911	Office of Harbor Masters	1925	Department of Correction
1884	Dairy Commission	1911	Conservation Commission	1925	Department of Mental Hygiene
1885	Forest Commission	1912	State Hospital Commission	1925	Division of Mental Disease
1886	Office of Factory Inspector	1913	Board of Estimate	1925	Department of Audit and Control
1886	Board of Mediation and Arbitration	1913	Department of Efficiency and Economy	1925	Department of Law
1889	Naval Militia	1913	Monuments Commission	1926	Division of the Budget

(*continued*)

Table 6.2. (*continued*)

Year Started	Agency	Year Started	Agency	Year Started	Agency
1889	Weather Bureau	1913	State Commission for the Blind	1926	Division of Parole
1891	Board of Port Wardens	1913	Public Health Council	1926	Board of Housing
1891	Board of Rapid Transit Commissioners	1913	Industrial Board	1926	Division of Military and Naval Affairs
1893	Department of Agriculture	1913	Workmen's Compensation Commission	1926	State Racing Commission
1894	Commission of Prisons	1914	Department of Foods and Markets	1926	Department of Charities/Social Affairs
1895	Fisheries, Forest and Game Commission	1915	Tax Commission	1926	Department of Social Welfare
1896	Commissioner of Excise	1915	Department of Taxation and Finance	1926	Department of Agriculture and Markets
1896	Board of Tax Commissioners	1915	Industrial Commission	1926	Department of Civil Service
1897	Inspector of Steam Vessels	1917	Division of State Police	1926	Department of Public Service
1897	Forest Preserve Board	1917	Department of Farms and Markets	1926	Department of State
1898	Metropolitan Election District Bureau	1917	Council of Defense	1927	Land Board
1899	Department of Architecture	1918	Commission for Mental Defectives	1927	Conservation Department
1900	State Fair Commission	1920	Commission on Boundary Waters	1931	Power Authority
1900	Forest, Fish and Game Commission	1920	Salt Water Bays Commission	1932	Division of Housing
1900	Tenement House Commission	1921	Transit Commission	1932	Banking Board
1901	Board of Commissioners on Paroled Prisoners	1921	Water Power Commission	1932	Bridge Authority

Source: New York State Archives and Records Administration, *Guide to Records in the New York State Archives* (Albany: University of the State of New York, State Education Department, State Archives and Records Administration, 1993).

(1915), recreation camps (1917), an employment bureau (1920), music, drama, and fine arts libraries (1921), golf courses (1922), symphony concerts (1925), a prison farm for women (1928), and a municipal lodging house (1930). The provision of such essential public services in municipalities became one of the foundations for the development of the new progressive concept of democratic administration.

Administration, Public and Democratic

There is no shortage of political, legal, and historical assessments of this modern administrative revolution. To date, however, the dominant interpretations have been captured by a single, overriding theme—the rise of modern bureaucracy and technocracy. Here the modern history of the administrative state is subsumed beneath a veritable bureaucracy fetish. Max Weber contributed the archetype, placing at the very center of modernity "the basic fact of the irresistible advance of bureaucratization," wherein "the bureaucratic apparatus" concentrates the "means of operation."[47] As Talcott Parsons once put it, "Roughly, for Weber, bureaucracy plays the part that the class struggle played for Marx."[48] Jürgen Habermas echoed, "For Weber, bureaucratization is a key to understanding modern societies."[49] Progress toward "bureaucratic officialdom" and the "bureaucratic state" became "the unambiguous yardstick" for assessing modernization and its turn toward systems of rationality, centralization, professionalization, expertise, and autonomous administration. "Routines of administration"— "adjudicating and administering according to rationally established law and regulation"—were necessary accoutrements of a modern system of rule necessarily and unavoidably bureaucratic.[50]

Of course, Max Weber was notoriously ambivalent about the normative implications of this modern governmental turn to bureaucratic administration. And his pessimistic assessments of modernity's "iron cage" and "shell of bondage" have been seconded by a legion of students of bureaucracy who see the administrative revolution as a troubling departure from original traditions of self-rule, popular governance, and political autonomy—raising concerns about technocracy, the relentless conquest of instrumental rationality, and roads to future serfdom and despotism. From propagandistic critiques like James Beck's *Wonderland of Bureaucracy* to popular explorations like Walter Lippmann's *The Phantom Public* to political and sociological assessments like James Burnham's *The Managerial Revolution* and C. Wright Mills's *The Power Elite*, treatments of modern administration as antidemocratic bureaucracy and elite technocracy abound.[51] For Habermas, "the mounting bureaucratization of the administration in state and society" and the rise of planning, distribution, and government intervention by "highly specialized experts" spelled the doom of the "critical publicity" of the bourgeois public sphere. Like his Frankfurt school colleagues, Habermas fretted about "the lure of technocracy," the divorce of organized system from ethical life, and the ultimate threat that "the technical means of destruction increases with the technical means of satisfying needs."[52] Even Pierre Rosanvallon assessed these turn-of-the-century administrative developments as bureaucratic, technocratic, and ultimately worrisome: "The themes of efficiency and rational administration reconnected in this way with the old cult of capacities," wherein "executive administrative power found a new centrality in both France and the United States." Such elite technocratic power reflected an inability or at least an unwillingness to "think government democratically."[53] Of course, a flood of late twentieth-century neoliberal critiques of the modern regulatory and social-welfare state loudly echoed such indictments of the dangerous, antidemocratic nature of bureaucratic administration.[54]

In law, this antibureaucratic position has a distinguished pedigree. Building on a nineteenth-century British constitutional literature increasingly aimed—in Henry Maine's words—at "applying the curb to popular impulses," Albert Venn Dicey made the formal legal case against administration as bureaucracy—as Gallican droit administratif.[55] Dicey viewed the historic English rule-of-law tradition as inherently antithetical to an administrative law that he deemed foreign and dangerous: "The whole scheme of administrative law was opposed to . . . essential characteristics of English institutions." He saw seeds of tyranny in administrators "who, if not actually part of the executive, are swayed by official sympathies, and who are inclined to consider the interest of the state or of the government more important than strict regard to the legal rights of individuals."[56] As Felix Frankfurter noted, "Few law books in modern times have had an influence comparable to that produced by the brilliant obfuscation of Dicey's *Law of the Constitution*." But despite what Frankfurter described as Dicey's "sociological sterility" and "misconceptions and myopia," about the "rule of law" versus "the development of administrative law," Dicey's indictment of administration as foreign statism has continued to influence "generations of judges and lawyers."[57] In but the most recent revival of the Diceyan critique, Philip Hamburger deemed the administrative power underwriting the modern American bureaucracy nothing short of "absolutist," "extralegal," "supralegal," "unconstitutional," and basically "unlawful."[58]

All these approaches to the modern administrative revolution curiously elide one of its foundational premises—democracy. Administration and administrative law were crucial parts of the transformation of public law that created a modern democratic state in the United States. In contrast to conventional interpretive emphasis on bureaucracy versus the rule of law, the actual founders of modern American administrative law explicitly claimed a democratic mandate. As early as 1887, Woodrow Wilson insisted that modern American administration was not about bureaucracy and technocracy: "To fear the creation of a domineering, illiberal officialism . . . is to miss altogether the principle upon which I wish most to insist. That principle is, that administration in the United States must be at all points sensitive to public opinion."[59] It was part of the "new meaning" of democratic government, Wilson insisted, "that its resources are not to be put at the disposal of a governing class or of any limited set of governing influences, but that it must exercise its authority . . . for the whole people." Wilson pointed to the neighborhood meetings, local assemblies, state conventions, and national conferences "held by people of every sort interested in every kind of occupation" that actually generated the claims increasingly being made on government in "the common interest."[60] Sentiments like these at the very foundation of modern American administration encapsulated the dominant themes of progressive new democracy—from its antiformalism to its substantive vision of democracy, from its critique of private power and plutocracy to its endorsement of public interest. While rationalization, systemization, and professionalization were certainly key aspects of modern governmental process, the administrative revolution was born of a radical reform energy and an insurgent self-consciousness concerning the new inequalities, exclusions, oppressions, and acute social needs that threatened the democratic legitimacy of American public and private life. In place of bureaucracy or technocracy, the history of the origins of the modern American administrative state must be understood in the context of such new democratic principles.

Indeed, the first thing to note about the architects of modern American administrative law is that they were radical antiformalists in the new democratic tradition. Frank Goodnow produced many technical treatises on administrative law, but he was also author of one of the era's most influential and radical critiques of formal law and conservative constitutionalism.[61] Joining Charles Beard's *Economic Interpretation of the Constitution of the United States* (1913) and J. Allen Smith's *The Spirit of American Government* (1907), Goodnow's *Social Reform and the Constitution* (1911) carved out new legal-constitutional space for the development of the new administrative state.[62] Taking note of the "tremendous changes in political and social conditions," Goodnow advocated a critical and pragmatic approach to law averse to the static anachronisms of formal juristic conservatism.

Echoing Smith's chapter "The Constitution as a Reactionary Document," Goodnow attacked "the superstitious reverence" that accepted the constitution as "the last word as to the proper form of government, suited to all times and conditions." Such an approach imported an eighteenth-century political theory of social compact and natural right, presupposing "that society was static rather than dynamic or progressive in character." The unfortunate result was "to fix upon the country for all time institutions which . . . may in this twentieth century be unsuitable because of the economic, social and political changes which have taken place in the last hundred years."[63] He extended Theodore Roosevelt's critique of the "false and mischievous" notion of the constitution as a "straight-jacket to be used for the control of an unruly patient—the people." Goodnow endorsed instead a progressive and dynamic approach to the constitution that would enable a new public law and administration—flexible, responsive to public opinion, and adaptable to the changing needs of modern public life. This was a new democratic vision of constitutional dynamism in the public interest: "Our constitutions are instruments designed to secure justice by securing the deliberate but effective expression of the popular will."[64]

Modern administrative law emerged directly out of such democratically oriented antiformalism. The constitutional critiques of reformers like Goodnow, Smith, and Beard provided the intellectual groundwork for a jurisprudential transition away from traditional ideas about quasi-private officeholders and formal constitutional limitations toward the public law legitimacy of broad-scale legislative and administrative action in the public interest.[65] Ernst Freund similarly emphasized the importance of freeing "American public law from what he conceived to be the crippling dominance of constitutional law."[66] Critical realism was integral to Goodnow and Freund's bold agenda to expand legislative and administrative powers to meet the demands of social reform for increased legislative regulation and public provision. Modern American administration was no mere elite technocratic project. It was radical, critical, and, in the end, democratic. In Walter Weyl's words, it involved a "not unreverential breaking of the tablets of tradition" in the midst of "a democratic revolt."[67] Freund acknowledged the "technical superiority" of existing forms of European bureaucracy, but he made it clear that the task of the age in America consisted of accommodating necessary administration to the historic project of self-government in an "extreme democratic spirit."[68]

Antiformalism created important new room in American law for the emergence of a more generalized and public—rather than particularized and private—conception of administrative action. The second new democratic idea at play in the development of the modern administrative state further extended this general public conception by centering a vision of democratic administration built on the protection of public over and against private interest. Here, substantive issues of economic inequality, political unfairness, and systemic bias and discrimination moved to the very center of the American administrative project. Indeed, one of the leading motivations for the turn to modern administration was an acute awareness of the troubling ascendancy of private special economic interests in turn-of-the-century American politics. Administration was an attempt to reclaim the democratic high ground in a political regime thoroughly beset by "plutocracy" and "corruption." Plutocracy and corruption were the ubiquitous political bywords of the day. And their meaning was clear and unambiguous to all observers—the antidemocratic capture of the public political sphere by corrupting private economic interests. Though today "regulatory capture" by special interests is usually associated with administrative agencies, it must be remembered that modern administration originally developed as an explicit response to the "capture" of supposedly democratic legislatures, councils, cities, states, and even courts by dominant economic interests. Antidemocratic capture, in other words, was not an unfortunate consequence of administration, it was arguably its raison d'être.[69]

"Our resplendent plutocracy" was Walter Weyl's moniker for the corrupt and aristocratic alliance of "political bosses" and "railroad kings" and "Senate oligarchs"—the new agglomerations of corporate wealth and political power that produced a dangerous new mixture of the age-old threat of private interest trumping public democracy.[70] Such "corruption" marked the rise of an "indifference to public concerns" that John Dewey and James Tufts saw as beginnings of an undermining of "the democratic ideal": "The control of the inner machinery of governmental power by a few who can work in irresponsible secrecy . . . incites to deliberate perversion of public functions into private advantages. As embezzlement is appropriation of trust funds to private ends, so corruption, 'graft,' is prostitution of public resources, whether of power or of money, to personal or class interests."[71] As Vernon Parrington put it, from this "degradation of democratic dogma," emerged the task of the times "to curb the ambitions of plutocracy and preserve the democratic quest for the common benefit of all"—to "wrest control of the government from the hands of the plutocracy that was befouling it, and to use it for democratic rather than plutocratic ends."[72] Administration and administrative law were at the center of that new democratic quest.

And though concern about private interests corrupting the public welfare was as old Plato's *Republic,* what was new at the turn of the twentieth century was an acute awareness of the unprecedented threat to democratic politics posed by the arrival of large-scale business, industrial, and corporate interests.[73] Richard L. McCormick called it "the discovery that business corrupts politics"—the awakening of the people to illicit private business influence in democratic political life—a discovery he placed at the very core of the entire progressive reform movement.[74] Ida Tarbell, Lincoln Steffens, Ray Stannard Baker, and countless other journalists spent enormous time and energy exposing the various frauds, thefts, bribes, extortions, and schemes that seemed to now permanently link selfish robber barons to corrupt politicos (to use Matthew Josephson's evocative terms). As Thorstein Veblen concluded in "Business Principles in Law and Politics," "Constitutional government has, in the main, become a department of the business organization and is guided by the advice of business men."[75]

Political corruption—and the pursuit of selfish economic advantage through the democratic public sphere—was seen as the central problem confronting American democracy at the turn of the century. And time after time, administration was offered up as a distinctly democratic solution. In the economic regulatory field, the reformer who most clearly articulated the explicit relationship between corruption and democratic administration was Charles Francis Adams Jr. A lawyer, a historian, regulator, railroad executive, and member of one of the most influential families in American politics and letters, Adams was also one of the central pioneers of modern administration as a response to the scandalous economic and political corruption that surrounded the so-called railroad problem. The picture Adams painted was ominous and urgent. In "A Chapter of Erie," he described the battle for control of the Erie Railroad between the Erie men—Jay Gould, Jim Fisk, and Daniel Drew—and Cornelius Vanderbilt as nothing less than the "Erie war": so rife with corruption that participants were literally running away with bags of money.[76] For Adams, the railroad problem involved not just the economic crisis of expensive "natural monopolies" operating in an atmosphere of "ruinous competition."[77] Rather, anticipating Richard McCormick, Adams contended that the railroad problem involved the explicitly political problem of private business interests corrupting the public body politic—"the sturdy corporation beggars who infested the lobby" of state legislatures. As Adams saw it, "Our legislatures are now universally becoming a species of irregular boards of railroad direction" creating persistent "scandal and alarm." "The effects upon political morality have been injurious," he suggested, adding that "many States in this country, and especially New York, New Jersey, Pennsylvania, and Maryland have now for years notoriously been controlled by their railroad corporations."[78]

So here was the original democratic problem posed by the railroads—the capture of the existing elected legislators and officeholders by the newly dominant private economic interests. Adams made it clear that "neither competition nor legislation have proved themselves effective agents for the regulation of the railroad system." And so, he probed further: "What other and more effective [instrument] is there within the reach of the American people?" Adams's answer was administration. Noting that "there is no power which can purify a corrupted legislature," Adams turned instead to the administrative regulatory commission—independent, permanent, and competent tribunals that he analogized to courts.[79] While it might be tempting to view this turn to an unelected special regulatory commission as inherently undemocratic and technocratic, the original impulse was quite the opposite. Adams noted developments in the Midwest, where administrative innovations like the Illinois Railroad and Warehouse Commission were explicitly demanded by popular uprisings and state constitutional conventions of the people. New democracy involved much more than the formal decisions of elected officials. As Adams put it, "The railroad corporations, necessarily monopolists, constitute a privileged class," and therein lay the substance of antidemocracy—in the private political-economic aggrandizement of special interests. Democracy required a response in the form of general laws and general regulations administered again so as to reestablish the priority of general advantage. Adams recommended a strengthening of governmental administrative power to vindicate the public interest: "The task of supervising in some way the railroads of a modern State does constitute one of the necessary functions of government."[80]

Now, at this critical juncture in the historical development of the modern administrative regulatory agency, it must be noted that Charles Francis Adams was under no illusion that administration was inherently democratic—forever magically immune from private influence, economic interest, or other forms of special pleading. On the contrary, he specifically anticipated the precise question of administrative capture as early as 1871: "But it will be said, Who will guard the virtue of the tribunal? Why should the corporations not deal with [the commissions just] as [they did] with the legislatures?" Who would guard the guardians? Adams's answer to such questions went to the pragmatic and historical heart of the new democratic reform project. In a self-governing democracy, there was no final guarantee, no silver bullet, no complete economic or political theory that could forever preclude the capture and corruption of governmental institutions for private gain and antidemocratic purpose. Democratic vigilance was as necessary as it was eternal. In popular forms of government, the only solution was the pragmatic, ongoing, never-ending tradition of, as Adams phrased it, continually developing "all the checks and balances that human ingenuity can devise" to secure more democratic results.[81] The solution to the crises of modern democracy, in short, was ever more democracy.

In the late nineteenth and early twentieth century, reformers turned to administration, independent agencies, and regulatory commissions as a new kind of democratic check on private economic corruption and public legislative capture. Rather than endorse bureaucracy as some kind of permanent technocratic response to political modernity, new democratic reformers explicitly emphasized the themes of corruption and democracy as a prelude to their administrative reform proposals. The peak years of muckraking disclosure from 1904 to 1908 were accompanied by a wave of legislative activity specifically designed to curb the influence of private interest and private money in American politics, including federal and state corrupt practices, laws regulating campaign contributions and the solicitation of funds from corporations, laws regulating legislative lobbying, laws prohibiting free transportation passes, and such political reforms as direct primaries.[82] The development of modern administration (as well as economic regulatory and police power measures) must be understood in this larger context of heightened concern about the susceptibility of existing democratic politics to capture and corruption by new organizations of private economic interest. And while economic regulation is a good site for tracing this relationship of new democracy and administration, municipal administration provided the classic case.

Municipal Administration: The Problem of Public Corruption

For the chief architects of progressive administration and reform, one of the key sites for the failure of democracy and the eclipse of the public at the turn of the century was the American city. Municipal administration was the question of the day. Frank Goodnow himself developed his general theory of administration on the foundation of multiple major works on city government, municipal government, municipal problems, and municipal home rule.[83] Charles Beard's general reflections on American constitutionalism and political economy were part and parcel of his early and lasting work in municipal reform.[84] And John Dewey and Jane Addams, of course, were totally immersed in the reform of Chicago politics and policy. Cities like Cleveland boasted armies of talented administrative reformers like Tom Johnson, Newton Baker, Fred Howe, and Peter Witt.[85] As Daniel Rodgers has established in some detail, "The struggle over economic doctrines that began in the 1880s first came to a political head in the 'great cities' of the 1890s."[86] And democratic administrative municipal reform was at the core.

Modern municipal administration became a central battleground because cities were central organs "for the satisfaction of local needs."[87] With the development of a modern, positive state directed toward the provision of public services, cities were harbingers of political-economic and administrative modernity. The concentration of population, the division of labor, the diversity of the local citizenry, and acute problems of complexity and scale made the administration of public goods, public services, public works, and public welfare in cities a task as imposing as it was necessary. New public problems of "health, poverty, and unemployment," Dewey and Tufts argued, required new "public agencies for the proper air, light, sanitary conditions of work and residence, cheap and effective transportation, pure food, decent educative and recreative facilities in schools, libraries, museums, parks." The enormous challenges and frightful consequences of municipal administration in this period were nicely summarized by Frank Prichard in 1892:

> It must, either directly or through grants of public franchises, supply the citizens with water and light, must provide for the removal of their waste, must secure their safe and rapid transportation, must look after their health and safety by suitable regulations, and must protect them by a disciplined army of police. . . . The scale on which such operations are conducted, increases both the danger and consequences of a mistake. Inefficient sanitary regulations may cause a sudden epidemic. . . . Unskillful engineering may cause a water famine, or send the germs of disease into every household. Inadequate transportation facilities or unwise building laws may check the growth of the city or crowd its poorer inhabitants into tenements. Improper harbor regulations may drive commerce from its doors. Ignorant or dishonest financing may bankrupt its treasury.

As Prichard concluded, "The happiness and prosperity of that large portion of the population which live in cities are directly dependent upon the administration by the government."[88]

By the turn of the twentieth century, as Lincoln Steffens's *The Shame of the Cities* made perfectly clear, this all-important administration of modern American cities had almost completely broken down. Despite the regular operation of the political machinery, substantive public participation in the formation and realization of generalized public interest was almost nonexistent. As in large segments of the industrializing economy, plutocracy and corruption were the name of the game. "The 'big business man,'" Steffens provocatively argued, "is busy with politics. . . . I found him buying boodlers in St. Louis, defending grafters in Minneapolis, originating corruption in Pittsburgh, sharing with bosses in Philadelphia, deploring reform in Chicago, and beating good government with corruption funds in New York." The unfortunate consequences for democracy were clear: "They boss the party and turn our municipal democracies into autocracies." Political machines betrayed the public interest. "Public spirit became private spirit, public enterprise became private greed," Steffens contended, as "'combines' of municipal legislators sold rights, privileges, and public franchises for their own individual profit, and at regularly scheduled rates."[89] Jane Addams's prose was more measured, but her conclusions about the failure of urban democracy and the private capture of public goods—corrupt aldermen, graft, bribery, corporate gifts—was just as thoroughgoing. Moreover, Addams emphasized that the "positive evils of corrupt government" fell heaviest on those least able to afford it: "When the water of Chicago is foul, the prosperous buy water bottled at distant springs; the poor have no alternative but the typhoid fever which comes from using the city's supply. When the garbage contracts are not enforced, the well-to-do pay for private service; the poor suffer the discomfort and illness which are inevitable from a foul atmosphere." In response, Addams urged "a transition to a new type of democratic relation" to "make clear to the voter that his individual needs are common needs, that is, public needs." Surely, Addams concluded, "the demand for a chance to work and obtain the fulness of life may be widened until it gradually embraces all the members of the community, and rises into a sense of the common weal."[90]

In a brilliant essay "Problems of Municipal Administration," Jane Addams put her finger directly on the central administrative obstacle impeding the municipal governments in the provision of modern public services. Despite democratic elections and popular electoral participation, Addams claimed that American cities continued to labor under an outdated administrative structure "strongly under the influence of the historians and doctrinaires of the eighteenth century." She held that the "admitted failure in municipal administration" was rooted in the "inadequacy of those eighteenth century ideals" concerned "more with the guarding of prerogative and with the rights of property than with the spontaneous life of the people." Municipal government, Addams argued, "became an entity by itself away from the daily life of the people." And the chief legal-administrative culprit was "the machinery of government incorporated in the charters of early American cities."[91]

By calling attention to the administrative limitations inherent in the special charter approach to municipal incorporation and urban governance, Addams identified a municipal problem with a long and complex legal history.[92] Despite some uneven movement in the direction of so-called general municipal incorporation, most larger American cities continued to labor under the strict governing restraints specifically outlined in their originating state legislative charter.[93] Moreover, the powers of the municipal corporation were further circumscribed by the rise of a rule of statutory interpretation known as "Dillon's rule," narrowly construing legislative delegations of municipal power against expansion, holding municipalities strictly to only specifically and formally expressed charter and legislative provisions.[94] Dillon's rule was rooted in the hybrid public-private character of many early nineteenth-century legislatively chartered associations—cities, towns, franchise corporations, charities, and so on—where strict state oversight proved a necessary and valuable control on the aggrandizement of private group power. And early American state legislatures did grant public municipalities fairly ample self-governing police powers for the baseline regulation of public health, safety, and order.[95] But with the rapid transformation of late nineteenth-century urban life, the municipal charter, state control, special supplementary legislation, and Dillon's rule combined to seriously impede the development of the expansive kinds of public provision, public services, and public works so urgently needed. Ancient and particularized public-private techniques like nuisance abatement, the poor law, the fee system, justices of the peace, private prosecution, the posse comitatus, and local licensing were not nearly sufficient administrative technologies to meet the more generalized public needs of burgeoning metropolises. Moreover, the existing state-controlled, municipal-incorporation regime seemed to only entrench and protect the kind of corrupt and plutocratic private bargaining power that urban reformers decried as a denial of democracy.

Indeed, the prevailing legal-administrative understanding of the city as distinctly limited corporate body and mere "creature of the state" reinforced a constrained vision of its public capabilities. Sam Bass Warner famously dubbed this "the private city"—"a closed corporation" lacking "concern for public management of the community," oriented instead around private enterprises: "profit-seeking builders, land speculators, and large investors."[96] John Dillon himself continued to hold as late as 1890 that "a modern American city was not so much a miniature State as it [was] a business corporation."[97] This legally particularized and piecemeal approach to specific charter provisions, special legislation, and "private bills," only increased the possibilities for privatized corruption in municipalities limited and controlled by the state political machines. As a New York municipal reform commission stated the problem: "The corrupt cliques and rings . . . were quick to perceive that in the business of procuring special laws concerning local affairs, they could easily outmatch the fitful and clumsy labors of disinterested citizens." The transfer of power over municipal resources "from the localities to the Capitol" likewise transferred "the methods and arts of corruption," making "the fortunes of our principal cities the traffic of the lobbies."[98] Fred Howe concluded, "We were abandoned to money-making in politics. . . . We had permitted the government to be seized by spoilsmen and politicians. It was from them that democracy must be reclaimed."[99]

Beyond these visible opportunities for corruption, graft, and private-public swindle that widely condemned turn-of-the-century American municipal administration, an even larger democratic governance issue concerned the consequent inability of cities to respond to the municipal public's increasing needs and demands. As J. Allen Smith put it, "Effective power to regulate municipal matters is withheld from the majority," and "the exercise of local self-government by our cities is to be regarded as a mere privilege and not a right." As Smith and other reformers saw it, this expropriation of local self-governing power undermined democracy, creating cities "less democratic than the government of either state or nation."[100] In *The City: The Hope of Democracy,* Fred Howe made clear the impact of such an undemocratic municipal administration on the provision of public services. Under Dillon's rule and state control, the city "cannot move beyond the limitations of state law, cannot even protect itself much less work out the solution of its own problems." Consequently, "the city cannot act as to its tenements or building laws, its parkage, its public baths, its civil service regulations; it cannot raise revenues as it will, or expend them, save as the state has ordered. The city cannot regulate the charges of the local companies for gas, electricity, or telephone service, save under authority delegated from the legislature; it cannot . . . inspect conditions of labor in the factories, cannot even pay the rate of wages that it charges, or determine the classification or discharge of employees."[101]

In response, reformers demanded more substantive and public democracy in American cities. Howe called for a new "City Republic"—with adequate public authority and democratic accountability to adequately address the needs of the people. Frank Goodnow insisted on "the public character of municipal corporations": "The statement of the proper position of the city in the governmental system is, therefore, that it is always a public, i.e., a governmental, corporation"—an organ explicitly designed "for the satisfaction of local needs." And John Commons too insisted that "whatever may have been its position in the time of the medieval guilds, in our day, a municipality is not a private or merely business corporation. . . . Its functions are public and not private, political and not mercantile."[102] From Chicago, Jane Addams viewed the transformation of municipal administration as nothing short of "new moral struggle" requiring "the acceptance of democracy": "back to the people."[103]

The struggle for home rule and modern municipal administration was the outgrowth of this reform quest for a more public and social vision of city governance democratically responsive to the actual needs of their citizenry. A city was neither a private corporation managed for shareholders nor a medieval jurisdiction for the extraction of profits and favors by state politicos, urban bosses, and economic powerbrokers. As David Barron put it, home rule reformers "arouse[d] a public realm too long dominated by private power" and succeeded in redefining city power as "public and political" rather than "quasi-private," corporate, or jurisdictional.[104] The policy consequences of this administrative transformation to a more public and democratic conception of city governance were legion. Indeed, they amounted to a veritable catalog of progressive reform, from structural changes in "central administration," "financial administration," "school administration," "police administration," "administration of charities and correction," "public health administration," and "public works administration" to more substantive reforms like tenement reform, juvenile justice reform, municipal courts, social settlements, social services reform, sanitary reform, vice commissions, zoning, city planning, and ultimately the municipal ownership of public services and public utilities.[105] Perhaps the most telling feature of this revolution in municipal administration was the extraordinary expansion of tax-supported public services, from schools, hospitals, museums, golf-courses, and municipal water supply to public markets, public wharves and docks, grain elevators, public warehousing facilities, public coal yards and public filling stations, municipally owned gas and electric plants, and municipally owned transport.[106]

The extraordinary on-the-ground stakes of this general battle for a more public and democratic municipal administration played out with special force in Tom Johnson's Cleveland. Johnson was surrounded by a "brains trust" of reformers like Fred Howe, eager to turn the city toward more effective management, public service, and the public good. As Howe put it, "The city appealed to me as a social agency of great possibilities": protecting the poor, opening playgrounds, public baths, and dance halls, developing the lake front, and turning charities into "public agencies." Such ambitious plans for a more democratic and public city, however, first needed to get past Dillon's rule, the Ohio Municipal Code, and . . . Mark Hanna. As Howe recalled, "The city was not free. It had only the shadow of self-government. It could not own or operate things or control property; it could not levy taxes as it willed. It could only borrow a limited amount of money and for limited uses." "Bound like Gulliver" through state restrictions that "crippled democracy," the people of Cleveland "were helpless before the bosses and business interests." Howe recalled that Ohio was "managed like a private estate" by barons with Mark Hanna's "feudal idea of society": "Some men must rule; the great mass of men must be ruled. Some men must own; the great mass of men must work for those who own."[107]

As in New York City, where Charles Beard and other reformers initiated a fifty-year battle over mass transit and rail, the struggle for home rule and municipal administration in Cleveland turned on the provision of municipal services in transportation.[108] Foreshadowing the crucial role that public utilities would come to play generally in the political economy of progressive reform, Tom Johnson put the municipal street railway question at the center of his radical 1901 mayoral platform: "home rule, a three-cent fare for street railways, municipal ownership of public utilities, the equalization of taxes, and the single tax."[109] As Johnson made clear, these specific policy initiatives were part of a much broader democratic agenda: "We are fighting for a free city, for a city for the whole people and not the few. We are fighting privilege and monopoly because privilege and monopoly stand for bad government."[110] The street railway question was intimately bound up not only with home rule but with monopoly, corruption, bossism, and the private extraction of public wealth from the city of Cleveland by bosses like Hanna. "He owned street-railways in Cleveland," Howe argued, and "monopoly was his religion," extracting "great wealth" by "using the State for private ends."[111] Cleveland's Johnson administration would go on to wage a seven year "three-cent" war in the attempt to bring public services under the more direct control—including price controls—of a local democratic public. When Johnson's lieutenant Newton D. Baker succeeded him as mayor, he continued the municipal fight for home rule (writing the 1912 state constitutional amendment and promoting the draft of the city's first home rule charter), "three-cent" utilities (including electric light, dance halls, and even three-cent fish), and the continued municipalization of public works and public services.[112]

From Cleveland to New York and across the country, the administrative project of home rule and ambitious programs for the expansion of municipal services were essential components of a broad reform effort to create a truly public city in a modern democratic state. Privatism, bossism, plutocracy, and corruption had been tried and found wanting. Amid obvious signs of a crisis in municipal government, reformers devised a bold alternative centered directly on the problem of modern administration. While many urban critics viewed the "shame of the cities" as further evidence of a historic weakness in democracy per se, reformers like Fred Howe delivered a powerful counterargument: "The trouble with our cities is not too much democracy, but too little democracy."[113] Municipal administration was a democratic reform—oriented around the problem of securing local self-government under modern conditions. Was a perfect democratic municipal administration attained? Certainly not. But just as certainly, the conception of the city in modern American life did overcome the privatized, corporate, and constitutional limitations of an earlier administrative inheritance. The National Municipal League eventually changed its name to the National Civic League—perhaps signaling the final decline of the old municipal corporation idea and the rise of a more modern vision of a city firmly embedded in the tasks of civic, governmental, public, and democratic service. Democracy was an ongoing public trust. As Jane Addams concluded, "If we could trust democratic government as over against and distinct from the older types—from those which repress, rather than release, the power of the people—then we should begin to know what democracy really is, and our municipal administration would at last be free to attain Aristotle's ideal of a city, 'where men live a common life for a noble end.'"[114]

Social Administration: The Problem of Public Provision

"A common life for a noble end"—that objective ably describes the other most important objective of the progressive era: the long fight to do something about material deprivation and economic inequality in the United States. Since Tocqueville, social and political theorists have posited that any truly democratic society required a modicum of equality and a minimum standard of living. Democracy was more than a political mechanism for assembling votes; it was a way of life predicated on relative social equality. True self-governance was possible only among equal citizens. Franklin Roosevelt articulated the basic intuition in his promotion of a second economic bill of rights: "Necessitous men are not free men. People who are hungry and out of a job are the stuff of which dictatorships are made."[115] In the late nineteenth and early twentieth century, Americans rediscovered poverty and precarity, as well as unprecedented socioeconomic inequality, at the very center of the democratic experiment.

The rediscovery of poverty as a modern social problem was as central to the American muckraking tradition as the revelation of economic and political corruption. B. O. Flower launched the socially conscious magazine *The Arena* in 1889 with an article by Helen Stuart Campbell whose Prisoners of Poverty series had already popularized the issue for the *New York Tribune*. "Our old equality is gone," Campbell noted. "Far from being the most equal people on the face of the earth, as we once boasted that we were, ours is now the most unequal of civilized nations." "Why are the masses so pitiably poor, and why are the classes so pitiably rich? What are the causes of this suffering?" Campbell voiced such increasingly common questions to publicly call the nation to account for "the present and ever increasing inequality in the distribution of wealth."[116] Robert Hunter's *Poverty* (1904) was more forensic, famously estimating that, "in fairly prosperous times, no less than 10 million persons in the United States are underfed, underclothed, and poorly housed." Beyond pauperism per se, Hunter drew attention to the especially troubling conditions plaguing the working poor—the "many thousand families" who, while working, were still receiving "too little of the common necessities" to "permit them to maintain a state of physical efficiency."[117] Sufficient food, adequate clothing, proper shelter, a living wage, and life expectancy itself were all struggling for survival in a socially Darwinian existence.[118] In *The New Democracy*, Walter Weyl noted the new misery, preventable death, sickness, hunger, and deprivation in America—the product of an unprecedented "disequilibrium between social surplus and social misery."[119]

Now, there are many ways to interrogate this proliferation of progressive interest in the social problem of American poverty, inequality, indigence, and deprivation.[120] From the perspective of public law, legislation. and regulation, two things are especially notable. First, progressive work on the poverty and necessity question shifted the terms of debate from a focus on issues of personal dependency and individual defect to a more social emphasis on insecurity, insufficiency, and inequality in basic human living standards and modern economic and labor conditions. Prior to progressive interventions, the social question was framed predominately in terms of various categories of dependency, debilitation, and incapacity. Legal treatises routinely carved out exceptions for various "delinquent" and "defective" classes, including treatment of the poor along with common drunkards, the insane, the feebleminded or epileptic, and the blind or the deaf.[121] Such categories imported highly moralistic theories of individual desert, while also legitimating strategies of social exclusion, expulsion, institutionalization, and various forms of second-class citizenship. Progressive social-welfare policy attempted to push this ancient discourse aside to make room for more structural and social-scientific analyses of economic inequality and public welfare. In place of the freighted language of dependence and defect, reformers created a new aspiration of social service and public assistance predicated on a more democratic, egalitarian, and inclusive conception of social citizenship.

Second and relatedly, progressive reformers understood the overriding problem of indigence and basic economic need as fundamentally a problem of administration (or maladministration). And once again, it is possible to detect an important underlying transformation in technologies of public action regarding poverty. Social welfare reformers endorsed a decided shift away from the more traditional, private, particularist, voluntarist, punitive, and common-law/criminal-law mechanisms of what they called a "charities and corrections" approach in favor of more modern and general forms of legislation, regulation, and administration. In the field of relief and social work, the unmistakable direction of change was away from the anachronisms of traditional poor law administration toward modern forms of public assistance—what Sophonisba Breckinridge called "public welfare administration."[122] In the field of work and employment (where issues of child labor, overwork, inadequate wages, and worker health and safety were all intertwined), a similar shift occurred away from the defunct framework of common-law master-servant toward what John Commons called modern "labor administration."[123] Curiously, half a century after the passage of the Thirteenth Amendment, both areas of policy innovation continued to struggle with remnants of various forms of private servitude and involuntary indenture. Increased public services via a modernized administration was the progressive alternative to the various forms of involuntary servitude, dependency, and deprivation that still prevailed in a purportedly democratic political economy.

One of the first places this new social-scientific and administrative approach to the problem of social welfare took hold was Chicago. With influences ranging from the truly extraordinary community of reformers gathered around Jane Addams's Hull House to an imposing network of municipal, civic, and educational organizations devoted to urban reform and social uplift, Chicago was a likely site for the development of a modern approach to public welfare administration. The presence of Ernst Freund, as well as John Dewey and James Tufts, at the University of Chicago added legal sophistication and philosophical depth to the entire enterprise. Sophonisba Breckinridge and Edith Abbott brought these Chicago networks and influences together in a rather audacious and relentless rethinking and reworking of traditional American approaches to poverty and inequality (including issues of education, housing, employment, juvenile justice, incarceration, immigration, and medical care). Together, their professional accomplishments in the field of law and social policy were unparalleled. They founded the professional school of Social Service Administration at the University of Chicago together with the aptly titled *Social Service Review* and the American Association of Schools of Social Work. Along with colleagues like Addams, Julia Lathrop, Florence Kelley, and Grace Abbott, one or both of them were literally on the front lines of almost every important initiative in the development of the modern social welfare state: mothers' pensions, state welfare administration, the Children's Bureau, the Sheppard-Towner Act, the Federal Emergency Relief Administration (FERA), and the Social Security Act. From a scholarly perspective, however, what was uniquely important about the work of Abbott and Breckinridge ("A and B" as they were called at the University of Chicago) was the way they keenly and meticulously traced the details and defects in early American poor law administration in voluminous works in quest of a radical new template for modern public welfare administration.[124]

That new template began with a reaffirmation of "public responsibility for those in need." As Abbott pointed out, public obligation was "an established American policy" since the first colonial settlements: "The care of the state for its dependent classes is considered by all enlightened people as a measure of its civilization, and the care of the poor is recognized as among the unquestioned objects of public duty." Abbott quoted Blackstone: "The law not only regards life and member and protects every man in the enjoyment of them, but also furnishes him with everything necessary for their support. For there is no man so indigent or wretched, but he may demand a supply sufficient for all the necessaries of life from the more opulent part of the community, by means of the several statutes enacted for the relief of the poor."[125] These were the English roots of the early American poor law regime—a system of local public responsibility written into the policies of the original states as well as the very earliest law of the old Northwest Territory (1790) authorizing quarter-sessions justices to appoint overseers of the poor as county public administrators. The administrators were to advise the justices in dispensing public relief by (a) taking "notice of all the poor and distressed families and persons residing in their township" and their means of support; (b) discovering persons or families "really suffering through poverty, sickness, accident, or any misfortune or inability, which might render him, her, or them a wretched and proper object of public charity"; and (c) notifying the justice of "all vagrant persons likely to become chargeable to the township" for support.[126] Breckinridge contributed exhaustive studies of the unfolding of this original poor law regime in Ohio, Indiana, Michigan, and Illinois. Like Grace Abbott, she acknowledged that the public obligation to aid the poor was "older than the constitution," but from that historic baseline, she produced a thoroughgoing dissection of the fundamental defects of this ancient tradition of local poor law administration.[127]

"Old pauper laws," Edith Abbott called them—vestiges of "the social thinking and social organization of the 17th and 18th centuries." Here, basic poor relief remained in the hands of erratic, incompetent, dishonest, and all-too-frequently cruel local authorities, providing what she called "a very *undemocratic, un-American* system of poor relief." Abbott and Breckinridge committed themselves to eradicating the old pauper system "with all its complex inefficiency and its harsh treatment of the men, women, and children who are in trouble through no fault of their own." They envisioned instead a "social revolution" in public administration that would "re-write" American poor law "from the standpoint of modern democracy."[128]

What was the problem with the old regime? Beyond the objectionable terminology of "pauperism" and "vagrancy," which Abbott deemed un-American, Malthusian, and "disgracefully opprobrious," the substantive provisions of these "undemocratic laws" were equally antiquated and problematic. As Abbott and Breckinridge wrote, fourteen states continued to deprive persons receiving poor relief of the right to vote. South Carolina's constitution withheld the vote from those receiving public assistance together with "persons who are idiots, insane, paupers, supported at the public expense, and persons confined in any public prison." That was only the beginning. Breckinridge's exhaustive histories of local poor law administration contained a parade of horribles involving capricious overseers and a seemingly arbitrary regime of forced removals, service auctions, coerced family support, involuntary servitudes, and various forms of indenture in dealing with local public charges, alleged vagrants, and destitute children. As Breckinridge summed up administration by local overseer in nineteenth-century Illinois, "All persons who were unable to earn a living due to unavoidable causes, who had relatives . . . financially able to assist, were to be supported by their relatives. If they had no such relatives, they were to be placed in the care of some person who would maintain them in return for their labor, if they were capable of any, plus a specified sum of money; or, in the counties where poorhouses had been established, they would be sent to the poorhouse."[129] Breckinridge's despairing accounts of abominable poorhouse and almshouse conditions in Illinois joined a long list of exposés documenting the horrors of late nineteenth-century institutionalization. In the 1890 *Atlantic Monthly*, Sarah Orne Jewett memorialized the harshness of the old regime in her fictional story "The Town Poor." Abbott added that the appalling nature of such investigative or fictional portraits was only surpassed by the "long lists" of "court reports" attesting to the many "indignities" of the "deterrent aspects" of the old pauper laws.[130]

While acknowledging a general public duty of indigent support, the old pauper law regime devolved vast amounts of administrative discretion to a "motley assortment" of justices of the peace, overseers of the poor, and local town, county, and municipal authorities. "Dogberrys and Bumbles," Abbott called them. In Ohio, approximately six thousand diverse and untrained officials ranging from "directors of safety" to township trustees to county commissioners were responsible for various administrations of poor relief.[131] The administrative result was an impossible "patchwork" of continually insufficient funds and ineffective, inconsistent, and frequently warring local poor law administrators. As Abbott summed things up, "The inadequacies of local relief funds and the inefficiency of relief administration under thousands of minor governmental authorities . . . created insurmountable difficulties in the way of reaching a minimum standard of social security even in a single state, and led to what might be described as an irrepressible conflict between the principle of public responsibility, on the one hand, and, on the other, the method of maintaining this principle by means of local support and local administration."[132] Breckinridge concurred, noting that researching her numerous long histories of "confused" and "halting" local poor law administration was a "painful experience." But both reformers had assiduously worked the legal-historical trenches in hopes that the transparency of such studies would soon speed the nation away from "local administration, family responsibility, and settlement restrictions" toward a more "modern program of adequate relief, social service, and state responsibility in carrying out a truly national policy of adequacy and security."[133]

"Abolish the pauper laws" was the battle cry of a new social welfare movement devoted to putting the issue of economic hardship and deprivation on a modern and more democratic footing. Given the "great social changes" of the modern era, welfare reformers demanded "fundamental and sweeping changes to make adequate provision for fellow-citizens who are in need of help" beyond the "old degrading method of poor law practice." Arguing that "our whole understanding of the fundamental rights of the common man has radically changed in the last generation," Abbott and her compatriots advocated the bold new theory that "certain minimum standards of living must be available for all." And they committed themselves to two basic causes to that effect: (a) "making new public services and new public aid available to all" and (b) bringing about "an increase in real wages."[134] Direct, professionally administered, equitably distributed public provision was to take the place of pauperism, charity, and corrections. A more continuous and competent administrative machinery staffed by professionally trained lawyers and social workers would administer new forms of public aid and public assistance allocated to bring all citizens up to a reasonable standard of living, including home assistance, mothers' pensions, old-age assistance, and disability pensions. Thus, Abbott and Breckinridge—along with an army of uniquely committed colleagues—launched the long progressive crusade for a new public administration of coordinated local, state, and national public assistance to address the problem of poverty in industrial America.

The actual policy reforms flowing from this modern revolution in social service administration ranged widely and reshaped all levels of American governmental assistance. At the local level, Abbott and Breckinridge worked through the Chicago Juvenile Court to develop the nation's first program of mothers' pensions for the support of women with dependent children.[135] At the state level, they promoted the administrative consolidation and departmentalization wherein state public welfare departments, boards, and agencies slowly secured professional supervisory authority over the old menagerie of local poor law practices. Though it was difficult to completely "rewrite the old pauper laws from the standpoint of modern democracy," as Abbott put it, the slow but unmistakable trend of social welfare reform was "progress toward the substitution of state responsibility . . . in place of, or in aid of, local support."[136] At the federal level, in their prodigious work for the Children's Bureau, Sheppard-Towner, and FERA, Abbott and Breckinridge helped to create a national progressive blueprint for subsequent New Deal social-welfare policy making. As Abbott put it, "The establishment of the United States Children's Bureau in 1912 was evidence of a new federal concern for social welfare. . . . Largely through the Bureau's initiative and support, came the demand for the protection of the nation's children through federal labor laws, through a federal birth registration system, and for federal help in the program to prevent infant and maternal mortality. Finally came the Bureau's new plan for federal grants-in-aid."[137] With "social legislation" like this, Helen Clarke declared the arrival of the modern American "Social Service State": "No longer is the protection of the laborer from exploitation, of women from masculine domination, of children from parental indifference and neglect, or of the poor from punitive relief dispensation a resisted or incidental governmental activity. Interference, regulation, prevention, and control by the government are justified on the theory that the welfare of the people is the supreme law of the land."[138]

Ultimately, however, the kind of public aid and assistance at the heart of mothers' pensions and social security was only part of the expansive agenda of social reform that drove "the Chicago Plan." Public education was always close at hand as a model of what could be attained through public service and public provision.[139] And Abbott and Breckinridge campaigned aggressively for housing and tenement reform, a "right to medical care," and increased attention to problems of criminal justice and incarceration.[140] But central as was the creation of a new state and federal platform for public aid and relief of the destitute, the second major plank of the progressive social services project involved labor, employment, the working poor, a living wage, and livable working conditions. True social security and social service included the need to reach deeper into the American workplace—a key contributor to the social problems of necessity and precarity in the Progressive Era. As Abbott put it in "The Wages of Unskilled Labor in the United States," "Complaints have not been wanting that the laboring man's share in these stupendous industrial gains has been pitifully small and mean; that the development of the machine system has tended to . . . depress the wages of all toward the lower wage-level of the unskilled."[141] Here, the concerns and unique energy of the Chicago Plan merged with the equally irrepressible force known as "the Wisconsin Idea."[142]

To date, the best short and simple account of the governmental program of the progressive reform movement remains Fred Howe's *Wisconsin: An Experiment in Democracy.* Dedicated to Robert La Follette—"whose work in Wisconsin laid the foundation for a Democratic Commonwealth"— Howe's account was a primer on the centrality of administration, public service, and social legislation to the creation of a new democratic state. As Howe recounted, "Democracy began to use its powers to serve people as well as business, to serve humanity as well as property. Democracy has begun a war on poverty, on ignorance, on disease, on human waste. The state is using its collective will to promote a programme of human welfare."[143] Howe's overview of administrative reform in Wisconsin was comprehensive and taxonomic, starting with the "agencies of political efficiency" and the electoral and municipal reforms through which La Follette and Wisconsin progressives were able to overthrow corrupt boss control of state political processes. He went on to underscore the importance of reform concerning "railways and public utility corporations" so as to rein in corporate domination of essential public infrastructure and public services. Taxation, education, and insurance experienced similar systematic reforms. Finally, Howe came to the all-important subject of "industrial and factory legislation"—where John R. Commons and the Wisconsin Industrial Commission pioneered a new, modern, and democratic approach to labor administration.[144]

Charles McCarthy rooted the Wisconsin Idea in the new "unequal conditions of contract" brought on by monopolies, trusts, high costs of living, and predatory wealth. The unprecedented concentrations of wealth and power in industrializing Wisconsin galvanized a statewide grassroots reform movement dedicated to "guarding of the governmental machinery from the corrupting force and might of concentrated wealth" and "the just regulation of the conditions of contract between the powerful and the weak whenever public interest demanded."[145] The progressive attempt to tame the

new sources of private power and domination came to Wisconsin with particular focus on questions of inequality, poverty, unemployment, and conditions of labor. The third issue of *La Follette's Weekly Magazine* (1911)
featured an article on unemployment by Carl Sandburg entitled "The Man,
the Boss, and the Job" as well as a lead piece on workers' injury law entitled "Our Judicial Oligarchy: Is the Poor Man on an Equality with the
Rich Man before the Courts?" The latter was a key source for Howe's
bleak account of the intersection of railroads, corporations, and worker
injury, noting, "War is safe compared to railroading in this country."
Howe and Gilbert Roe decried the "reckless and wanton disregard of the
safety and lives of the employed . . . which is a constant menace to our
society and government."[146] The Wisconsin Idea involved using some of
the same legal and regulatory technologies devised in the fight against railroads and monopolies to address the equally challenging problems facing
modern American labor. Wisconsin pioneered new techniques of labor
administration—in the fight to better regulate unequal "contract conditions
by special administrative agencies of the people."[147]

When Richard T. Ely's institutional economics fused with John Commons's labor economics at the University of Wisconsin, a new approach to
labor administration emerged—something of an analog to the modern
social service administration pioneered by Abbott and Breckinridge at
Chicago. Commons's first forays into labor administration began with a
research position at the National Civic Federation, where he worked assiduously to bring the interests of both capital and labor to the table so as
to ameliorate economic disputes. There he gained experience with labor
administration and arbitration while also confronting the persistent labor
problem of low wages and risky work environments. "Adam Smith had
stated that accepting risky jobs would get higher wages than others," he
noted, but employers "were slow in raising wages to compensate for
risk."[148] With La Follette in Wisconsin, Commons went on to draft two of
the most important pieces of progressive state reform legislation—the Wisconsin Civil Service Law of 1905 and the Public Utilities Law of 1907.[149]

Commons's experience with civil service and public utilities reform prepared him to make some rather remarkable inroads into the field of labor
administration. There, the interconnections between police power legislation, public utility regulation, and administrative innovation became central as Commons worked to forge a modern law of labor relations beyond
the traditional common-law limitations of master and servant. Commons
was explicit about this path of modern legal development. "While working
on the public utility law of 1907," he noted, he "wondered why similar
administrative machinery could not be set up for the conflicts of capital and

labor." He immediately shipped a graduate student off to Belgium to study the Belgian Superior Council of Labor—an administrative body set up outside of parliament and composed "of representatives of capital, labor and the public." He then introduced Wisconsin to the Industrial Commission idea. In 1911, Wisconsin brought together all of the "piecemeal labor laws . . . going back to their beginnings in 1867," added a new workers' compensation law, and placed them under a new council of labor and capital. As Commons put it, "The older laws were repealed, to take effect when the Commission issued its 'orders.'"[150]

Commons was clear about the importance of the railroad regulation and public utility frameworks. Here, the constitutional issue had been solved by delegating "to an administrative body the power to make rules." In the case of railroads and utilities, commissioners were "to investigate, ascertain and fix 'reasonable values' and 'reasonable services.'" In the case of the relationship of employer and employees, the issue revolved around the reasonableness not of values but of labor practices. Accordingly, a staggering array of labor issues came under the supervision of Wisconsin's Industrial Commission: "safety, health, child labor, moral well-being, wage-bargaining, hours of labor, minimum wages for women and children, labor disputes, and free employment offices."[151] Though the overthrow of the common law of tort concerning workers' injuries has been frequently highlighted as the centerpiece of this reform legislation,[152] the innovative and capacious administrative authority granted the Industrial Commission established an institutional design that would guide the development of modern labor relations and the safety, health, and well-being of employees for the next quarter century. As Commons put it, "The industrial commission law applies the same theory and procedure to the relation of capital and labor that the railroad commission law applies to the relations of public corporations and consumers." It was a "fourth branch" of state government—a "legislature continually in session," "an executive sharing with the governor the enforcement of laws," and "a court deciding cases that the judiciary formerly decided."[153] Fred Howe assessed the democratic nature of the administrative achievement: "Wisconsin has undertaken the most comprehensive programme of human conservation in any state in the Union. The state lays down the principle that every one has a right to be protected from the dangers, diseases, and exhaustion of modern industry. The laws enacted are a declaration, too, that the state has an interest in the health of its people; that property must be used so as not to injure humanity; that the purpose of organized government is to promote the well-being and working efficiency of its citizens." For Howe, Wisconsin labor administration was fundamentally about public provision and social service—"provision for old age, for sickness, for accident," provision for the education of children, and social provision for adequate wages and a reasonable standard of living. As Charles McCarthy concluded, despite its appointive rather than elective foundation, the administrative commission was "an aid to democracy."[154]

In 1930, Felix Frankfurter opened the timely topic of "expert administration and democracy" with a prescient one-two punch: "Epitaphs for democracy are the fashion of the day. . . . But it is simply not true that the area of democratic government has contracted."[155] As scholars and intellectuals have attempted to come to terms with the extraordinary growth of the modern American administrative state, they have most often worked with the highly visible and theorized themes of bureaucracy, technocracy, science, management, and expertise. And more frequently than not, the tendency has been to view those governmental changes as one-dimensional and fundamentally at odds with democratic governance as in Democracy versus Administration or Man versus the State. Just as frequently, scholars have proffered solutions to the "problem of administration" by invoking some kind of intermediating, moderating influence: for example, the rule of law, an ancient or original constitution, civil society, the public sphere, social movements, or the market. But historically, we should not forget that the main impulse behind modern American administration was political. The turn to contingent administrative solutions—as John Dewey, Jane Addams, Charles Francis Adams, Edith Abbot, Sophonisba Breckinridge, John Commons, and Fred Howe constantly reminded us—was part of a broader political-economic struggle and a social contest in favor of more democracy: a new democracy. Reformers witnessed traditional democratic procedures at the national, state, and municipal level too easily manipulated by urban machines, state legislative politicos, and resurgent economic and industrial interests so as to corruptly turn the res publica to private service. The administrative state was not emblematic of a "crisis in democracy"; it was the new democratic response. Like the creation of a modern constitution (which was also the product of intense political struggle and contest), the modern administrative state was created for the service of larger public and human ends. Progressive and democratic administration was but a first step on the road to the kind of public and social service-oriented state endorsed by Franklin D. Roosevelt in 1935:

> to increase the security and happiness of a large number of people in all occupations of life and in all parts of the country; to give them more of the good things of life; to give them a greater distribution not only of

wealth in the narrow terms but of wealth in the wider terms; to give them places to go in the summer time—recreation; to give them assurance that they are not going to starve in their old age; to give honest business a chance to go ahead and make a reasonable profit; and to give everyone a chance to earn a living.[156]

As Roosevelt saw it, the administrative reforms of the New Deal were part of this new democratic tradition: "We have made the exercise of all power more democratic; for we have begun to bring private autocratic powers into their proper subordination to the public's government."[157]

With the arrival of the New Deal, the administrative state found new prophets and advocates from Felix Frankfurter to James Landis. In some sense, they consummated the revolution in modern administrative governance pioneered by the likes of Goodnow, Freund, and Wyman. As Frankfurter noted in 1936, it was "Frank J. Goodnow and Ernst Freund, who as early as the '90s saw general tendencies towards an administrative law" and a new regulatory state where others saw only unrelated, individual occurrences. In *The Public and Its Government,* Frankfurter synthesized and popularized the several themes worked out by previous generations of political and legal thinkers and reformers: the demands of modern society on government, the need for a more positive and instrumental conception of law and legislation, the new democratic idea of public service in the public interest, and the need for modern administration in a democratic state.[158] These were the crucial building blocks of the revolution in governance and transformation of public law that created a new state in modern America. Well before James Landis, as former chair of the Securities and Exchange Commission and dean of Harvard Law School, wrote his great defense of the administrative regulatory system, *The Administrative Process* (1938), the main lines of American administrative state development had already been well established. And as Landis concluded, that "growth of the administrative process shows little sign of being halted. . . . Its extraordinary growth in recent years, the increasing frequency with which government has come to resort to it, the extent to which it is creating new relationships between the individual, the body economic, and the state, already have given it great stature."[159] The stature that modern administration and administrative law had already achieved in the United States by 1932 set the stage for another round of development in Franklin Roosevelt's New Deal.

CONCLUSION
The Myth of the New Deal State

———

The relativity of all human concepts is the
last word of the historical vision of the world.
—WILHELM DILTHEY

The United States was in the middle of a deep and unprecedented financial and economic crisis. Fear itself gripped the nation and captured
the imagination of more than a few of its chief chroniclers. Out of the sound
and fury of an unusual presidential campaign, there emerged a bold and
charismatic American leader. Talk turned immediately to the radical possibilities of a new administration, a new era, indeed a "New Deal." The year
was 2008.

"Franklin Delano Obama" declared the *New York Times*'s Paul Krugman:
"Everything old is New Deal again. Reagan is out; F.D.R. is in." Proclaiming
a "*New* New Deal," the cover of *Time* magazine on November 24, 2008,
featured Barack Obama's face and hands cropped into a vintage picture of
Roosevelt—cigarette holder, fedora, and 1930s automobile bending historical time as well as ahistorical minds. CBS News chose a 1939 photo of a
Works Progress Administration sign from the White Fringed Beetle Project
in Louisiana to hail "FDR's New Deal Blueprint for Obama." The *Nation*
kept up the steady drumbeat of journalistic calls for Obama's New Deal,
and even the independent socialist *Monthly Review* joined the endless
parade of repetitive, ostensibly historical New Deal observations.[1] Professional historians, political scientists, and sociologists were more circum-
spect and sophisticated in excavating the links between past and present,
but they too could not resist the ever-present lure of the New Deal analogy.
All "in the shadow of Roosevelt" is how a leading history summed up
American presidential administrations from Truman to Obama.[2] That long
shadow continued to cloud the return of progressive politics in 2020 as calls
for a more radical policy agenda were readily dubbed a "Green New Deal."

Such is the power of the New Deal to capture and circumscribe the imagination of the American democratic political. And such is the tenacity of the myth of the New Deal state.

A central premise of the myth of the New Deal state is the idea that the creation of a distinctly modern state and a refurbished social democracy in American history awaited the historic events of the mid-twentieth century: depression, executive reorganization, and world war. Before FDR, before the New Deal revolution, conventional wisdom too frequently suggests, American politics and policy making were trapped beneath the weight of the anachronistic inheritances of small government, classical political economy, and constitutional limitations. The central myths challenged by this book—of a weak state, laissez-faire, and Lochnerism—thus very much burnished the image of the New Deal as the crucial turning point, a new beginning, in the construction of the modern American state.

Like most myths, the one about the New Deal state has roots in a rather dramatic and exceptionalist origin story as the New Deal is lifted out of the prosaic stream of American secular history and placed on new, higher ground. Principal actors take on almost mythic proportions, and extraordinary causal force is imputed to their quotidian personal interactions. In the end, the seismic historical event is itself transformed into a new foundation for national historical narrative and aspiration—the new departure and point of renewal for the entire "American political tradition."

Such narrative tropes, of course, tacitly deploy all of the structure and trappings of timeless mythology rather than time-bound analytical history. Indeed, origin stories frequently assume the status of quasi-theological creation myths. Mircea Eliade is the classic authority on these archetypes (as well as on the crucial differences that should separate earthly history from cosmic mythos). As he put it, "Myth narrates a sacred history; it relates an event that took place in primordial Time, the fabled time of the 'beginnings.' . . . Myth, then, is always an account of a 'creation.'"[3] Eliade painstakingly outlined the key attributes of a sacred mythology at odds with profane historical interpretation. Beyond the primordial creation myth itself (ab origine, from the beginning), they included such things as the symbolism of a new power center (a new axis mundi); notions of recurrence, return, repetition, and imitation; an embrace of repetitive cycles of time versus the distinctive, irreversible linearity of history; the personification of power and efficacy; narratives built around images of rise and fall and rebirth; and more than a dab of nostalgia for the "Great Time" or a yearning for its resurrection or restoration. Such forms disguise a basic flight from the "terror of history" as well as from the more ephemeral realities of the temporal human condition.

And though it may seem a stretch to invoke such a mythic or archaic ontology when referring to conventional legal-political events like the New Deal, the narrative arc of some standard accounts continues to reflect the general contours of myth and legend. In his *Political Theology*, Carl Schmitt criticized the use of such "secularized theological concepts" as more appropriate to early church history than the study of contemporary political institutions.[4] Eliade attributed the continued predominance of myth in modern thinking to the consoling "antihistorical character" of a "popular memory" unwilling to reckon with "historical reality."[5] In the context of analyses of the modern American political, such mythological constructions have made it more difficult to discern the actual history of the modern American state. Moreover, the adaptability and mutability of mythic tropes also render them especially susceptible to reversal and subversion—a fact not lost on vociferous critics of the New Deal.[6] In the interest of resisting such tendencies, it is worth taking a closer look at some of the key features of the myth of the New Deal state.

Arthur M. Schlesinger Jr. began his influential, multivolume history of the New Deal with an epigraph from Emerson that set the stage for future histories: "Every revolution was first a thought in one man's mind." Revolution, thought, one man—classic signs the reader is about to embark on a hero's journey. Schlesinger followed with a prologue of imagery straight out of Genesis. March 4, 1933, began in darkness—"midnight," "gray," "bleak," "clouds," "cast-iron skies," "colorless light," "fog," "dark clouds."[7] As Hoover and Roosevelt rode together to the inauguration, Hoover was a ghost—"expressionless," "downcast," "motionless," "cold," "silent"—death incarnate at "the end of our rope." The family Bible on which FDR took the oath of office was open to 1 Corinthians 13: "through a glass, darkly." And then the worm turned. Roosevelt declared a new day of "national consecration." He invoked the "money changers." Cavalry bugles. Horsemen. "Men and women now curiously awakened from apathy and daze." And "across the land the fog began to lift." From darkness to light, from death to life—a history of the New Deal launched in sacred time.[8]

Though not all New Deal history deploys such literary and mythic tropes so conspicuously, the more secular image of a new beginning and a revolution is unmistakable in classic accounts. William Leuchtenburg's New Deal is not quite "the Roosevelt Revolution" heralded by the journalist Ernest Lindley seven months after the inauguration, but it is a new and radical departure from the past.[9] Indeed, Leuchtenburg's conclusion in 1940 is perhaps a perfect bookend to Schlesinger's prologue in 1933 as Henry Wallace declared: "We are children of the transition—we have left Egypt but we have not yet arrived at the Promised Land." And by the time Leuchtenburg turned his own attention the courts in a *Supreme Court Reborn,* he acknowledged nothing less than a "Constitutional Revolution" in "the Age of Roosevelt." In constitutional history, Bruce Ackerman's portrait of the New Deal as the third American constitutional revolution is a commonplace, featuring New Dealers engaged "in self-conscious acts of constitutional creation that rivaled the Founding Federalists' in their scope and depth."[10] The New Deal regularly takes center stage in a historical dramaturgy featuring revolutionary cycles of rise, fall, and renewal at the heart of American political tradition.[11] The notion of "the rise and fall of the New Deal order" is only the latest reincarnation of the New Deal as a "dominant order of ideas, public policies, and political alliances" whose "ghost still hovers over a troubled polity."[12]

Especially important to the mythic proportions of the New Deal in American historical narrative is the personification of political power, especially in the personality of the president and his "brain trust"—sometimes approaching the status of a new axis mundi. "Although the influence of great men is usually exaggerated," Richard Hofstadter argued, Franklin Roosevelt was an exception: "No personality has ever expressed the American popular temper so articulately or with such exclusiveness."[13] Like large swaths of the Old Testament, New Deal histories often detour into the long lists of names of New Dealers coupled with biographies of agency heads that culminate in "presidential synthesis"—a classic form of national historical narrative built upon the "old skeleton" of wars and presidential administration.[14] Hofstadter himself long ago called for an end to such normatively charged chronicles as "an engaging and moving simplicity, accessible to the casual reader of history," made way for "a new awareness of the multiplicity of forces."[15] In legal history, Willard Hurst voiced similar concerns about traditional constitutional narrative as a "recital of Great Cases," which "tends to take the cream off the top of the bottle and let the nutritious skimmed stuff flow down the drain because it is bulky to handle and not so pleasing to taste." "With intelligent diligence and some literary flair anyone can make a good story out of the spotlighted star acts, like the Federal Convention . . . or the Court-packing bill," Hurst contended, "but the spotlighted acts could not go on without stage crew and audience, and without a complicated environing pattern of activity which produced a theatre, a city, and an economic surplus sufficient to allow the luxury of star performances."[16]

The creation of a modern American state has also played a key role in elevating the New Deal to mythic status. As Alan Brinkley argued in "The New Deal and the Idea of the State," the problem of the state is at the very center of the history of the New Deal.[17] But too frequently in conventional renderings, the New Deal is conflated with the modern American state itself, and the history of the New Deal becomes even more magnified as the defining and contested moment in the advent of a modern state. The myth of the New Deal state reinforces the tendency to look for that state precisely in those characters and categories that reinforce the notion of the New Deal as the epitome of modern statecraft—the national presidency and high-level officialdom. Fiscal-military imperatives are privileged, and measures of federal expenditures and personnel provide the New Deal with a special quantifiable claim to "making" the American state modern. This national story line, of course, provides a perfect backdrop to the tale of executive reorganization, court-packing, the constitutional revolution of 1937, and a Supreme Court supposedly "reborn." The stage is thus set for the essentially polemical condition that Pierre Rosanvallon lamented as well in *L'État en France:* "The state as a political problem, or as a bureaucratic phenomenon, is at the heart of heightened political passions while more important philosophical debates about the nature of the state evade serious historical scrutiny."[18]

A crucial legacy of the myth of the New Deal state has been the tendency to downplay American state development before the Roosevelt Revolution. Alan Brinkley drew on an expansive history and social science literature concerning the distinctive "limits" of American state capacity in his portrayal of the huge governmental challenges greeting the New Deal's emergence:

The United States was one of the slowest of the advanced industrial nations to define an important social and economic role for its national government. The American state did not remain static, certainly, in the last decades of the nineteenth century and the first decades of the twentieth century; but *it grew slowly, haltingly, incompletely.* The Great Depression, which would have been a difficult challenge for any state, was doubly intimidating in the United States because Americans had as yet made few decisions about what their government should do and how it should do it. As a result, the New Deal was not only an effort to deal with the particular problems of the 1930s; it was also a process of building government institutions where *none existed.*[19]

Ira Katznelson's recent epic history also emphasizes the structural limitations of pre–New Deal statecraft: "It was not clear at all that America's constitutional state possessed the means to meet the era's challenges," underscoring Pendleton Herring's worry: "Our government was originally designed for no such complex necessities." Katznelson's New Deal state is thus unmistakably a revolution, a creation—indeed "the origins of our time." Katznelson ascribed to the New Deal "an import almost on a par with that of the French Revolution," and that import concerned the state: "The New Deal made many historic contributions, but its most enduring one was a novel national state."[20] This characterization comports fully with Bruce Ackerman's notion of a third American constitutional revolution finally overcoming "the Founding notion that the national government had limited powers over economic and social development." Henceforth, "the federal government would operate as a truly national government," Ackerman concluded. "All of us live in the modern era that begins with the Supreme Court's 'switch in time' in 1937, in which an activist, regulatory state is finally accepted as an unchallengeable constitutional reality."[21]

This book has offered up an alternative account of the rise of an activist, regulatory state in America, challenging the overweening centrality of the New Deal in the creation of modern America. In place of presidential prophets and promised lands, it has focused instead on the seventy years in the wilderness before darkness purportedly turned to light on March 4, 1933. Much of the heavy lifting in terms of the creation of a modern American state was done before the so-called Hundred Days. The reason the New Deal was possible as a response to the Great Depression was because of the legal, institutional, socioeconomic, and democratic revolutions of the preceding decades. It takes more than a financial crisis and a charismatic presidential candidate to create something like a New Deal.

After Reconstruction, but before the ascendancy of Franklin Roosevelt, a new kind of American state unmistakably came into being—a modern legislative, regulatory, and administrative state. This structural transformation of the American political sphere was not the product of a sudden new "moment" of constitutional change or popular revolution; nor did it entail a complete break with all earlier American traditions of governance (though it certainly did with some). Rather, it was a less conspicuous revolution. It involved a fundamental shift in the scale, scope, techniques, and legitimating rationales of governance, but the character of these governmental changes ran a bit underground. One does not find the most important markers in the usual sites of national political history: elections, party platforms, campaign addresses, inaugurals, floor speeches, or even the most famous Supreme Court opinions. Rather, the key transformations that made up this revolution—new conceptions of citizen and state, the rise of legal positivism and legal realism, the transformation of police power and administrative law, new ideas of public service and public utility and public welfare—were the products of larger, more disparate, and more subterranean processes of legal and political, as well as social and economic, change. Together these changes amounted to a transformation of American public law—a fundamental reworking of the legitimating basis for governmental action in the

United States. That transformation of American public law created a polity far more legislated, regulated, and administered than before the Civil War. And it marked the ascendancy of a distinctly modern form of statecraft in America. One thing is certain, American governance by 1932 bore little resemblance to nineteenth-century practice. And legal and public policy making had acquired some of the distinctive characteristics—a new kind of sustained and systemic legal interventionism—that would continue to drive American governance into the twenty-first century. These were the public law beginnings of the kind of modern American state that could launch a New Deal.

Barely a generation after the United States defeated the oldest and gravest threat to its democratic aspirations—that is, the scourge of slavery—American progressives faced a new and dangerous triple threat. In the late nineteenth century, radical shifts in political economy forever transformed American finance, business, labor, and politics, unsettling established relationships between the governors and the governed, the business classes and the working classes, urban America and rural America, new corporate-financial interests and prevailing conceptions of the public interest. On the ground, unprecedented forms of populist unrest and extreme conflict—some called it a social war—unleashed an endless cycle of violence, protests, political scandals, and volatile socioeconomic uncertainty and insecurity. Progressives viewed this state of affairs as nothing short of a full-blown crisis in American democracy (and pessimists like Brooks and Henry Adams fretted over the impending death of the entire noble experiment).[22]

Though this book has identified innumerable concerns in the reform movement that stretched from 1866 to 1932, new democratic energies coalesced around three primary public policy challenges that continue to resonate to this very day: (a) the rise of corporate economic power and its subsequent abuse; (b) the consequent corruption (or capture) of American politics by such special private interests; and (c) the increased socioeconomic inequality, precarity, and deprivation on the ground that seemed to so betray American democratic ideals and aspirations.

It is impossible to exaggerate the centrality of the new problem of corporate power to new democracy. Indeed, progressive reformers were stunned that so soon after vanquishing an old aristocratic slavocracy and land monopoly that a new economic power center could reemerge so quickly to again challenge American democratic commitments. From the monopolistic machinations of the new Railroad Barons at the heart of *Chapters of Erie* to the Standard Oil Trust made famous in Ida Tarbell's muckraking exposé to the pure financial domination of the House of

Morgan in Louis Brandeis's still relevant *Other People's Money,* the over-riding concern about the threat posed to democracy by unprecedented concentrations of economic wealth and corporate power was at the very core of the reform crusade. The thrust of progressive critique was clear—such new agglomerations of private economic authority within a newly industrialized and financialized capitalism were sources of private coercion and economic domination, upending the existing balance of socioeconomic power, exacerbating inequality, and ultimately threatening the project of popular self-governance. The problem of monopoly and the concentration of economic power galvanized an ambitious program of progressive economic reforms, running the gambit from railroad rate regulation and anti-trust to public utility and financial regulation to social insurance and labor administration.

But beyond the challenges to economic citizenship posed by the concentration of economic power, big business in the Gilded Age generated a secondary concern—an obsession with political capture and the rediscovery of "the prevalence of illicit business influence in politics." As one historian summed up this second priority: progressives "discovered how big business interests were corrupting politics in quest of special privileges and an outraged people acted to reform the perceived evils."[23] Political concern about "the politicos"—the political bosses, the party machines, and the spoils of patronage politics—now joined original progressive economic concern with "the robber barons" themselves.[24] Progressives used "corruption" in its classical sense indicating the despoiling of a distinctly public sphere (a commonwealth supposedly devoted to res publica—public things) by private economic interests. But the ancient worry about the corrupt bending of public governing institutions to private, selfish ends took on new democratic content given the general scale of the threat to self-government illuminated by scandals like Crédit Mobilier, the Whiskey and Tweed Rings, and Teapot Dome.[25] Beyond the well-known exposés of the muckraking journalists Ida Tarbell, Lincoln Steffens, and Ray Stannard Baker who gathered around *McClure's Magazine,* progressive reformers, legislators, jurists, and social scientists maintained a steady drumbeat of exposure and criticism against political-economic corruptions of the Gilded Age, large and small. The progressive discovery that private business and economic interests were systematically capturing the main instruments of American democratic politics precipitated an insurgent, broad-based campaign to change American attitudes, policies, and practices to insulate the public sphere from private corruption. They included some of the most ambitious attempts to reform the democratic process, from the underlying mechanics of suffrage, direct primaries, and initiative/referendum/recall to more substantive policies of municipal home rule, the regulation of lobbying, and the restriction of corporate political spending and favors via the so-called corrupt practices acts.

Perhaps most importantly, progressives coupled worry about economic concentration and political corruption with an abiding concern for intensifying inequality and socioeconomic necessity. Jacob Riis's *How the Other Half Lives* (1890), and Robert Hunter's *Poverty* (1904) were just two landmarks in a wave of progressive attempts to bring attention to the perilous way economic concentration and political corruption were creating conditions of privation and need among large swaths of a supposedly democratic citizenry.[26] As future empirical research on life expectancy would confirm, an extraordinarily large number of Gilded Age Americans were living lives that were poor, nasty, brutish, and short—literally working too long, resting too little, struggling with disease and substandard conditions in housing and work, with wages that didn't even support adequate caloric intake.[27] New democrats viewed this problem of baseline socioeconomic inequality not as an externality or a temporary maladjustment in supply and demand or an unfortunate byproduct of industrialism but as a fundamental failure of a vision of substantive democracy in which democracy stood for no more than mere adjustments in the formal political machinery. Substantive democracy was ultimately bound up with equality and socioeconomic justice—that is, the development of each and every human personality. New democracy implicated a new "way of life, social and individual," predicated on the equal participation of "every mature human being" in the formation of the values, rules, and social institutions that regulated collective life together.[28] New democrats redirected discussion away from traditional nineteenth-century frameworks of charity, exclusion, and dependency toward a more modern policy conversation about economic insecurity, inadequate standards of living, and the unequal distribution of wealth. A substantive democratic mandate translated into an ambitious policy agenda of socioeconomic provisioning that stretched from revising an obsolete American poor law to the wholesale revision of American labor law, from hours and wages to workers' compensation and collective bargaining.

And the first thing to underscore about the extensive policy innovations that transformed American society and economy between 1866 and 1932 is that new democrats were not "tinkerers"—they had as little patience for accommodationist, incremental, and technocratic policy "nudges" as they had for conservative, laissez-faire apologetics. Whether talking about antimonopoly or juvenile justice, the Federal Reserve or social insurance, food and drug laws or zoning and city planning, this was a radical, substantive, and transformative policy agenda deeply rooted in the critical-realist and social-democratic commitments and aspirations of the day. Progressive proposals rested on a seriously thought-out, rigorous underlying philosophical pedigree. Indeed, new democracy was coincident with the rise of professional academic social science as well as the extraordinary beginnings of American pragmatism and legal realism. Their revolt against formalism involved a full-throated critical assault on the sclerotic orthodoxies obstructing progressive reform and social-democratic improvement—ideas like natural law, liberty of contract, laissez-faire liberalism, A. V. Dicey's anti-administrative constitutionalism, and Herbert Spencer's social statics.

But as important as pragmatic, realist, and antiformalist big ideas were to emancipating the progressive quest for bold solutions, it is equally important to acknowledge the role of popular participation, organization, infrastructure, and social movements in various policy successes (as well as failures). New democracy involved a sprawling social movement built on a vast network of reform institutions, civic organizations, voluntary associations, labor unions, professional associations, universities, institutes, magazines, and newspapers. The 1,300 fine-print, double-columned pages of the *New Encyclopedia of Social Reform* published in 1908 (which attempts to list such organizations) bears witness to the vast scale and scope of the progressive social network.

The mobilization of such a democratic multitude of participants and associations was key to what Walter Weyl viewed as the "general movement toward a new democracy"—a movement toward a common end but composed "along divergent lines by people holding separate interests":

> One group in the community strives to end the exploitation of child labor. Other groups seek to extend and improve education, to combat tuberculosis, to reform housing conditions, to secure direct primaries, to obtain the referendum, to punish force and fraud at the polls, to secure governmental inspection of foods, to regulate railroad rates, to limit the issue of stocks and bonds of corporations doing an interstate business, to change the character and incidence of taxation, to protect and recreate our forests, to reserve and conserve our mines, to improve the lot of the farmer, to build up trade-unions among workingmen, to Americanize incoming immigrants, to humanize prisons and penal laws, to protect the community against penury caused by old age, accident, sickness, and invalidity, to prevent congestion in cities, to divert to the public a larger share of the unearned increment, to accomplish a thousand other results for the general welfare.[29]

Together these forces allowed for what Vernon Parrington called "an extension of democratic control" over the "forces of exploitation." For Parrington, the goal of new democracy was "to wrest control of the government from the hands of the plutocracy that was befouling it, and to use it for democratic rather than plutocratic ends."[30] New democratic means and ends were brought together in a more realistic and substantive conception of the state, not as an abstract sovereignty or a supreme command but as a modern governmental institution rooted in the provision of public services in the interest of the public welfare. This pragmatic reorientation of a reorganized government emphasized the public duties, legal obligations, and social functions of a modern democratic state in solving pressing social and economic problems in the service of a democratic public. It was this more common, social, and democratic vision of a modern American state that united the widely divergent policies and practices of this re-formative era.

Thus, well before 1932, the rights of American citizens were increasingly hammered out in relationship to a new democratic state. That new state already boasted a new institutional identity as a modern governmental organization consisting of an expanded positive legislative power, an unprecedented administrative regulatory range, and prolific new instrumentalities of public law. As Charles Beard surveyed the "huge complex of wealth, political institutions, military engines, economic undertakings, and technological activities" that made up American government by 1930, he could do no better than to characterize this vast new assemblage of power as nothing less than an American Leviathan—a "powerful and bewildering Titan."[31] This modern revolution in American governance was rooted in the new functions demanded of modern democratic states—the new jobs that the new state was constantly being asked to perform in the service of ever-growing public needs. Beard listed just some of the more significant public obligations facing the new American democratic leviathan: taxation, finance, and supplies; money and banking; transportation (inland and coastal waters, railways, express, pipelines, highways, aviation); communications (postal service, wire communications, radio); the promotion of business enterprise (tariff, unfair competition, antitrust, trademarks, copyrights, and patents); labor and immigration policy; agricultural promotion and regulation; the conservation of natural resources; public health, safety, and morals; measurements and planning (standards, surveying, mapping, statistics); and the nature and conduct of foreign relations. And, as this book suggests, this was but the tip of an ever-expanding iceberg. In the actual output of the modern legislative and regulatory state, one gains a better appreciation of the dramatic changes in social and economic life entailed by this formative revolution in American government before the New Deal. The legacy of this new democracy in ideas, organization, law, and policy innovation made the New Deal a historic possibility. And it might continue to hold out some important lessons for American democracy in a new era of crisis and concern.

We live today in an era that some have likened to a "Second Gilded Age." And indeed, given increased economic inequality, growing social and racial stratification, burgeoning anti-immigrant and xenophobic sentiment, failing infrastructure, resurgent corporate capital and financial assertiveness, the return of dark money in political campaigns, and the revival of plutocracy and oligarchy, it is easy to see grounds for surface historical comparisons. Contemporary notions of democracy and political freedom have shriveled as private economic liberty and celebrity entrepreneurship again overtake public traditions of self-government, collective welfare, and public accountability. Indeed, the latent political-economic orientation of our times—sometimes captured by the telling catchphrase *neoliberalism*—features the unmistakable return of a discourse about the American political tradition confined again to its most undemocratic and least egalitarian dimensions. The rightward strand in American political-economic thought has not been as aggressive in the United States since the original polemics of Herbert Spencer and William Graham Sumner. In law, formalism, originalism, and constitutional limitations (sometimes dubbed a "New First Amendment Lochnerism") are again ascendant—as they have not been since the inventive doctrinalism of the likes of Christopher Tiedeman and Rufus Peckham.[32] The democratic deficit in recent social and political trends is all too apparent as modern democracy seems to have given up the substantive guarantees and enlightened aspirations that John Dewey and his compatriots knew were the very heart of the matter. One cannot help but worry that contemporary America is being systematically de-democratized. We seem dangerously too close to living again in what Hannah Arendt called "dark times"—periods in which the "public realm" has become so "obscured," so "dubious," and so "despised" that people ask no more of politics than that it serve personal, private, and ultimately "petty" interests.[33]

Under such circumstances, resignation and political pessimism are perhaps in order. But because of a focus on the past as well as the present, historians offer an alternative approach—seeing the constant opportunity for rediscovery and reinvention in the never-ending dialectic of past possibilities and present conditions. The classicist Werner Jaeger perhaps captured it best when he reflected on what moderns could possibly gain by turning attention back to an earlier time: "Inevitably toward the end of a historical period, when thought and custom have petrified into rigidity, and when the elaborate machinery of civilization opposes and represses man's heroic qualities, life stirs again beneath the hard crust." At just such times, Jaeger contended, "A deep-seated historical instinct drives one not only to go back to the resources of their own national culture, but also to live once more in that earlier age when the spirit . . . was still fervently alive, and from its ardent life was creating the forms which eternalized its ardour and its genius."[34]

Jaeger was writing in 1939 when the petrified crust of "dark times" was unbearably heavy. Yet in the turn to the past—to an age where the original spirit was still fervently alive—Jaeger saw infinite possibility for the renewal of culture and civilization. The past is indeed a useful schoolhouse. In something of that same spirit, this book invites a rediscovery of the possibilities of American democratic politics through a turn to another age. In the late nineteenth and early twentieth century, American thinkers and reformers rediscovered and reinvented American democracy for a new era. In a period when prevailing theories of social Darwinism deemed activism, instrumental change, and progressive reform increasingly futile, these new democrats transformed every corner of American life. They rewrote the rules of the entire game from law and society to state and economy, from public and private to collective and individual. This was a generation still in touch and in tune with an original Enlightenment aspiration of change, human creativity, progress, and social and political emancipation. From Kant's famous injunction, "Dare to know," they dared to act. With that original and ardent spirit, they built a modern state and a new democracy.

NOTES

Introduction

1. Gordon S. Wood, *The Creation of the American Republic, 1776–1787* (Chapel Hill: University of North Carolina Press, 1969).
2. Richard Hofstadter, *The Age of Reform: From Bryan to F. D. R.* (New York: Alfred A. Knopf, 1955); Samuel P. Hays, *The Response to Industrialism, 1885–1914* (Chicago: University of Chicago Press, 1957); Robert H. Wiebe, *The Search for Order, 1877–1920* (New York: Hill and Wang, 1967).
3. William J. Novak, *The People's Welfare: Law and Regulation in Nineteenth-Century America* (Chapel Hill: University of North Carolina Press, 1996).
4. John F. Manning and Matthew C. Stephenson, eds., *Legislation and Regulation: Cases and Materials* (New York: Foundation, 2010); William N. Eskridge Jr., Philip P. Frickey, Elizabeth Garrett, and James J. Brudney, eds., *Legislation and Regulation: Statutes and the Creation of Public Policy: Cases and Materials,* 5th ed. (St. Paul, MN: West Academic, 2014); Jerry L. Mashaw, Richard A. Merrill, Peter M. Shane, M. Elizabeth Magill, Mariano-Florentino Cuéllar, and Nicholas R. Parrillo, eds., *Administrative Law: The American Public Law System: Cases and Materials,* 7th ed. (St. Paul, MN: West Academic, 2014); Lisa Schultz Bressman, Edward L. Rubin, and Kevin M. Stack, eds., *The Regulatory State* (New York: Aspen Publishers, 2010).
5. James Willard Hurst, "Consensus and Conflict in Twentieth-Century Public Policy," *Daedalus: Journal of the American Academy of Arts and Sciences* 105 (1976): 89; Hurst, "Legal History: A Research Program," *Wisconsin Law Review* 1942 (1942): 331–332. Of course, Hurst's two great histories *Law and the Conditions of Freedom in the Nineteenth-Century United States* (Madison: University of Wisconsin Press, 1956) and *Law and Economic Growth: The Legal History of the Lumber Industry in Wisconsin, 1836–1915* (Cambridge, MA: Harvard University Press, 1964) provide more detail on the nature of this modern transformation in law and governance. For a fuller

discussion of Hurst's overarching historical sociology, see William J. Novak, "Law, Capitalism, and the Liberal State: The Historical Sociology of James Willard Hurst," *Law and History Review* 18 (2000): 97–145.

6. The literature is voluminous. In addition to the classic syntheses of Hofstadter, Hays, and Wiebe, see Gabriel Kolko, *The Triumph of Conservatism: A Reinterpretation of American History, 1900–1914* (New York: Free Press, 1963); James Weinstein, *The Corporate Ideal in the Liberal State, 1900–1918* (New York: Farrar Straus & Giroux, 1971); Martin J. Sklar, *The Corporate Reconstruction of American Capitalism, 1890–1916: The Market, the Law, and Politics* (New York: Cambridge University Press, 1988); Alfred D. Chandler Jr., *The Visible Hand: The Managerial Revolution in American Business* (Cambridge, MA: Harvard University Press, 1977); Morton Keller, *Affairs of State: Public Life in Late Nineteenth Century America* (Cambridge, MA: Harvard University Press, 1977); Duncan Kennedy, *The Rise and Fall of Classical Legal Thought* (Washington, DC: Beard Books, 2006); Morton J. Horwitz, *The Transformation of American Law, 1870–1960: The Crisis of Legal Orthodoxy* (New York: Oxford University Press, 1992); Theda Skocpol, *Protecting Soldiers and Mothers: The Political Origins of Social Policy in the United States* (Cambridge, MA: Harvard University Press, 1992); Stephen Skowronek, *Building a New American State: The Expansion of National Administrative Capacities, 1877–1920* (New York: Cambridge University Press, 1982); James T. Kloppenberg, *Uncertain Victory: Social Democracy and Progressivism in European and American Thought, 1870–1920* (New York: Oxford University Press, 1986); Daniel T. Rodgers, *Atlantic Crossings: Social Politics in a Progressive Age* (Cambridge, MA: Harvard University Press, 1998); Alice Kessler Harris, *In Pursuit of Equity: Women, Men, and the Quest for Economic Citizenship in 20th-Century America* (New York: Oxford University Press, 2001); Dorothy Sue Cobble, *For the Many: American Feminists and the Global Fight for Democratic Equality* (Princeton, NJ: Princeton University Press, 2021).

7. Novak, *People's Welfare;* William J. Novak, "The Myth of the 'Weak' American State," *American Historical Review* 113 (2008): 752–772. See also James T. Sparrow, William J. Novak, and Stephen W. Sawyer, eds., *Boundaries of the State in US History* (Chicago: University of Chicago Press, 2015); William J. Novak, Stephen W. Sawyer, and James T. Sparrow, "Beyond Stateless Democracy," *Tocqueville Review/La Revue Tocqueville* 36 (2015): 21–164.

8. John Dewey, *The Public and Its Problems,* in *John Dewey: The Later Works, 1925–1953,* vol. 2, ed. Jo Ann Boydston (Carbondale: University of Southern Illinois Press, 1984), 241, 256, 264, 279.

9. Novak, "Myth of the 'Weak.'" "*AHR* Exchange: On the 'Myth' of the 'Weak' American State," *American Historical Review* 115 (2010): 766–800.

10. Alexis de Tocqueville, *Democracy in America,* trans. George Lawrence, ed. J. P. Mayer (New York: Harper and Row, 1988), 394–395; Georg Wilhelm Friedrich Hegel, *The Philosophy of History,* trans. J. Sibree (New York: Dover, 1956), 85–86.

11. Ernst Cassirer, *Language and Myth,* trans. Susanne K. Langer (New York: Harper and Brothers, 1946); Cassirer, *The Philosophy of the Enlightenment,* trans. Fritz C. A. Koelln and James P. Pettegrove (Princeton, NJ: Princeton University Press, 1951).

12. Vernon Louis Parrington, *Main Currents in American Thought: Volume Three; The Beginnings of Critical Realism in American, 1860–1920* (New York: Harcourt, Brace & World, 1930).

13. Albert Shaw, "The American State and the American Man," *Contemporary Review* 51 (1887): 696.

14. Arthur M. Schlesinger, *Paths to the Present* (New York: Macmillan, 1949), 22.

15. Max M. Edling, *A Revolution in Favor of Government: Origins of the U.S. Constitution and the Making of the American State* (New York: Oxford University Press, 2003); Max M. Edling, *A Hercules in the Cradle: War, Money, and the American State, 1783–1867* (Chicago: University of Chicago Press, 2014); Jerry L. Mashaw, *Creating the Administrative Constitution: The Lost One Hundred Years of American Administrative Law* (New Haven, CT: Yale University Press, 2012); Nicholas R. Parrillo, *Against the Profit Motive: The Salary Revolution in American Government, 1780–1940* (New Haven, CT: Yale University Press, 2013); Richard R. John, "Governmental Institutions as Agents of Change: Rethinking American Political Development in the Early Republic, 1787–1835," *Studies in American Political Development* 11 (Fall 1997): 347–380; Richard White, *"It's Your Misfortune and None of My Own": A New History of the American West* (Norman: University of Oklahoma Press, 1991); Patricia Nelson Limerick, *The Legacy of Conquest: The Unbroken Past of the American West* (New York: W. W. Norton, 1987); Colleen A. Dunlavy, *Politics and Industrialization: Early Railroads in the United States and Prussia* (Princeton, NJ: Princeton University Press, 1994); Mae M. Ngai, *Impossible Subjects: Illegal Aliens and the Making of Modern America* (Princeton, NJ: Princeton University Press, 2005); Nayan Shah, *Contagious Divides: Epidemics and Race in San Francisco's Chinatown* (Berkeley: University of California Press, 2001); Sarah Barringer Gordon, *The Mormon Question: Polygamy and Constitutional Conflict in Nineteenth-Century America* (Chapel Hill: North Carolina University Press, 2002); Karen M. Tani, *States of Dependency: Welfare, Rights, and American Governance, 1935–1972* (New York: Cambridge University Press, 2016); Michele Landis Dauber, *Sympathetic State: Disaster Relief and the Origins of the American Welfare State* (Chicago: University of Chicago Press, 2003); Christopher Howard, *The Hidden Welfare State: Tax Expenditures and Social Policy in the United States* (Princeton, NJ: Princeton University Press, 1997); Jennifer Klein, *For All These Rights: Business, Labor, and the Shaping of America's Public-Private Welfare State* (Princeton, NJ: Princeton University Press, 2003); James T. Sparrow, *Warfare State: World War II Americans and the Age of Big Government* (New York: Oxford University Press, 2011); Jennifer Mittelstadt, *The Rise of the Military Welfare State* (Cambridge, MA: Harvard University Press, 2015).

16. Franz L. Neumann, "The Change in the Function of Law in Modern Society," in *The Rule of Law under Siege: Selected Essays of Franz L. Neumann and*

Otto Kirchheimer, ed. William E. Scheuerman (Berkeley: University of California Press, 1996), 101.

17. See, for example, the pioneering articles of Friedrich Pollock, "State Capitalism: Its Possibilities and Limitations," and Max Horkheimer, "The Authoritarian State," in *The Essential Frankfurt School Reader*, ed. Andrew Arato and Eike Gebhardt (New York: Continuum, 1982), 71–94, 95–117.

18. William J. Novak, Stephen W. Sawyer, and James T. Sparrow, "Beyond Stateless Democracy," *Tocqueville Review/La Revue Tocqueville* 36 (2015): 21–41.

19. Louis Hartz, *The Liberal Tradition in America* (New York: Harcourt Brace Jovanovich, 1955), 60, 62.

20. Pierre Bourdieu, *On the State: Lectures at the Collège de France, 1989–1992*, trans. David Fernbach (Cambridge: Polity, 2014), 5–6.

21. Quoted in Graham Burchell, Colin Gordon, and Peter Miller, eds., *The Foucault Effect: Studies in Governmentality* (Chicago: University of Chicago Press, 1991), ix.

22. The classics remain J. G. A. Pocock, *The Machiavellian Moment: Florentine Political Thought and the Atlantic Republican Tradition* (Princeton, NJ: Princeton University Press, 1975); Caroline Robbins, *The Eighteenth-Century Commonwealthman: Studies in the Transmission, Development and Circumstances of English Liberal Thought from the Restoration of Charles II until the War with the Thirteen Colonies* (New York: Atheneum, 1968); Bernard Bailyn, *The Ideological Origins of the American Revolution* (Cambridge, MA: Harvard University Press, 1967); Pauline Maier, *From Resistance to Revolution: Colonial Radicals and the Development of American Opposition to Britain, 1765–1776* (New York: Alfred A. Knopf, 1972); Quentin Skinner, *Liberty before Liberalism* (Cambridge: Cambridge University Press, 1998); Philip Pettit, *Republicanism: A Theory of Freedom and Government* (Oxford: Oxford University Press, 1997). Also see the bibliographies in Robert E. Shalhope, "Toward a Republican Synthesis: The Emergence of an Understanding of Republicanism in American Historiography," *William and Mary Quarterly* 29 (1972): 49–80; Robert E. Shalhope, "Republicanism in Early American Historiography," *William and Mary Quarterly* 39 (1982): 334–356; and Daniel T. Rodgers, "Republicanism: The Career of a Concept," *Journal of American History* 79 (1992): 11–38.

23. Max Weber, "Politics as a Vocation," in *From Max Weber: Essays in Sociology*, ed. H. H. Gerth and C. Wright Mills (New York: Oxford University Press, 1946), 78.

24. Max Weber, *Economy and Society*, ed. Guenther Roth and Claus Wittich, 2 vols. (Berkeley: University of California Press, 1968), 1:220–221. I discuss the advantages and disadvantages of the Weberian approach to the state in more detail in Novak, "Beyond Max Weber: The Need for a Democratic (Not Aristocratic) Theory of the Modern State," *Tocqueville Review/La Revue Tocqueville* 36 (2015): 43–92.

25. Theda Skocpol, "Bringing the State Back In: Strategies of Analysis in Current Research," in *Bringing the State Back In*, ed. Peter B. Evans, Dietrich Reue-

schemeyer, and Theda Skocpol (Cambridge: Cambridge University Press, 1985), 3–42; Stephen Skowronek, *Building a New American State: The Expansion of National Administrative Capacities, 1877–1920* (New York: Cambridge University Press, 1982); Andrew Abbott, "A Brief Note on Pasturization," *International Journal of Comparative Sociology* 47 (2006): 343–348.

26. John R. Gillis, *The Prussian Bureaucracy in Crisis, 1840–1860: Origins of an Administrative Ethos* (Stanford, CA: Stanford University Press, 1971), 16.

27. G. W. F. Hegel, *Elements of the Philosophy of Right,* ed. Allen W. Wood, trans. H. B. Nisbet (Cambridge: Cambridge University Press, 1991), 328–329, 333, 336.

28. G. R. Elton, *Political History: Principles and Practice* (London: A. Lane, 1970), 70.

29. Karl Marx, "Critique of Hegel's Doctrine of State," in *Karl Marx: Early Writings,* trans. Rodney Livingstone and Gregor Benton (New York: Vintage, 1975), 86–88, 108, 109, 127. Charles Taylor offered a similar critique of Hegel's embrace of bureaucracy. Taylor, *Hegel* (Cambridge: Cambridge University Press, 1975), 442–443.

30. Walter Weyl, *The New Democracy* (New York: Macmillan, 1912), 159.

31. Richard Hofstadter, *The American Political Tradition* (New York: Alfred A. Knopf, 1948). See, for example, Allan G. Bogue, "The New Political History in the 1970s," in *The Past before Us,* ed. Michael Kammen (Ithaca, NY: Cornell University Press, 1980), 231–251; Peter B. Evans, Dietrich Rueschemeyer, and Theda Skocpol, eds., *Bringing the State Back In* (New York: Cambridge University Press, 1985); Karen Orren and Stephen Skowronek, *The Search for American Political Development* (New York: Cambridge University Press, 2004); Chris Beneke, "The New, New Political History," *Reviews in American History* 33 (2005): 314–324.

32. Stephen W. Sawyer, "Neoliberalism and the Crisis of Democratic Theory," in *In Search of the Liberal Moment: Democracy, Antitotalitarianism and Intellectual Politics in France since the 1950s,* ed. Stephen W. Sawyer and Iain Stewart (New York: Palgrave, 2016); Stephen W. Sawyer, "Foucault and the State," *Tocqueville Review / La Revue Tocqueville* 36 (2015): 135–164.

33. Andrew Arato and Eike Gebhardt, eds., *The Essential Frankfurt School Reader* (New York: Continuum, 1982); William E. Scheuerman, *The Rule of Law under Siege: Selected Essays of Franz L. Neumann and Otto Kirchheimer* (Berkeley: University of California Press, 1996); Jürgen Habermas, *The Structural Transformation of the Public Sphere: An Inquiry into a Category of Bourgeois Society,* trans. Thomas Burger (Cambridge, MA: MIT Press, 1989); Axel Honneth, *Freedom's Right: The Social Foundations of Democratic Life,* trans. Joseph Ganahl (New York: Columbia University Press, 2014).

34. Theda Skocpol, "Bringing the State Back In: Strategies of Analysis in Current Research," in Evans, Rueschemeyer, and Skocpol, *Bringing the State Back In,* 4, 7. For an overview of this basic dispute, see Sean D. Stryker, "The Rationalization of the Political Field: Beyond the State- and Society-Centered Theories of Policy Change" (working paper, Center for Culture, Organization, and Politics, Berkeley, CA, 1999).

35. For further discussion, see Steven Pincus and William Novak, "Political History after the Cultural Turn," *Perspectives on History: The Newsmagazine of the American Historical Association,* May 2011; Geoff Eley and Keith Nield, "Why Does Social History Ignore Politics?," *Social History* 5 (1980): 249–271; Victoria de Grazia, "For a Social History of Politics," *Radical History Review* 1980 (1980): 3–7.

36. Mitchell Dean and Kaspar Villadsen, *State Phobia and Civil Society: The Political Legacy of Michel Foucault* (Stanford, CA: Stanford University Press, 2016).

37. Brian Balogh, "The State of the State among Historians," *Social Science History* 27 (2003): 455; Eric A. Nordlinger, *On the Autonomy of the Democratic State* (Cambridge, MA: Harvard University Press, 1981); Michael Mann, "The Autonomous Power of the State: Its Origins, Mechanisms, and Results," *European Journal of Sociology* 25 (1985): 185–213.

38. Tony Judt, "A Clown in Regal Purple," *History Workshop* 7 (1989): 87–88.

39. Carl Schmitt, *The Concept of the Political,* trans. George Schwab (Chicago: University of Chicago Press, 1996), 22; Hannah Arendt, *On Revolution* (New York: Viking, 1963).

40. Pierre Rosanvallon, "Toward a Philosophical History of the Political," in *Democracy Past and Future,* ed. Samuel Moyn (New York: Columbia University Press, 2006), 60; "Inaugural Lecture, Collège de France," 36.

41. Pierre Rosanvallon, *L'État en France de 1789 à nos jours* (Paris: Seuil, 1990), 14 (pers. translation).

42. Rosanvallon, "Toward a Philosophical History," 36–37. See also Marcel Gauchet, "Democracy: From One Crisis to Another," trans. Natalie Doyle, *Social Imaginaries* 1 (2015): 166.

43. Michel Foucault, "The Mesh of Power," *Viewpoint Magazine,* https://viewpointmag.com/2012/09/12/the-mesh-of-power; Paolo Napoli, *Naissance de la police moderne. Pouvoir, normes, société* (Paris: La Découverte, 2003); Sawyer, "Foucault and the State."

44. Foucault, "Mesh of Power"; Foucault, *Discipline and Punish,* trans. Alan Sheridan (New York: Vintage Books, 1979), 26–27.

45. Honneth, *Freedom's Right;* Alex Honneth, *The Struggle for Recognition: The Moral Grammar of Social Conflicts,* trans. Joel Anderson (Cambridge, MA: MIT Press, 1995); Alex Honneth, *The Critique of Power: Reflective Stages in a Critical Social Theory,* trans. Kenneth Baynes (Cambridge, MA: MIT Press, 1991), viii.

46. Morton G. White, *Social Thought in America: The Revolt against Formalism* (New York: Viking, 1949).

47. Kloppenberg, *Uncertain Victory;* Rodgers, *Atlantic Crossings;* Dorothy Ross, *The Origins of American Social Science* (New York: Cambridge University Press, 1991); Thomas L. Haskell, *The Emergence of Professional Social Science: The American Social Science Association and the Nineteenth-Century Crisis of Authority* (Urbana: University of Illinois Press, 1977); Robert B. Westbrook, *John Dewey and American Democracy* (Ithaca, NY: Cornell University Press, 1991).

48. John Dewey, "The Historic Background of Corporate Legal Personality," *Yale Law Journal* 35 (1926): 660–661.

49. Roscoe Pound, *The Spirit of the Common Law* (Boston: Marshall Jones, 1921); Edward S. Corwin, *The "Higher Law" Background of American Constitutional Law* (Ithaca, NY: Cornell University Press, 1955), back cover; Edward S. Corwin, "The Basic Doctrine of American Constitutional Law," *Michigan Law Review* 12 (1914): 247–276, 538–572.

50. Julius Goebel Jr., *The Oliver Wendell Holmes Devise History of the Supreme Court of the United States, Volume I: Antecedents and Beginnings to 1801* (New York: Macmillan, 1971), 1–2 (emphasis added).

51. Sir Henry Sumner Maine, *Popular Government: Four Essays* (New York: Henry Holt, 1886); A. V. Dicey, *Lectures on the Relation between Law and Public Opinion in England during the Nineteenth Century*, 2nd ed. (London: Macmillan, 1914), 505; Friedrich A. Hayek, *The Constitution of Liberty* (Chicago: University of Chicago Press, 1960). Dicey's references to the United States in *Law and Public Opinion* are few but significant: "legal conservatism in," "respect for the obligation of contracts in," "individual freedom in"—fragments of the basic position on the American rule of law versus droit administratif that he articulated in *Introduction to the Study of the Law of the Constitution*, 8th ed. (London: Macmillan, 1920).

52. Such works are of an ilk. See, for example, Edwin Meese III, ed., *The Heritage Guide to the Constitution* (Washington, DC: Heritage, 2005); Randy E. Barnett, *Restoring the Lost Constitution: The Presumption of Liberty* (Princeton, NJ: Princeton University Press, 2004); Richard A. Epstein, *The Classical Liberal Constitution: The Uncertain Quest for Limited Government* (Cambridge, MA: Harvard University Press, 2014). For an alternative perspective rooted in sociolegal history research, see Larry D. Kramer, *The People Themselves: Popular Constitutionalism and Judicial Review* (New York: Oxford University Press, 2004).

53. James Willard Hurst, "Problems of Legitimacy in the Contemporary Legal Order," *Oklahoma Law Review* 24 (1971): 228; Hurst, *Conditions of Freedom*; Morton J. Horwitz, "The Conservative Tradition in the Writing of American Legal History," *American Journal of Legal History* 17 (1973): 275–294; Morton J. Horwitz, *The Transformation of American Law, 1780–1860* (Cambridge, MA: Harvard University Press, 1977).

54. James Willard Hurst, "The Law in United States History," *Proceedings of the American Philosophical Society* 104 (1960): 521.

55. Michael Mann, *The Sources of Social Power, Volume 1: A History of Power from the Beginning to AD 1760* (New York: Cambridge University Press, 1986), 170.

56. Martin Loughlin, *Foundations of Public Law* (New York: Oxford University Press, 2010), 407.

57. Erich Kahler, *Man the Measure: A New Approach to History* (Cleveland: World Publishing, 1943), 639–640.

58. Bruce Ackerman, *We the People: Transformations* (Cambridge, MA: Harvard University Press, 1998); Akhil Amar, *The Bill of Rights: Creation and Reconstruction* (New Haven, CT: Yale University Press, 1998).

59. Three constitutional syntheses from three different eras bear out this persistent interpretive convention. Robert G. McCloskey, *The American Supreme Court* (Chicago: University of Chicago Press, 1960), ch. 5, "Constitutional Evolution in the Gilded Age, 1865–1900," and ch. 6, "The Judiciary and the Regulatory State, 1900–1937"; Alfred H. Kelly, Winfred A. Harbison, and Herman Belz, eds. *The American Constitution: Its Origins and Development*, 6th ed. (New York: W. W. Norton, 1983): ch. 20, "The Supreme Court and Entrepreneurial Liberty," and ch. 21, "Progressive Constitutionalism"; Barry Friedman, *The Will of the People: How Public Opinion Has Influenced the Supreme Court and Shaped the Meaning of the Constitution* (New York: Farrar, Straus and Giroux, 2009).

60. Jürgen Habermas, *The Philosophical Discourse of Modernity: Twelve Lectures,* trans. Frederick G. Lawrence (Cambridge, MA: MIT Press, 1987); Robert B. Pippin, *Modernism as a Philosophical Problem*, 2d ed. (Oxford: Blackwell, 1999); Honneth, *Freedom's Right*.

61. Max Horkheimer and Theodor W. Adorno, *Dialectic of Enlightenment*, trans. John Cummings (New York: Continuum, 1987).

62. Some classic statements on this "democratic crisis" are Edward A. Purcell Jr., *The Crisis of Democratic Theory: Scientific Naturalism and the Problem of Value* (Lexington: University of Kentucky Press, 1973); Carl Schmitt, *The Crisis of Parliamentary Democracy*, trans. Ellen Kennedy (Cambridge, MA: MIT Press, 1985); Pierre Rosanvallon, *Democratic Legitimacy: Impartiality, Reflexivity, Proximity,* trans. Arthur Goldhammer (Princeton, NJ: Princeton University Press, 2011), 3; Gauchet, "Democracy."

63. W. E. H. Lecky, *Democracy and Liberty,* new ed., 2 vols. (New York: Longmans, Green, 1903), 1:vi, viii, 25. The old aristocratic theme that pervaded this and so many other critiques of democracy in this period included the racist and classist assumption that most people were simply "unfit" for self-governance. See Madison Grant, *The Passing of the Great Race: Or the Racial Basis of European History* (New York: Charles Scribner's Sons, 1916); Lothrop Stoddard, *The Rising Tide of Color against White World-Supremacy* (New York: Charles Scribner's Sons, 1920).

64. Anthony M. Ludovici, *A Defence of Aristocracy: A Text Book for Tories* (Boston: LeRoy Phillips, 1915), viii–ix; Anthony M. Ludovici, *The False Assumptions of "Democracy"* (London: Heath Cranton, 1921); Emile Faguet, *The Cult of Incompetence*, trans. Beatrice Barstow (New York: E. P. Dutton, 1916), 234; Ralph Adams Cram, *The Nemesis of Mediocrity* (Boston: Marshall Jones, 1917), 21–22, 38. For a succinct summary of the "antagonists of democratic theory" in this period, see Malcolm M. Willey, "Some Recent Critics and Exponents of the Theory of Democracy," in *A History of Political Theories: Recent Times,* ed. Charles Edward Merriam and Harry Elmer Barnes (New York: Macmillan, 1924), 46–79.

65. Maine, *Popular Government*; John Austin, *A Plea for the Constitution,* 2nd ed. (London: John Murray, 1859), vi. Austin's critique was explicitly aristocratic: Dicey, *Law of the Constitution*; Ernest Barker, "The Discredited State," *Political Quarterly*, o.s., vol. 2 (1915): 101.

66. Maine, *Popular Government,* 59–61, 63, 70, 98.
67. William Graham Sumner, *Folkways: A Study of the Sociological Importance of Usages, Manners, Customs, Mores, and Morals* (Boston: Ginn, 1906), 98, 180, 194, 376, 631; William Graham Sumner, *The Challenge of Facts and Other Essays* (New Haven, CT: Yale University Press, 1914), 223, 286.
68. Rosanvallon, *Democratic Legitimacy,* 3; Purcell, *Crisis of Democratic Theory.*
69. Moisei Ostrogorski, *Democracy and the Organization of the Political Parties,* trans. Frederick Clarke (New York: Macmillan, 1903); Hillaire Belloc and Cecil Chesterton, *The Party System* (London: Stephen Swift, 1911); Dorman B. Eaton, *The Government of Municipalities* (New York: Macmillan, 1899); Robert Michels, *Political Parties* (New York: Free Press, 1962); Walter Lippmann, *Public Opinion* (New York: Harcourt, Brace & Company, 1922); Carl Schmitt, *Crisis of Parliamentary Democracy,* 19.
70. Sumner, *Challenge of Facts,* 275.
71. Albion W. Small, "Review of Ostrogorski," *American Journal of Sociology* 8 (1903): 565.
72. Jane Addams, *Democracy and Social Ethics* (New York: Macmillan, 1905), 11–12. Dewey, *Public and Its Problems,* 325.
73. John Dewey, "The Ethics of Democracy," *University of Michigan Philosophical Papers,* 2nd ser. (Ann Arbor, MI: Andrews, 1888), 2, 20, 22, 25.
74. John Dewey, "Creative Democracy," in *John Dewey: The Later Works, 1925–1953,* vol. 14, ed. Jo Ann Boydston (Carbondale: University of Southern Illinois Press, 1984), 225; Dewey, "Ethics of Democracy," 12.
75. White, *Social Thought in America;* F. O. Matthiessen, *American Renaissance: Art and Expression in the Age of Emerson and Whitman* (New York: Oxford University Press, 1941). In law, this theme animates Horwitz, *Transformation of American Law.* Both Perry Miller and David Brion Davis hinted at the links between antiformalism in early American religious and legal/political thought. Perry Miller, *The Life of the Mind in America: From the Revolution to the Civil War* (New York: Harcourt, Brace & World, 1965); David Brion Davis, *Challenging the Boundaries of Slavery* (Cambridge, MA: Harvard University Press, 2003), 51–52.
76. Dewey, "Ethics of Democracy," 1.
77. Dewey, 3, 6–7, 9, 17–18.
78. Dewey, "Creative Democracy," 225–226. This basic sentiment was ubiquitous in this period. See James Russell Lowell, "On Democracy," quoted in Dewey, "Ethics of Democracy," 17; Henry Carter Adams, "Democracy," *New Englander* 40 (1881): 756–757. See also Andrew C. McLaughlin, "American History and American Democracy," *American Historical Review* 20 (1915): 255–276, 356.
79. John Dewey, "Democracy and Educational Administration," in *Problems of Men* (New York: Philosophical Library, 1946), 58.
80. Westbrook, *Dewey,* xv.
81. Dewey, "Democracy and Educational Administration," 57–58; Addams, *Democracy and Social Ethics,* 221–223.

82. Weyl, *New Democracy*, 2.

83. Dewey, "Ethics of Democracy," 25–26.

84. James H. Tufts, *Our Democracy: Its Origins and Its Tasks* (New York: Henry Holt, 1917), 268.

85. Graham Wallas, *The Great Society: A Psychological Analysis* (New York: Macmillan, 1914); Dewey, *Public and Its Problems*, 325–350.

86. John Dewey and James H. Tufts, *Ethics* (New York: Henry Holt, 1908), 435 (emphasis added).

87. Dewey, "Creative Democracy," 225; Weyl, *New Democracy*, 4.

88. Dewey, *Public and Its Problems*, 254.

89. Thomas C. Leonard, *Illiberal Reformers: Race, Eugenics and American Economics in the Progressive Era* (Princeton, NJ: Princeton University Press, 2016); Kolko, *Triumph of Conservatism*.

90. Frederick Engels, *The Condition of the Working Class in England in 1844*, trans. Florence Kelley Wischnewetzky (New York: John W. Lovell, 1887), 202.

91. "Hearings before a Special Committee to Investigate Communist Activities in the United States," 71st Cong., 2nd Sess. (June 9 and 13, 1930) US House of Representatives.

92. Wendy Brown, *Undoing the Demos: Neoliberalism's Stealth Revolution* (New York: Zone Books, 2015).

1. Citizenship

1. Abraham Lincoln, "Speech on the Kansas-Nebraska Act at Peoria, Illinois," in *Speeches and Writings, 1832–1858*, ed. Don E. Fehrenbacher (New York: Library of America, 1989), 339–340.

2. Alexis de Tocqueville, *The Old Regime and the French Revolution*, trans. Gilbert Stuart (New York: Anchor, 1955), vii.

3. Charles A. Beard and Mary R. Beard, *The Rise of American Civilization* (New York: Macmillan, 1927); James M. McPherson, *Abraham Lincoln and the Second American Revolution* (New York: Oxford University Press, 1991); Stephen Sawyer and William J. Novak, "Emancipation and the Creation of Modern Liberal States in America and France," *Journal of the Civil War Era* 3 (2013): 467–500.

4. George Ticknor, *Life, Letters, and Journals of George Ticknor*, 2 vols. (Boston: James R. Osgood, 1876), 2:486; Morton Keller, "The Weight of the War," in *Affairs of State: Public Life in Late Nineteenth Century America* (Cambridge: Harvard University Press, 1977), 1–33.

5. Roman J. Hoyos, "Peaceful Revolution and Popular Sovereignty: Reassessing the Constitutionality of Southern Secession," in *Signposts: New Directions in Southern Legal History*, ed. Patricia Hagler Minter and Sally E. Hadden (Athens: University of Georgia Press, 2013), 241–264; John Alexander Jameson, *A Treatise on Constitutional Conventions: Their History, Powers, and Modes of Proceeding* (Chicago: Callaghan, 1887), 243–247.

6. Broadly construed, this is what Jack M. Balkin and Sanford Levinson dub "the dangerous Thirteenth Amendment." Balkin and Levinson, "The Dan-

gerous Thirteenth Amendment," *Columbia Law Review* 112 (2012): 1459–1500. For provocative discussions of some of the historic limitations of this broad theoretical mandate, see Risa L. Goluboff, *The Lost Promise of Civil Rights* (Cambridge, MA: Harvard University Press, 2007).

7. Sidney George Fisher, *The Trial of the Constitution* (Philadelphia: J. B. Lippincott, 1862); John Alexander Jameson, *The Constitutional Convention* (New York: C. Scribner, 1867); Orestes A. Brownson, *The American Republic: Its Constitution, Tendencies, and Destiny* (New York: P. O'Shae, 1866); Eric Foner, *The Second Founding: How the Civil War and Reconstruction Remade the Constitution* (New York: Norton, 2019); Bruce Ackerman, *We the People: Transformations* (Cambridge, MA: Harvard University Press, 1998); Akhil Amar, *The Bill of Rights: Creation and Reconstruction* (New Haven, CT: Yale University Press, 1998); Robert J. Kaczorowski, *The Politics of Judicial Interpretation: The Federal Courts, Department of Justice, and Civil Rights, 1866–1876* (New York: Fordham University Press, 2005); Michael Vorenberg, *Final Freedom: The Civil War, the Abolition of Slavery, and the Thirteenth Amendment* (New York: Cambridge University Press, 2001).

8. Charles Edward Merriam, *American Political Ideas: Studies in the Development of American Political Thought, 1865–1917* (New York: Augustus M. Kelley, 1969), 215.

9. Harold M. Hyman, "An Adequate Constitution," in *A More Perfect Union: The Impact of the Civil War and Reconstruction on the Constitution* (New York: Alfred A. Knopf, 1973), ch. 8, 124–140; Timothy Farrar, "Adequacy of the Constitution," *New Englander* 21 (1862): 51–73.

10. Robert J. Kaczorowski, "To Begin the Nation Anew: Congress, Citizenship, and Civil Rights after the Civil War," *American Historical Review* 92 (1987): 45–68. See also Michael Vorenberg, "Bringing the Constitution Back In: Amendment, Innovation, and Popular Democracy during the Civil War," in *The Democratic Experiment: New Directions in American Political History,* ed. Meg Jacobs, William J. Novak, and Julian E. Zelizer (Princeton, NJ: Princeton University Press, 2003), 120–145.

11. Perhaps the opening wedge in this new dispensation was Lincoln's Emancipation Proclamation in 1863. James M. McPherson, *Battle Cry of Freedom: The Civil War Era* (New York: Oxford University Press, 1988), 557–567.

12. William Yates, *Rights of Colored Men to Suffrage, Citizenship and Trial by Jury* (Philadelphia: Merrihew and Gunn, 1838), v.

13. Pierre Rosanvallon, *Le sacre du citoyen. Histoire du suffrage universel en France* (Paris: Gallimard nrf, 1992), 15.

14. T. H. Marshall, "Citizenship and Social Class," in *Citizenship and Social Class,* ed. Tom Bottomore (London: Pluto, 1992), 3–51.

15. *The Oxford Dictionary of Difficult Words* (Oxford: Oxford University Press, 2004), 394.

16. Quoted in Eric Foner, *Nothing But Freedom: Emancipation and Its Legacy* (Baton Rouge: Louisiana State University Press, 1983), 6. *Slaughter-House Cases,* 83 U.S. 36 (1873); *Bradwell v. Illinois,* 83 U.S. 130 (1873); *United States v. Cruikshank,* 92 U.S. 542 (1875); *Civil Rights Cases,* 108 U.S. 3 (1883); *Plessy v. Ferguson,* 163 U.S. 537 (1896).

17. Bethany R. Berger, "Birthright Citizenship on Trial: *Elk v. Wilkins* and *Wong Kim Ark*," *Cardozo Law Review* 37 (2016): 1191; Maggie Blackhawk, "Federal Indian Law as a Paradigm within Public Law," *Harvard Law Review* 132 (2019): 1787–1877; Ian Haney López, *White by Law: The Legal Construction of Race* (New York: New York University Press, 2006); Gregory Ablavsky, "'With the Indian Tribes': Race, Citizenship, and Original Constitutional Meanings," *Stanford Law Review* 70 (2018): 1025–1076; Lucy E. Salyer, *Laws Harsh as Tigers: Chinese Immigrants and the Shaping of Modern Immigration Law* (Chapel Hill: University of North Carolina Press, 2000).

18. Hannah Arendt, *The Origins of Totalitarianism* (New York: Harcourt Brace Jovanovich, 1973), 301.

19. See Derrick Bell, *And We Are Not Saved: The Elusive Quest for Racial Justice* (New York: Basic Books, 1987), 255.

20. Kate Masur, *Until Justice Be Done: States' Rights and the Struggle for Racial Equality from the Revolution to Reconstruction* (New York: Norton, 2021); Martha S. Jones, *Birthright Citizens: A History of Race and Rights in Antebellum America* (New York: Cambridge University Press, 2018); Rebecca J. Scott, "Asserting Citizenship and Refusing Stigma: New Orleans Equal-Rights Activists Interpret 1803 and 1848," in *New Orleans, Louisiana, and Saint Louis, Senegal: Mirror Cities in the Atlantic World, 1659–2000s*, ed. Emily Clark, Cecile Vidal, and Ibrahima Thioub (Baton Rouge: Louisiana State University Press, 2019), 146. See also William J. Novak, "The Legal Transformation of Citizenship in Nineteenth-Century America," in Jacobs, Novak, and Zelizer, *Democratic Experiment*, 85–119.

21. G. W. F. Hegel, *Elements in the Philosophy of Right*, ed. Allen W. Wood (Cambridge: Cambridge University Press, 1991), 23.

22. To Tocqueville's "born equal," Hartz added Santayana's "referring to American democracy" as "a 'natural' phenomenon." Louis Hartz, *The Liberal Tradition in America: An Interpretation of American Political Thought since the Revolution* (New York: Harcourt Brace Jovanovich, 1955), i, 5. See also Benjamin Fletcher Wright, *Consensus and Continuity, 1776–1787* (Boston: Boston University Press, 1958).

23. Rogers M. Smith, *Civic Ideals: Conflicting Visions of Citizenship in U.S. History* (New Haven, CT: Yale University Press, 1997), 1, 6.

24. Linda K. Kerber, *No Constitutional Right to Be Ladies: Women and the Obligations of Citizenship* (New York: Hill and Wang, 1998), xx.

25. Arthur Conan Doyle, *Sherlock Holmes #15: The Adventure of Silver Blaze* (Baltimore: Gunston Trust, 2018).

26. Articles of Confederation, art. 4. James Madison defended the establishment of a uniform rule of naturalization. James Madison, *Federalist* no. 42, "On the Powers of the Federal Government: Relations with Foreign Nations, and other Provisions of Article I, Section 8," in *The Debate on the Constitution*, 2 vols., ed. Bernard Bailyn (New York: Library of America, 1993), 2:68–69.

27. Joseph Story, *Commentaries on the Constitution of the United States* (Boston: Hilliard, Gray, 1833), 383.

28. George Bancroft, *History of the United States: From the Discovery of the Continent: Volume IX* (Boston: Little, Brown, 1866), 447–448; George Ban-

croft, *History of the Formation of the Constitution of the United States of America*, 2 vols. (New York: D. Appleton, 1885), 1:218.

29. "Judge Drayton's Speech," in *Principles and Acts of the Revolution in America*, ed. Hezekiah Niles (Baltimore: William Ogden Niles, 1822), 100, 110.

30. *Lemmon v. People,* 20 N.Y. 562 (1860); New York Court of Appeals, *Report of the Lemmon Slave Case: Containing Points and Arguments of Counsel on Both Sides, and Opinions of All the Judges* (New York: Horace Greeley, 1861), 58-59.

31. United States Constitution, art. 1, sec. 8; art. 2, sec. 1; art. 4, sec. 2; Alexander Hamilton, *Federalist* no. 80, "On the Bounds and Jurisdiction of the Federal Courts," in Bailyn, *Debate,* 2:479.

32. Charles Pinckney, "Observations on the Plan of Government Submitted to the Federal Convention in Philadelphia," in *The Records of the Federal Convention of 1787,* 4 vols., ed. Max Farrand (New Haven, CT: Yale University Press, 1937), 3:112; "Charles Pinckney in the House of Representatives," in Farrand, *Records,* 3:445-446.

33. Alexander M. Bickel, *The Morality of Consent* (New Haven, CT: Yale University Press, 1975), 33.

34. Louis Henkin, "'Selective Incorporation' in the Fourteenth Amendment," *Yale Law Journal* 73 (1963): 74. In the official 1953 House and Senate authorized revised edition of the Annotated Constitution of the United States of America, Edward S. Corwin strangely annotated the preamble by citing Roger Taney in *Dred Scott:* "The words 'people of the United States' and 'citizens' are synonymous terms, and mean the same thing." Corwin, ed., *The Constitution of the United States of America: Analysis and Interpretation* (Washington, DC: Government Printing Office, 1953), 59.

35. William Blackstone, *Commentaries on the Laws of England: A Facsimile of the First Edition of 1765-1769,* 4 vols. (Chicago: Chicago University Press, 1979), 1:354-356. Blackstone's discussion followed closely the logic of Edward Coke's often-cited argument in *Calvin's Case,* 7 Co. Rep. 4 (1608).

36. Story, *Commentaries,* 3:565-566.

37. James Kent, *Commentaries on American Law,* 4 vols. (1826; Boston: Little, Brown, 1873), 2:53-54, 65.

38. The legislature of the state of New York passed over 2,660 special statutes between 1777 and 1857 authorizing aliens to purchase and hold real estate in New York. See *General Index of the Laws of the State of New York, 1777-1857* (Albany, 1859), 30-72. See also Kent, *Commentaries,* 2:63-64.

39. *Corfield v. Coryell,* 6 Fed. Cas. 546 (C.C.E.D. Pa., 1823), 551-552.

40. *Corfield v. Coryell,* 552.

41. Kent, *Commentaries,* 2:71.

42. Edward Bates, *Opinion of Attorney General Bates on Citizenship* (Washington, DC: Government Printing Office, 1862), 3-4.

43. William J. Novak, *The People's Welfare: Law and Regulation in Nineteenth-Century America* (Chapel Hill: University of North Carolina Press, 1996). Or for that matter, the contemporary human rights project. See William J. Novak, "Legal Realism and Human Rights," *History of European Ideas* 37 (2011): 168-174.

44. Benjamin Constant, "The Liberty of the Ancients Compared with That of the Moderns," in *Political Writings,* ed. Biancamaria Fontana (Cambridge: Cambridge University Press, 1988), 311.

45. Henry Maine, *Ancient Law* (New York: E. P. Dutton, 1931 [1861]).

46. Blackstone, *Commentaries,* 1:119, 142; Kent, *Commentaries,* 2:1.

47. Florien Giauque, *A Manual for Guardians and Trustees of Minors, Insane Persons, Imbeciles, Drunkards, and for Guardians Ad Litem, Resident and Non-Resident Affected by the Laws of Ohio* (Cincinnati: Robert Clarke, 1881); Clark D. Knapp, *A Treatise on the Laws of the State of New York Relative to the Poor, Insane, Idiots and Habitual Drunkards* (Rochester, NY: Williamson & Higbie, 1887).

48. Kent, *Commentaries,* 2:253, 277–78.

49. Christopher Tomlins, *Law, Labor, and Ideology in the Early American Republic* (New York: Cambridge University Press, 1993); Robert J. Steinfeld, *The Invention of Free Labor: The Employment Relation in English and American Law and Culture, 1350–1870* (Chapel Hill: University of North Carolina Press, 1991); Ariela J. Gross, *Double Character: Slavery and Mastery in the Antebellum Southern Courtroom* (Princeton, NJ: Princeton University Press, 2000); Ariela J. Gross, *What Blood Won't Tell: A History of Race on Trial in America* (Cambridge, MA: Harvard University Press, 2008); Thomas D. Morris, *Southern Slavery and the Law, 1619–1860* (Chapel Hill: University of North Carolina Press, 1996); Kerber, *No Constitutional Right;* Hendrik Hartog, *Man and Wife in America: A History* (Cambridge, MA: Harvard University Press, 2000); Nancy F. Cott, *Public Vows: A History of Marriage and the Nation* (Cambridge, MA: Harvard University Press, 2000); Michael Grossberg, *Governing the Hearth: Law and Family in Nineteenth-Century America* (Chapel Hill: University of North Carolina Press, 1985); Michael B. Katz, *In the Shadow of the Poorhouse: A Social History of Welfare in America* (New York: Basic Books, 1986).

50. Frederick Pollock and Frederic William Maitland, *The History of English Law before the Time of Edward I,* 2nd ed., 2 vols. (Washington, DC: Lawyers' Literary Club, 1959); Frederic William Maitland, *Township and Borough* (Cambridge: Cambridge University Press, 1898); H. D. Hazeltine, G. Lapsley, and P. H. Winfield, eds., *Maitland: Selected Essays* (Cambridge: Cambridge University Press, 1936). Maitland underscored the vast scale and scope of the law of association. Maitland, "Translator's Introduction," in Otto Gierke, *Political Theories of the Middle Age,* trans. Frederic William Maitland (Boston: Beacon, 1958), xxvii.

51. For a fuller explication, see William J. Novak, "The American Law of Association: The Legal-Political Construction of Civil Society," *Studies in American Political Development* 15 (2001): 163–188. One quick indicator of the public quality of early American associations was their formal creation and regulation by state governments. Between 1777 and 1857, for example, the state of New York passed hundreds of special statutes recognizing and incorporating associations. *General Index of the Laws of the State of New York, 1777–1857* (Albany, 1859). See also *Resolves and Private Laws of the State*

of Connecticut, 1789–1865, 5 vols. (New Haven, 1837–1871); *Private Laws of the State of Illinois, 1851, 1853, 1855,* 3 vols. (Springfield, 1851–1855); *Private and Special Laws of the State of Maine, 1820–1839,* 4 vols. (Portland, 1828).

52. George Bailey, in Frank Capra, dir., *It's a Wonderful Life* (RKO Radio Pictures, 1946); Novak, *People's Welfare*; Ernst Freund, *The Police Power: Public Policy and Constitutional Rights* (Chicago: Callaghan, 1904); John F. Dillon, *Treatise on the Law of Municipal Corporations* (Chicago: James Cockcroft, 1872).

53. *Commonwealth v. Stewart,* 1 S&R 342 (Pa., 1815), 345; *Smith v. Commonwealth,* 42 Ky. 21 (1845).

54. Novak, *People's Welfare,* 53.

55. *Barron v. Baltimore,* 32 U.S. 243 (1833), 250–251.

56. See Michael B. Katz, *The Undeserving Poor: From the War on Poverty to the War on Welfare* (New York: Pantheon, 1989), 12–15; Douglas L. Jones, "The Transformation of the Law of Poverty in Eighteenth-Century Massachusetts," in *Law in Colonial Massachusetts, 1630–1800,* ed. Daniel R. Coquillette (Boston: Colonial Society of Massachusetts, 1984), 153–190; Gerald L. Neuman, *Strangers to the Constitution: Immigrants, Borders, and Fundamental Law* (Princeton, NJ: Princeton University Press, 1996), 23–29; and Kunal M. Parker, "Citizenship, Poverty and Territory: The Legal Construction of Immigrants in Antebellum Massachusetts," *Law and History Review* 19 (2001): 583–643.

57. *Laws of Maine* (1821), c. 124, s. 6 and 7; *Nott's Case,* 11 Me. 208 (1834), 211.

58. *Portland v. Bangor,* 42 Me. 403 (1856), 404, 410. See also *Shafer v. Mumma,* 17 Md. 331 (1861).

59. *People v. Hall,* 4 Cal. 399 (1854).

60. *In Re Perkins,* 2 Cal. 424 (1852); *United States v. Skiddy,* 36 U.S. 73 (1837). Edgar Whittlesey Camp, "Hugh C. Murray: California's Youngest Chief Justice," *California Historical Society Quarterly* 20 (1941): 365–373.

61. *People v. Hall,* 402–403.

62. *People v. Hall,* 404–405.

63. Bates, *Opinion on Citizenship,* 3–4.

64. Jones, *Birthright Citizens.*

65. Thomas Jefferson, "A Bill Declaring Who Shall be Deemed Citizens of this Commonwealth," in *The Papers of Thomas Jefferson,* ed. Julian P. Boyd (Princeton, NJ: Princeton University Press, 1950), 2:476–478. Jefferson's bill was adopted by the Virginia legislature in May 1779. "An Act Declaring Who Shall be Deemed Citizens of this Commonwealth," in *The Statutes at Large: Being a Collection of All of the Laws of Virginia,* ed. William Waller Hening (Richmond: George Cochran, 1822), ch. 55, 10:129–130.

66. St. George Tucker, *Blackstone's Commentaries: With Notes of Reference, to The Constitution and Laws, of the Federal Government of the United States,* 5 vols. (Philadelphia: William Young Birch and Abraham Small, 1803).

67. Tucker, *Blackstone's Commentaries*, vol. 1, appendix "Note G: The Right of Conscience; and of the Freedom of Speech and of the Press," 3–30; "Note H: On the State of Slavery in Virginia," 31–85. Tucker, *A Dissertation on Slavery with a Proposal for the Gradual Abolition of It in the State of Virginia* (Philadelphia: Mathew Carey, 1796), 9.

68. Tucker, *Dissertation on Slavery*, 94–95.

69. Tucker himself claimed to be opposed to banishment. But his own plan employed multiple means of coercion. Tucker, 92.

70. Smith, *Civic Ideals;* Peter H. Schuck and Rogers M. Smith, *Citizenship without Consent: Illegal Aliens in the American Polity* (New Haven, CT: Yale University Press, 1985); James H. Kettner, *The Development of American Citizenship, 1608–1870* (Chapel Hill: University of North Carolina Press, 1978); Robert D. Putnam, *Bowling Alone: The Collapse and Revival of American Community* (New York: Simon and Schuster, 2000); Theda Skocpol and Morris P. Fiorina, eds., *Civic Engagement in American Democracy* (Washington, DC: Brookings, 1999).

71. Jones, *Birthright Citizens;* Rebecca J. Scott and Jean M. Hebrard, *Freedom Papers: An Atlantic Odyssey in the Age of Emancipation* (Cambridge, MA: Harvard University Press, 2012); Nathan Perl-Rosenthal, *Citizen Sailors: Becoming American in the Age of Revolution* (Cambridge, MA: Harvard University Press, 2015); *Report of the Arguments of Counsel in the Case of Prudence Crandall* (Boston: Garrison and Knapp, 1834). Useful summaries of some of the key cases and controversies can be found in William M. Wiecek, *The Sources of Antislavery Constitutionalism in America, 1760–1848* (Ithaca, NY: Cornell University Press, 1977); Gerald L. Neumann, *Strangers to the Constitution: Immigrants, Borders, and Fundamental Law* (Princeton, NJ: Princeton University Press, 1996).

72. Yates, *Rights of Colored Men*, iii–v.

73. Missouri Constitution of 1820, art. 3, sec. 26, in Francis Newton Thorpe, *The Federal and State Constitutions*, 7 vols. (Washington, DC: Government Printing Office, 1909), 4:2154. There was not just one Missouri Compromise but at least three. If the first and most famous focused intense national attention on the question of slavery in the territories, the second drew almost as much attention to the explicit issue of citizenship. Glover Moore, *The Missouri Controversy, 1819–1921* (Lexington: University of Kentucky Press, 1943).

74. *Federalist*, no. 80.

75. Missouri Constitution of 1820, art. 3, sec. 26, in Thorpe, *Federal and State Constitutions*, 4:2154.

76. Abraham Lincoln, "'House-Divided' Speech at Springfield Illinois," in Lincoln, *Speeches and Writings, 1832–1858* (New York: Library of America, 1989), 432.

77. Moore, *Missouri Controversy*, 151.

78. In Indiana, the legislative lower house passed a similar resolution, but it did not pass the upper house. Moore, 139.

79. 37 *Annals of Cong.*, 16th Cong., 2nd sess. (1820–1821), 23, 79–80.

80. 37 *Annals of Cong.*, 16th Cong., 2nd sess. (1820–1821), 45–48, 57–61.
81. 37 *Annals of Cong.*, 16th Cong., 2nd sess. (1820–1821), 92, 93, 98.
82. "An Act to Restrain the Emancipation of Slaves and to Prevent Free Persons of Colour from Entering Into this State," *Acts and Resolutions of the General Assembly of the State of South-Carolina, Passed in December 1820* (Columbia, SC, 1821), 22–24.
83. "An Act for Regulating the Police of Towns in this Commonwealth, and to Restrain the Practice of Negroes going at Large," *Acts Passed at a General Assembly of the Commonwealth of Virginia,* 1793 (Richmond, VA, 1794), ch. 22, 27.
84. "An Act to Prevent the Migration of Free Negroes and Mulattoes into this Commonwealth," *Acts Passed at a General Assembly of the Commonwealth of Virginia,* 1793 (Richmond, VA, 1794), ch. 23, 28.
85. "An Act to Prohibit the Emigration of Free Negroes Into this State," *A Session of the General Assembly of Maryland, 1806* (Annapolis, MD, 1807) ch. 56, 32; "An Act to Prohibit the Emigration of Free Negroes or Mulattoes Into this State," *Laws of the State of Delaware, 1811* (Dover, DE, 1811), ch. 146, 400–404; "An Act Prescribing the Mode of Manumitting Slaves in this State, To Prevent the Future Migration of Free Persons of Color Thereto; To Regulate Such Free Persons of Color," *Acts of the General Assembly of the State of Georgia, 1818* (Milledgeville, GA, 1818), 126; *Report of the Debates and Proceedings of the Convention for the Revision of the Constitution of the State of Indiana* (Indianapolis: H. Fowler, 1850), 1:583ff. For more general discussion of the regulation of free African Americans, see John Hope Franklin, *The Free Negro in North Carolina, 1790–1860* (Chapel Hill: University of North Carolina Press, 1943); Leon F. Litwack, *North of Slavery: The Negro in the Free States, 1790–1860* (Chicago: University of Chicago Press, 1961); Ira Berlin, *Slaves without Masters: The Free Negro in the Antebellum South* (New York: Pantheon Books, 1974).
86. "An Act to Restrain the Emancipation of Slaves and to Prevent Free Persons of Colour from Entering Into this State," *Acts and Resolutions of the General Assembly of the State of South-Carolina, Passed in December 1820* (Columbia, SC, 1821), 22–23.
87. "An Act for the Better Regulation and Government of Free Negroes and Persons of Colour" *Acts and Resolutions of the General Assembly of the State of South-Carolina Passed in December, 1822* (Columbia, SC, 1823), ch. 3, 11–14.
88. William Wirt, "Rights of Free Virginia Negroes," *Official Opinions of the Attorneys General of the United States* (Washington, DC: Robert Farnham, 1852), 1:507.
89. Perl-Rosenthal, *Citizen Sailors;* Michael A. Schoeppner, "Status across Borders: Roger Taney, Black British Subjects, and a Diplomatic Antecedent to the Dred Scott Decision," *Journal of American History* 100 (2013): 46–67; W. Jeffrey Bolster, *Black Jacks: African American Seamen in the Age of Sail* (Cambridge, MA: Harvard University Press, 1997).

90. *Elkison v. Deliesseline,* 8 F. Cas. 493 (C.C.D.S.C., 1823); *Gibbons v. Ogden,* 22 U.S. 1 (1824); Donald G. Morgan, *Justice William Johnson: The First Dissenter* (Columbia: University of South Carolina Press, 1954).

91. "Free Colored Seamen—Majority and Minority Reports," *H.R. Report,* 27th Cong., 3rd sess., ser. 426, doc. 80 (1843), 1–3.

92. H. Jefferson Powell, "Attorney General Taney and the South Carolina Police Bill," *Green Bag* 5 (2001): 84–85.

93. Notably, the next item on the Maryland Senate's agenda concerned "a bill, entitled, and act to authorize Joseph Stewart, of Dorchester county to sell the negro man therein named." *Journal of the Proceedings of the Senate of Maryland,* Jan. 16, 1832, 55; Carl Brent Swisher, *Roger B. Taney* (New York: Macmillan, 1935), 146–149.

94. "An Act for the Admission and Settlement of Inhabitants of Towns," May 24, 1833, *Connecticut Public Acts,* ch. 9, 420.

95. William Jay, *An Inquiry into the Character and Tendency of the American Colonization and American Anti-Slavery Societies* (New York: Leavitt, Lord, 1835), 28–48, 50; Yates, *Rights of Colored Men,* 54–75.

96. William Goodell, *The American Slave Code* (New York: American and Foreign Anti-Slavery Society, 1853), 355.

97. Frederick Douglass, "In what New Skin Will the Old Snake Come Forth?," in *The Frederick Douglass Papers: Series One,* ed. John W. Blassingame and John R. McKivigan (New Haven, CT: Yale University Press, 1991), 81–82.

98. Bates, *Opinion on Citizenship,* 26–27.

99. Francis Lieber, "Amendments of the Constitution, Submitted to the Consideration of the American People," in *Contributions to Political Science* (Philadelphia: J. B. Lippincott, 1881), 138, 179.

100. Joseph Story, *Commentaries on the Constitution of the United States,* ed. Thomas Cooley, 2 vols. (Boston: Little, Brown, 1873), 2:632–704.

101. James Bradley Thayer, *Cases on Constitutional Law,* 2 vols., (Cambridge, MA: Charles W. Sever, 1895), 1:449. See also Westel Woodbury Willoughby, "American Citizenship," in *The Constitutional Law of the United States,* 2 vols. (New York: Baker, Voorhis, 1910), 1:258–279.

102. See, for example, Alexander Porter Morse, *A Treatise on Citizenship, By Birth and by Naturalization: With Reference to the Law of Nations, Roman Civil Law, Law of the United States of America, and the Law of France* (Boston: Little, Brown, 1881); Prentiss Webster, *A Treatise on the Law of Citizenship in the United States: Treated Historically* (Albany, NY: Matthew Bender, 1891); Frederick Van Dyne, *Citizenship of the United States* (Rochester, NY: Lawyers' Co-operative, 1904); John S. Wise, *A Treatise on American Citizenship* (Northport, NY: Edward Thompson, 1906).

103. Theophilus Parsons, *The Political, Personal, and Property Rights of a Citizen of the United States: How to Exercise and How to Preserve Them* (Cincinnati: National Publishing, 1875).

104. David P. Currie, "The Reconstruction Congress," *University of Chicago Law Review* 75 (2008): 383–495.

105. Foner, *Second Founding,* 7.

106. Frederick Douglass, "Reconstruction," *The Atlantic,* 18 (Dec. 1866): 761–765.

107. W. E. B. Du Bois, *Black Reconstruction in America: Toward a History of the Part Which Black Folk Played in the Attempt to Reconstruct Democracy in America, 1860–1980* (New York: Harcourt, Brace, 1935), 325.

108. *Congressional Globe,* 39th Cong., 1st sess. (Dec. 4, 1866), 2.

109. "An Act to Establish a Bureau for the Relief of Freedmen and Refugees," *Statutes at Large,* 13 (Mar. 3, 1865), 507–508.

110. The Second Freedman's Bureau Bill passed the Senate on January 25, 1866, and the House on February 6. *Congressional Globe,* 39th Cong., 1st sess. (Jan. 12, 1866), 210–211.

111. Mark A. Graber, "The Second Freedmen's Bureau Bill's Constitution," *Texas Law Review* 94 (2016): 1402.

112. *Congressional Globe,* 39th Cong., 1st sess. (Dec. 13, 1865), 39.

113. *Congressional Globe,* 39th Cong., 1st sess. (Jan. 29, 1866), 474; *Corfield v. Coryell,* 4 Wash. C.C. 371 (1823).

114. *Congressional Globe,* 39th Cong., 1st sess. (Jan. 29, 1866), 474–475.

115. *Roberts v. City of Boston,* 59 Mass. 198 (1850); Charles Sumner, "Equality Before the Law," in *His Complete Works* (Boston: Lee and Shepard, 1900), 3:65–66.

116. *Congressional Globe,* 42nd Cong., 1st sess. (March 31, 1871), appendix, 84. For an excellent discussion, see Amar, *Bill of Rights.*

117. *People v. Washington,* 36 Cal. 658 (1869), 665.

118. *Portland v. Bangor,* 65 Me. 120 (1876), 121.

119. See, for example, Foner, *Nothing But Freedom;* Pamela Brandwein, *Rethinking the Judicial Settlement of Reconstruction* (New York: Cambridge University Press, 2011); Laura F. Edwards, *A Legal History of the Civil War and Reconstruction: A Nation of Rights* (New York: Cambridge University Press, 2015); Heather Cox Richardson, *The Death of Reconstruction: Race, Labor and Politics in the Post–Civil War North, 1865–1901* (Cambridge, MA: Harvard University Press, 2001).

120. "An Act to Amend the Naturalization Laws and to Punish Crime Against the Same," 16 Stat. 254 (1870), 256. See Berger, "Birthright Citizenship on Trial"; Sarah H. Cleveland, "Powers Inherent in Sovereignty: Indians, Aliens, Territories, and the Nineteenth Century Origins of Plenary Power over Foreign Affairs," *Texas Law Review* 81 (2002): 1–284.

121. See *United States v. Bhagat Singh Thind,* 261 U.S. 204 (1923), 211; *Ozawa v. United States,* 260 U.S. 178 (1922); *In re Mohan Singh,* 257 Fed. 207 (1919). For the definitive discussion of the so-called racial prerequisite cases, see López, *White by Law.*

122. *People v. Washington,* 36 Cal. 658 (1869), 666. Indeed, in *People v. Brady,* 40 Cal. 198 (1870), the California court retreated further from the limited equalitarian sentiments of *Washington.* William E. Nelson, *The Fourteenth Amendment: From Political Principle to Judicial Doctrine* (Cambridge, MA: Harvard University Press, 1988); J. A. C. Grant, "Testimonial Exclusion Because of Race: A Chapter in the History of Intolerance in California," in

Chinese Immigrants and American Law, ed. Charles McClain (New York: Garland, 1994), 82–91.

123. For a discussion of the decision in the context of antebellum public health and offensive trade regulation, see Novak, *People's Welfare,* 230–233.

124. *Slaughter-House Cases,* 83 U.S. 36 (1872), 74, 77.

125. *Slaughter-House Cases,* 79.

126. James G. Blaine, *Twenty Years of Congress: From Lincoln to Garfield,* 2 vols. (Norwick: Henry Bill, 1884–1886), 2:419.

127. *Plessy v. Ferguson,* 163 U.S. 537 (1896), 162–163.

128. Amar, *Bill of Rights,* 290.

129. Risa Goluboff, *Vagrant Nation: Police Power, Constitutional Change, and the Making of the 1960s* (New York: Oxford University Press, 2016); Ruth Bloch and Naomi Lamoreaux, "Corporations and the Fourteenth Amendment," in *The Corporation and American Democracy,* ed. Ruth Bloch and Naomi Lamoreaux (Cambridge: Harvard University Press, 2017), 286–328.

130. Foner, *Second Founding,* 175.

131. Story, *Commentaries,* 1:216 (emphasis added).

132. John C. Hurd, *The Theory of Our National Existence, as Shown by the Action of the Government of the United States Since 1861* (Boston: Little, Brown, and Company, 1881); John C. Hurd, *The Law of Freedom and Bondage in the United States,* 2 vols. (Boston: Little, Brown, 1858); Francis Lieber, "Fragments of Political Science on Nationalism and Internationalism," in *Miscellaneous Writings of Francis Lieber,* 2 vols. (Philadelphia: J. B. Lippincott, 1881), 2:221–243, 243.

133. See, for example, Charles Sumner, *Are We a Nation? Address of Hon. Charles Sumner* (New York: New York Young Men's Republican Union, 1867); Frederick Douglass, "Our Composite Nationality," in *The Frederick Douglass Papers,* ed. John W. Blassingame and John R. McKivigan (New Haven, CT: Yale University Press, 1991), 4:240–259.

134. Francis Lieber, "What is Our Constitution? First Lecture," in *Miscellaneous Writings of Francis Lieber,* 2 vols. (Philadelphia: J. B. Lippincott, 1881), 1:89. See also Michael G. Kammen, *A Machine that Would Go of Itself: The Constitution in American Culture* (New York: Transaction, 1986).

135. Harold M. Hyman and William M. Wiecek, *Equal Justice under Law: Constitutional Development, 1835–1875* (New York: HarperCollins,1982), 234; Hyman, *A More Perfect Union,* 121–140.

136. John Norton Pomeroy, *An Introduction to the Constitutional Law of the United States* (New York: Hurd and Houghton, 1870), 24–25.

137. Pomeroy, *Introduction,* 60, 78.

2. Police Power

1. See Steven Pincus and William J. Novak, "Revolutionary State Formation: The Origins of the Strong American State," in *State Formations: Global Histories and Cultures of Statehood,* ed. John L. Brooke, Julia C. Strauss, and Greg Anderson (New York: Cambridge University Press, 2018), 138–155. See also

Max M. Edling, *A Revolution in Favor of Government: Origins of the U.S. Constitution and the Making of the American State* (New York: Oxford University Press, 2003); Richard R. John, *Spreading the News: The American Postal System from Franklin to Morse* (Cambridge, MA: Harvard University Press, 1995); Jerry R. Mashaw, *Creating the Administrative Constitution: The Lost One Hundred Years of American Administrative Law* (New Haven, CT: Yale University Press, 2012); Nicholas R. Parrillo, *Against the Profit Motive: The Salary Revolution in American Government, 1780–1940* (New Haven, CT: Yale University Press, 2013).

2. John Brewer, *The Sinews of Power: War, Money and the English State, 1688–1783* (Cambridge, MA: Harvard University Press, 1988); Max M. Edling, *A Hercules in the Cradle: War, Money, and the American State, 1783–1867* (Chicago: University of Chicago Press, 2014); Ira Katznelson and Martin Shefter, eds., *Shaped by War and Trade: International Influences on American Political Development* (Princeton, NJ: Princeton University Press, 2002); Gautham Rao, *National Duties: Custom Houses and the Making of the American State* (Chicago: University of Chicago Press, 2016).

3. William J. Novak, "The American Law of Association: The Legal-Political Construction of Civil Society," *Studies in American Political Development* 15 (2001): 163–188.

4. Morton J. Horwitz, *The Transformation of American Law, 1780–1860* (Cambridge, MA: Harvard University Press, 1977), xii

5. Oliver Wendell Holmes Jr., *The Common Law,* ed. Mark DeWolfe Howe (Cambridge, MA: Harvard University Press, 1963), 5; James Kent, *Commentaries on American Law,* 12th ed., ed. Oliver Wendell Holmes Jr., 4 vols. (Boston: Little, Brown,1873).

6. For a more complete portrait of this old regime, see William J. Novak, *The People's Welfare: Law and Regulation in Nineteenth-Century America* (Chapel Hill: University of North Carolina Press, 1996).

7. Max Weber, *The Theory of Social and Economic Organization* (New York: Oxford University Press, 1947), 154–156; Max Weber, *Economy and Society: An Outline of Interpretive Sociology,* ed. Guenther Roth and Claus Wittich, 2 vols. (Berkeley: University of California Press, 1978), 1:217–220. For an excellent presentation, see Reinhard Bendix's discussion of Weber's view in his "The Modern State and Its Legitimacy," in *Max Weber: An Intellectual Portrait* (Garden City, NY: Anchor Books, 1962), 417–423.

8. David R. Mayhew, "Lawmaking as a Cognitive Enterprise," in *Living Legislation: Durability, Change, and the Politics of American Lawmaking,* ed. Jeffrey A. Jenkins and Eric M. Patashnik (Chicago: University of Chicago Press, 2012): 255–264; John Dewey, ed., *Creative Intelligence: Essays in the Pragmatic Attitude* (New York: Henry Holt, 1917).

9. Francis Lieber, *The Miscellaneous Writings of Francis Lieber,* 2 vols. (Philadelphia: J. B. Lippincott, 1881), 2:222.

10. Sidney George Fisher, *The Trial of the Constitution* (Philadelphia: J. B. Lippincott, 1862); John Alexander Jameson, *The Constitutional Convention* (New York: C. Scribner, 1867); Orestes A. Brownson, *The American Republic:*

Its Constitution, Tendencies, and Destiny (New York: P. O'Shae, 1865); John C. Hurd, *The Theory of our National Existence, As Shown by the Action of the Government of the United States Since 1861* (Boston: Little, Brown, 1881); Elisha Mulford, *The Nation: The Foundations of Civil Order and Political Life in the United States* (New York: Hurd and Houghton, 1870).

11. Fisher, *Trial of the Constitution*, 199; Hurd, *Theory of our National*, 97; C. Edward Merriam, *A History of American Political Theories* (New York: Macmillan, 1915), 296. For a fuller discussion, see George M. Frederickson, *The Inner Civil War: Northern Intellectuals and the Crisis of the Union* (New York: Harper & Row, 1965); and Morton Keller, *Affairs of State: Public Life in Late Nineteenth Century America* (Cambridge, MA: Harvard University Press, 1977), ch. 1.

12. Stephen Sawyer and William J. Novak, "Emancipation and the Creation of Modern Liberal States in America and France," *Journal of the Civil War Era* 3 (2013): 467–500.

13. Harold M. Hyman, *A More Perfect Union: The Impact of the Civil War and Reconstruction on the Constitution* (New York: Alfred A. Knopf, 1973); Richard Franklin Bensel, *Yankee Leviathan: The Origins of Central State Authority in America, 1859–1877* (New York: Cambridge University Press, 1990); Eric Foner, *Reconstruction: America's Unfinished Revolution, 1863–1877* (New York: Harper & Row, 1988); Robert H. Bremner, *The Public Good: Philanthropy and Welfare in the Civil War Era* (New York: Alfred A. Knopf, 1980).

14. John Austin, *The Province of Jurisprudence Determined* (London: J. Murray, 1832); Johann Kaspar Bluntschli, *The Theory of the State*, trans. D. G. Ritchie, P. E. Matheson, and R. Lodge (Kitchener, Canada: Batoche Books, 2000).

15. Vernon Louis Parrington, *Main Currents in American Thought: Volume Three: The Beginnings of Critical Realism in America: 1860–1920* (New York: Harcourt, Brace & World, 1930), 117, 125. Unfortunately, this crucial section of Parrington's famous tract remained unfinished.

16. James Bryce, "The United States Constitution as Seen in the Past: The Predictions of Hamilton and Tocqueville," in *Studies in History and Jurisprudence*, 301–358 (New York: Oxford University Press, 1901), 349; Thomas L. Haskell, *The Emergence of Professional Social Science: The American Social Science Association and the Nineteenth-Century Crisis of Authority* (Urbana: University of Illinois Press, 1977); Dorothy Ross, *The Origins of American Social Science* (New York: Cambridge University Press, 1991).

17. Francis Lieber, *Manual of Political Ethics, Designed Chiefly for the Use of Colleges and Students at Law*, 2 vols. (Boston: C. C. Little & J. Brown, 1838); Theodore D. Woolsey, *Political Science or The State Theoretically and Practically Considered*, 2 vols. (New York: Scribner, Armstrong, 1878).

18. Woolsey, *Political Science*, 1:190. Some of this portrait of political ethics conforms closely to what I have previously called the early nineteenth-century "common law vision of a well-regulated society." Novak, *People's Welfare*, ch. 1.

19. Parrington, *Main Currents*, 124.

20. Woolsey, *Political Science;* John W. Burgess, *Political Science and Comparative Constitutional Law,* 2 vols. (Boston: Ginn, 1890); Woodrow Wilson, *The State: Elements of Historical and Practical Politics,* rev. ed. (1890; Boston: D. C. Heath, 1904); Westel Woodbury Willoughby, *An Examination of the Nature of the State: A Study in Political Philosophy* (New York: Macmillan, 1896).

21. For another indicator of this important shift in orientation, note that Tocqueville began his classic 1835 investigation of American politics and culture with a chapter titled "The Need to Study What Happens in the States before Discussing the Government of the Union." In contrast, James Bryce began his 1888 *American Commonwealth* directly with "The National Government." Alexis de Tocqueville, *Democracy in America,* trans. George Lawrence, ed. J. P. Mayer (New York: Harper and Row, 1988), 61–98; Bryce, *American Commonwealth,* 3 vols. (New York: Macmillan, 1888). On Bryce's vision of himself as following in the footsteps of the great commentators on American politics, see Bryce, "Hamilton and Tocqueville."

22. See, for example, Otto von Gierke, *Political Theories of the Middle Age,* trans. Frederic William Maitland (Cambridge: Cambridge University Press, 1900); Frederic William Maitland, *Selected Essays,* ed. H. D. Hazeltine, G. Lapsley, and P. H. Winfield (Freeport, NY: Books for Libraries, 1968); Harold J. Laski, *Studies in the Problem of Sovereignty* (New Haven, CT: Yale University Press, 1917). For the best secondary discussion of this historical issue, see David Runciman, *Pluralism and the Personality of the State* (Cambridge: Cambridge University Press, 1997).

23. G. W. F. Hegel, *Elements of the Philosophy of Right,* ed. Allen W. Wood (Cambridge: Cambridge University Press, 1991), 279; Bluntschli, *Theory of the State,* 7, 69. Bluntschli characterized his differences with Hegel thus: "Hegel's State is however only a logical abstraction, not a living organism, a mere logical notion, not a person."

24. Westel Woodbury Willoughby, *The Fundamental Concepts of Public Law* (New York: Macmillan, 1924), 10, 31.

25. Morris Cohen, "Communal Ghosts and Other Perils in Social Philosophy," *Journal of Philosophy* 16 (1919): 673–690. See also Runciman, *Pluralism,* 262; Ernest Barker, *Principles of Social and Political Theory* (Oxford: Oxford University Press, 1951), 75.

26. Wilson, *State,* 13.

27. Willoughby, *Nature of the State,* 141; Lester Frank Ward, *The Psychic Factors of Civilization* (Boston: Ginn, 1893), 304.

28. Bluntschli, *Theory of the State,* 261–262.

29. Wilson, *State,* 631–632.

30. Willoughby, *Nature of the State,* 345–346.

31. John Dewey, *The Public and Its Problems,* in *John Dewey: The Later Works, 1925–1953,* vol. 2, ed. Jo Ann Boydston (Carbondale: University of Southern Illinois Press, 1984), 241, 256, 264, 279. For a brilliant contemporary version, see Axel Honneth, "Democracy as Reflexive Cooperation: John Dewey and the Theory of Democracy Today," *Political Theory* 6 (1998): 763–783.

32. John Dewey, "Liberalism and Social Action," in *John Dewey: The Later Works, 1925–1953*, vol. 11, ed. Jo Ann Boydston (Carbondale: University of Southern Illinois Press, 1987), 21.

33. Michael Freeden, *New Liberalism: An Ideology of Social Reform* (Oxford: Oxford University Press, 1978); Peter Weiler, *The New Liberalism: Liberal Social Theory in Great Britain, 1889–1914* (New York: Routledge, 2017); James Meadowcraft, ed., *L. T. Hobhouse: Liberalism and Other Writings* (Cambridge: Cambridge University Press, 1994). For a comprehensive analysis of the links between American and European new liberal traditions, see James T. Kloppenberg, *Uncertain Victory: Social Democracy and Progressivism in European and American Thought, 1870–1920* (New York: Oxford University Press, 1988).

34. Morton White, *Social Thought in America: The Revolt against Formalism* (Boston: Beacon, 1957); Walter Lippmann, *A Preface to Politics* (1913; New York: Macmillan, 1933), 202.

35. Herbert Spencer, *Social Statics, Abridged and Revised; Together with The Man Versus the State* (London: Williams and Norgate, 1892), 357.

36. Lester Frank Ward, "The Laissez Faire Doctrine Is Suicidal," in *Glimpses of the Cosmos: A Mental Biography*, 3 vols. (New York: Putnam, 1913), 3:301–305.

37. Frank J. Goodnow, *Social Reform and the Constitution* (New York: Macmillan, 1911), 308; J. Allen Smith, *The Spirit of American Government*, ed. Cushing Strout (1907; Cambridge, MA: Harvard University Press, 1965), 307, 308–309.

38. John Dewey, "Individualism, Old and New," in *The Later Works, 1925–1953*, ed. Jo Ann Boydston (1929; Carbondale: Southern Illinois University Press, 1988), 5:41–123; Dewey, "Liberalism and Social Action," in *The Later Works, 1925–1953*, ed. Jo Ann Boydston (1935; Carbondale: Southern Illinois University Press, 1991), 11:1–65.

39. Stefan Collini, ed., *John Stuart Mill: On Liberty and Other Writings* (Cambridge: Cambridge University Press, 1989), 13.

40. Albert Venn Dicey, *Lectures on the Relation between Law and Public Opinion in England during the Nineteenth Century*, 2nd ed. (London: Macmillan, 1914), liii–lv.

41. *Lochner v. New York*, 198 U.S. 45 (1905), 75; *Budd v. New York*, 143 U.S. 517 (1892), 549.

42. The most recent adherent to this old, negative liberal philosophy is Richard A. Epstein, *Simple Rules for a Complex World* (Cambridge, MA: Harvard University Press, 1995); Richard A. Epstein, *Principles for a Free Society: Reconciling Individual Liberty with the Common Good* (Cambridge, MA: Perseus Books, 1998). I apply some of these arguments to a critique of Epstein's positions on public health law in "Private Wealth and Public Health: A Critique of Richard Epstein's Defense of the 'Old' Public Health," *Perspectives in Biology and Medicine* 46 (Summer supplement, 2003): S176–S198.

43. Roscoe Pound, "Liberty of Contract," *Yale Law Journal* 18 (1909): 456, 484.

44. Pound, "Liberty of Contract," 457, 460.

45. Roscoe Pound, *Outlines of Lectures on Jurisprudence,* 2nd ed. (Cambridge, MA: Harvard Law School, 1914), 58.

46. Thomas Hill Green, "Liberal Legislation and Freedom of Contract," in *The Political Theory of T. H. Green,* ed. John R. Rodman, 43–74 (New York: Appleton-Century-Crofts, 1964), 51–52; Thomas Hill Green, *Lectures on the Principles of Political Obligation* (London: Longmans, Green, 1895).

47. Green, "Liberal Legislation," 53.

48. See the comprehensive analysis of Kloppenberg, *Uncertain Victory,* 396–397.

49. Novak, *People's Welfare.*

50. John Dewey and James H. Tufts, *Ethics* (New York: Henry Holt, 1908), 437–438.

51. Dewey and Tufts, *Ethics,* 286, 292, 294–295.

52. Dewey and Tufts, 298, 482–483.

53. Jane Addams, *A New Conscience and an Ancient Evil* (New York: Macmillan, 1914), 10; Walter Weyl, *The New Democracy: An Essay on Certain Political and Economic Tendencies in the United State* (New York: Macmillan, 1913), 160–161.

54. Marietta Kies, *The Ethical Principle and Its Application in State Relations* (Ann Arbor, MI: Inland, 1892), i.

55. Léon Duguit, *Law in the Modern State,* trans. Frida Laski and Harold Laski (London: George Allen & Unwin, 1921), xxxv.

56. Roscoe Pound, "The Need of a Sociological Jurisprudence," *The Green Bag* 19 (1907): 607. Pound began his famous discussion in "Mechanical Jurisprudence," *Columbia Law Review* 8 (1908): 605, by quoting Frederick Pollock: "There is no way by which modern law can escape from the scientific and artificial character imposed on it by the demand of modern societies for full, equal, and exact justice."

57. The key secondary works on this intellectual transformation are Morton White, *Social Thought in America: The Revolt against Formalism* (Boston: Beacon, 1957); Morton J. Horwitz, *The Transformation of American Law, 1870–1960: The Crisis of Legal Orthodoxy* (New York: Oxford University Press, 1992); Duncan Kennedy, *The Rise and Fall of Classical Legal Thought* (Washington, DC: BeardBooks, 2006); John Henry Schlegel, *American Legal Realism and Empirical Social Science* (Chapel Hill: University of North Carolina Press, 1995); Laura Kalman, *Legal Realism at Yale, 1927–1960* (Chapel Hill: University of North Carolina Press, 1986); and Edward A. Purcell Jr., *The Crisis of Democratic Theory: Scientific Naturalism and the Problem of Value* (Lexington: University Press of Kentucky, 1973).

58. Donald R. Kelley's wonderful synthesis *The Human Measure: Social Thought in the Western Legal Tradition* (Cambridge, MA: Harvard University Press, 1990), xi, provides a good measure of the early legal roots of this tradition.

59. See Roscoe Pound, "The Scope and Purpose of Sociological Jurisprudence III," *Harvard Law Review* 25 (1912): 489. For an excellent brief synopsis of Comte's contribution, see Raymond Aron, "Auguste Comte," in *Main Currents in Sociological Thought,* 2 vols. (Garden City, NY: Anchor Books, 1968), 1:73–143.

60. John Austin, *The Province of Jurisprudence Determined* (London: John Murray, 1832); John Austin, *Lectures on Jurisprudence or The Philosophy of Positive Law,* ed. Robert Campbell, 2 vols. (London: John Murray, 1869).

61. John Chipman Gray, *The Nature and Sources of the Law* (New York: Columbia University Press, 1909), 86–87.

62. Morris R. Cohen, "John Austin," in *Encyclopaedia of the Social Sciences,* 8 vols. (New York: Macmillan, 1930) 2:318.

63. Austin, *Province of Jurisprudence,* 1.

64. Roscoe Pound, "The Scope and Purpose of Sociological Jurisprudence I," *Harvard Law Review* 24 (1911): 594–595. For an even greater sign of the enormous influence of the positivists on Pound, see his *Outlines of Lectures on Jurisprudence,* 2nd ed. (Cambridge, MA: Harvard Law School, 1914), which is replete with analytical sources.

65. Felix S. Cohen, "The Problems of a Functional Jurisprudence," *Modern Law Review* 1 (1937): 8.

66. See, for example, John Dewey, "Austin's Theory of Sovereignty," *Political Science Quarterly* 9 (1894): 31–52; John R. Commons, *A Sociological View of Sovereignty* (New York: Reprints of Economic Classics, 1965).

67. Julius Stone, *The Province and Function of Law* (London: Stevens & Sons, 1947), 70–71; Roscoe Pound, *Social Control through Law* (New Haven, CT: Yale University Press, 1942), 94.

68. Perry Miller, *The Life of the Mind in America: From the Revolution to the Civil War* (New York: Harcourt, Brace & World, 1965); David Brion Davis, *Challenging the Boundaries of Slavery* (Cambridge, MA: Harvard University Press, 2003), 51–53.

69. Pound, "Sociological Jurisprudence III," 516.

70. Duncan Kennedy, *The Rise and Fall of Classical Legal Thought* (Washington, DC: BeardBooks, 2006); Morton J. Horwitz, "The Structure of Classical Legal Thought, 1870–1905," in *Transformation of American Law,* 9–32. For a useful introduction to legal realism in general, see William W. Fisher III, Morton J. Horwitz, and Thomas A. Reed, eds., *American Legal Realism* (New York: Oxford University Press, 1993).

71. Charles A. Beard, *An Economic Interpretation of the Constitution of the United States* (New York: Macmillan, 1913), 8–13.

72. Oliver Wendell Holmes Jr., "The Path of the Law," *Harvard Law Review* 10 (1897): 457–478. The roots of Holmes's perspective are already discernible in his critique of Christopher Columbus Langdell's contracts casebook. Oliver Wendell Holmes Jr., "Book Notices," *American Law Review* 14 (1880): 234.

73. Philip P. Wiener, *Evolution and the Founders of Pragmatism* (Gloucester, UK: P. Smith, 1969); Bruce Kuklick, *The Rise of American Philosophy, 1860–1930* (New Haven, CT: Yale University Press, 1970); Kloppenberg, *Uncertain Victory.* See also Louis Menand, *The Metaphysical Club: A Story of Ideas in America* (New York: Farrar, Straus, and Giroux, 2001).

74. William James, *Pragmatism and the Meaning of Truth* (Cambridge, MA: Harvard University Press, 1975), 32, 34, 169.

75. Holmes was famously not so keen on Dewey's eloquence. Mark DeWolf Howe, ed., *Holmes-Pollock Letters: The Correspondence of Mr. Justice Holmes and Sir Frederick Pollock, 1874–1932* (Cambridge, MA: Harvard University Press, 1941), 2:287.

76. John Dewey, "My Philosophy of Law," in *My Philosophy of Law: Credos of Sixteen American Scholars,* ed. Julius Rosenthal Foundation for General Law (Boston: Boston Law, 1941), 73–85.

77. Richard Rorty, *Consequences of Pragmatism: Essays, 1972–1980* (Minneapolis: University of Minnesota Press, 1982), 166.

78. Dewey, "My Philosophy of Law."

79. Karl N. Llewellyn, *The Bramble Bush: Some Lectures on Law and Its Study* (New York: Oceana Publications, 1930), 3–5. See also John R. Commons, *A Sociological View of Sovereignty* (New York: A. M. Kelly, 1965).

80. Robert M. Cover, "Violence and the Word," *Yale Law Journal* 95 (1986): 1601–1629.

81. This objective was made quite explicit in an extraordinary volume published by the American Association of Law Schools entitled *The Rational Basis of Legal Institutions* (New York: Macmillan, 1923), xx, xxi.

82. Franz L. Neumann, "The Change in the Function of Law in Modern Society," in *The Rule of Law under Siege: Selected Essays of Franz L. Neumann and Otto Kirchheimer,* ed. William E. Scheuerman (Berkeley: University of California Press, 1996), 101–141; Jürgen Habermas, *Between Facts and Norms: Contributions to a Discourse Theory of Law and Democracy,* trans. William Rehg (Cambridge, MA: MIT Press, 1996), 431.

83. Paul Vinogradoff, "Modern Tendencies in Jurisprudence," in *Outlines of Historical Jurisprudence,* 2 vols. (London: Oxford University Press, 1920), 1:149.

84. Harold Laski, "Introduction," in Duguit, *Law in the Modern State,* x.

85. Roscoe Pound, "General Introduction," in *Cases and Readings on Law and Society,* 3 vols., ed. Sidney Post Simpson and Julius Stone (St. Paul: West Publishing, 1949), xvii; Pound, "Sociological Jurisprudence I," 591–619; Pound, "Sociological Jurisprudence III," 141–168, 489–516.

86. James Willard Hurst, *Law and Social Order in the United States* (Ithaca, NY: Cornell University Press, 1977), 138–139.

87. Elihu Root, "Address to the American Law Institute," *American Law Institute Proceedings* 1 (1923): 49.

88. Charles E. Merriam, "Government and Society," in *Recent Social Trends in the United States: Report of the President's Research Committee on Social Trends,* vol. 1 (New York: McGraw-Hill Book, 1933), 1515; R. F. Fuchs, "Quantity of Regulatory Legislation," *St. Louis Law Review* 16 (1930): 52.

89. As early as 1910, James W. Garner listed numerous functions of the modern state (beyond the basic maintenance of peace, order, and safety) as subjects of constant state and federal legislation. James W. Garner, *Introduction to Political Science: A Treatise on the Origin, Nature, Functions, and Organization of the State* (New York: American, 1910), 318–320.

90. *Laws of New York, 1781–1801,* 2 vols. (Albany: State of New York, 1802). The tale of these developments is basically the subject of Novak, *People's Welfare.*

91. *Commonwealth v. Alger,* 7 Cush. 53 (Mass., 1851), 53; *People v. Budd,* 117 N.Y. 1 (1889), 14–15, 29.

92. Collins Denny Jr., "The Growth and Development of the Police Power of the State," *Michigan Law Review* 20 (1921): 173; Lewis Hockheimer, "Police Power," *Central Law Journal* 44 (1897): 158. Also, see generally Ernst Freund, *The Police Power and Public Rights* (Chicago: University of Chicago Press, 1904).

93. *District of Columbia v. Brooke,* 214 U.S. 138 (1909), 149; *Vanderbilt v. Adams,* 7 Cow. 349 (N.Y., 1827), 351–352.

94. Nikolas Rose, *Powers of Freedom: Reframing Political Thought* (Cambridge: Cambridge University Press, 1999); Mitchell Dean, *Governmentality: Power and Rule in Modern Society* (London: Sage, 1999); Pasquale Pasquino, "Theartum Politicum: The Genealogy of Capital—Police and the State of Prosperity," *Ideology and Consciousness* 4 (1978): 41–54. Also see generally the essays in Markus D. Dubber and Mariana Valverde, *The New Police Science: The Police Power in Domestic and International Governance* (Stanford, CA: Stanford University Press, 2006).

95. Marc Raeff, "The Well-Ordered Police State and the Development of Modernity," *American Historical Review* 80 (1975): 1226.

96. Michel Foucault, "Omnes et Singulatim: Towards a Criticism of 'Political Reason,'" in *Tanner Lectures on Human Values* (Stanford, CA: Stanford University Press, 1979), 248–249.

97. B. J. Ramage, "Social Progress and the Police Power of a State," *American Law Review* 36 (1902): 685.

98. Michel Foucault, *Power/Knowledge: Selected Interviews and Other Writings, 1972–1977,* ed. Colin Gordon (New York: Pantheon Books, 1980), 170.

99. This analysis thus parts ways with the important work of Markus Dubber and Christopher Tomlins, which insists on a clearer separation of the police and rule-of-law traditions. Christopher L. Tomlins, *Law, Labor, and Ideology in the Early American Republic* (New York: Cambridge University Press, 1993), 45; Markus D. Dubber, "Criminal Police and Criminal Law in the Rechtsstaat," in *Police and the Liberal State,* ed. Markus Dubber and Mariana Valverde (Stanford, CA: Stanford University Press, 2008), 98–88; Novak, "Police Power and the Hidden Transformation of the American State," in Dubber and Valverde, *Police and the Liberal State,* 54–73.

100. *Brown v. Maryland,* 12 Wheat. 419 (U.S., 1827); *Commonwealth v. Alger,* 7 Cush. 53 (Mass., 1851); Leonard W. Levy, *The Law of the Commonwealth and Chief Justice Shaw* (Cambridge, MA: Harvard Univ. Press, 1957).

101. Novak, *People's Welfare,* ch. 1.

102. Thomas M. Cooley, *A Treatise on the Constitutional Limitations Which Rest Upon the Legislative Power of the States of the American Union* (Boston: Little, Brown, 1868), 594–595.

103. *Wynehamer v. People*, 13 N.Y. 402 (1856), 451–452.
104. W. P. Prentice, *Police Powers Arising Under the Law of Overruling Necessity* (New York: Banks & Brothers, 1894), 7.
105. Ernst Freund, *The Police Power: Public Policy and Constitutional Rights* (Chicago: University of Chicago Press, 1904); Ernst Freund, *Standards of American Legislation* (Chicago: University of Chicago Press, 1917); Ernst Freund, *Administrative Powers over Persons and Property: A Comparative Survey* (Chicago: University of Chicago Press, 1928); Ernst Freund, *Legislative Regulation: A Study of the Ways and Means of Written Law* (New York: Commonwealth Fund, 1932). In addition to his legal writings, Freund was active in progressive Illinois and Chicago politics. Jane Addams memorialized Freund in "The Friend and Guide of Social Workers," *University Record* 19 (1933): 43–44. For a serviceable introduction to Freund's career and writing, see Oscar Kraines, *The World and Ideas of Ernst Freund: The Search for General Principles of Legislation and Administrative Law* (Tuscaloosa: University of Alabama Press, 1974).
106. Francis A. Allen, "Ernst Freund and the New Age of Legislation," in *Standards of American Legislation*, 1965 ed. (Chicago: University of Chicago Press, 1965), vii–xlvi; Ernst Freund, "The Problem of Intelligent Legislation," *Proceedings of the American Political Science Association* 4 (1907): 70.
107. Freund, *Legislative Regulation*, 12; Ernst Freund, *Jurisprudence and Legislation* (St. Louis: Congress of Arts and Science, Universal Exposition, 1904), 11.
108. Freund, *Police Power;* W. G. Hastings, "The Development of Law as Illustrated by the Decisions Relating to the Police Power of the State," *Proceedings of the American Philosophical Society* 39 (1900): 359–554; Alfred Orendorff, "Public Policy and the Police Power of the State," *Chicago Legal News* 14 (1882): 256–257; B. J. Ramage, "Social Progress and the Police Power of a State," *American Law Review* 36 (1902): 681–699; J. M. Blayney Jr., "The Term 'Police Power,'" *Central Law Journal* 59 (1904): 486–492; Walter Wheeler Cook, "What Is the Police Power?," *Columbia Law Review* 7 (1907): 322–336; George Wickersham, "The Police Power, the Product of the Rule of Reason," *Harvard Law Review* 27 (1914): 297–316; Thomas Reed Powell, *The Supreme Court and State Police Power, 1922–1930* (Charlottesville, VA: Michie, 1932).
109. *Sic utere tuo ut alienum non laedas* (use your own so as not to injure another). For more on the nuisance law roots of police power, see Novak, *People's Welfare*, 44–71.
110. Freund, *Standards of American Legislation*, 66–71.
111. Freund, *Police Power*, 5–6.
112. Freund, iii; Lewis Hockheimer, "Police Power," *Central Law Journal* 44 (1897): 158.
113. *Bacon v. Walker*, 204 U.S. 311 (1907), 317–318. For statements to similar effect concerning the police power and general welfare, see *Barbier v. Connolly*, 113 U.S. 27 (1885); and *Manigault v. Springs*, 199 U.S. 473 (1905). Also see the general discussion in Scott M. Reznick, "Empiricism and the

Principle of Conditions in the Evolution of the Police Power: A Model for Definitional Scrutiny," *Washington University Law Quarterly* 1978 (1978): 31–32.

114. Harrison H. Brace, "To What Extent May Government in the Exercise of its Police Power, Take, Destroy or Damage Private Property Without Giving Compensation Therefor?" *Chicago Legal News* 18 (1886): 339–341, 341; Ramage, "Social Progress," 698.

115. Samuel P. Hays, "The Social Analysis of American Political History, 1880–1920," *Political Science Quarterly* 80 (1965): 391.

116. Leonard D. White, "Public Administration," in *Recent Social Trends in the United States* (New York: McGraw-Hill , 1933), 1394; Walter Thompson, *Federal Centralization: A Study and Criticism of the Expanding Scope of Congressional Legislation* (New York: Harcourt, Brace, 1923).

117. *United States v. Dewitt*, 76 U.S. 41 (1870). *Dewitt* concerned a federal statute of 1867 regulating the sale of naphtha and other dangerous illuminating oils. Chase cited *The License Cases,* 5 Howard, 504 (U.S., 1847); *The Passenger Cases,* 7 How. 283 (U.S., 1849); and *The License Tax Cases,* 5 Wallace, 470 (U.S., 1866) to establish the "obvious" and "fully explained" antebellum consensus about federal regulations of internal state police. For a discussion of *Barron,* see Ch. 1. *Barron v. Baltimore,* 32 U.S. 243 (1833), 250–251.

118. Charles Evans Hughes, "New Phases of National Development," *American Bar Association Journal* 4 (1918): 93–94.

119. Ernst Freund, "The New German Constitution," *Political Science Quarterly* 35 (1920): 181; Walter Thompson, *Federal Centralization: A Study and Criticism of the Expanding Scope of Congressional Legislation* (New York: Harcourt, Brace, 1923), 10.

120. Robert E. Cushman, *The Independent Regulatory Commissions* (New York: Oxford University Press, 1941).

121. Robert Eugene Cushman, *Studies in the Police Power of the National Government* (Minneapolis: Minnesota Law Review, 1919–1920), 291; James A. Lyons, "Development of a National Police Power," *Tennessee Law Review* 14 (1935): 11–20.

122. Austin F. MacDonald, *Federal Aid: A Study of the American Subsidy System* (New York: Thomas Y. Crowell, 1928); Harry N. Scheiber, "Federalism and the American Economic Order, 1789–1910," *Law and Society Review* 10 (1975): 57–118.

123. *Mayor of New York v. Miln,* 36 U.S. 102 (1837); *Passenger Cases,* 48 U.S. 283 (1849); *Henderson v. Mayor of the City of New York,* 92 U.S. 259 (1875). For an excellent summary of this development, see Matthew J. Lindsay, "Immigration, Sovereignty, and the Constitution of Foreignness," *Connecticut Law Review* 45 (2013): 743–812.

124. "An Act to Execute Certain Treaty Stipulations Relating to Chinese," *U.S. Statutes at Large* (1882): 58–61; *Chae Chan Ping v. United States,* 130 U.S. 581 (1889), 597.

125. "An Act for the Suppression of Trade in and Circulation of Obscene Literature and Articles of Immoral Use," *U.S. Statutes at Large* 17 (1873): 598–

600; "An Act to Further Regulate Interstate and Foreign Commerce by Prohibiting the Transportation Therein for Immoral Purposes of Women and Girls," *U.S. Statutes at Large* 36 (1910): 825–828. For further discussion, see the essays in Nancy Cott, Margot Canaday, and Robert Self, eds., *Intimate States: Gender, Sexuality, and Governance in Modern US History* (Chicago: University of Chicago Press, 2021).

126. Walter Wyman, "Quarantine and Commerce," *Annual Report of the Supervising Surgeon-General of the Marine-Hospital Service of the United States* (Washington, DC: Government Printing Office, 1901), 240; Edwin Maxey, "Federal Quarantine Laws," *American Law Review* 43 (1909): 382–396.

127. "An Act to Provide Further for the national Security and Defense by Encouraging the Production, Conserving, the Supply, and Controlling the Distribution of Food Products and Fuel," *U.S. Statutes at Large* 40 (1917): 276–287; Senator James A. Reed, *Congressional Record,* 55 (1917), 3597. Clinton Rossiter enumerated the most important statutory delegations of further emergency power to the president. Clinton L. Rossiter, *Constitutional Dictatorship: Crisis Government in the Modern Democracies* (Princeton, NJ: Princeton University Press, 1948), 243.

128. J. Reuben Clark Jr., *Emergency Legislation Passed Prior to December, 1917 Dealing with the Control and Taking of Private Property for the Public Use, Benefit, or Welfare* (Washington, DC: Government Printing Office, 1918).

129. *Lochner v. New York,* 198 U.S. 45 (1905), 53; "An Act to Regulate the Manufacture of Flour and Meal Food Products," *Laws of the State of New York* (Albany: James B. Lyon, 1895), ch. 518, 305–307. Also see Peckham's opinion in *Allgeyer v. Louisiana,* 165 U.S. 578 (1897).

130. Charles A. Beard, *Contemporary American History, 1877–1913* (New York: Macmillan, 1914), 54.

131. The best treatments of this trend in "progressive historiography" more generally are Richard Hofstadter, *The Progressive Historians: Turner, Beard, Parrington* (Chicago: University of Chicago Press, 1968); Lee Benson, *Turner and Beard: American Historical Writing Reconsidered* (Glencoe, IL: Free Press, 1960); and Morton J. Horwitz, "Progressive Legal Historiography," *Oregon Law Review* 63 (1984): 679–687.

132. Louis B. Boudin, *Government by Judiciary,* 2 vols. (New York: William Godwin, 1932); J. Allen Smith, *The Growth and Decadence of Constitutional Government* (New York: Henry Holt, 1930); Edward S. Corwin, *Court over Constitution: A Study of Judicial Review as an Instrument of Popular Government* (New York: P. Smith, 1938); Frank J. Goodnow, *Social Reform and the Constitution* (New York: Macmillan, 1911); Gustavus Myers, *The History of the Supreme Court of the United States* (Chicago: C. H. Kerr, 1912).

133. Goodnow, *Social Reform,* v; J. Allen Smith, *The Spirit of American Government* (New York: Macmillan, 1907), vii; Boudin, *Government by Judiciary,* viii.

134. Vernon L. Parrington, "Introduction," in J. Allen Smith, *The Growth and Decadence of Constitutional Government* (New York: Henry Holt, 1930), xii.

135. Max Lerner, "The Supreme Court and American Capitalism," *Yale Law Journal* 42 (1933): 672.
136. Benjamin Twiss brought this vision to bear on the constitutional revolution of 1937. Benjamin R. Twiss, *Lawyers and the Constitution: How Laissez Faire Came to the Supreme Court* (Princeton, NJ: Princeton University Press, 1942), 114, 260; Clyde E. Jacobs, *Law Writers and the Courts: The Influence of Thomas M. Cooley, Christopher G. Tiedeman, and John F. Dillon upon American Constitutional Law* (Berkeley: University of California Press, 1954); Arnold M. Paul, *Conservative Crisis and the Rule of Law: Attitudes of Bar and Bench, 1887–1895* (Ithaca, NY: Cornell University Press, 1960); Sidney Fine, "Laissez Faire Becomes the Law of the Land," in *Laissez Faire and the General-Welfare State: A Study of Conflict in American Thought, 1865–1901* (Ann Arbor: University of Michigan Press, 1956), ch. 5, 126, 164.
137. Jack N. Rakove, *Original Meanings: Politics and Ideas in the Making of the Constitution* (New York: A. A. Knopf, 1996); Akhil Reed Amar, *The Bill of Rights: Creation and Reconstruction* (New Haven, CT: Yale University Press, 1998); Bruce A. Ackerman, *We the People: Volume 1, Foundations* (Cambridge, MA: Harvard University Press, 1991).
138. William E. Forbath, *Law and the Shaping of the American Labor Movement* (Cambridge, MA: Harvard University Press, 1991), x, 169–171; Christopher L. Tomlins and Andrew J. King, eds., *Labor Law in America: Historical and Critical Essays* (Baltimore: Johns Hopkins University Press, 1992). For an alternative perspective on the relationship of law, labor, and state, see Kate Andrias, "An American Approach to Social Democracy: The Forgotten Promise of the Fair Labor Standards Act," *Yale Law Journal* 128 (2019): 616–709.
139. See Theda Skocpol, *Protecting Soldiers and Mothers: The Political Origins of Social Policy in the United States* (Cambridge, MA: Harvard University Press, 1992), 227; Stephen Skowronek, *Building a New American State: The Expansion of National Administrative Capacities, 1877–1920* (New York: Cambridge University Press, 1982), 287; Daniel T. Rodgers, *Atlantic Crossings: Social Politics in a Progressive Age* (Cambridge, MA: Harvard University Press, 1998), 201.
140. For excellent examples of the continued resonance of the *Lochner* critique, see Amanda Shanor, "The New *Lochner*," *Wisconsin Law Review* 2016 (2016): 133–208; Jeremy K. Kessler, "The Early Years of First Amendment Lochnerism," *Columbia Law Review* 116 (2016): 1915–2004; Jedediah Purdy, "Neoliberal Constitutionalism: Lochnerism for a New Economy," *Law and Contemporary Problems* 77 (2014): 195–213.
141. Charles Warren, "The Progressiveness of the United States Supreme Court," *Columbia Law Review* 13 (Apr. 1913): 294; Charles Warren, "A Bulwark to the State Police Power—the United States Supreme Court," *Columbia Law Review* 13 (Dec. 1913): 667, 695.
142. Ernst Freund, "Tendencies of Legislative Policy and Modern Social Legislation," *International Journal of Ethics* 27 (1916): 1.

143. *Muller v. Oregon,* 208 U.S. 412 (1908); *Ives v. South Buffalo Railway Co.,* 201 N.Y. 271 (1911); *New York Central Railroad Co. v. White,* 243 U.S. 188 (1917).

144. *Bunting v. Oregon,* 243 U.S. 426 (1917), 437–439.

145. John R. Commons, *Labor and Administration* (New York: Sentry, 1913); John R. Commons and John B. Andrews, *Principles of Labor Legislation* (New York: Harper & Brother, 1916).

146. John R. Commons, *Legal Foundations of Capitalism* (New York: Macmillan, 1924); Richard T. Ely, *Property and Contract in their Relations to the Distribution of Wealth* (New York: Macmillan, 1914); Freund, *Police Power.*

147. Lawrence M. Friedman, *A History of American Law,* 2nd ed. (New York: Simon and Schuster, 1985), 358–360; Edward S. Corwin, *The Twilight of the Supreme Court: A History of Our Constitutional Theory* (New Haven, CT: Yale University Press, 1934), 78.

148. *Wynehamer v. New York,* 13 N.Y. 378 (1856); *In Re Jacobs,* 98 N.Y. 98 (1885); *Godcharles v. Wigeman,* 113 Pa. 431 (Pa. 1886); *Ritchie v. People,* 155 Ill. 98 (1895); and *Lochner v. New York* (1905).

3. Public Utility

1. See, for example, William Letwin, *Law and Economic Policy in America: The Evolution of the Sherman Antitrust Act* (Chicago: University of Chicago Press, 1954); Ellis W. Hawley, *The New Deal and the Problem of Monopoly: A Study in Economic Ambivalence* (Princeton, NJ: Princeton University Press, 1966); Martin J. Sklar, *The Corporate Reconstruction of American Capitalism: The Market, the Law, and Politics* (New York: Cambridge University Press, 1988); Alan Brinkley, *The End of Reform: New Deal Liberalism in Recession and War* (New York: Knopf, 1995).

2. For a perfect example of this, see the overlapping and definitive treatments in the treatises of Bruce Wyman on rate regulation, public service corporations, and administrative law. Joseph Henry Beale and Bruce Wyman, *Railroad Rate Regulation: With Special Reference to the Power of the Interstate Commerce Commission,* 2nd ed. (New York: Baker, Voorhis, 1915); Bruce Wyman, *The Special Law Governing Public Service Corporations and All Others Engaged in Public Employment,* 2 vols. (New York: Baker, Voorhis, 1911); Bruce Wyman, *The Principles of the Administrative Law Governing the Relations of Public Officers* (St. Paul, MN: Keefe-Davidson, 1903).

3. For a preliminary account of this larger legal-economic discourse concerning the "social control of capitalism," see William J. Novak, "Law and the Social Control of American Capitalism," *Emory Law Journal* 60 (2010): 377–405.

4. The classic statement is A. V. Dicey, "Lecture VI: The Period of Benthamism or Individualism" in *Lectures on the Relation between Law and Public Opinion in England during the Nineteenth-Century,* 2nd ed. (London: MacMillan, 1914), 126–210. For a more revisionist perspective, see Graham

Wallas, "Jeremy Bentham," *Political Science Quarterly* 38 (1923): 45–56; J. B. Brebner, "Laissez Faire and State Intervention in Nineteenth-Century Britain," *Journal of Economic History,* supplement (1948), 59–70; Oliver MacDonagh, "The Nineteenth-Century Revolution in Government: A Reappraisal," *Historical Journal* 1 (1958): 52–67; David Roberts, "Jeremy Bentham and the Victorian Administrative State," *Victorian Studies* 3 (1959): 193–210.

5. Henry C. Adams, "Relation of the State to Industrial Action" and "Economics and Jurisprudence," in *Two Essays by Henry Carter Adams,* ed. Joseph Dorfman (New York: Augustus M. Kelley, 1969); John R. Commons, *Legal Foundations of Capitalism* (New York: Macmillan, 1924); Louis Brandeis, *Other People's Money and How the Bankers Use It* (New York: Harper Torchbooks, 1967), 43.

6. Richard T. Ely, "Statement of Dr. Richard T. Ely," in *Publications of the American Economic Association, Volume 1* (American Economic Association, 1887), 16. See also Richard T. Ely, *Property and Contract in their Relations to the Distribution of Wealth,* 2 vols. (New York: Macmillan, 1914).

7. James Willard Hurst, "Problems of Legitimacy in the Contemporary Legal Order," *Oklahoma Law Review* 24 (1971): 225–226.

8. See, for example, William K. Jones, *Cases and Materials on Regulated Industries* (New York: Foundation, 1967); Richard J. Pierce Jr. and Ernest Gellhorn, *Regulated Industries in a Nutshell* (St. Paul, MN: West Publishing, 1999); Joseph D. Kearney and Thomas W. Merrill, "The Great Transformation of Regulated Industries Law," *Columbia Law Review* 98 (1998): 1323–1409.

9. Kenneth Culp Davis, *Administrative Law and Government* (St. Paul, MN: West Publishing, 1960), 13–17.

10. Wyman, *Special Law,* 1:29–33.

11. Wyman, 1:39–134.

12. Felix Frankfurter, *The Public and Its Government* (New Haven, CT: Yale University Press, 1930), 83.

13. See, for example, Randal C. Picker, "Materials on Network Industries" (University of Chicago Law School, 2014). On the contemporary revival of the public utility idea in contemporary policy making, see K. Sabeel Rahman, "The New Utilities: Private Power, Social Infrastructure, and the Revival of the Public Utility Concept," *Cardozo Law Review* 39 (2017–2018): 1621–1692; Lina M. Khan, "The Separation of Platforms and Commerce," *Columbia Law Review* 119 (2019): 973–1098; Tim Wu, *The Master Switch: The Rise and Fall of Information Empires* (New York: Alfred A. Knopf, 2010); and Nicholas Bagley, "Medicine as a Public Calling," *Michigan Law Review* 114 (2015): 57–106. An additional problem is terminology. See Charles K. Burdick, "The Origin of the Peculiar Duties of Public Service Companies," pt. 1, *Columbia Law Review* 11 (1911): 514–638, 515; Leverett S. Lyon and Victor Abramson, *Government and Economic Life: Development and Current Issues of American Public Policy,* vol. 2 (Washington, DC: Brookings Institution, 1940), 616.

14. *Nebbia v. New York,* 291 U.S. 502 (1934).

15. Frank J. Goodnow, *The American Conception of Liberty and Government* (Providence, RI: Standard Printing, 1916), 28–29.

16. R. H. Coase, "The Federal Communications Commission," *Journal of Law and Economics* 2 (1959): 1–40; George J. Stigler and C. Friedland, "What Can Regulators Regulate? The Case of Electricity," *Journal of Law and Economics* 5 (1962): 1–16; Harold Demsetz, "Why Regulate Utilities?," *Journal of Law and Economics* 11 (1968): 55–65; Sam Peltzman, "Pricing in Public and Private Enterprise: Electric Utilities in the United States," *Journal of Law and Economics* 14 (1971): 109–47; Richard A. Posner, "Taxation by Regulation," *Bell Journal of Economics and Management Science* 2 (1971): 22–50. See also Ronald Coase, "The Theory of Public Utility Pricing and Its Application," *Bell Journal of Economics and Management Science* 1 (1970): 113–114; Harry M. Trebing, "The Chicago School versus Public Utility Regulation," *Journal of Economic Issues* 10 (1976): 97–126. For an overview of the critique of regulation focused on regulatory capture, see William J. Novak, "A Revisionist History of Regulatory Capture," in *Preventing Regulatory Capture: Special Interest Influence and How to Limit It*, ed. Daniel Carpenter and David A. Moss (Cambridge: Cambridge University Press, 2013), 25–48.

17. See Edward Adler's survey of "common" activities from Leet Jurisdiction of Norwich between 1374 and 1391. Edward A. Adler, "Business Jurisprudence," *Harvard Law Review* 28 (1914): 149–151.

18. On the distinctive history of the law of public callings, see Wyman, "Historical Introduction," in *Public Service Corporations*, 1–36; Charles K. Burdick, "The Origin of the Peculiar Duties of Public Service Corporations," *Columbia Law Review* 11 (1911): 514–531, 616–638; Norman F. Arterburn, "The Origin and First Test of Public Callings," *University of Pennsylvania Law Review* 75 (1927): 411–428; Benjamin F. Small, "Anti-Trust Laws and Public Callings: The Associated Press Case," *North Carolina Law Review* 23 (1944): 1–24.

19. William Blackstone, *Commentaries on the Laws of England: A Facsimile of the First Edition of 1765–1769*, vol. 3 (Chicago: University of Chicago Press, 1979), 164.

20. *Lane v. Cotton*, 12 Mod. 472 (Eng., 1701), 484–485.

21. Wyman, "Historical Introduction," 14. Wyman added, "No more significant phrases were ever penned."

22. Molly Selvin, "The Public Trust Doctrine in American Law and Economic Policy," *Wisconsin Law Review* 1980 (1980): 1403–1442; Harry N. Scheiber, "The Road to *Munn*: Eminent Domain and the Concept of Public Purpose in the State Courts," *Perspectives in American History* 5 (1971): 327–402. Hale's text was so influential that his argument was published verbatim as an appendix to the New York case, *Ex Parte Jennings*, 6 Cow. 518 (N.Y., 1826).

23. Matthew Hale, "De Portibus Maris," in *A Collection of Tracts Relative to the Law of England*, ed. Francis Hargrave (London: T. Wright, 1787), 77–78.

24. See William J. Novak, *The People's Welfare: Law and Regulation in Nineteenth-Century America* (Chapel Hill: University of North Carolina Press, 1996), 115–148.

25. Joseph K. Angell, *A Treatise on the Law of Carriers of Goods and Passengers, By Land and By Water* (Boston: Little and Brown, 1848); Isaac F. Redfield, *The Law of Carriers of Goods and Passengers, Private and Public, Inland and Foreign, By Railway, Steamboat, and other Modes of Transportation; Also, The Construction, Responsibility, and Duty of Telegraph Companies, The Responsibility and Duty of Innkeepers, and the Law of Bailments* (Cambridge, MA: Houghton, 1869). See also, Oliver Wendell Holmes Jr., "Common Carriers and the Common Law," *American Law Review* 13 (1879): 609–631.

26. Joseph Henry Beale Jr., *The Law of Innkeepers and Hotels: Including Other Public Houses, Theatres, Sleeping Cars* (Boston: William J. Nagel, 1906), iii. Also see James Schouler, *A Treatise on the Law of Bailments: Including Carriers, Innkeepers, and Pledge* (Boston, 1880); and Emlin McClain, *A Selection of Cases on the Law of Bailments and Carriers: including Ordinary Bailments, Pledges, Warehousemen, Wharfingers, Innkeepers, Postmasters and Public Carriers of Goods and Passengers*, 3rd ed. (Boston: Little, Brown, 1914).

27. Note the progression of publication: Joseph Henry Beale Jr., *A Selection of Cases on the Law of Carriers* (Cambridge, MA: Harvard Law Review Publishing Association, 1898); Joseph Henry Beale and Bruce Wyman, *Cases on Public Service Companies: Public Carriers, Public Works, and Other Public Utilities* (Cambridge, MA: Harvard Law Review Publishing Association, 1902); Beale and Wyman, *Law of Railroad Rate Regulation* (1906). After this Beale handed off the development of the ideas of public calling, public service corporation, and public utility law to Wyman and Frankfurter. Beale, *Innkeepers*, iii.

28. For some overviews of this nineteenth-century transformation to police power, see Ernst Freund, *The Police Power: Public Policy and Constitutional Rights* (Chicago: Callaghan, 1904); Ernst Freund, *Standards of American Legislation* (Chicago: University of Chicago Press, 1917); John F. Dillon, *Treatise on the Law of Municipal Corporations* (Chicago: James Cockcroft, 1872); Novak, *People's Welfare*.

29. *Commonwealth v. Alger*, 7 Cushing 53 (Mass., 1851), 84.

30. These headings are culled from *Laws of New York, 1781–1801*, 2 vols. (Albany, 1802). See also *The Revised Statutes of the State of Michigan* (Detroit, 1838); *The Revised Statutes of the Commonwealth of Massachusetts* (Boston, 1836).

31. "An Act Concerning Passenger Carriers," *Acts and Resolves of Massachusetts* (1840), ch. 80, 224; "An Act Concerning Effects of Passengers Transported by Railroad Corporations and Other Common Carriers," *Acts and Resolves of Massachusetts* (1851), ch. 147, 645–647.

32. *The Charter and Ordinances of the City of Boston, Together with the Acts of the Legislature Relating to the City: Collected and Revised* (Boston, 1834), ch. 28, "Licensed Houses," 203–210. Boston's authority to regulate innkeepers and other public callings in the city was derived from the legislature. "An Act for the Due Regulation of Licensed Houses," *Acts and Resolves of Massachusetts* (1832).

33. For the assize of bread see *Mayor of Mobile v. Yuille*, 3 Ala. 137 (1841); On the mill acts, see the discussion in Morton J. Horwitz, *The Transformation of*

American Law, 1780–1860 (Cambridge, MA: Harvard University Press, 1977); On rate setting in the canal era, see Harry N. Scheiber, "The Rate-Making Power of the State in the Canal Era: A Case Study," *Political Science Quarterly* 77 (1962): 397–413; see also *Public Laws of the State of New York* (Albany, 1835), ch. 119, 37.

34. Freund, *Standards of Legislation*, iii, 68, 72; Edmund Burke, *A Letter to the Sheriffs of Bristol*, ed. James Hugh Moffatt (Philadelphia: Hinds, Noble & Eldredge, 1904), 9, 45.

35. See the still important study George Heberton Evans Jr., *Business Incorporations in the United States, 1800–1943* (New York: National Board of Economic Research, 1948), 10.

36. *Resolves and Private Laws of the State of Connecticut, 1789–1865*, 5 vols. (New Haven, 1837–1871). For a more elaborate discussion of this phenomenon, see William J. Novak, "The American Law of Association: The Legal-Political Construction of Civil Society," *Studies in American Political Development* 15 (2001): 163–188.

37. For excellent revisionist overviews of the special charter period and the important transition to more general laws, see Eric Hilt, "Early American Corporations and the State," and Jessica Hennessey and John Wallis, "Corporations and Organizations in the United States After 1840," in *Corporations and American Democracy*, ed. Naomi Lamoreaux and William J. Novak (Cambridge, MA: Harvard University Press, 2017).

38. This is crucial, for much ink has been spent delineating the private benefits to corporations of state chartering, and fewer pages have been devoted to figuring out the exact dimensions of this enlarged regulatory power. Freund, *Police Power*, 358.

39. Freund provided a useful listing of the typical kinds of charter restrictions. Freund, 359.

40. In addition to the sources cited in Hilt, "Early American Corporations," and Hennessey and Wallis, "Corporations and Organizations," see Adolf A. Berle and Gardiner C. Means, *The Modern Corporation and Private Property*, rev. ed. (New York: Macmillan, 1968), 11; Joseph S. Davis, *Essays in the Earlier History of American Corporations*, 2 vols. (Cambridge, MA: Harvard University Press, 1917), 2:24–27; Novak, *People's Welfare*, 106.

41. James Willard Hurst, *The Legitimacy of the Business Corporation* (Charlottesville: University of Virginia Press, 1970), 17.

42. John F. Stover, *History of the Baltimore and Ohio Railroad* (West Lafayette, IN: Purdue University Press, 1987), 24.

43. *Thorpe v. Rutland and Burlington Railroad Company*, 27 Vt. 140 (1855), 142–143. See also Isaac Redfield, "Regulation of Interstate Traffic on Railways by Congress," *American Law Register* 13 (1974): 9.

44. *Thorpe v. Rutland*, 150, 153–154.

45. *Lumbard v. Stearns*, 4 Cush. 60 (1849); Joseph H. Beale, "Lemuel Shaw," in *Great American Lawyers*, vol. 3, ed. William Draper Lewis (Philadelphia: John C. Winston, 1907), 484.

46. *Hazen v. Essex Co.*, 12 Cush. 475 (1832), 477–478. See also the extended discussion of the mill act cases in Leonard W. Levy, *The Law of the*

Commonwealth and Chief Justice Shaw (New York: Oxford University Press, 1957), 255–259.

47. "An Act to Incorporate the Springfield Acqueduct Company," *Acts and Resolves of the State of Massachusetts* (1848), ch. 303.
48. *Lumbard v. Stearns*, 61–62.
49. Scheiber, "Road to *Munn*"; Beale, "Lemuel Shaw"; Levy, *Law of the Commonwealth;* Breck P. McAllister, "Lord Hale and Business Affected with a Public Interest," *Harvard Law Review* 43 (1930): 759–791.
50. Léon Duguit, *Law in the Modern State*, trans. Frida Laski and Harold Laski (New York: B. W. Huebsch, 1919; London: George Allen & Unwin, 1921).
51. Freund, *Police Power*, 3–5. For a more elaborate discussion, see William J. Novak, "Police Power and the Hidden Transformation of the American State," in *Police and the Liberal State*, ed. Markus Dubber and Mariana Valverde (Stanford, CA: Stanford University Press, 2008), 54–73.
52. John Dewey, *The Public and Its Problems*, in *John Dewey: The Later Works, 1925–1953*, vol. 2, ed. Jo Ann Boydston (Carbondale: University of Illinois Press, 1984), 266, 303.
53. Frankfurter, *Public and Its Government*, 81.
54. On this point, also see Richard R. John, *Spreading the News: The American Postal System from Franklin to Morse* (Cambridge, MA: Harvard University Press, 1995); and Richard R. John, *Network Nation: Inventing American Telecommunications* (Cambridge, MA: Belknap Press of Harvard University Press, 2010).
55. Duguit, *Law in the Modern State*, 32–33, 38, 46–48.
56. Frank J. Goodnow, *Comparative Administrative Law: An Analysis of the Administrative Systems, National and Local, of the United States, England, France and Germany* (New York: G. P. Putnam's Sons, 1893); Freund, *Police Power.*
57. Ernst Freund, "Police Power," in *Cyclopedia of American Government*, 3 vols., ed. Andrew C. McLaughlin and Albert Bushnell Hart (New York: D. Appleton, 1914), 2:708. See also Freund, *Police Power*, 4–7; W. G. Hastings, "The Development of Law as Illustrated by the Decisions Relating to the Police Power of the State," *Proceedings of the American Philosophical Society* 39 (1900): 359–554.
58. Rexford G. Tugwell, *The Economic Basis of Public Interest* (Menasha, WI: Collegiate, 1922), v.
59. Felix Frankfurter, "Foreword," *Yale Law Journal* 47 (1938): 517–518.
60. Beale, *Selection of Cases;* Beale and Wyman, *Law of Railroad Rate Regulation;* Joseph Henry Beale and Bruce Wyman, *Cases on Public Service Companies;* Wyman, *Principles;* Frankfurter, *Selection of Cases.*
61. William Howard Taft, "Proceedings on the Death of Chief Justice White," 257 U.S. xxv–xxvi (1922).
62. Goodnow, *American Conception of Liberty.*
63. The literature on utilitarianism and the "nineteenth-century revolution in government" is voluminous. Two excellent overviews are Oliver MacDonagh, "The Nineteenth-Century Revolution in Government: A Reappraisal," *Historical Journal* 1 (1958): 52–67; and Arthur J. Taylor, *Laissez-Faire and State*

Intervention in Nineteenth-Century Britain (London: Macmillan, 1972). Also see David Hume, *A Treatise on Human Nature,* ed. T. H. Green and T. H. Grose, 2 vols. (London: Longmans, Green, 1874); Jeremy Bentham, *A Fragment on Government* (Oxford: Clarendon, 1891).

64. Tugwell, *Economic Basis,* v.

65. Tugwell, 23, 124.

66. For an early statement of the relation of monopoly and trust to problems of public utility, see Bruce Wyman, "The Law of Public Callings as a Solution of the Trust Problem," *Harvard Law Review* 17 (1904): 157–173.

67. Tugwell, *Economic Basis,* 80–108, 102.

68. Bagley, "Medicine."

69. Wyman, *Public Service Corporations,* xi.

70. Oliver Wendell Holmes Jr., *The Common Law* (Boston: Little, Brown, 1881), 5.

71. Frankfurter, *Public and Its Government,* 31.

72. See, for example, Shaw Livermore's discussion of the Lynn Iron Works of 1645. Shaw Livermore, *Early American Land Companies: Their Influence on Corporate Development,* 2nd ed. (Cambridge, MA: Harvard University Press, 1968), 42–45.

73. Jerry L. Mashaw, *Creating the Administrative Constitution: The Lost One Hundred Years of American Administrative Law* (New Haven, CT: Yale University Press, 2012); Nicholas R. Parrillo, *Against the Profit Motive: The Salary Revolution in American Government, 1780–1940* (New Haven, CT: Yale University Press, 2013). Also see the early pioneering work of Leonard White, nicely introduced in Richard R. John's synthetic review, "In Retrospect: Leonard D. White and the Invention of American Administrative History," *Reviews in American History* 24 (1996): 344–360.

74. "Resolve Incorporating the New-York and Stonington Rail Road Company" (passed May 1832), *Resolves and Private Laws of the State of Connecticut from the Year 1789 to the Year 1836,* 2 vols. (Hartford, 1837), 1019–1023.

75. Leonard D. White, "The Origin of Utility Commissions in Massachusetts," *Journal of Political Economy* 29 (1921): 185.

76. Frankfurter, *Public and Its Government,* 84–85. See also Robert Eugene Cushman, *Studies in the Police Power of the National Government* (Minneapolis: Minnesota Law Review, 1919–1920).

77. Alfred D. Chandler Jr., ed., *The Railroads: The Nation's First Big Business* (New York: Harcourt, Brace & World, 1965).

78. Frankfurter, *Public and Its Government,* 82.

79. Charles Francis Adams, "A Chapter of Erie," *North American Review* 109 (1869): 30.

80. Arthur T. Hadley, *Railroad Transportation: Its History and Its Laws* (New York: G. P. Putnam's Sons, 1902), 134.

81. Hurst, "Problems of Legitimacy," 225–226.

82. Charles Francis Adams Jr., "The Railroad System," in Charles Francis Adams Jr. and Henry Adams, *Chapters of Erie and other Essays* (Boston, 1871), 414. See also Hadley, *Railroad Transportation.*

83. New Hampshire county commissioners were ultimately consolidated into a State Board of Railroad Commissioners in 1844—technically the first state

board in the country. New Hampshire Railroad Commissioners, *Reports of the Railroad Commissioners: Exhibiting the Condition of the Several Railroads in New Hampshire* (Concord, NH: Butterfield & Hill, 1849). Other states experimented early with various kinds of temporary boards or commissioners to arbitrate disputes concerning railroads. Frederick C. Clark, "State Railroad Commissions and How They May be Made Effective," *Publications of the American Economic Association* 6 (1891): 11–110, 23–26.

84. "An Act to Establish a Board of Railroad Commissioners," *Acts and Resolves Passed by the General Court of Massachusetts in the Year 1868* (Boston: Wright and Potter, 1869), ch. 408, 699–700.

85. On the significance of early American legislative petitioning, see Daniel Carpenter and Benjamin Schneer, "Party Formation through Petitions: The Whigs and the Bank War of 1832–1834," *Studies in American Political Development* 29 (2015): 213–234; Maggie McKinley, "Petitioning and the Making of the Administrative State," *Yale Law Journal* 127 (2017): 1538–1637. Adams was a fierce critic of the undue influence railroads seemed to be exerting on the Massachusetts legislature. White, "Origins of Utility Commissions," 186; Thomas K. McCraw, *Prophets of Regulation* (Cambridge, MA: Harvard University Press, 1984).

86. On the move from "private bills" to "general laws," see Naomi R. Lamoreaux and John Joseph Wallis, eds., *Organizations, Civil Society, and the Roots of Development* (Chicago: University of Chicago Press, 2017); Naomi R. Lamoreaux and John Joseph Wallis, "States, Not Nation: The Sources of Political and Economic Development in the Early United States," unpub. mss., 2015.

87. *First Annual Report of the Board of Railroad Commissioners* (Boston: Wright & Potter, 1870); *Second Annual Report of the Board of Railroad Commissioners* (Boston: Wright and Potter, 1871).

88. *New London Northern Railroad Company v. Boston & Albany Railroad Company*, 102 Mass. 386 (1869), 387–388. By 1873, the court just as matter-of-factly sustained such things as the board's expanding powers to supervise and regulate the details of certain kinds of railroad and station construction. *Attorney General v. Norwich and Worcester Railroad Company*, 113 Mass. 161 (1873), 168–169.

89. The Massachusetts legislature passed almost a hundred other special and general railroad measures in the 1869 session alone. "An Act to Establish a Board of Railroad Commissioners," *Acts and Resolves Passed by the General Court of Massachusetts* (1869), ch. 408, 699–703.

90. *Annual Report of the Massachusetts Board of Railroad Commissioners*, 24 (1892), 13–15. Irston R. Barnes, *Public Utility Control in Massachusetts: A Study in the Commission Regulation of Security Issues and Rates* (New Haven, CT: Yale University Press, 1930), 13, 94.

91. Clark, "State Railroad Commissions," 32.

92. Colorado, Connecticut, Iowa, Kentucky, Maine, Massachusetts, Michigan, Nebraska, New York, Ohio, Rhode Island, Vermont, Virginia, and Wisconsin, as well as the territory of Dakota. Robert E. Cushman, *The Independent Regulatory Commissions* (New York: Oxford University Press, 1941), 25.

93. "An Act to Establish a Board of Railroad and Warehouse Commissioners, and Prescribe their Powers and Duties," *Public Laws of the State of Illinois* (1871), 618–625.

94. The Constitution of the State of Illinois (1870), art. 11, sec. 12 and 15; art. 13, sec. 6 and 7. Similar railroad policy constitutional provisions made their way into the new state constitutions of Iowa in 1874, Nebraska and Alabama in 1875, and California in 1879.

95. "An Act to Regulate Public Warehouses, and the Warehousing and Inspection of Grain," *Public Laws of the State of Illinois* (1871), 762–774. "An Act to Provide for the Incorporation of Associations that may be Organized for the Purposes of Constructing Railways, Maintaining and Operating the Same; For Prescribing and Defining the Duties and Limiting the Powers of such Corporations when so Organized"; "An Act to Prevent Injury to Persons or Property at Railroad Junctions or Crossings"; "An Act to Prevent Unjust Discriminations and Extortions in the Rates to be Charged by the Different Railroads in this State for the Transportation of Freight on Said Roads"; "An Act Regulating the Receiving, Transportation and Delivery of Grain by Railroad Corporations"; "An Act to Establish a Reasonable Maximum Rate of Charges for the Transportation of Passengers on Railroads in this State"; and "An Act Authorizing the Formation of Union Depots and Stations for Railroads in this State," *Public Laws of the State of Illinois* (1871), 625–643.

96. "An Act to Establish a Board of Railroad and Warehouse Commissioners, and Prescribe their Powers and Duties, *Public Laws of the State of Illinois* (1871), 618–625, 622.

97. "An Act to Prevent Extortion and Unjust Discrimination in the Rates Charged for the Transportation of Passengers and Freights on Railroads in this State," *Public Laws of the State of Illinois* (1873), 135–140; "Schedule of Maximum Rates," *Public Laws of the State of Illinois* (1874), 129.

98. Alabama, California, Georgia, Illinois, Kansas, Minnesota, Mississippi, Missouri, New Hampshire, and South Carolina. Cushman, *Independent Regulatory Commissions,* 26.

99. *First Report of the Railroad and Warehouse Commission of the State of Illinois,* 4–7.

100. *Report of the Senate Select Committee on Interstate Commerce* (Washington, DC: Government Printing Office, 1886), 1:110.

101. *First Report,* 6–7.

102. *First Report,* 6.

103. *First Report,* 17. Ira Y. Munn et. al. v. The People of the State of Illinois, 69 Ill. 80 (1873).

104. *Fourth Annual Report of the Railroad and Warehouse Commission of the State of Illinois* (Springfield, IL: State Journal Steam Print, 1874), 14–16.

105. *Fourth Annual Report,* 370–377.

106. *Fourth Annual Report,* 22.

107. Stephen Breyer, *Regulation and Its Reform* (Cambridge, MA: Harvard University Press, 1982), 36–70. Stephen G. Breyer, Richard B. Stewart, Cass R. Sunstein, and Matthew L. Spitzer, *Administrative Law and Regulatory Policy,* 5th ed. (New York: Aspen Law & Business, 2002), 267.

108. See, for example, the extraordinary "Report of J. H. Rowell," Illinois state's attorney, on his argument pursued at the commission's initiative in *People v. Chicago and Alton Railroad Company. Second Annual Report of Railroad and Warehouse Commission,* 43–114.

109. *Sixth Annual Report of the Railroad and Warehouse Commission of the State of Illinois* (Springfield, IL: D. W. Lusk, State Printer, 1876), 11.

110. *Gibbons v. Ogden,* 22 U.S. 1 (1824); *Brown v. Maryland,* 25 U.S. 419 (1927); *Willson v. Black Bird Creek Marsh Company,* 27 U.S. 245 (1829); Felix Frankfurter, *The Commerce Clause under Marshall, Taney and Waite* (Chapel Hill: University of North Carolina Press, 1937).

111. *Peik v. Chicago and Northwestern Railway,* 94 U.S. 164 (1877), 177–178.

112. *Wabash, St. Louis and Pacific Railway v. Illinois,* 118 U.S. 557 (1886), 573, 577.

113. Cushman, *Independent Regulatory Commissions,* 38, 40–41.

114. I. L. Sharfman, "The Interstate Commerce Commission: An Appraisal," *Yale Law Journal* 46 (1937): 915.

115. "An Act to Regulate Commerce," *U.S. Statutes at Large* 24 (1887): 379–387.

116. Shelby M. Cullom, "Report of the Senate Select Committee on Interstate Commerce (with Appendix)," 49th Cong., 1st sess. (Washington, DC: Government Printing Office, 1886).

117. Cullom, "Report," 180–181.

118. U. H. Painter, *Interstate Commerce: Debate in Forty-Ninth Congress on the Bill to Establish a Board of Commissioners on Interstate Commerce,* (Washington, DC: Government Printing Office, 1887), 507, 658–659.

119. "An Act to Regulate Interstate Commerce," sec. 13–16.

120. *Proceedings of a General Conference of Railroad Commissioners Held at the Office of the Interstate Commerce Commission* (Washington, DC: Government Printing Office, 1889), 97.

121. See, for example, David E. Lilienthal, "The Regulation of Public Utility Holding Companies," *Columbia Law Review* 29 (1929): 404–440.

122. Henry Carter Adams, "The Relation of the State to Industrial Action," *Publications of the American Economic Association* 1 (1887): 84.

123. Charles Fairman suggested that the name was something of a pejorative— emanating from the dissenting opinion of Justice Field in *Stone v. Wisconsin*— "an unfriendly hand." Charles Fairman, "The So-Called Granger Cases, Lord Hale, and Justice Bradley," *Stanford Law Review* 5 (1953): 587.

124. *Munn v. Illinois,* 94 U.S. 113 (1877); *Chicago, Burlington, and Quincy Railroad Company v. Iowa,* 94 U.S. 155 (1877); *Peik v. Chicago and Northwestern Railway Company* and *Lawrence v. North-western Railway Company,* 94 U.S. 164 (1877); *Chicago, Milwaukee, and St. Paul Railroad Company v. Ackley,* 94 U.S. 179 (1877); *Winona and St. Peter Railroad Company v. Blake,* 94 U.S. 180 (1877); *Stone v. Wisconsin,* 94 U.S. 181 (1877).

125. Frankfurter inaugurated a long tradition of routinely starting modern discussion of the legal regulation of public utilities with *Munn v. Illinois.* Felix Frankfurter and James Forrester Davison, *Cases and Other Materials on Administrative Law* (Chicago: Commerce Clearing House, 1932), 685. See also

Young B. Smith, Noel T. Dowling, and Robert L. Hale, *Cases on the Law of Public Utilities* (St. Paul, MN: West Publishing, 1936), 7.

126. Chief Justice Breese elaborated for the Illinois Supreme Court on this distinctly legislative power. *Munn v. People*, 88.

127. *Munn v. People*, 124–125.

128. *Munn v. People*, 124–125.

129. And, indeed, in *Nebbia v. New York*, 291 U.S. 502 (1934), the US Supreme Court would ultimately come back to just such a straightforward application of the police power.

130. *Nebbia v. New York*, 126.

131. *Nebbia v. New York*, 126–134.

132. *Chicago, Burlington, and Quincy Railroad Company v. Iowa*, 161.

133. Bruce Wyman, "The Law of the Public Callings as a Solution of the Trust Problem II," *Harvard Law Review* 17 (1904): 222.

134. Max Lerner, "The Triumph of Laissez-Faire," in *Paths of American Thought*, ed. Arthur M. Schlesinger Jr., and Morton White (Boston: Houghton and Mifflin, 1963), 159.

135. Fairman, "So-Called Granger Cases," 588; *Nebbia v. New York*, 291 U.S. 502 (1934).

136. Harry N. Scheiber, "Law and Political Institutions," in *Encyclopedia of American Economic History: Studies of the Principal Movements and Ideas*, 3 vols., ed. Glenn Porter (New York: Charles Scribner's Sons, 1980), 2:501–502. See also Owen Fiss, *Troubled Beginnings of the Modern State, 1888–1910* (New York: Macmillan, 1993), ch. 7, 185–222; Robert Rabin, "Federal Regulation in Historical Perspective," *Stanford Law Review* 38 (1986): 1211.

137. See Stephen Skowronek, *Building a New American State: The Expansion of National Administrative Capacities, 1877–1920* (New York: Cambridge University Press, 1982), 138–160.

138. *Civil Rights Cases*, 109 U.S. 3 (1883), 42.

139. *Western Turf Association v. Greenberg*, 204 U.S. 359 (1907), 362.

140. For a broad survey of state appellate usage of *Munn* to uphold regulation (as well as an excellent presentation of the legal and historical rationale), see Justice Samuel Blatchford's opinion in *Budd v. New York*, 143 U.S. 517 (1892).

141. *Schmidinger v. Chicago*, 226 U.S. 578 (1913); *Holden v. Hardy*, 169 U.S. 366 (1898).

142. For an excellent survey, see Carl D. Thompson, *Public Ownership: A Survey of Public Enterprises, Municipal, State, and Federal in the United States and Elsewhere* (New York: Thomas Y. Crowell, 1925).

143. Felix Frankfurter and Henry M. Hart Jr., "Rate Regulation," in *Encyclopaedia of the Social Sciences*, 15 vols., ed. Edwin R. A. Seligman (New York: Macmillan, 1934), 13:104.

144. Tugwell, *Economic Basis*, 95; Wyman, *Special Law*.

145. Ben W. Lewis, "Public Utilities," in *Government and Economic Life: Development and Current Issues of American Public Policy*, 2 vols., ed. Leverett S. Lyon and Victor Abramson (Washington, DC: Brookings Institution, 1940), 2:616.

146. Wyman, *Public Service Corporations,* 1:x.

147. Mary L. Barron, *State Regulation of the Securities of Railroads and Public Service Companies* (Philadelphia: University of Pennsylvania Press, 1918); Delos F. Wilcox, "The Public Regulation of Wages, Hours, and Conditions of Labor of the Employees of Public Service Corporations," *National Municipal Review* 6 (1917): 31–40.

148. *Wabash, St. Louis & Pacific Railway Company v. Illinois,* 118 U.S. 557 (1886); *Chicago, Milwaukee & St. Paul Railway Company v. Minnesota,* 134 U.S. 418 (1890); *Smyth v. Ames,* 169 U.S. 466 (1898).

4. Social Legislation

1. Edward Alsworth Ross, *Social Control: A Survey of the Foundations of Order* (1901; New York: Macmillan, 1929), 436.

2. Brooks Adams, "Introductory Note," in Henry Adams, *The Degradation of the Democratic Dogma* (1919; repr., New York: Harper & Row, 1969), xxx; Louis Adamic, *Dynamite: The Story of Class Violence in America* (New York: Viking, 1931).

3. Richard Hofstadter, *The Age of Reform: From Bryan to F. D. R.* (New York: Alfred A. Knopf, 1955); Samuel P. Hays, *The Response to Industrialism, 1885–1914* (Chicago: University of Chicago Press, 1957); Robert H. Wiebe, *The Search for Order, 1877–1920* (New York: Hill and Wang, 1967); Alan Dawley, *Struggles for Justice: Social Responsibility and the Liberal State* (Cambridge, MA: Harvard University Press, 1991); Daniel T. Rodgers, *Atlantic Crossings: Social Politics in a Progressive Age* (Cambridge, MA: Harvard University Press, 1998).

4. Oliver Wendell Holmes Jr., *The Common Law,* ed. Mark DeWolfe Howe (1881; Boston: Little, Brown, 1963), 5. This externalist and contextualist perspective is at the heart of the modern approach to legal history as well as the law and society movement. See Robert W. Gordon, "J. Willard Hurst and the Common Law Tradition in American Legal Historiography," *Law and Society Review* 10 (1975): 9–55; Lawrence M. Friedman, "The Law and Society Movement," *Stanford Law Review* 38 (1986): 763–780.

5. On this methodological point, see William J. Novak, "The Concept of the State in American History," in *Boundaries of the State in U.S. History,* ed. James T. Sparrow, William J. Novak, and Stephen W. Sawyer (Chicago: University of Chicago Press, 2015), 325–350; Novak, "Beyond Max Weber: The Need for Democratic (Not Aristocratic) Theory of the Modern State," *Tocqueville Review/La Revue Tocqueville* 36 (2015): 43–91.

6. The literature on modern social welfare and social policing is enormous. On social police, I have found most useful Michel Foucault, *Security, Territory, Population: Lectures at the College de France, 1977–1978,* ed. Michel Senellart (New York: Palgrave Macmillan, 2007); Jacques Donzelot, *The Policing of Families* (New York: Random House, 1979); François Ewald, "A Concept of Social Law," in *Dilemmas of Law in the Welfare State,* ed. Gunther Teubner (New York: Walter de Gruyter, 1988), 40–75; Nikolas Rose, *Powers of*

Freedom: Reframing Political Thought (Cambridge: Cambridge University Press, 1999); David Garland, *The Culture of Control: Crime and Social Order in Contemporary Society* (Chicago: University of Chicago Press, 2001); Dario Melossi, *The State of Social Control: A Sociological Study of Concepts of State and Social Control in the Making of Democracy* (New York: St. Martin's, 1990). On social provisioning and social welfare, I have found most useful Karen M. Tani, *States of Dependency: Welfare, Rights, and American Governance, 1935–1972* (New York: Cambridge University Press, 2016); Michael B. Katz, *The Price of Citizenship: Redefining the American Welfare State* (Philadelphia: University of Pennsylvania Press, 2001); Michele Landis Dauber, *The Sympathetic State: Disaster Relief and the Origins of the American Welfare State* (Chicago: University of Chicago Press, 2013); David Garland, *Punishment and Welfare: A History of Penal Strategies* (Aldershot, UK: Gower, 1985); George Steinmetz, *Regulating the Social: The Welfare State and Local Politics in Imperial Germany* (Princeton, NJ: Princeton University Press, 1993).

7. John Maurice Clark, *The Social Control of Business* (Chicago: University of Chicago Press, 1926); American Economic Association, *Readings in the Social Control of Industry* (Philadelphia: Blakiston, 1942).

8. Walter I. Trattner, ed., *Social Welfare or Social Control? Some Historical Reflections on Regulating the Poor* (Knoxville: University of Tennessee Press, 1983); Daniel T. Rodgers, "In Search of Progressivism," *Reviews in American History* 10 (1982): 113–132; Julilly Kohler-Hausmann, "Guns and Butter: The Welfare State, the Carceral State, and the Politics of Exclusion in the Postwar United States," *Journal of American History* 102 (2015): 87–99.

9. See Michel Foucault, "Governmentality," in *The Foucault Effect: Studies in Governmentality,* ed. Graham Burchell, Colin Gordon, and Peter Miller (Chicago: University of Chicago Press, 1991), 87–104; and Michel Foucault, "*Omnes et Singulatim*: Towards a Criticism of 'Political Reason,'" in *The Tanner Lectures of Human Values II,* ed. Sterling McMurrin (Salt Lake City: University of Utah Press, 1981), 225–254.

10. Ewald, "Social Law," 41. The work of Emile Durkheim is particularly attuned to the important relationship of law and modern social regulation generally. Emile Durkheim, *The Division of Labor in Society,* trans. W. D. Halls (New York: Free Press, 1984); Roger Cotterrell, *Emile Durkheim: Law in a Moral Domain* (Stanford, CA: Stanford University Press, 1999), esp. 18.

11. Alexis de Tocqueville, *Democracy in America,* trans. Arthur Goldhammer (New York: Library of America, 2004), ch. 3; John Stuart Mill, "M. de Tocqueville on Democracy in America," in *Dissertations and Discussions: Political, Philosophical, and Historical,* 2. vols. (London: John W. Parker and Son, 1859), 2:3–4. For an extensive discussion of this pivotal moment see, Stephen W. Sawyer, *Demos Assembled: Democracy and the International Origins of the Modern State, 1840–1880* (Chicago: University of Chicago Press, 2018).

12. Michel Foucault, *Discipline and Punish: The Birth of the Prison,* trans. Alan Sheridan (New York: Vintage Books, 1979), 213.

13. E. R. A. Seligman, ed., *Encyclopaedia of the Social Sciences,* 15 vols. (New York: Macmillan, 1935).

14. William D. P. Bliss and Rudolph M. Binder, *The New Encyclopedia of Social Reform, including All Social-Reform Movements and Activities, and the Economic, Industrial, and Sociological Facts and Statistics of All Countries and All Social Subjects* (New York: Funk and Wagnalls, 1908).

15. Peter Stein, *Legal Evolution: The Story of an Idea* (Cambridge: Cambridge University Press, 1980); Roger Cotterrell, *Law's Community: Legal Theory in Sociological Perspective* (Oxford: Oxford University Press, 1995).

16. Richard Hofstadter, *Social Darwinism in American Thought* (Philadelphia: University of Pennsylvania Press, 1944), 7.

17. Thomas L. Haskell, *The Emergence of Professional Social Science: The American Social Science Association and the Nineteenth-Century Crisis of Authority* (Urbana: University of Illinois Press, 1977); Dorothy Ross, *The Origins of American Social Science* (New York: Cambridge University Press, 1991); Daniel T. Rodgers, *Atlantic Crossings: Social Politics in a Progressive Age* (Cambridge, MA: Harvard University Press, 2000).

18. Thomas A. Green, "Freedom and Criminal Responsibility in the Age of Pound: An Essay on Criminal Justice," *Michigan Law Review* 93 (1995): 1915–2053; Michael Willrich, *City of Courts: Socializing Justice in Progressive Era Chicago* (New York: Cambridge University Press, 2003).

19. Winston Churchill, *Liberalism and the Social Problem* (London: Hodder and Stoughton, 1909), 317.

20. Graham Wallas, *The Great Society: A Psychological Analysis* (New York: Macmillan, 1914), 3.

21. C. Wright Mills, *Sociology and Pragmatism: The Higher Learning in America* (New York: Paine-Whitman, 1964), 448.

22. Robert B. Pippin, "Hegel, Modernity, and Habermas," *The Monist* 74 (1991): 333–334; Robert B. Pippin, *Modernism as a Philosophical Problem: On the Dissatisfactions of European High Culture,* 2nd ed. (Oxford: Blackwell, 1999); Robert B. Pippin, *The Persistence of Subjectivity: On the Kantian Aftermath* (New York: Cambridge University Press, 2005); Terry Pinkard, *German Philosophy, 1760–1860: The Legacy of Idealism* (New York: Cambridge University Press, 2002).

23. Richard Rorty, "Review of *The Persistence of Subjectivity,*" *Notre Dame Philosophical Review: An Electronic Journal,* http://ndpr.nd.edu/news/the-persistence-of-subjectivity-on-the-kantian-aftermath.

24. William James, *The Principles of Psychology,* 2 vols. (New York: Henry Holt, 1890), 1:104–127, 193–196, 224–290. George Herbert Mead, "The Social Self," *Journal of Philosophy, Psychology and Scientific Methods* 10 (1913): 374–380.

25. John Dewey, "From Absolutism to Experimentalism," in *Contemporary American Philosophy: Personal Statements,* ed. George P. Adams and William Pepperell Montague (New York: Macmillan, 1930): 25.

26. John Dewey, "Liberalism and Social Action," in *John Dewey: The Later Works, 1925–1953,* vol. 11, ed. Jo Ann Boydston (Carbondale: University of

Southern Illinois Press, 1987), 48–49. John Dewey, *Human Nature and Conduct: An Introduction to Social Psychology* (New York: Henry Holt, 1922), 314.

27. John Dewey, "Democracy and Educational Administration," in *Problems of Men* (New York: Philosophical Library, 1946), 59–60; John Dewey and James H. Tufts, *Ethics* (New York: Henry Holt, 1932), 408.

28. William James, *The Meaning of Truth: A Sequel to "Pragmatism"* (New York: Longmans, Green, 1909), vi.

29. Dewey and Tufts, *Ethics,* 433.

30. John Dewey, "The Philosophy of Thomas Hill Green," in *John Dewey: The Early Works, 1882–1898,* vol. 3, ed. Jo Ann Boydston (Carbondale: University of Southern Illinois Press, 1969), 16, 27.

31. Dewey and Tufts, *Ethics,* 433.

32. Mead, "Social Self," 374. Mead also drew attention to the "democratic" nature of such an epistemological and sociological position. George Herbert Mead, "Cooley's Contribution to American Social Thought," *American Journal of Sociology* 35 (1930): 694–695.

33. Dewey, *Human Nature and Conduct,* 317.

34. Dewey, "The Ethics of Democracy," *University of Michigan Philosophical Papers,* 2nd ser., no. 1 (Ann Arbor, MI: Andrews, 1888), 7.

35. Albion Small, *General Sociology: An Exposition of the Main Development in Sociological Theory from Spencer to Ratzenhofer* (Chicago: University of Chicago Press, 1905), 3, 20–21, 47. See also Franklin Henry Giddings, *The Theory of Socialization: A Syllabus of Sociological Principles* (New York: Macmillan, 1897), 1.

36. Woodrow Wilson, *The New Freedom: A Call for the Emancipation of the Generous Energies of a People* (New York: Doubleday, Page, 1913), 7; Jane Addams, *Democracy and Social Ethics* (New York: Macmillan, 1915), 142, 207; Scott Nearing, *Social Sanity: A Preface to the Book of Social Progress* (New York: Moffart, Yard, 1913); Walter E. Weyl, *The New Democracy: An Essay on Certain Political and Economic Tendencies in the United States* (New York: Macmillan, 1912), 160. The "old individualism," Weyl contended, "would have meant impotence and social bankruptcy."

37. Dewey, "Liberalism and Social Action," in Boydston, *John Dewey,* 11:13.

38. Dewey and Tufts, *Ethics,* 296; Dewey, "Liberalism and Social Action," 11–12.

39. Dewey and Tufts, *Ethics,* 294–295, 303–304.

40. Dewey, "Liberalism and Social Action, 14.

41. Arthur John Taylor, *Laissez-Faire and State Intervention in Nineteenth-Century Britain* (New York: Macmillan, 1972); J. Bartlett Brebner, "Laissez Faire and State Intervention in Nineteenth-Century Britain," *Journal of Economic History* 8 (1948): 59–73; Oliver MacDonagh, "The Nineteenth-Century Revolution in Government: A Reappraisal," *Historical Journal* 1 (1958): 52–67; Henry Parris, "The Nineteenth-Century Revolution in Government: A Reappraisal Reappraised," *Historical Journal* 3 (1960): 17–37. See also Ellen Frankel Paul, *Moral Revolution and Economic Science: The*

Demise of Laissez-Faire in Nineteenth-Century British Political Economy (Westport, CT: Greenwood, 1979), 76.

42. A. V. Dicey, *Lectures on the Relation between Law and Public Opinion in England* (London: Macmillan, 1914), 288, 299, 310.

43. Both Roscoe Pound and Julius Stone categorized Jhering as a "social utilitarian." Julius Stone, *The Province and Function of Law: Law as Logic, Justice, and Social Control; A Study in Jurisprudence* (London: Stevens & Sons, 1947), 300; Roscoe Pound, "The Scope and Purpose of Sociological Jurisprudence II," *Harvard Law Review* 25 (1911): 142 (quoting Theodor Sternberg).

44. Paul Vinogradoff, *Outlines of Historical Jurisprudence,* 2 vols. (London: Oxford University Press, 1920), 1:149, 151; Eugen Ehrlich, *Fundamental Principles of the Sociology of Law* (Cambridge, MA: Harvard University Press, 1936); Léon Duguit, *Études de droit public,* 2 vols. (Paris: Albert Fontemoing, 1903).

45. Pound's most complete statement of the dramatically changed social order came in his provocatively entitled article "The New Feudalism," *American Bar Association Journal* 16 (1930): 557.

46. Roscoe Pound, "The Scope and Purpose of Sociological Jurisprudence I," *Harvard Law Review* 24 (1911): 611.

47. Roscoe Pound, *Social Control through Law* (New Haven, CT: Yale University Press, 1942), 75–78.

48. Willrich, *City of Courts,* 98.

49. Roscoe Pound, "The Scope and Purpose of Sociological Jurisprudence III," *Harvard Law Review* 25 (1912): 516 (emphasis added).

50. Roscoe Pound, "The Need of a Sociological Jurisprudence," *The Green Bag* 19 (1907): 614–615 (emphasis added). On the turn to "social justice," also see Westel Woodbury Willoughby, *Social Justice: A Critical Essay* (New York: Macmillan, 1900).

51. I explore some of this lineage in "The Common-Law Vision of a Well-Regulated Society," in William J. Novak, *The People's Welfare: Law and Regulation in Nineteenth-Century America* (Chapel Hill: University of North Carolina Press, 1996), ch. 1, 26–35. See also Donald R. Kelley, *The Human Measure: Social Thought in the Western Legal Tradition* (Cambridge, MA: Harvard University Press, 1990); and Walter Ullmann, *The Medieval Idea of Law: As Represented by Lucas de Penna* (New York: Routledge, 2010), 143.

52. Robert Pippin quoted in *University of Chicago Chronicle* 15 (2001): chronicle.uchicago.edu/011115/pippin.shtml; Axel Honneth, *The Struggle for Recognition: The Moral Grammar of Social Conflicts* (Cambridge, MA: MIT Press, 1996), 13.

53. T. H. Marshall, *Citizenship and Social Class* (Cambridge: Cambridge University Press, 1950), 8.

54. Weyl, *New Democracy,* 161–162.

55. Dewey and Tufts, *Ethics,* 438, 441.

56. Weyl, *New Democracy,* 161–162.

57. Dewey and Tufts, *Ethics,* 565–570.

58. Durkheim, *Division of Labor,* 3.

59. Scott Nearing, *Social Adjustment* (New York: Macmillan, 1911), 322, 325.

60. Roscoe Pound, "Legislation as a Social Function," *American Journal of Sociology* 18 (1913): 756, 762.

61. Ernst Freund, *Standards of American Legislation: An Estimate of Restrictive and Constructive Factors* (Chicago: University of Chicago Press, 1917).

62. Ernst Freund, *The Police Power: Public Policy and Constitutional Rights* (Chicago: Callaghan, 1904), 5; Ernst Freund, "Tendencies of Legislative Policy and Modern Social Legislation," *International Journal of Ethics* 27 (1916): 16.

63. Mary Stevenson Callcott, *Principles of Social Legislation* (New York: Macmillan, 1932), 12–13.

64. Freund, "Modern Social Legislation," 16, 23.

65. Helen I. Clarke, *Social Legislation: American Laws Dealing with Family, Child, and Dependent* (New York: D. Appleton-Century, 1940), 5.

66. John R. Commons and John B. Andrews, *Principles of Labor Legislation* (New York: Harper & Brothers, 1916), 17.

67. Clarke, *Social Legislation,* 7 (emphasis added). For a similar perspective, see Grace Abbott, "The Social Services as a Public Responsibility," in *From Relief to Social Security: The Development of the New Public Welfare Services and Their Administration* (Chicago: University of Chicago Press, 1941), 3–48.

68. Callcott, *Principles of Social Legislation;* Clarke, *Social Legislation.* See also W. Jethro Brown, *The Underlying Principles of Modern Legislation* (New York: E. P. Dutton, 1915); Jeremiah W. Jenks, *Governmental Action for Social Welfare* (New York: Macmillan, 1910); Robert D. Leigh, *Federal Health Administration* (New York: Harper & Brothers, 1927).

69. John Henry Crooker, *Problems in American Society: Some Social Studies* (Boston: George H. Ellis, 1889); Samuel George Smith, *Social Pathology* (New York: Macmillan, 1911); Charles A. Ellwood, *The Social Problem: A Reconstructive Analysis* (New York: MacMillan, 1919); Lyman P. Powell, *The Social Unrest* (New York: Review of Reviews, 1919); James Ford, *Social Problems and Social Policy: Principles Underlying Treatment and Prevention of Poverty, Defectiveness and Criminality* (Boston: Ginn, 1923); Ezra Thayer Towne, *Social Problems: A Study of Present-Day Social Conditions* (New York: MacMillan, 1924); Henry S. Spalding, ed., *Social Problems and Agencies* (New York: Benziger Brothers, 1925); Grove Samuel Dow and Edgar B. Wesley, *Social Problems of Today* (New York: Thomas Y. Crowell, 1925); Stuart Alfred Queen and Delbert Martin Mann, *Social Pathology* (New York: Thomas Y. Crowell, 1925); Mabel A. Elliott and Francis E. Merrill, *Social Disorganization* (New York: Harper & Brothers, 1934). See also Ross L. Finney, *Causes and Cures for the Social Unrest* (New York: Macmillan, 1922); Ernest R. Groves, *Social Problems and Education* (New York: Longmans, Green, 1925).

70. Towne, *Social Problems.* Dow and Wesley's *Social Problems of Today* follows an almost identical topical development while deploying a less social-scientific articulation of today's social problems. Other texts merged these social problems with a focus on pertinent economic issues, as in Richard

Henry Edwards, ed., *Studies in American Social Conditions, Issues 1–7* (Madison, WI, 1908–1910).

71. Ford, *Social Problems*.

72. Queen and Mann, *Social Pathology*, esp. 153–194; Smith, *Social Pathology*.

73. Asaheal Stearns and Lemuel Shaw, eds., *General Laws of Massachusetts, 1780–1822*, 2 vols. (Boston, 1823), vol. 1 (1787), c. 54, 322. For a fuller discussion of these early vagrancy regulations, see Novak, *People's Welfare*, 167–171. For the definitive treatment of recent American vagrancy law, see Risa Goluboff, *Vagrant Nation: Police Power, Constitutional Change, and the Making of the 1960s* (New York: Oxford University Press, 2016).

74. Clark D. Knapp, *Treatise on the Laws of the State of New York in Relation to the Poor, Insane, Idiots, and Habitual Drunkards* (Rochester: Williamson & Higbie, 1887). See also Florien Giauque, *A Manual for Guardians and Trustees of Minors, Insane Persons, Imbeciles, Idiots, Drunkards* (Cincinnati: Robert Clarke, 1881); Charles Richard Henderson, *Introduction to the Study of the Dependent, Defective, and Delinquent Classes and of their Social Treatment* (Boston: D. C. Heath, 1893).

75. Foucault, *Discipline and Punish*, 80–81.

76. For a complete listing of Mann's acknowledged social organizations and periodicals on which he drew, see Stuart Alfred Queen and Jennette Rowe Gruener, *Social Pathology: Obstacles to Social Participation*, rev. ed. (New York: Thomas Y. Crowell, 1940), vii–viii.

77. Queen and Gruener, *Social Pathology*, viii, xi, 681. See also Manuel Conrad Elmer, *Social Surveys of Urban Communities* (Menasha, WI: Collegiate, 1914), 2–3.

78. Nearing, *Social Adjustment*, vii; Nearing, *Social Sanity*, 20.

79. See William J. Novak, "Public Morality: Disorderly Houses and Demon Rum," in *People's Welfare*, 149–189.

80. Ross, *Social Control*; Edward Alsworth Ross, *Sin and Society: An Analysis of Latter-Day Iniquity, with a Letter from President Roosevelt* (Boston: Houghton Mifflin, 1907); Edward Alsworth Ross, *The Social Trend* (New York: Century, 1922), 96–97.

81. Harold Begbie, *The Crisis of Morals: An Analysis and a Programme* (New York: Fleming H. Revell, 1914), 158. See also Harold Begbie, *Twice-Born Men: A Clinic in Regeneration* (New York: Fleming H. Revell, 1909).

82. Austin Phelps, *Religion, Temperance, Tobacco* (Chicago: University of Chicago Library, n.d.), iii.

83. James Hayden Tufts, *America's Social Morality: Dilemmas of the Changing Mores* (New York: Henry Holt, 1933), 7, 21. See also Arthur T. Hadley, *Standards of Public Morality* (New York: Macmillan, 1912); Walter Rauschenbusch, *Christianity and the Social Crisis* (New York: Macmillan, 1907); Walter Rauschenbusch, *Christianizing the Social Order* (New York: Macmillan, 1912).

84. Jane Addams, "Public Recreation and Social Morality," *Charities and the Commons* 18 (1907): 492–94.

85. Charles W. Margold, *Sex Freedom and Social Control* (Chicago: University of Chicago Press, 1926), vii, 4, 7–8, 16, 30.

86. Jane Addams, *A New Conscience and an Ancient Evil* (New York: Macmillan, 1912); Harry Elmer Barnes and Willoughby C. Waterman, "A Scientific View of Sex Problems," *Social Forces* 3 (1924): 149–154; Maurice A. Bigelow, *Sex Education: A Series of Lectures concerning Knowledge of Sex in Its Relation to Human Life* (New York: Macmillan, 1916); Havelock Ellis, *Sex in Relation to Society: Studies in the Psychology of Sex, Vol. VI* (London: Heinemann, 1946); M. J. Exner, *Rational Sex Life for Men* (New York: Association Press, 1914); T. W. Galloway, *The Sex Factor in Human Life* (New York: American Social Hygiene Association, 1921); William J. Robinson, *Sexual Problems of To-Day* (New York: Critic and Guide, 1912); A. Maude Royden, *Sex and Common Sense* (New York: G. P. Putnam's Sons, 1922); W. I. Thomas, *Sex and Society: Studies in the Social Psychology of Sex* (Chicago: University of Chicago Press, 1907).

87. Queen and Mann, *Social Pathology,* 162–165.

88. Elliot and Merrill, "Social Control of Prostitution," in *Social Disorganization,* 181–183, 186, 190. For this list, the authors relied on Ben L. Reitman's *The Second Oldest Profession: A Study of the Prostitute's "Business Manager"* (New York: Vanguard, 1931).

89. Queen and Mann, *Social Pathology,* 162–165; George B. Mangold, *Born out of Wedlock: A Sociological Study of Illegitimacy* (Columbia: University of Missouri Press, 1921); Percy Kammerer, *The Unmarried Mother: A Study of Five Hundred Cases* (London: William Heinemann, 1918); William Healy, *The Individual Delinquent: A Text-Book or Diagnosis and Prognosis for All Concerned in Understanding Offenders* (Boston: Little, Brown, 1915); W. I. Thomas, *The Unadjusted Girl: With Cases and Standpoint for Behavior Analysis* (Boston: Little, Brown, 1923). Notably, Kammerer, and Thomas were published as "Criminal Science Monographs" of the American Institute of Criminal Law and Criminology—the first such monograph bespeaks the steady expansion of the "criminal" category along these lines: William Healy and Mary Tenney Healy, *Pathological Lying, Accusation and Swindling: A Study in Forensic Psychology* (Boston: Little, Brown, 1915).

90. Francis A. Allen, "Criminal Justice, Legal Values and the Rehabilitative Ideal," *Journal of Criminal Law, Criminology, and Police Science* 50 (1959): 226. See also Francis A. Allen, *The Borderland of Criminal Justice: Essays in Law and Criminology* (Chicago: University of Chicago Press, 1964); and Francis A. Allen, *The Decline of the Rehabilitative Ideal: Penal Policy and Social Purpose* (New Haven, CT: Yale University Press, 1981).

91. William J. Stuntz, *The Collapse of American Criminal Justice* (Cambridge, MA: Harvard University Press, 2011), 31.

92. Roscoe Pound, *Criminal Justice in America* (New York: Henry Holt, 1930), 23; Allen, *Borderland,* 3.

93. Stuntz, *Collapse,* 158–159.

94. Roscoe Pound, "Do We Need a Philosophy of Law?," *Columbia Law Review* 5 (1905): 347; Roscoe Pound, "Society and the Individual," in *Proceedings of the National Conference of Social Work,* ed. National Conference of Social Work (Chicago: Rogers and Hall, 1920), 104. See also Thomas Andrew Green,

Freedom and Criminal Responsibility in American Legal Thought (New York: Cambridge University Press, 2014), 68–84.

95. Roscoe Pound, "Introduction," in Francis Bowes Sayre, *A Selection of Cases on Criminal Law: With an Introduction by Roscoe Pound,* abridged ed. (Rochester: Lawyers Co-operative, 1930), xxxiv–xxxv.

96. Markus Dirk Dubber, "Policing Possession: The War on Crime and the End of Criminal Law," *Journal of Criminal Law and Criminology* 91 (2001): 850–851.

97. Freund, *Police Power,* 4–7. See also Aya Gruber, "Duncan Kennedy's Third Globalization, Criminal Law, and the Spectacle," *Comparative Law Review* 3 (2012): 1–26.

98. Francis Bowen Sayre, "Public Welfare Offenses," *Columbia Law Review* 33 (1933): 68. *U.S. v. Balint,* 258 U.S. 250 (1922), 251–252.

99. Sayre, "Public Welfare Offenses," 84–88 (citing more than four hundred cases).

100. Dubber, "Policing Possession," 852–853.

101. Stuntz, *Collapse,* 159.

102. David J. Pivar, *Purity Crusade: Sexual Morality and Social Control, 1868–1900* (Westport, CT: Greenwood, 1973); David J. Pivar, *Purity and Hygiene: Women, Prostitution, and the "American Plan," 1900–1930* (Westport, CT: Greenwood, 2002).

103. Prince A. Morrow, "Foreword: A Plea for the Organization of a 'Society of Sanitary and Moral Prophylaxis,'" *Transactions of the American Society of Sanitary and Moral Prophylaxis* 1 (1906): 17. See also Prince A. Morrow, *Social Diseases and Marriage: Social Prophylaxis* (New York: Lea Brothers, 1904).

104. Charles W. Eliot, "The American Social Hygiene Association," *Social Hygiene* 1 (1914): 2. The very first issue of *Social Hygiene* also included other important articles, for example, Franklin Hichborn, "California's Fight for a Red Light Abatement Law," 6–14; Abraham Flexner, "The Regulation of Prostitution in Europe," 15–28; G. Stanley Hall, "Education and the Social Hygiene Movement," 29–35; Clark W. Hetherington, "Play Leadership in Sex Education," 36–43; and Vernon L. Kellogg, "The Bionomics of War: Race Modification by Military Selection," 44–52.

105. Eliot, "American Social Hygiene Association," 4. See also in this issue George J. Fisher, "Sex Education in the Young Men's Christian Association," *Social Hygiene* 1 (1914): 226–230.

106. "Resume of Legislation upon Matters Relating to Social Hygiene Considered by the Various States during 1914, *Social Hygiene* 1 (1914): 93–107, 107–120. Issues also regularly concluded with equally detailed book reviews and reading recommendations, including "approved" works like Jane Addams, *New Conscience and an Ancient Evil* (1912), Maurice A. Bigelow, *Sex Instruction as a Phase of Social Education* (1913), Charles B. Davenport, *Eugenics* (1910), Havelock Ellis, *The Task of Social Hygiene* (1912), E. Lyttelton, *Training of the Young in Laws of Sex* (1906), C. W. Saleeby, *Woman and Womanhood* (1911), and Thompson and Geddes, *Problems of Sex* (1912);

"approved under supervision" works like the *Reports* of the municipal vice commissions and Abraham Flexner, *Prostitution in Europe* (1914); and "disapproved" works like Iwan Bloch, *Sexual Life of Our Times* (1913), August Forel, *The Sexual Question* (1908), and Robert N. Willson, *American Boy and Social Evil* (1905).

107. "Social Hygiene Legislation in 1915: A Summary of Bills Bearing upon Social Hygiene, Introduced in the Several State Legislatures Having Sessions in 1915," *Social Hygiene* 2 (1915): 245–256. See also Ronald Hamowy, "Medicine and the Crimination of Sin: 'Self-Abuse' in 19th-Century America," *Journal of Libertarian Studies* 1 (1977): 229–270.

108. Joseph Mayer, "Social Hygiene Legislation in 1917," *Social Hygiene* 5 (1917): 67–82.

109. For the classics in a voluminous historiography, see Mark Thomas Connelly, *The Response to Prostitution in the Progressive Era* (Chapel Hill: University of North Carolina Press, 1980); Ruth Rosen, *The Lost Sisterhood: Prostitution in America, 1900–1918* (Baltimore: Johns Hopkins University Press, 1982); Mara L. Keire, "The Vice Trust: A Reinterpretation of the White Slavery Scare in the United States, 1907–1917," *Journal of Social History* 35 (2001): 5–41; Allan M. Brandt, *No Magic Bullet: A Social History of Venereal Disease in the United States since 1880* (New York: Oxford University Press, 1987); Daniel J. Kevles, *In the Name of Eugenics: Genetics and the Uses of Human Heredity* (Cambridge, MA: Harvard University Press, 1998): David J. Langum, *Crossing Over the Line: Legislating Morality and the Mann Act* (Chicago: University of Chicago Press, 1994).

110. Maude E. Miner, "Report of the Committee on Prostitution of the National Conference of Charities and Correction," *Social Hygiene,* 1 (1915): 81–82.

111. Connelly, *Response to Prostitution,* 93; Thomas C. Mackey, *Red Lights Out: A Legal History of Prostitution, Disorderly Houses, and Vice Districts, 1870–1917* (New York: Garland, 1987); Peter C. Hennigen, "Property War: Prostitution, Red-Light Districts, and the Transformation of Public Nuisance Law in the Progressive Era," *Yale Journal of Law and the Humanities* 16 (2004): 123–198; Stephen G. Sylvester, "Avenue for Ladies Only: The Soiled Doves of East Grand Forks, 1887–1915," *Minnesota History* 51 (1989): 290–300.

112. Franklin Hichborn, "The Fight for a Red Light Abatement Law," *Social Hygiene* 1 (1915): 6–8; Miner, "Report of the Committee," 81–92.

113. Ala. Laws 1919 no. 53; Ariz. Rev. St. 1913 § 4340; Cal. Gen. Laws 1915 no. 2798; Colo. Laws 1915, c. 123; Conn. Gen. Stat. 1918 § 2705; D.C. (1913) 38 Stat. 280; Ga. Laws 1917, 177; Idaho Comp. Stat. 1919 § 7042; Ill. Laws 1915, 371; Ind. Ann. Stat. 1918 § 293a; Iowa Laws 1915, c. 71; Ky. Stat. 1918 § 3941m; La. Laws 1918 no. 47; Mass. Laws 1914, c. 624; Mich. Comp. Laws 1915 § 7781; Minn. Gen. Stat. 1913 § 8717; Miss. Laws 1918, c. 193; Mont. Laws 1917, c. 95; Neb. Rev. Laws 1913 § 8775; N. H. Laws 1919, c. 95; N. J. Laws 1916, 315; N. C. Laws 1913, c. 761; N. D. Comp. Laws 1913 § 9644; Ohio Laws 1917, 514; Ore. Laws 1913, c. 274; S. C. Laws 1918, 814; S. D. Rev. Code 1919 § 2078; Utah Comp. Laws 1917 § 4275; Va. Laws 1916, c. 463; Wash. Rem. 1915 Code § 946; Wis. Stat. 1917

§ 3185b. See also Kans. Gen. Stat. 1915 § 3650; Maine Rev. Stat. 1916 c. 23; Md. Laws 1918 c. 84; N. Y. Laws 1914 c. 365; Pa. Laws 1913 no. 852; Tenn. Laws 1913, 2nd sess., c. 2; Tex. Pen. Code 1916 art. 501. Charles S. Ascher and James M. Wolf, "'Red Light' Injunction and Abatement Acts," *Columbia Law Review* 20 (1920): 605–608.

114. Bascom Johnson, "Good Laws . . . Good Tools: Injunctions and Abatements versus Houses of Prostitution," *Journal of Social Hygiene* 38 (1952): 204–211; Robert McCurdy, "The Use of the Injunction to Destroy Commercialized Prostitution in Chicago," *Journal of Criminal Law* 19 (1929): 513–517.

115. Felix Frankfurter and Nathan Green, *The Labor Injunction* (New York: Macmillan, 1930); William G. Peterkin, "Government by Injunction," *Virginia Law Register* 3 (1897): 549–563.

116. *Neaf v. Palmer,* 45 S.W. 506 (1898); Novak, "Public Morality."

117. *Eden on Injunctions* (New York, 3rd ed., 1852), 2:259; Olin L. Browder Jr., Roger A. Cunningham, Joseph R. Julin, and Allan F. Smith, eds., *Basic Property Law* (St. Paul, MN: West Publishing, 1979), 116; James W. Eaton, *Handbook of Equity Jurisprudence* (St. Paul, MN: West Publishing, 1901), 588.

118. William Blackstone, *Commentaries on the Laws of England* (Oxford, 1769), 4:167.

119. *Attorney General v. Utica Insurance Co.,* 2 Johns. Ch. Rep. 371 (N.Y., 1817), 378.

120. *Attorney General v. Richard,* 2 Anstr. 603 (Eng., 1795); *Columbus v. Jaques,* 30 Ga. 506 (1860); *State v. Mayor of Moblie,* (Ala. 1838). John C. Bagwell, "The Criminal Jurisdiction of Equity—Purpresture and Other Public Nuisance Affecting Health and Safety," *Kentucky Law Journal* 20 (1932): 163–165.

121. *Hamilton v. Whitridge,* 11 Md. 128 (1857), 147. See also *Cranford v. Tyrell,* 128 N.Y. 341 (1891).

122. *State v. Crawford,* 28 Dan. 726 (1882), 733–734; *State ex. rel. Crow v. Canty,* 207 Mo. 439 (1907).

123. On direct injunctive action by state attorney general, see *Mugler v. Kansas,* 123 U.S. 623 (1887); *State of Texas v. Patterson,* 14 Tx. Civ. App. 456 (1896);

124. "An Act Relating to Sale of Intoxicating Liquors," *Acts and Resolutions of the General Assembly of the State of Iowa* (1884), ch. 143, § 12, 149.

125. Hennigen, "Property War," 138–146.

126. *Mugler v. Kansas,* 669.

127. *Massachusetts Acts and Resolves* 1914, 589.

128. *Chase v. Revere House,* 232 Mass. 88 (1918), 96.

129. *People v. Smith,* 275 Ill. 256 (1916), 259–260.

130. *Chicago Tribune,* "Vice Raids Aid U.S. and City in Health Drive," Apr. 5, 1918, 15.

131. *War and Navy Departments Commission on Training Camp Activities, Standard Forms of Laws for the Repression of Prostitution, the Control of Venereal Diseases, the Establishment and Management of Reformatories for Women and Girls, and Suggestions for a Law Relating to Feeble-Minded Persons* (Washington, DC, 1919), 2, 4, 7.

132. *War and Navy Departments Commission,* 6, 12, 14–16.

133. For an excellent overview, see Kimberley A. Reilly, "'A Perilous Venture for Democracy': Soldiers, Sexual Purity, and American Citizenship in the First World War," *Journal of the Gilded Age and Progressive Era* 13 (2014): 223–255.

5. Antimonopoly

1. Felix Frankfurter and Henry M. Hart Jr., "Rate Regulation," *Encyclopaedia of the Social Sciences,* 15 vols., ed. Edwin R. A. Seligman (New York: Macmillan, 1934), 13:104.
2. Alfred D. Chandler, ed., *The Railroads: The Nation's First Big Business* (New York: Harcourt, Brace & World, 1965).
3. Arthur T. Hadley, *Railroad Transportation: Its History and Laws* (New York: G. P. Putnam's Sons, 1886), 65; Arthur T. Hadley, "Private Monopolies and Public Rights," *Quarterly Journal of Economics* 1 (1886): 28; Arthur T. Hadley, "The Good and Evil of Industrial Combinations," *Atlantic Monthly* 79 (1897): 377–385.
4. John C. Welch, "The Standard Oil Company," *North American Review* 136 (1883): 191–200. Lloyd's essays were ultimately compiled in Henry Demarest Lloyd, *Lords of Industry* (New York: G. P. Putnam's Sons, 1910), also including "Servitudes Not Contracts" (1889) and "The Sugar Trust" (1897).
5. Welch, "Standard Oil Company," 191.
6. Henry Demarest Lloyd, *Wealth Against Commonwealth* (New York: Harper & Brothers, 1894); Henry George, *Progress and Poverty: An Inquiry into the Cause of Industrial Depression* (New York: D. Appleton, 1879); Tamara Venit Shelton, *A Squatter's Republic: Land and the Politics of Monopoly in California, 1850–1900* (Berkeley: University of California Press, 2013).
7. Henry Carter Adams, "The Relation of the State to Industrial Action," *Publications of the American Economic Association* 1 (1887): 47–48; Adams, *Description of Industry: An Introduction to Economics* (New York: Henry Holt, 1918), 264; Hadley, "Private Monopolies," 40.
8. Adams, "Relation of the State," 64. Morton Horwitz, *The Transformation of American Law: The Crisis of Legal Orthodoxy, 1870–1960* (New York: Oxford University Press, 1992), 80–83.
9. Fanny Borden, "Monopolies and Trusts in America, 1895–1899," *Bulletin of the New York State Library* 67 (1901): 1–33.
10. John Lewson, *Monopoly and Trade Restraint Cases: Including Conspiracy, Injunction, Quo Warranto, Pleading and Practice and Evidence,* 2 vols. (Chicago: T. H. Flood, 1908), 1:vii.
11. Richard R. John, "Rethinking the Monopoly Question: Commerce, Land, and Industry," in *Antimonopoly and American Democracy,* ed. Daniel Crane and William J. Novak (forthcoming, 2022); Richard White, "From Antimonopoly to Antitrust," in Crane and Novak, *Antimonopoly and American Democracy.*
12. Roscoe Pound, "The New Feudalism," *American Bar Association Journal* 16 (1930): 553–558. For similar critiques today, see Tim Wu, *The Curse of*

Bigness: Antitrust in the New Gilded Age (New York: Columbia Global Reports, 2018); Lina Khan, "Amazon's Antitrust Paradox," *Yale Law Journal* 126 (2017): 710–805.

13. 21 *Congressional Record* (1890), 2456–2457.

14. *Appalachian Coals v. United States,* 288 U.S. 344 (1933), 359. On the Sherman Act as a superstatute, see William N. Eskridge Jr. and John Ferejohn, "Super-Statutes," *Duke Law Journal* 50 (2001): 1215–1276.

15. Louis D. Brandeis, "The Regulation of Competition versus the Regulation of Monopoly," *Yearbook of the Economic Club of New York,* vol. 3 (New York: G. P. Putnam's Sons, 1913), 17, 19.

16. Lina Khan, "The New Brandeis Movement: America's Antimonopoly Debate," *Journal of European Competition Law and Practice* 9 (2018): 131.

17. Zephyr Teachout, *Break 'Em Up: Recovering Our Freedom from Big Ag, Big Tech, and Big Money* (New York: All Points Books, 2020); Matt Stoller: *Goliath: The 100-Year War between Monopoly Power and Democracy* (New York: Simon & Schuster, 2020); Barry C. Lynn, *Cornered: The New Monopoly Capitalism and the Economics of Destruction* (Hoboken, NJ: John Wiley & Sons, 2010).

18. Edward A. Adler, "Business Jurisprudence," *Harvard Law Review* 28 (1914): 135–162; See also Edward A. Adler, "Labor, Capital, and Business at Common Law," *Harvard Law Review* 29 (1916): 241–276.

19. Jürgen Habermas, *Legitimation Crisis* (Boston: Beacon, 1975), 33. See also Jürgen Habermas, *The Theory of Communicative Action, Volume II: Lifeworld and System,* trans. Thomas McCarthy (Boston: Beacon, 1987), 306; Max Weber, "The Bureaucratization of Politics and the Economy," in *Max Weber: Essays in Economic Sociology,* ed. Richard Swedberg (Princeton, NJ: Princeton University Press, 1999), 110.

20. Friedrich Pollock, "State Capitalism: Its Possibilities and Limitations," in *The Essential Frankfurt School Reader,* ed. Andrew Arato and Eike Gebhardt, 71–94 (New York: Continuum, 1994), 78. See also Michael Aglietta, *A Theory of Capitalist Regulation: The U.S. Experience* (London: Verso, 1979); Robert Boyer, *The Regulation School: A Critical Introduction* (New York: Columbia University Press, 1990); Robert Boyer and J. Rogers Hollingsworth, eds., *Contemporary Capitalism: The Embeddedness of Capitalist Institutions* (Cambridge: Cambridge University Press, 1997).

21. Bob Jessop, "Survey Article: The Regulation Approach," *Journal of Political Philosophy* 5 (1997): 289; Andrew Shonfield, *Modern Capitalism: The Changing Balance of Public and Private Power* (New York: Oxford University Press, 1965).

22. Walton Hamilton, *The Politics of Industry* (New York: Knopf, 1957), 6–7.

23. Karl Polanyi, *The Great Transformation: The Political and Economic Origins of Our Time* (Boston: Beacon, 1957), 250. See also Adam Smith, *Lectures on Justice, Police, Revenue, and Arms* (1763; Oxford: Clarendon, 1869); Emma Rothschild, *Economic Sentiments: Adam Smith, Condorcet, and the Enlightenment* (Cambridge, MA: Harvard University Press, 2002).

24. William J. Novak, "Public Economy: The Well-Ordered Market," in *The People's Welfare: Law and Regulation in Nineteenth-Century America* (Chapel Hill: University of North Carolina Press, 1996), 87; Oscar Handlin and Mary Flug Handlin, *Commonwealth: A Study of the Role of Government in the American Economy: Massachusetts, 1774–1861* (New York: Oxford University Press, 1947); Harry N. Scheiber, "Government and the Economy: Studies of the 'Commonwealth' Policy in Nineteenth-Century America," *Journal of Interdisciplinary History* 3 (1972): 135–151.

25. This is not to say, however, that national or administrative controls were *invented* in this period. See the wonderfully revisionist work of Max Edling, *A Revolution in Favor of Government: Origins of the U.S. Constitution and the Making of the American State* (New York: Oxford University Press, 2003); Jerry L. Mashaw, *Creating the Administrative Constitution: The Lost One Hundred Years of American Administrative Law* (New Haven, CT: Yale University Press, 2012); and Nicholas R. Parrillo, *Against the Profit Motive: The Salary Revolution in American Government, 1790–1940* (New Haven, CT: Yale University Press, 2014).

26. Claudia Goldin and Gary D. Libecap, eds., *The Regulated Economy: A Historical Approach to Political Economy* (Chicago: University of Chicago Press, 1994); Morton Keller, *Regulating a New Economy: Public Policy and Economic Change in America, 1900–1933* (Cambridge, MA: Harvard University Press, 1996); Howard Brick, *Transcending Capitalism: Visions of a New Society in Modern American Thought* (Ithaca, NY: Cornell University Press, 2006); William J. Novak, "Law and the Social Control of American Capitalism," *Emory Law Journal* 60 (2010): 377–405.

27. Walter E. Weyl, *The New Democracy: An Essay on Certain Political and Economic Tendencies in the United States* (New York: Macmillan, 1913), viii, 276–277.

28. John R. Commons, *The Distribution of Wealth* (New York: Macmillan, 1893); Richard T. Ely, *Property and Contract in Their Relations to the Distribution of Wealth*, 2 vols. (New York: Macmillan, 1914).

29. Henry Carter Adams, "Relation of the State to Industrial Action" and "Economics and Jurisprudence," in *Two Essays by Henry Carter Adams*, ed. Joseph Dorfman (New York: Augustus M. Kelley, 1969); Thorstein Veblen, "The Preconceptions of Economic Science," in *What Veblen Thought: Selected Writings of Thorstein Veblen*, ed. Wesley C. Mitchell (New York: Viking, 1936), 39–150; and Thorstein Veblen, *Theory of Business Enterprise* (New York: Charles Scribner's Sons, 1904); Ely, *Property and Contract;* Commons, *Legal Foundations of Capitalism;* John Maurice Clark, *Social Control of Business* (Chicago: University of Chicago Press, 1926); Bruce Wyman, *Control of the Market: A Legal Solution of the Trust Problem* (New York: Moffat, Yard, 1911); Walton Hale Hamilton, *The Politics of Industry* (New York: Alfred A. Knopf, 1957); Wesley C. Mitchell, *Business Cycles* (Berkeley: University of California Press, 1913); Mitchell, *What Veblen Taught;* Samuel P. Orth, ed., *Readings on the Relation of Government to Property and Industry* (Boston:

Atheneum, 1915); Robert Lee Hale, *Freedom through Law: Public Control of Private Governing Power* (New York: Columbia University Press, 1952); and Rexford G. Tugwell, *The Economic Basis of Public Interest* (Menasha, WI: Collegiate, 1922).

30. The significance of the institutionalist revolution in American economic thinking has to some extent been eclipsed by the revanchism of the late twentieth-century Chicago school. Ronald H. Coase, "The New Institutional Economics," *Journal of Institutional and Theoretical Economics* 140 (1984): 230. Donald R. McCloskey, *The Rhetoric of Economics* (Madison: University of Wisconsin Press, 1985); Malcolm Rutherford, "Chicago Economics and Institutionalism," in *The Elgar Companion to the Chicago School of Economics,* ed. Ross B. Emmett (Northampton, UK: Edward Elgar, 2010), 25–39.

31. The survey that follows emphasizes the broad commonalities within the institutionalist tradition. For a more thoroughgoing examination of the variety of influences, separate schools, and important debates within institutional economics proper, see Malcolm Rutherford, *The Institutionalist Movement in American Economics, 1918–1947: Science and Social Control* (New York: Cambridge University Press, 2011).

32. For two able introductions, see Daniel T. Rodgers, *Atlantic Crossings: Social Politics in a Progressive Age* (Cambridge, MA: Harvard University Press, 1998), 76–111; Dorothy Ross, *The Origins of American Social Science* (New York: Cambridge University Press, 1991).

33. John Maurice Clark worried about a "terrible catastrophe" that echoed E. A. Ross's fear of a "grand crash" owing to "the thrust of new, blind, economic forces we have not learned to regulate." Clark, *Social Control of Business,* 3–4; E. A. Ross, *Social Control: A Survey of the Foundations of Order* (New York: Macmillan, 1901), 432–433, 435.

34. Thomas Carlyle, *Past and Present* (London: Chapman and Hall, 1897), 210–211; Karl Marx, *Capital: A Critique of Political Economy* (New York: International Publishers, 1967); John Ruskin, *Unto This Last and Other Writings,* ed. Clive Wilmer (New York: Penguin Books, 1997), 202.

35. "Report of the Organization of the American Economic Association," *Publications of the American Economic Association* 1 (1886): 10.

36. Richard T. Ely, "Statement of Dr. Richard T. Ely," *Publications of the American Economic Association* 1 (1886): 16–17. On the broader effects of social Darwinism on American thought in this period, see Richard Hofstadter, *Social Darwinism in American Thought* (Philadelphia: University of Pennsylvania Press, 1944).

37. "Report of the Organization," 10–11. The *Oberlin Review* at exactly the same time noted the same article in the *Christian Union* announcing the new approach, "The Duty of the Universities," 130.

38. Vernon Louis Parrington, *The Beginnings of Critical Realism in America: Main Currents in American Thought* (New York: Harcourt, Brace, 1927); Morton G. White, *Social Thought in America: The Revolt against Formalism* (New York: Viking, 1949); Richard Hofstadter, *Social Darwinism in Amer-*

ican Thought (Boston: Beacon, 1944); H. Stuart Hughes, *Consciousness and Society* (New York: Alfred A. Knopf, 1958); James T. Kloppenberg, *Uncertain Victory: Social Democracy and Progressivism in European and American Thought, 1870–1920* (New York: Oxford University Press, 1988).

39. Geoffrey M. Hodgson, *The Evolution of Institutional Economics: Agency, Structure and Darwinism in American Institutionalism* (New York: Routledge, 2004).

40. Thorstein Veblen, "Why Is Economics Not an Evolutionary Science?," in *The Place of Science in Modern Civilization and Other Essays* (New York: B. W. Huebsch, 1919), 56–81; Wesley C. Mitchell, ed., *What Veblen Taught: Selected Writings of Thorstein Veblen* (New York: Viking, 1936), xxiii–xiv.

41. Walton H. Hamilton, "The Institutional Approach to Economic Theory," *American Economic Review* 9 (1919): 314–315.

42. Walton Hamilton, "Charles Horton Cooley," *Social Forces* 8 (1929): 183–185.

43. Charles Horton Cooley, *Human Nature and the Social Order* (New York: Charles Scribner's Sons, 1902); Charles Horton Cooley, *Social Organization* (New York: Charles Scribner's Sons, 1909); and Charles Horton Cooley, *Social Process* (New York: Charles Scribner's Sons, 1918). On Cooley's influence, also see John Maurice Clark, *Economic Institutions and Human Welfare* (New York: Alfred A. Knopf, 1957), 57.

44. Hamilton, "Cooley," 185–187; Walton Hamilton and Associates, *Price and Price Policies* (New York: McGraw-Hill, 1938), 1.

45. William James, *Principles of Psychology*, 2 vols. (New York: Henry Holt, 1890); George Herbert Mead, *Mind, Self and Society* (Chicago: University of Chicago Press, 1934).

46. Hamilton, "Institutional Approach," 316–317. See also Veblen, "Preconceptions of Economics," 109–110.

47. John Dewey, "Individualism, Old and New," in *The Later Works, 1925–1953*, ed. Jo Ann Boydston (1929; Carbondale: Southern Illinois University Press, 1988), 5:49.

48. Hamilton, "Institutional Approach," 309, 311, 313.

49. Joan Robinson, *The Economics of Imperfect Competition* (London: Macmillan, 1933); E. H. Chamberlin, *The Theory of Monopolistic Competition* (Cambridge, MA: Harvard University Press, 1933); Gardiner C. Means, *Industrial Prices and Their Relative Inflexibility*, Sen. Doc. 13, 74th Cong., 1st sess. (Washington, DC, 1935); Caroline F. Ware and Gardiner C. Means, *The Modern Economy in Action* (New York: Harcourt Brace, 1936).

50. Hamilton, *Price and Price Policies*; see also Hamilton's pioneering investigations of the coal industry: Walton Hamilton and Helen R. Wright, *The Case of Bituminous Coal* (New York: Macmillan, 1925); Walton Hamilton and Wright, *A Way of Order for Bituminous Coal* (New York: Macmillan, 1928). This deep background on the coal industry greatly informed Hamilton's noted critique of the US Supreme Court's decision in *Carter v. Carter Coal Co.* Walton Hale Hamilton and Douglass Adair, *The Power to Govern: The*

Constitution—Then and Now (New York: W. W. Norton, 1937). See also Walton Hale Hamilton and Stacy May, *The Control of Wages* (New York: George H. Doran, 1923).

51. Hamilton, *Price and Price Policies,* vii.
52. Hamilton, "Institutional Approach," 312.
53. Clark, *Social Control of Business,* 12–13.
54. Hamilton, "Institutional Approach," 313; Wesley C. Mitchell, "Commons on Institutional Economics," *American Economic Review* 25 (1935): 638. See also Wesley C. Mitchell, "Commons on the *Legal Foundations of Capitalism,*" *American Economic Review* 14 (1924): 240–253.
55. "Platform," *Publications of the American Economic Association* 1 (1886): 6.
56. Henry Carter Adams, "Relation of the State to Industrial Action" (1887), in Dorman, *Two Essays,* 119, 125. For an excellent discussion of the economics and jurisprudence of Adams, see Ajay K. Mehrotra, *Making the Modern American Fiscal State: Law, Politics, and the Rise of Progressive Taxation, 1877–1929* (New York: Cambridge University Press, 2013).
57. Adams, "State and Industrial Action," 59–60, 62; Henry Carter Adams, *Description of Industry: An Introduction to Economics* (New York: Henry Holt, 1918), 247.
58. Commons, *Legal Foundations of Capitalism;* Ely, *Property and Contract.*
59. Morris R. Cohen, "Property and Sovereignty," *Cornell Law Quarterly* 13 (1927): 12, 22; Robert Lee Hale, "Coercion and Distribution in a Supposedly Non-Coercive State," *Political Science Quarterly* 38 (1923): 470–494. See also Wesley Newcomb Hohfeld, "Fundamental Legal Conceptions as Applied in Judicial Reasoning," *Yale Law Journal* 26 (1917): 710–770; Barbara H. Fried, *The Progressive Assault on Laissez Faire: Robert Hale and the First Law and Economics Movement* (Cambridge, MA: Harvard University Press, 2001); Joseph William Singer, "Legal Realism Now," *California Law Review* 76 (Mar. 1988): 465–544.
60. Cohen, "Property and Sovereignty," 16. For a compelling recent statement of this theme, see Larry M. Bartels, *Unequal Democracy: The Political Economy of the New Gilded Age* (Princeton, NJ: Princeton University Press, 2008).
61. James Willard Hurst, "Problems of Legitimacy in the Contemporary Legal Order," *Oklahoma Law Review* 24 (1971): 225. For a more complete discussion of Hurst's perspective, see William J. Novak, "Law, Capitalism, and the Liberal State: The Historical Sociology of James Willard Hurst," *Law and History Review* 18 (2000): 97–145.
62. James Willard Hurst, "Law and the Balance of Power: The Federal Anti-Trust Laws," unpub. ms., 2.
63. Hale, *Freedom through Law;* Hale, "Coercion and Distribution," 470.
64. Robert H. Bork, *The Antitrust Paradox: A Policy at War with Itself* (New York: Basic Books, 1978), 61–63; Richard A. Posner, *Antitrust Law: An Economic Perspective* (Chicago: University of Chicago Press, 1976); Aaron Director and Edward H. Levi, "Law and the Future: Trade Regulation," *Northwestern Law Review* 51 (1956–1957): 281–296.

65. Thomas K. McCraw, "Rethinking the Trust Question," in *Regulation in Perspective*, 5; Thomas K. McCraw, "Louis D. Brandeis Reappraised," *American Scholar* 54 (1985): 525, 527. For an excellent overview of McCraw's position, see Richard R. John, "Prophet of Perspective: Thomas K. McCraw," *Business History Review* 89 (2015): 129–153.

66. Robert H. Bork, "Legislative Intent and the Policy of the Sherman Act," *Journal of Law and Economics* 9 (1966): 11–12. Lest the point be missed, Bork used the term "efficiency" fifty-one times in his forty-one-page article. Bork's historical research on the Sherman Act has been vigorously challenged by Robert Lande and Herbert Hovenkamp, among others. Robert Lande, "Wealth Transfers as the Original and Primary Concern of Antitrust: The Efficiency Interpretation Challenged," *Hastings Law Journal* 34 (1982): 65–151; Herbert Hovenkamp, "Antitrust's Protected Classes," *Michigan Law Review* 88 (1989): 22; Daniel A. Crane, "The Tempting of Antitrust: Robert Bork and the Goals of Antitrust Policy," *Antitrust Law Journal* 79 (2014): 835.

67. William Letwin, *Law and Economic Policy in America: The Evolution of the Sherman Antitrust Act* (Chicago: University of Chicago Press, 1956), 7. Notably, Letwin's study was a direct product of Edward Levi and Aaron Director's Antitrust Research Project at the University of Chicago Law School. Daniel R. Ernst, "The New Antitrust History," *New York Law School Law Review* 35 (1990): 879–892.

68. Ellis W. Hawley, *The New Deal and the Problem of Monopoly: A Study in Economic Ambivalence* (Princeton, NJ: Princeton University Press, 1966), vii, 4–5. Martin Sklar also caricatured America's common-law traditions. Martin J. Sklar, *The Corporate Reconstruction of American Capitalism: The Market, the Law, and Politics* (New York: Cambridge University Press, 1988), 100–101. See also Rudolph Peritz, *Competition Policy in America: History, Rhetoric, Law* (New York: Oxford University Press, 2001), 11–12. For a broader analysis of this interpretive problem, see William J. Novak, "The Myth of the 'Weak' American State," *American Historical Review* 113 (2008): 752–772.

69. *Santa Clara v. Southern Pacific Railroad*, 118 U.S. 394 (1886).

70. Morton Horwitz, "*Santa Clara* Revisited: The Development of Corporate Theory," in *The Transformation of American Law, 1870–1960* (New York: Oxford University Press, 1992), 65–107; Gerard Carl Henderson, *The Position of Foreign Corporations in American Constitutional Law* (Cambridge, MA: Harvard University Press, 1918).

71. Joel Seligman, "A Brief History of Delaware's Corporation Law of 1899," *Delaware Journal of Corporate Law* 1 (1976): 273. Also see Adam Winkler, *We the Corporations: How American Businesses Won Their Civil Rights* (New York: W. W. Norton, 2018). For an alternative portrait of the complexities of corporation law in this period, see Naomi Lamoreaux and William J. Novak, eds., *Corporations and American Democracy* (Cambridge, MA: Harvard University Press, 2017).

72. Horwitz, "Corporate Theory," 104.

73. Myron W. Watkins, "Federal Incorporation, III," *Michigan Law Review* 17 (1919): 242.

74. Myron W. Watkins, "The Economic Philosophy of Anti-Trust Legislation," *Annals of the American Academy of Political and Social Science* 147 (1930): 15, 23

75. Walton Hamilton, "Common Right, Due Process, and Antitrust," *Law and Contemporary Problems* 7 (1940): 24.

76. Oliver Wendell Holmes Jr., *The Common Law* (Boston: Little, Brown, 1881), 1.

77. Richard T. Ely, *Problems of To-Day: A Discussion of Protective Tariffs, Taxation, and Monopolies* (New York: Thomas Y. Crowell, 1888), 112.

78. Ely, *Problems,* 117.

79. Ely, 111–113.

80. Ely, 210.

81. Ely, 108.

82. Ely, 181.

83. Richard T. Ely, *Monopolies and Trusts* (New York: Macmillan, 1900), 264–268.

84. Joseph Henry Beale and Bruce Wyman, "Monopolies," *Cyclopedia of Law and Procedure,* ed. William Mack and Howard P. Nash, 40 vols. (New York: American Law Book, 1901–1912), 27:888–915.

85. Beale and Wyman, "Monopolies," 898.

86. Bruce Wyman, *Control of the Market: A Legal Solution of the Trust Problem* (New York: Moffat, Yard,1911), v.

87. Wyman, *Control of the Market,* v–vi.

88. George Stewart Brown, "Municipal Ownership of Public Utilities," *North American Review* 182 (1906): 707.

89. *A Survey of State Laws on Public Utility Commission Regulation in the United States: Analyzing the Principal Powers and Jurisdiction of State Public Utility Regulatory Commissions, including the Bonbright Utility Regulation Chart* (New York: Bonbright, 1928).

90. Laura Phillips Sawyer, *American Fair Trade: Proprietary Capitalism, Corporatism, and the New Competition, 1890–1940* (New York: Cambridge University Press, 2018).

91. *Proceedings of the Special Committee on Railroads Appointed Under a Resolution of the Assembly to Investigate Alleged Abuses in the Management of the Railroads Chartered by the State of New York* (New York: Evening Post Steam Presses, 1879).

92. *Report of the Senate Select Committee on Interstate Commerce as to the Regulation of Interstate Commerce,* 49th Cong., 1st sess. (Washington, DC: Government Printing Office, 1886).

93. 21 *Congressional Record* (1890), 2458; *Richardson v. Buhl,* 77 Mich. 632 (1889). Sherman's other cited cases included *Handy v. Cleveland & M.R. Co.,* 31 Fed. 689 (C.C. Ohio, 1887); *Craft v. McConoughy,* 79 Ill. 346 (1875); *Chicago Gas Light Co. v. People's Gase and Coke Co.,* 121 Ill. 530 (1887); *People v. North River Sugar Refining Co.,* 22 Abb. N.C. 164 (1889); *Commonwealth v. Carlisle,* Brightly N.P. 32 (Pa., 1821).

94. Walton Hamilton, "The Problem of Capitalistic Monopoly," in Hamilton, *Current Economic Problems,* 429.
95. Milton Handler, "Unfair Competition," in *Readings in the Social Control of Industry,* ed. American Economic Association (Philadelphia: Blakiston, 1942), 134.
96. "An Act Authorizing the Appointment of a Nonpartisan Commission to collate Information and to Consider and Recommend Legislation to Meet the Problems Presented by Labor, Agriculture, and Capital," *U.S. Statutes at Large* 30 (1898): 476–477; US Industrial Commission, *Final Report of the Industrial Commission* (Washington, DC: Government Printing Office, 1902), ix.
97. US Industrial Commission, *Final Report,* 595.
98. The Industrial Commission's reports also had an important impact on institutional economics as both Thorstein Veblen and John Commons drew on the wealth of new information now available on business enterprise. David Hamilton, "Veblen, Commons, and the Industrial Commission," in *The Founding of Institutional Economics: The Leisure Class and Sovereignty,* ed. Warren J. Samuels (London: Routledge, 1998), 3–13. Laura Weinrib has argued that the Industrial Commission's report on labor "helped shape the agenda for labor reform in the Progressive Era." Weinrib, *The Taming of Free Speech: America's Civil Liberties Compromise* (Cambridge, MA: Harvard University Press, 2016), 23.
99. "An Act to Establish the Department of Commerce and Labor," *U.S. Statutes at Large* 32 (1903): 828.
100. US Commissioner of Corporations, *Report on the Petroleum Industry* (Washington, DC: Government Printing Office, 1907); US Industrial Commission, *Preliminary Report on Trusts and Industrial Combinations* (Washington, DC: Government Printing Office, 1900), 719–726. US Commissioner of Corporations, *Report on the Tobacco Industry* (Washington, DC: Government Printing Office, 1909). See also Civic Federation of Chicago, *Chicago Conference on Trusts* (Chicago: Civic Federation, 1900).
101. "An Act to Amend an Act Entitled 'An Act to Regulate Commerce,'" *U.S. Statutes at Large* 34 (1906): 584–596.
102. Myron Watkins, *Public Regulation of Competitive Practices in Business Enterprise* (New York: National Industrial Conference Board, 1940), 15.
103. *Standard Oil v. United States,* 221 U.S. 1 (1910); *United States v. American Tobacco Co.,* 221 U.S. 106 (1911); *United States v. Patterson,* 201 Fed. 697 (1912); 205 Fed. 292 (1913); 222 Fed. 599 (1915); *United States v. International Harvester Co.,* 214 Fed. 987 (1917); *United States v. American Can Co.,* 230 Fed. 859 (1916).
104. Watkins, *Public Regulation,* 17–18. For an exhaustive list of offenses, cases, and decrees, see Handler, "Unfair Competition," 125–130.
105. Bruce Wyman, "Competition and the Law," *Harvard Law Review* 15 (1902): 427–445; Handler, 121–122; Myron Watkins, "Failure of Common Law Doctrine to Reach New Types of Unfair Competition," in *Regulation of Competitive Practices,* 28–32.
106. US Industrial Commission, *Trusts and Industrial Combinations* (Washington, DC: Government Printing Office, 1900), 3.

107. Handler, 142–149.

108. Elizabeth Kimball MacLean, "Joseph E. Davies: The Wisconsin Idea and the Origins of the Federal Trade Commission," *Journal of the Gilded Age and Progressive Era* 6 (2007): 248–284; Charles McCarthy, *The Wisconsin Idea* (New York: Macmillan, 1912).

109. Joseph E. Davies, *Trust Laws and Unfair Competition* (Washington, DC: Government Printing Office, 1916).

110. Joseph E. Davies, "Memorandum of Recommendations as to Trust Legislation," in *Papers of Woodrow Wilson,* ed. Arthur S. Link (Princeton, NJ: Princeton University Press, 1979), 29:78–85, 30:420.

111. *Interstate Commerce Commission v. Brimson,* 154 U.S. 447 (1897).

112. "An Act to Create a Federal Trade Commission," *U.S. Statutes at Large* 38 (1914): 717–724; Davies, *Trust Laws,* 22.

113. "An Act to Supplement Existing Laws against Unlawful Restraints and Monopolies," *U.S. Statutes at Large* 38 (1914): 730–740.

114. The list excludes specifically sanctioned Clayton Act violations. "Types of Unfair Competition: Practices Condemned in Orders to Cease and Desist," in *Annual Report of the Federal Trade Commission for the Fiscal Year Ended June 30, 1935* (Washington, DC: Government Printing Office, 1935), 67–71; Handler, "Unfair Competition," 159–164.

115. Watkins, *Regulation of Competitive Practices,* 275, 300–317.

116. Clark, *Social Control of Business,* 4.

117. Clark, 4–5.

118. Milton Handler, *Cases and Other Materials on Trade Regulation* (Chicago: Foundation, 1937), vii.

119. *McKinney's Consolidated Laws of New York, Annotated,* 67 vols. (New York, 1931).

120. Handler, *Trade Regulation,* 2.

121. Handler, 3–4.

122. *Nebbia v. New York,* 291 U.S. 502 (1934); *Hegeman Farms Corp v. Baldwin,* 293 U.S. 502 (1934); *Borden's Farm Products v. Baldwin,* 293 U.S. 194 (1934); *G. Seelig, Inc. v. Baldwin,* 294 U.S. 511 (1935); *Borden's Farm Products v. Ten Eyck,* 297 U.S. 251 (1936); *Mayflower Farms, Inc. v. Ten Eyck,* 297 U.S. 266 (1936).

123. Handler, *Trade Regulation,* 9–10.

124. Handler, 13–14 (emphasis added).

125. John A. Lapp, *Important Federal Laws* (Indianapolis: B. F. Bowen, 1917); John A. Lapp, *Federal Rules and Regulations* (Indianapolis: B. F. Bowen, 1918). Stuart Chase went further, highlighting the even more rapid proliferation of federal economic regulations in the aftermath of World War I and also during what he termed "Mr. Hoover's New Deal." Chase, *Government in Business,* 28–29.

126. Dexter Merriam Keezer and Stacy May, *The Public Control of Business: A Study of Antitrust Law Enforcement, Public Interest Regulation, and Government Participation in Business* (New York: Harper & Brothers, 1930), 3–4.

127. Handler, *Trade Regulation,* 18.

128. Gerard Carl Henderson, *The Position of Foreign Corporations in American Constitutional Law* (Cambridge, MA: Harvard University Press, 1918), 3.

129. Bruce Wyman, *The Special Law Governing Public Service Corporations and All Others Engaged in Public Employment,* 2 vols. (New York: Baker, Voorhis, 1911); Joseph Henry Beale and Bruce Wyman, *Railroad Rate Regulation: With Special Reference to the Power of the Interstate Commerce Commission,* 2nd ed. (New York: Baker, Voorhis, 1915); Felix Frankfurter, *A Selection of Cases under the Interstate Commerce Act* (Cambridge, MA: Harvard University Press, 1915). For the modern regulated industries approach, see Handler, *Trade Regulation;* William K. Jones, *Cases and Materials on Regulated Industries* (Brooklyn: Foundation, 1967).

130. Joseph D. Kearney and Thomas W. Merrill, "The Great Transformation of Regulated Industries Law," *Columbia Law Review* 98 (1998): 1333–1334.

131. Hurst, "Balance of Power," 3.

132. Harry W. Laidler, "More Government in Business," *Annals of the American Academy of Political and Social Science* 178 (1935): 148.

133. Gail Radford, *The Rise of Public Authority: Statebuilding and Economic Development in Twentieth-Century America* (Chicago: University of Chicago Press, 2013).

134. "Government Competition with Private Enterprise," *Report of the Special Committee Appointed to Investigate Government Competition with Private Enterprise,* H.R. 1985, 72nd Cong., 2nd sess. (Washington, DC: Government Printing Office, 1933), 10–13.

135. Laidler, "More Government in Business," 148–149.

136. Franklin D. Roosevelt, campaign address in Portland, OR, "Public Utilities and the Development of Hydro-Electric Power," Sept. 21, 1932, in *The Public Papers and Addresses of Franklin D. Roosevelt,* vol. 1, *The Genesis of the New Deal, 1928–1932* (New York: Random House, 1938), 727–742.

137. Thurman Arnold, "An Inquiry into the Monopoly Issue," *New York Times,* Aug. 21, 1938; Franklin D. Roosevelt, "Acceptance Speech at the Democratic National Convention," July 27, 1936, in *The Public Papers and Addresses of Franklin D. Roosevelt,* vol. 5, *The People Approve, 1936* (New York: Random House, 1938), 229–236.

6. Democratic Administration

1. Bruce Wyman, *The Principles of the Administrative Law Governing the Relations of Public Officers* (St. Paul, MN: Keefe-Davidson, 1903), 1.

2. US Bureau of the Census, *1957 Census of Governments* (Washington, DC: Government Printing Office, 1957), 1.

3. Ernst Freund, "The Law of the Administration in America," *Political Science Quarterly* 9 (1894): 404; Frank J. Goodnow, *Comparative Administrative Law,* 2 vols. (New York: Putnams, 1893), 1:7.

4. *American Banana Company v. United Fruit Co.,* 213 U.S. 347, 350 (1909). Felix Frankfurter, "Foreword," *Yale Law Journal* 47 (1938): 517, 518.

5. Charles Evans Hughes, "Speech before Federal Bar Association," *New York Times,* Feb. 13, 1931, 18, col. 1.

6. Felix Frankfurter and J. Forrester Davison, eds., *Cases and Other Material on Administrative Law* (New York: Commerce Clearing House, 1932), vii; Kenneth Culp Davis, *Administrative Law and Government* (St. Paul, MN: West Publishing, 1960), 13. See also Joanna Grisinger, *The Unwieldy American State: Administrative Politics since the New Deal* (New York: Cambridge University Press, 2012), 2.

7. Theodore J. Lowi, *The End of Liberalism: The Second Republic of the United States,* 2nd ed. (New York: W. W. Norton, 1979), 21.

8. See, for example, Stephen Skowronek, *Building a New American State* (New York: Cambridge University Press, 1982); Daniel P. Carpenter, *The Forging of Bureaucratic Autonomy: Reputations, Networks, and Policy Innovation in Executive Agencies, 1862–1928* (Princeton, NJ: Princeton University Press, 2001); Daniel R. Ernst, *Tocqueville's Nightmare: The Administrative State Emerges in America, 1900–1940* (New York: Oxford University Press, 2014); Robert H. Wiebe, *The Search for Order, 1877–1920* (New York: Hill and Wang, 1967); Louis Galambos, "The Emerging Organizational Synthesis in Modern American History," *Business History Review* 44 (1970): 279–290; John A. Rohr, *To Run a Constitution: The Legitimacy of the Administrative State* (Lawrence: University Press of Kansas, 1986); Brian J. Cook, *Bureaucracy and Self-Government: Reconsidering the Role of Public Administration in American Politics* (Baltimore: Johns Hopkins University Press, 1996); Richard J. Stillman II, *Creating the American State: The Moral Reformers and the Modern Administrative World They Made* (Tuscaloosa: University of Alabama Press, 1998).

9. Martin Loughlin, *Foundations of Public Law* (Oxford: Oxford University Press, 2010), 407.

10. Friedrich A. Hayek, *The Road to Serfdom* (Chicago: University of Chicago Press, 1944). For similar critiques of bureaucracy, see Ludwig von Mises, *Bureaucracy* (New Haven, CT: Yale University Press, 1944); James Burnham, *The Managerial Revolution: What Is Happening in the World* (New York: Van Rees, 1941); Gaetano Mosca, *The Ruling Class* (New York: McGraw-Hill, 1939); Robert Michels, *Political Parties: A Sociological Study of the Oligarchical Tendencies of Modern Democracy* (Glencoe, IL: Free Press, 1915).

11. Key works in this revisionist tradition are Stephen W. Sawyer, *Demos Assembled: Democracy and the International Origins of the Modern State, 1840–1880* (Chicago: University of Chicago Press, 2018); Karen M. Tani, *States of Dependency: Welfare, Rights, and American Governance: 1935–1972* (New York: Cambridge University Press, 2016); Jeremy K. Kessler, "The Struggle for Administrative Legitimacy," *Harvard Law Review* 129 (2016): 718–773; Gillian E. Metzger, "1930s Redux: The Administrative State under Siege," *Harvard Law Review* 131 (2017): 2–95; Reuel E. Schiller, "The Era of Deference: Courts, Expertise, and the Emergence of New Deal Administrative Law," *Michigan Law Review* 106 (2007): 399–441; Risa L. Goluboff, *The Lost Promise of Civil Rights* (Cambridge, MA: Harvard University Press, 2007);

Sophia Z. Lee, *The Workplace Constitution from the New Deal to the New Right* (New York: Cambridge University Press, 2014).

12. Loughlin, *Foundations of Public Law,* 407. Loughlin's *potestas / potentia* distinction shares important similarities with the distinction Michael Mann draws between "despotic" and "infrastructural" power in the making of modern states. Michael Mann, "The Autonomous Power of the State: Its Origins, Mechanisms, and Results," *European Journal of Sociology* 25 (1984): 185–213.

13. John Dewey, *The Public and Its Problems*, in *John Dewey: The Later Works, 1925–1953*, vol. 2, ed. Jo Ann Boydston (Carbondale: University of Southern Illinois Press, 1984).

14. Frederic Clemson Howe, *Wisconsin: An Experiment in Democracy* (New York: Charles Scribner's Sons, 1912), 3.

15. Jacob A. Riis, *How the Other Half Lives: Studies Among the Tenements of New York* (New York: Charles Scribner's Sons, 1890); Edith Abbott, *Public Assistance: American Principles and Policies* (Chicago: University of Chicago Press, 1940); Grace Abbott, *From Relief to Social Security* (Chicago: University of Chicago Press, 1941); John R. Commons, *Labor and Administration* (New York: Macmillan, 1913).

16. The radical departure argument is as perennial as it is misguided. For the most recent version, see Philip Hamburger, *Is Administrative Law Unlawful?* (Chicago: University of Chicago Press, 2014). The best critical response to this kind of polemical historical argument is exemplified by Adrian Vermeule, "No," *Texas Law Review* 93 (2015): 1547–1566.

17. My favorite example is Bill Miller's wonderful discussion of administrative functions and the *hreppr* (which administered a primitive poor law and community insurance regime) in medieval Iceland between the eleventh and thirteenth centuries. William Ian Miller, *Bloodtaking and Peacemaking: Feud, Law, and Society in Saga Iceland* (Chicago: University of Chicago Press, 1990).

18. Bernard Bailyn, *The Origins of American Politics* (New York: Vintage Books, 1968), 102–104.

19. Hendrik Hartog, "The Public Law of a County Court: Judicial Government in Eighteenth Century Massachusetts," *American Journal of Legal History* 20 (1976): 284, 288, 323.

20. Alexis de Tocqueville, *Democracy in America*, trans. George Lawrence, ed. J. P. Mayer (New York: Harper and Row, 1988), 79–81.

21. John Stuart Mill, "De Tocqueville on Democracy in American (I)," in *Collected Works of John Stuart Mill*, vol. 18, ed. J. M. Robson (Toronto: University of Toronto Press, 1977), 59–60. This reading of Tocqueville and Mill draws on Stephen Sawyer's revisionist account of "Tocqueville's democratic state" concerning administration and police power in Sawyer, *Demos Assembled: Democracy and the International Origins of the Modern State, 1840–1880* (Chicago: University of Chicago Press, 2018), 48–51.

22. Steve Pincus, *1688: The First Modern Revolution* (New Haven, CT: Yale University Press, 2009), 36; John Brewer, *The Sinews of Power: War, Money and the English State, 1688–1783* (Cambridge, MA: Harvard University Press,

1989), xvii. See also Charles Tilly, *Coercion, Capital, and European States: AD 990–1990* (Oxford: Blackwell, 1990).

23. *Final Report of the Attorney General's Committee on Administrative Procedure* (S.D. 8, 77th Cong., 1941), 8–9. Leonard D. White, *The Federalists: A Study in Administrative History* (New York: Macmillan, 1948); Leonard D. White, *The Jeffersonians: A Study in Administrative History, 1801–1829* (New York: Macmillan, 1951); Leonard D. White, *The Jacksonians: A Study in Administrative History, 1829–1861* (New York: Macmillan, 1954). For an overview of White's historical contribution, see Richard R. John, "Leonard D. White and the Invention of American Administrative History," *Reviews in American History* 24 (1996): 344–360.

24. Jerry L. Mashaw, *Creating the Administrative Constitution: The Lost One Hundred Years of American Administrative Law* (New Haven, CT: Yale University Press, 2012), 5, 187.

25. Nicholas R. Parrillo, *Against the Profit Motive: The Salary Revolution in American Government, 1790–1940* (New Haven, CT: Yale University Press, 2014), 1.

26. Parrillo, *Against the Profit Motive*, 92. On a similar trend from private to public prosecution in criminal justice, see Allen Steinberg, *The Transformation of Criminal Justice: Philadelphia, 1800–1880* (Chapel Hill: University of North Carolina Press, 1989); William J. Stuntz, *The Collapse of American Criminal Justice* (Cambridge, MA: Harvard University Press, 2011).

27. On officeholding, see, for example, Montgomery H. Throop, *Public Officers and Sureties in Official Bonds* (Chicago: T. H. Flood, 1892); Karen Orren, "Officers Rights: Toward a Unified Field Theory of American Constitutional Development," *Law and Society Review* 34 (2000): 873–905.

28. On the political culture of generality, see Pierre Rosanvallon, *Democratic Legitimacy: Impartiality, Reflexivity, Proximity*, trans. Arthur Goldhammer (Princeton, NJ: Princeton University Press, 2011), esp. 38–43; Marcel Gauchet, "Democracy: From One Crisis to Another," trans. Natalie Doyle, *Social Imaginaries* 1 (2015): 163–187; Wim Weymans, "Freedom through Political Representation: Lefort, Gauchet and Rosanvallon on the Relationship between State and Society," *European Journal of Political Theory* 4 (2005): 263–282.

29. Léon Duguit, *Law in the Modern State*, trans. Frida Laski and Harold Laski (London: George Allen & Unwin, 1921), 51; Rosanvallon, *Democratic Legitimacy*, 38–39.

30. Harold J. Laski, "The Responsibility of the State in England: To Roscoe Pound," *Harvard Law Review* 32 (1919): 462, 472.

31. Felix Frankfurter, *The Public and Its Government* (Boston: Beacon, 1930), 2, 81.

32. Duguit, *Law in the Modern State*, 243.

33. Freund, "Law of Administration," 404.

34. Woodrow Wilson, "New Meaning of Government" (1912), reprinted in *Public Administration Review* 44 (1984): 194.

35. Woodrow Wilson, "The Study of Administration," *Political Science Quarterly* 2 (1887): 201.

36. Felix Frankfurter, "The Task of Administrative Law," *University of Pennsylvania Law Review* 75 (1927): 617; Leonard D. White, *Introduction to the Study of Public Administration* (New York: Macmillan, 1926), 2.

37. Herbert Croly, "State Political Reorganization," *American Political Science Review* 6 (1912): 132.

38. Charles Evans Hughes, *Addresses and Papers of Charles Evans Hughes, Governor of New York* (New York: G. P. Putnam's Sons, 1908), 90; Frankfurter, *Public and Its Government,* 86, 88.

39. Frankfurter, 89, 134.

40. For excellent overviews, see Dwight Waldo, *The Administrative State: A Study of the Political Theory of American Public Administration* (New York: Ronald Press, 1948); White, *Introduction.*

41. Frankfurter, *Public and Its Government,* 27. A more complete and definitive compilation and discussion from this period is Robert E. Cushman, *The Independent Regulatory Commissions* (New York: Oxford University Press, 1941).

42. George Cyrus Thorpe, *Federal Departmental Organization and Practice* (St. Paul, MN: West Publishing, 1925), v–vi (emphasis added). At a similar moment in time, John A. Lapp compiled a register of important federal laws, rules, and regulations to keep citizens appraised of rapidly expanding federal administration. John A. Lapp, *Important Federal Laws* (Indianapolis: B. F. Bowen, 1917); John A. Lapp, *Federal Rules and Regulations* (Indianapolis: B. F. Bowen, 1918).

43. This accounting considers something an agency where either it was expressly called an agency or had express funding earmarked for its purposes in the *Official Register of the United States* (or other federal budget) and could be distinguished from a functional division of another agency (e.g., by a different mission statement or leadership).

44. Samuel P. Hays, *Conservation and the Gospel of Efficiency: The Progressive Conservation Movement, 1890–1920* (Pittsburgh: University of Pittsburgh Press, 1999), x.

45. Frank M. Stewart, *Officers, Boards and Commissions of Texas* (Austin, TX: Legislative Reference Division, 1916).

46. Leverett S. Lyon and Victor Abramson, eds., *Government and Economic Life: Development of Current Issues of American Public Policy,* 2 vols. (Washington: Brookings Institution, 1940), 2:1103–1106; Lent D. Upson, *The Growth of a City Government* (Detroit: Detroit Bureau of Governmental Research, 1942).

47. Max Weber, "The Bureaucratization of Politics and the Economy," in *Essays in Economic Sociology,* ed. Richard Swedberg (Princeton, NJ: Princeton University Press, 1999), 109–110, 114. The heightened attention to bureaucracy in Weber was only exacerbated by an American reception that first translated and fixated on the "bureaucratic" aspects of his oeuvre. Max Weber, "Bureaucracy," in *From Max Weber: Essays in Sociology,* ed. H. H. Gerth and C. Wright Mills (New York: Oxford University Press, 1946), 196–244. Robert K. Merton's *Social Theory and Social Structure* contained no index

entry for "state" but seventeen separate entries for various discussions of "bureaucracy" and "bureaucratization." Merton, *Social Theory and Social Structure* (New York: Free Press, 1949), 195–224.

48. Talcott Parsons, *The Structure of Social Action*, 2 vols. (New York: Free Press, 1968), 2:509.

49. Jürgen Habermas, *The Theory of Communicative Action: Volume Two: Lifeworld and System: A Critique of Functionalist Reason*, trans. Thomas McCarthy (Boston: Beacon, 1987), 306.

50. Weber, "Bureaucratization," 109–110. In *Economy and Society*, Weber expanded these categories into eight more specific attributes of modern "legal authority with a bureaucratic administrative staff." Weber, *Economy and Society*, 1:218–219, 220–221.

51. James M. Beck, *The Wonderland of Bureaucracy: A Study of the Growth of Bureaucracy in the Federal Government, and Its Destructive Effect upon the Constitution* (New York: Macmillan, 1932); Walter Lippmann, *Public Opinion* (New York: Harcourt, Brace, 1922); Walter Lippmann, *The Phantom Public* (New York: Harcourt, Brace, 1925); Burnham, *Managerial Revolution;* James Burnham, *The Machiavellians: Defenders of Freedom* (New York: John Day, 1943); Kenneth E. Boulding, *The Organizational Revolution: A Study in the Ethics of Economic Organization* (New York: Harper & Brothers, 1953); C. Wright Mills, *The Power Elite* (New York: Oxford University Press, 1956); William H. Whyte Jr., *The Organization Man* (New York: Simon and Schuster, 1956).

52. Jürgen Habermas, *The Structural Transformation of the Public Sphere: An Inquiry into a Category of Bourgeois Society*, trans. Thomas Burger (Cambridge, MA: MIT Press, 1991), 233, 235. Habermas, *Theory of Communicative Action*, 306–307.

53. Pierre Rosanvallon, *Le bon gouvernement* (Paris: Seuil, 2015), 94–95.

54. Hayek, *Road to Serfdom;* Hayek's *The Constitution of Liberty* (Chicago: University of Chicago Press, 1960) provided the critique along these lines—taking explicit issue with the entire canon on the modern administrative state. Gary S. Becker, "Competition and Democracy," *Journal of Law and Economics* 1 (1958): 105–109; Charles Murray, *Losing Ground: American Social Policy, 1950–1980* (New York: Basic Books, 1984); World Bank, *From Plan to Market: World Development Report 1996* (New York: Oxford University Press, 1996); Daniel Yergin and Joseph Stanislaw, *The Commanding Heights: The Battle between Government and the Marketplace that Is Remaking the Modern World* (New York: Simon & Schuster, 1998); David Harvey, *A Brief History of Neoliberalism* (New York: Oxford University Press, 2005); Angus Bergin, *The Great Persuasion: Reinventing Free Markets since the Depression* (Cambridge, MA: Harvard University Press, 2012).

55. Sir Henry Sumner Maine, *Popular Government: Four Essays* (London: John Murray, 1886), xi.

56. A. V. Dicey, *Introduction to the Study of the Law of the Constitution*, 6th ed. (London: Macmillan, 1902), 349, 334. For earlier and later juxtapositions of

Anglican versus Gallican liberty, see Francis Lieber, "Anglican and Gallican Liberty," in *Miscellaneous Writings,* 2 vols. (Philadelphia: J. B. Lippincott, 1881), 369–388; and Friedrich A. Hayek, "Freedom, Reason, and Tradition," *Ethics* 68 (1958): 229.

57. Frankfurter, "Foreword," 517.
58. Hamburger, *Is Administrative Law Unlawful?* See also Ernst, *Tocqueville's Nightmare,* 1. For an excellent critical overview of these current debates, see Jeremy K. Kessler, "The Struggle for Administrative Legitimacy," *Harvard Law Review* 129 (2016): 733.
59. Wilson, "Study of Administration," 216.
60. Wilson, "New Meaning of Government," 194.
61. Goodnow, *Comparative Administrative Law;* Frank J. Goodnow, *Politics and Administration* (New York: Macmillan, 1900); Frank J. Goodnow, *Principles of the Administrative Law of the United States* (New York: G. P. Putnam, 1905); Frank J. Goodnow, *Selected Cases on American Administrative Law with Particular Reference to the Law of Officers* (Chicago: Callaghan, 1906); Frank J. Goodnow, *Selected Cases on Government and Administration* (Chicago: Callaghan, 1906); Frank J. Goodnow, *Principles of Constitutional Government* (New York: Harper & Brothers, 1916); see also Charles G. Haines and Marshall E. Dimock, eds., *Essays on the Law and Practice of Governmental Administration: A Volume in Honor of Frank Johnson Goodnow* (Baltimore: Johns Hopkins University Press, 1935), v.
62. Frank J. Goodnow, *Social Reform and the Constitution* (New York: Macmillan, 1911); Goodnow, *Politics and Administration;* Charles A. Beard, *An Economic Interpretation of the Constitution of the United States* (New York: Macmillan, 1913); J. Allen Smith, *The Spirit of American Government: A Study of the Constitution; Its Origin, Influence and Relation to Democracy* (New York: Macmillan, 1907). The other truly radical tract in this legal-constitutional tradition is Louis B. Boudin, *Government by Judiciary,* 2 vols. (New York: William Godwin, 1932).
63. Goodnow, *Social Reform,* 1, 8–9, 308, 359.
64. Theodore Roosevelt, "The Right of the People to Rule: An Address at Carnegie Hall, New York City, Under the Auspices of the Civic Forum," Mar. 20, 1912; Goodnow, *Principles of Constitutional Government,* 11.
65. Goodnow, *Politics and Administration,* 39, 74–77, 82. On the move away from the fee system, see Parrillo, *Against the Profit Motive,* 117. On the constitutional transformation of a common law of "office," see Karen Orren, "Officers' Rights: Toward a Unified Field Theory of American Constitutional Development," *Law and Society Review* 34 (2000): 873–909. Also see Floyd R. Mechem, *A Treatise on the Law of Public Offices and Officers* (Chicago: Callaghan, 1890).
66. Francis A. Allen, "Ernst Freund," *University of Chicago Law School Record* 29 (1983): 8; Anonymous student note, "Ernst Freund: Pioneer of Administrative Law," *University of Chicago Law Review* 29 (1962): 756.
67. Walter Weyl, *The New Democracy* (New York: Macmillan, 1912), 4, 155.
68. Freund, "Law of Administration," 424–425.

69. William J. Novak, "A Revisionist History of Regulatory Capture," in *Preventing Regulatory Capture: Special Interest Influence and How to Limit It*, ed. Daniel Carpenter and David A. Moss (New York: Cambridge University Press, 2014), 25–48.

70. Weyl, *New Democracy*, 2, 78.

71. John Dewey and James H. Tufts, *Ethics* (New York: Henry Holt, 1908), 474, 477.

72. Vernon Louis Parrington, *Main Currents in American Thought: Volume Three: The Beginnings of Critical Realism in American, 1860–1920* (New York: Harcourt, Brace & World, 1930), 227, 283; Henry Adams, *The Degradation of the Democratic Dogma*, with an introduction by Brooks Adams (New York: Macmillan, 1920).

73. Plato, *The Republic: The Complete and Unabridged Jowett Translation* (New York: Vintage, 1991), bk. 4, 129–130. Aristotle also decried the corrupting effects of private interest and private vice on the commonwealth. Aristotle, *The Politics and the Constitution of Athens* (Cambridge: Cambridge University Press, 1996), bk. 3, 71.

74. Richard L. McCormick, "The Discovery that Business Corrupts Politics: A Reappraisal of the Origins of Progressivism," *American Historical Review* 86 (1981): 247–274.

75. Matthew Josephson, *The Robber Barons: The Great American Capitalists, 1861–1901* (New York: Harcourt, Brace, 1934); Matthew Josephson, *The Politicos, 1865–1896* (New York: Harcourt, Brace, 1938); Thorstein Veblen, *The Theory of Business Enterprise* (New York: Charles Scribner's Sons, 1904), 287.

76. Charles Francis Adams Jr., "A Chapter of Erie," in Charles Francis Adams Jr. and Henry Adams, *Chapters of Erie and Other Essays* (Boston, 1871), 1–99, 6.

77. On the complicated economics of railroad regulation, see Herbert Hovenkamp, *Enterprise and American Law, 1836–1937* (Cambridge, MA: Harvard University Press, 1991).

78. Charles Francis Adams Jr., "The Railroad System," in Adams and Adams, *Chapters of Erie*, 417–418, 427.

79. C. F. Adams, "Railroad System," 414, 417–418.

80. C. F. Adams, 416–417, 428–429.

81. C. F. Adams, 427.

82. McCormick, "Business Corrupts Politics," 266–267; Earl Ray Sikes, *State and Federal Corrupt Practices Legislation* (Durham, NC: Duke University Press, 1928); Helen M. Rocca, *Corrupt Practices Legislation* (Washington, DC: National League of Women Voters, 1928); Tabatha Abu El-Haj, "Changing the People: Legal Regulation and American Democracy," *New York University Law Review* 86 (2011): 1–68.

83. Frank J. Goodnow, *Municipal Home Rule: A Study in Administration* (New York: Macmillan, 1895); Frank J. Goodnow, *Municipal Problems* (New York: Macmillan, 1895); Frank J. Goodnow, *City Government in the United States* (New York: Century, 1904); Frank J. Goodnow, *Municipal Government* (New York: Century, 1919).

84. Luther Gulick, "Beard and Municipal Reform," in *Charles A. Beard, an Appraisal*, ed. Howard K. Beale (Lexington: University of Kentucky Press, 1954), 47–60; Charles A. Beard, *American City Government: A Survey of New Tendencies* (New York: Century, 1912); Charles A. Beard, *The Administration and Politics of Tokyo: A Survey and Opinions* (New York: Macmillan, 1923); National Municipal League, *A Municipal Program* (New York: Macmillan, 1900).

85. Hoyt Landon Warner, *Progressivism in Ohio, 1897–1917* (Columbus: Ohio State University Press, 1964); Mark C. Hoffman, "City Republic, Civil Religion, and the Single Tax: The Progressive Era Founding of Public Administration in Cleveland, 1901–1915" (PhD diss., Cleveland State University, 1998); Kim K. Bender, "Cleveland, a Leader among Cities: The Municipal Home Rule Movement of the Progressive Era, 1900–1915" (PhD diss., University of Oklahoma, 1996).

86. Daniel T. Rodgers, *Atlantic Crossings: Social Politics in a Progressive Age* (Cambridge, MA: Harvard University Press, 1998), 112.

87. Goodnow, *Municipal Government*, vii.

88. Frank P. Prichard, "The Study of the Science of Municipal Government," *Annals of the American Academy of Political and Social Science* 2 (1892): 19–20.

89. Lincoln Steffens, *The Shame of the Cities* (New York: McClure, Phillips, 1904), 5, 9, 11, 30–34, 103.

90. Jane Addams, *Democracy and Social Ethics* (New York: Macmillan, 1905), 260, 269, 272.

91. Jane Addams, "Problems of Municipal Administration," *American Journal of Sociology* 10 (1905): 425, 426–427.

92. On the original problem of the municipal corporation in American law, see Hendrik Hartog, *Public Property and Private Power: The Corporation of the City of New York in American Law, 1730–1870* (Chapel Hill: University of North Carolina Press, 1983). Similarly for English law, see Sidney Webb and Beatrice Webb, *The Development of English Local Government, 1689–1835* (London: Oxford University Press, 1963). On positions developed in the home rule movement that rose up against the administrative limits of municipal incorporation, see David J. Barron, "The Promise of Cooley's City: Traces of Local Constitutionalism," *University of Pennsylvania Law Review* 147 (1999): 487–612; David J. Barron, "Reclaiming Home Rule," *Harvard Law Review* 116 (2003): 2255–2386.

93. Jessica L. Hennessey and John Joseph Wallis, "Corporations and Organizations in the United States after 1840," in *Corporations and American Democracy*, ed. Naomi Lamoreaux and William J. Novak (Cambridge, MA: Harvard University Press, 2017), 74–108.

94. Hartog, *Public Property*, 223. See also John F. Dillon, *Treatise on the Law of Municipal Corporations* (Chicago: James Cockroft, 1872), 101–102.

95. William J. Novak, *The People's Welfare: Law and Regulation in Nineteenth-Century America* (Chapel Hill: University of North Carolina Press, 1996).

96. Sam Bass Warner, *The Private City: Philadelphia in Three Periods of Its Growth*, 2nd ed. (Philadelphia: University of Pennsylvania Press, 1987), 4;

Eric H. Monkkonen, *America Becomes Urban: The Development of U.S. Cities and Towns, 1780–1980* (Berkeley: University of California Press, 1988); Barron, "Reclaiming Home Rule," 2281–2285.

97. John F. Dillon, *Commentaries on the Law of Municipal Corporations*, 4th ed., 2 vols. (Boston: Little, Brown, , 1890), 34.

98. *Report of the Commission to Devise a Plan for the Government of Cities of the State of New York* (New York: Jerome B. Parmenter, 1877), 16.

99. Frederic C. Howe, *The Confessions of a Reformer* (Chicago: Quadrangle Books, 1967), 7.

100. J Smith, *Spirit of American Government*, 251–253, 255; Goodnow, *Municipal Problems*, 9.

101. Frederic C. Howe, *The City: The Hope of Democracy* (New York: Charles Scribner's Sons, 1905), 162–163.

102. Goodnow, *Municipal Home Rule*, 11; Goodnow, *Municipal Problems*, 26; John R. Commons, "State Supervision for Cities," *Annals of the American Academy of Political and Social Science* 5 (1895): 37.

103. Addams, *Democracy and Social Ethics*, 275–277.

104. Barron, "Reclaiming Home Rule," 2309.

105. Goodnow, *City Government*. Luther Gulick provided another able catalog. Gulick, "Beard and Municipal Reform," 48.

106. Lyon and Abramson, *Government and Economic Life*, 2:1130–1132.

107. Howe, *Confessions*, 110, 147, 157.

108. Charles A. Beard, *The Traction Crisis in New York* (New York: Bureau of Municipal Research, 1919); Gulick, "Beard and Municipal Reform."

109. Warner, *Progressivism in Ohio*, 55.

110. Johnson quoted in Hoffman, "Progressive-Era Founding," 132.

111. Howe, *Confessions*, 151.

112. Clarence H. Cramer, *Newton D. Baker: A Biography* (New York: Garland, 1979), 51. On the scale and ambition of the original municipalization movement, see Barron, "Reclaiming Home Rule," 2315–2316.

113. Howe, *City*, 163.

114. Addams, "Problems of Municipal Administration," 444.

115. Franklin D. Roosevelt, "State of the Union Message to Congress," Jan. 11, 1944.

116. Helen Campbell, "Certain Convictions as to Poverty," *The Arena* 1 (1889): 103–104. See also Riis, *How the Other Half Lives*; Robert A. Woods, William T. Elsing, and Jacob A. Riis, "The Poor in Great Cities," *Scribner's Magazine* 11 (1892): 399–400; Washington Gladden, "The Problem of Poverty," *The Century* 45 (1892–1893): 245–256.

117. Robert Hunter, *Poverty* (New York: Macmillan, 1904), v–vi, 5–6.

118. Robert Fogel's research corroborates some of these dire depictions on the ground. Robert William Fogel, *The Fourth Great Awakening and the Future of Egalitarianism* (Chicago: University of Chicago Press, 2000), 165–166.

119. Weyl, *New Democracy*, 197–198.

120. For the most useful overviews, see Robert H. Bremner, *From the Depths: The Discovery of Poverty in the United States* (New York: New York University Press, 1956); William I. Trattner, *From Poor Law to Welfare State: A History*

of Social Welfare in America (New York: Free Press, 1974); Michael B. Katz, *In the Shadow of the Poorhouse: A Social History of Welfare in America* (New York: Basic Books, 1986); Karen M. Tani, *States of Dependency: Welfare, Rights, and American Governance, 1935–1972* (New York: Cambridge University Press, 2016).

121. See, for example, Clark D. Knapp, *Treatise on the Laws of the State of New York in Relation to the Poor, Insane, Idiots, and Habitual Drunkards* (Rochester, NY: Williamson & Higbie, 1887); Florien Giauque, *A Manual for Guardians and Trustees of Minors, Insane Persons, Imbeciles, Idiots, Drunkards* (Cincinnati: Robert Clarke, 1881); Charles Richard Henderson, *Introduction to the Study of the Dependent, Defective, and Delinquent Classes and of their Social Treatment* (Boston: D. C. Heath, 1893); Bureau of the Census, *Summary of State Laws Relating to Dependent Classes* (Washington, DC: Government Printing Office, 1914). See the discussion in Chapter 4.

122. Sophonisba P. Breckinridge, *Public Welfare Administration in the United States* (Chicago: University of Chicago Press, 1927); E. Abbott, *Public Assistance;* G. Abbott, *Relief to Social Security.*

123. Commons, *Labor and Administration;* John R. Commons and John B. Andrews, *Principles of Labor Legislation* (New York: Harper & Brothers, 1916).

124. Two of the best recent works highlighting this extraordinary collaboration are Anya Jabour, *Sophonisba Breckinridge: Championing Women's Activism in Modern America* (Champagne-Urbana: University of Illinois Press, 2019); Felice Batlan, *Women and Justice for the Poor: A History of Legal Aid, 1863–1945* (New York: Cambridge University Press, 2015).

125. E. Abbott, *Public Assistance,* 3; William M. McKinney and Burdett A. Rich, eds., *Ruling Case Law* (Northport, NY: Edward Thompson, 1918), 21:701; William Blackstone, *Commentaries on the Laws of England* (12th ed., London, 1793), 1:131.

126. "An Act to Authorize and Require the Courts of General Quarter Sessions of the Peace to Divide the Counties into Townships and to Alter the Boundaries of the Same when Necessary, and Also to Appoint Constables, Overseers of the Poor, and Clerks of the Townships, and for Other Purposes Mentioned," *Laws Passed in the Territory of the United States North-West of the River Ohio* (Philadelphia: Francis Childs and John Swaine, 1791), 47–52.

127. G. Abbott, *Relief to Social Security,* "The Social Services a Public Responsibility," 5; Aileen Kennedy and Sophonisba P. Breckinridge, *The Ohio Poor Law and Its Administration* (Chicago: University of Chicago Press, 1934); Alice Shaffer, Mary W. Keefer, and Sophonisba P. Breckinridge, *The Indiana Poor Law* (Chicago: University of Chicago Press, 1936); Sophonisba P. Breckinridge, *The Michigan Poor Law* (Chicago: University of Chicago Press, 1936); Sophonisba P. Breckinridge, *The Illinois Poor Law and Its Administration* (Chicago: University of Chicago Press, 1939), 9.

128. E. Abbott, *Public Assistance,* vii, 125–126, 511.

129. Breckinridge, *Illinois Poor Law,* 18–21, 25.

130. E. Abbott, *Public Assistance,* 127–131; Sarah Orne Jewett, "The Town Poor," in *Novels and Stories* (New York: Library of America, 1994), 722–733.

131. Edith Abbott, "Abolish the Pauper Laws," *Social Service Review* 8 (1934): 9.

132. E. Abbott, *Public Assistance,* 509.

133. Breckinridge, *Illinois Poor Law,* viii.

134. E. Abbott, "Abolish the Pauper Laws," 3–4, 7–8.

135. Edith Abbott and Sophonisba Breckinridge, *The Administration of the Aid-to-Mothers Law in Illinois* (Washington, DC: Government Printing Office, 1921). See Joanne L. Goodwin, *Gender and the Politics of Welfare Reform: Mothers' Pensions in Chicago, 1911–1929* (Chicago: University of Chicago Press, 1997).

136. E. Abbott, *Public Assistance,* "From Local Responsibility to State Aid for Public Relief," 509, 511; Breckinridge, *Public Welfare Administration,* "Departmentalization of State Government Including Public Welfare Activities," 557–561.

137. E. Abbott, *Public Assistance,* "The Long History of the Movement Toward Federal Aid for Social Welfare," 651; Breckinridge, *Public Welfare Administration,* "A National Program and Proposals for a Federal Department of Public Welfare," 739–742.

138. Helen I. Clarke, *Social Legislation: American Laws Dealing with Family, Child, and Dependent* (New York: D. Appleton-Century, 1940), 7.

139. Abbott consistently used the success of public provision of education as a model for other forms of public assistance. E. Abbott, *Public Assistance,* 645.

140. Sophonisba Breckinridge and Edith Abbott, *The Housing Problem in Chicago* (Chicago: University of Chicago Press, 1910); Edith Abbott and Sophonisba Breckinridge, *The Tenements of Chicago, 1908–1935* (Chicago: University of Chicago Press, 1936); E. Abbott, *Public Assistance,* "Local Responsibility and Medical Care," 349–508; Edith Abbott, *The Real Jail Problem* (Chicago: Juvenile Protective Association, 1915); Edith Abbott, *The One Hundred and One County Jails of Illinois and Why They Ought to Be Abolished* (Chicago: Juvenile Protective Association, 1916).

141. Edith Abbott, "The Wages of Unskilled Labor in the United States, 1850–1900," *Journal of Political Economy* 13 (1905): 321. See also Edith Abbott, *Women in Industry: A Study in American Economic History* (New York: D. Appleton, 1910).

142. Charles McCarthy, *The Wisconsin Idea* (New York: Macmillan, 1912).

143. Howe, *Wisconsin,* 190.

144. Howe, 193–196.

145. McCarthy, *Wisconsin Idea,* 2, 16, 18.

146. Gilbert E. Roe, "Our Judicial Oligarchy: Why the People Distrust the Courts; Is the Poor Man on an Equality with the Rich Man before the Courts?," *La Follette's Weekly Magazine* 3 (1911): 6–8; Carl Sandburg, "The Man, the Boss and the Job: How Milwaukee, with the Aid of Experts, Grappled with the Problems of Unemployment," *La Follette's Weekly Magazine* 3 (1911): 5; Howe, *Wisconsin,* 89.

147. McCarthy, *Wisconsin Idea,* 16.

148. John R. Commons, *Myself: The Autobiography of John R. Commons* (Madison: University of Wisconsin Press, 1963), 90.

149. "An Act in Relation to the Civil Service of the State of Wisconsin," in *The Laws of Wisconsin Passed at the Biennial Session of the Legislature, 1905* (Madison:

Democrat Printing, 1905), 570–588; "An Act Giving the Wisconsin Railroad Commission Jurisdiction Over Public Utilities, Providing for the Regulation of Such Public Utilities," in *The Laws of Wisconsin Passed at the Biennial Session of the Legislature, 1907* (Madison: Democrat Printing, 1907), 446–483.
150. Commons, *Myself*, 133–134.
151. Commons, 135.
152. For the best histories of the legal transformations involved in the progressive quest for workers' compensation, see John Fabian Witt, *The Accidental Republic: Crippled Workingmen, Destitute Widows, and the Remaking of American Law* (Cambridge, MA: Harvard University Press, 2004); James Willard Hurst and Lloyd K. Garrison, eds., *Law in Society: A Course Designed for Undergraduates and Beginning Law Students; Cases and Other Materials* (Madison, WI: College Typing, 1941).
153. Commons, *Labor and Administration*, 385, 396.
154. Howe, *Wisconsin*, 115–116; McCarthy, *Wisconsin Idea*, 172.
155. Felix Frankfurter, "Expert Administration and Democracy," *Public and Its Government*, 123.
156. Franklin D. Roosevelt, "The Two Hundred and Eleventh Press Conference," June 7, 1935, in *The Public Papers and Addresses of Franklin D. Roosevelt*, vol. 4, *The Court Disapproves, 1935* (New York: Random House, 1938), 237.
157. Franklin D. Roosevelt, "Second Inaugural Address," Jan. 20, 1937, in *Inaugural Addresses of the Presidents of the United States* (Washington, DC: Government Printing Office, 1969), 241.
158. Felix Frankfurter, "Foreword: Courts and Administrative Law," *Harvard Law Review* 49 (1936): 427; Frankfurter, *Public and Its Government*.
159. James M. Landis, *The Administrative Process* (New Haven, CT: Yale University Press, 1938), 5.

Conclusion

1. Paul Krugman, "Franklin Delano Obama?," *New York Times*, Nov. 10, 2008; "The New New Deal," *Time*, Nov. 24, 2008, cover; Chip Reid, "FDR's New Deal Blueprint for Obama," CBS News, Dec. 14, 2009; William P. Jones, "Obama's New Deal," *The Nation*, Nov. 13, 2008; John Bellamy Foster and Robert W. McChesney, "A New New Deal under Obama?," *Monthly Review*, February, 2009. See also Mike Allen and Jonathan Martin, "Obama Unveils 21st Century New Deal," *Politico*, Dec. 6, 2008.
2. William E. Leuchtenburg, *In the Shadow of FDR: From Harry Truman to Barack Obama* (Ithaca, NY: Cornell University Press, 2009); Thomas J. Sugrue, *Not Even Past: Barack Obama and the Burden of Race* (Princeton, NJ: Princeton University Press, 2010).
3. Mircea Eliade, *Myth and Reality* (New York: Harper and Row, 1963), 5; Mircea Eliade, *Cosmos and History: The Myth of the Eternal Return*, trans. Willard R. Trask (New York: Harper and Row, 1959), viii.
4. Carl Schmitt, *Political Theology: Four Chapters on the Concept of Sovereignty*, trans. George Schwab (Chicago: University of Chicago Press, 2005), 36.

5. Eliade, *Cosmos and History*, 46.

6. Richard A. Epstein, *How Progressives Rewrote the Constitution* (Washington, DC: Cato Institute, 2006); Randy E. Barnett, *Restoring the Lost Constitution: The Presumption of Liberty* (Princeton, NJ: Princeton University Press, 2004); Jeffrey Rosen, "The Unregulated Offensive," *New York Times Magazine*, April 17, 2005; Adam Cohen, "What's New in the Legal World? A Growing Campaign to Undo the New Deal," *New York Times*, Dec. 14, 2004.

7. The number of times Schlesinger tells us that the sky is dark in the first pages of his epic suggests a clear and self-conscious deployment of mythic literary tropes. Arthur M. Schlesinger Jr., *The Age of Roosevelt: The Crisis of the Old Order, 1919–1933* (New York: Houghton Mifflin Company, 1957), 1–3. Schlesinger's second volume continues in this mode with a new epigraph from Machiavelli: "There is nothing more difficult to carry out, nor more doubtful of success, nor more dangerous to handle, than to initiate *a new order of things.*" Schlesinger, *The Age of Roosevelt: The Coming of the New Deal, 1933–1935* (New York: Houghton Mifflin Company, 1958), xv (emphasis added).

8. Schlesinger, *Crisis*, 8.

9. Ernest K. Lindley, *The Roosevelt Revolution* (New York: Viking, 1933); William E. Leuchtenberg, *Franklin D. Roosevelt and the New Deal, 1932–1940* (New York: Harper & Row, 1963), 347; William E. Leuchtenburg, *The Supreme Court Reborn: The Constitutional Revolution in the Age of Roosevelt* (New York: Oxford University Press, 1995), vii, 75; Carl N. Degler, "The Third American Revolution," in *Out of Our Past: The Forces That Shaped Modern America* (New York: Harper & Row, 1959), 379–413.

10. Bruce Ackerman, *We the People: Foundations* (Cambridge, MA: Harvard University Press, 1991), 44, 105. Akhil Amar also borrows this basic tripartite structure of constitutional revolution. For the requisite "third act," Amar highlights Hugo Lafayette Black, a gesture to the subsequent rights revolution of the Warren court. Akhil Reed Amar, *The Law of the Land: A Grand Tour of Our Constitutional Republic* (New York: Basic Books, 2015).

11. Of course, it was Arthur Schlesinger Sr. who pioneered the cycles concept. Arthur M. Schlesinger, "The Tides of National Politics," in *Paths to the Present* (New York: Macmillan, 1949), 89–103; Arthur M. Schlesinger Jr., *The Cycles of American History* (Boston: Houghton Mifflin, 1986).

12. Steve Fraser and Gary Gerstle, ed., *The Rise and Fall of the New Deal Order, 1930–1980* (Princeton, NJ: Princeton University Press, 1989), ix.

13. Richard Hofstadter, *The American Political Tradition* (New York: Alfred A. Knopf, 1948), 315.

14. Thomas C. Cochran, "The 'Presidential Synthesis' in American History," *American Historical Review* 53 (1948): 749.

15. Richard Hofstadter, *The Progressive Historians: Turner, Beard, Parrington* (Chicago: University of Chicago Press, 1968), 442. In a pioneering essay, Hofstadter exhorted historians to move beyond traditional disciplinary limitations and embrace the broader social sciences (sociology, psychology, political

science, economics, and even critical theory) thereby enhancing the "methodological self-consciousness" and the "analytical dimension" of their work. Richard Hofstadter, "History and the Social Sciences," in *The Varieties of History: From Voltaire to the Present,* ed. Fritz Stern (New York: Meridian Books, 1956), 359.

16. James Willard Hurst, *Law and Social Process in United States History* (Ann Arbor: University of Michigan Press, 1960), 18–19.

17. Alan Brinkley, "The New Deal and the Idea of the State," in Fraser and Gerstle, *Rise and Fall,* 85–121; see also Alan Brinkley, *The End of Reform: New Deal Liberalism in Recession and War* (New York: Knopf, 1995).

18. Pierre Rosanvallon, *L'État en France de 1789 à nos jours* (Paris: Seuil, 1990), 9 (pers. trans.).

19. Brinkley, "Idea of the State," 86 (emphasis added). Theda Skocpol, "Political Response to Capitalist Crisis," *Politics and Society* 10 (1980): 155–201; Theda Skocpol and Kenneth Finegold, "State Capacity and Economic Intervention in the New Deal, *Political Science Quarterly* 97 (1982): 255–278; Morton Keller, *Affairs of State: Public Life in Late Nineteenth-Century America* (Cambridge, MA: Harvard University Press, 1977); Stephen Skowronek, *Building an American State: The Expansion of National Administrative Capacities, 1877–1920* (Cambridge: Cambridge University Press, 1982); James T. Patterson, *The New Deal and the States: Federalism in Transition* (Princeton, NJ: Princeton University Press, 1969), 201–207.

20. Ira Katznelson, *Fear Itself: The New Deal and the Origins of Our Time* (New York: W.W. Norton, 2013), 8–9, 18–20.

21. Ackerman, *We the People,* 40, 105.

22. Henry Adams, *The Degradation of the Democratic Dogma* (New York: Macmillan, 1920); Brooks Adams, *The Law of Civilization and Decay: An Essay on History* (New York: Macmillan, 1895).

23. Richard L. McCormick, "The Discovery that Business Corrupts Politics: A Reappraisal of the Origins of Progressivism," *American Historical Review* 86 (1981): 247.

24. Matthew Josephson, *The Robber Barons: The Great American Capitalists, 1861–1901* (New York: Harcourt, Brace, 1934); Matthew Josephson, *The Politicos, 1865–1896* (New York: Harcourt, Brace, 1938)

25. Edward L. Glaeser and Claudia Goldin, eds., *Corruption and Reform: Lessons from America's Economic History* (Chicago: University of Chicago Press, 2006).

26. Robert Hunter, *Poverty* (New York: Macmillan, 1904); Jacob A. Riis, *How the Other Half Lives: Studies Among the Tenements of New York* (New York: Charles Scribner's Sons, 1890).

27. Robert W. Fogel, *The Fourth Great Awakening and the Future of Egalitarianism* (Chicago: University of Chicago Press, 2000).

28. John Dewey, "Democracy and Educational Administration," in *Problems of Men* (New York: Philosophical Library, 1946), 64.

29. Walter Weyl, *The New Democracy* (New York: Macmillan, 1912), 166–167.

30. Vernon Louis Parrington, *The Beginnings of Critical Realism in America: Main Currents in American Thought, Volume III* (New York: Harcourt, Brace, 1927), 283.

31. Charles A. Beard and William Beard, *American Leviathan: The Republic in the Machine Age* (New York: Macmillan, 1930), vii.

32. Amanda Shanor, "The New Lochner," *Wisconsin Law Review* 2016 (2016): 133–208; Jedediah Purdy, "Neoliberal Constitutionalism: Lochnerism for a New Economy," *Law and Contemporary Problems* 77 (2014): 195–213; Jeremy K. Kessler, "The Early Years of First Amendment Lochnerism," *Columbia Law Review* 116 (2016): 1915–2004.

33. Hannah Arendt, *Men in Dark Times* (New York: Harcourt Brace Jovanovich, 1968), 11.

34. Werner Jaeger, *Paideia: The Ideals of Greek Culture, Volume I: Archaic Greece: The Mind of Athens*, trans. Gilbert Highet (New York: Oxford University Press, 1939), xviii.

ACKNOWLEDGMENTS

With long-term research and writing projects such as this, one accumulates so many debts and graces that it is futile to try to acknowledge them individually and completely. Nonetheless, a few institutions and people deserve special mention for supererogatory contributions to the production of this volume.

The University of Michigan Law School saved me and patiently coaxed this book into existence. Prior to my arrival in Ann Arbor, I didn't know such places existed, humbly combining intellectual rigor and public commitment with joyous collegiality and mutual regard and respect. Dean Mark West sustained these communal values through crisis times and, in the process, enabled me as a scholar and teacher in unprecedented ways. I am grateful for the support of each and every one of my Michigan colleagues, but for special, indispensible interventions and contributions on my behalf, I particularly thank Kate Andrias, Sam Bagenstos, Nick Bagley, Evan Caminker, Rich Friedman, Bruce Frier, Monica Hakimi, Don Herzog, Jim Hines, John Hudson, Martha Jones, Matt Lassiter, Nina Mendelson, Bill Miller, Julian Mortenson, Sallyanne Payton, Emily Prifogle, Richard Primus, Adam Pritchard, Gabriel Rauterberg, Margo Schlanger, Rebecca Scott, Gil Seinfeld, and, last but never least in the eyes of our ever appreciative family, Mike Steinberg and David Uhlmann.

The Tobin Project similarly supported this author and this project in exceptional ways. Working with Dan Crane and Naomi Lamoreaux on co-edited volumes on American antimonopoly and the American corporation provided me with the foundation for this volume's chapters on political economy as well as a model for cooperative intellectual endeavor. The unique academic fellowship so ably curated by David Moss and John Cisternino at Tobin brought together some of my favorite collaborators: Jess Davis, Gary Gerstle, Richard John, Lina Khan, Kate Masur, Joel Michaels, Sabeel Rahman, Laura Phillips Sawyer, Ganesh Sitaraman, Melanie Wachtell Stinnett, John Wallis, and Richard White. Ajay Mehrotra has long been an integral part of the extended Tobin community, and like Bryant Garth, he offered further invaluable support as executive director of the American Bar Foundation. As the Tobin Project honed my approach to economic regulation, the Intimate States collaboration organized by Margot Canaday, Nancy Cott, and Robert Self wonderfully advanced my understanding of modern social regulation and social police. Similarly, the amazing scholars and activists at the Law and Political Economy Project, convened by Amy Kapczynski, David Grewal, and Jed Purdy, only increased my faith in the future possibility of a new, more equitable democracy.

One of the advantages of taking a long time to write a book is that one gets to watch students turn into prominent teachers, scholars, and professionals in their own right. What a gift it has been to explore legal history with the likes of Brad Asher, Rabia Belt, Danny Blinderman, Kat Brausch, Kathy Brosnan, Nancy Buenger, Cathleen Cahill, Kate Caldwell, Pedro Cantisano, Andrew Cohen, Chad Cover, Elizabeth Dale, Scott De Orio, Jacqueline Edelberg, Sam Erman, Bridget Fahey, Kathy Frydl, Laila Galvão, Susan Gaunt, Allie Goodman, Michelle Grisé, Jamie Grishkan, Joanna Grisinger, Elizabeth Harmon, Hunter Harris, Roman Hoyos, Mollie Hudgens, Mac James, Maria Jhai, Susan Karr, James Kirwan, Zach Kopin, Nora Krinitsky, Andrew Lanham, Ted Lawrence, Mordechai Levy-Eichel, Lauren Libby, Scott Lien, Matthew Lindsay, Danielle Lipow, Kate Markey, Betsy Mendelsohn, Maureen Tracey Mooney, Maribel Morey, Jim Morrison, Mithi Mukherjee, Amol Naik, Jessica Neptune, Bob Olender, Devin Pendas, Alyssa Pennick, Kim Phillips-Fein, Peter Pihos, Steve Porter, Gautham Rao, Kimberley Reilly, Katie Rosenblatt, Mark Schmeller, Pat Selmi, Nayan Shah, Aviram Shahal, Charles Smith, Charlotte Smith, Stephen Smith, Leela de Souza, Laurel Spindel, Ronit Stahl, Michael Stamm, Tracey Steffes, Andrew Sandoval Strausz, David Tanenhaus, Anthony Todd, Kyle Volk, Pat Waldron, Jeffrey Webb, Barbara Welke, Michael Willrich, Stewart Winger, and Madeleine Young.

At Harvard University Press, Kathleen McDermott guided this project through to completion with a seemingly endless supply of both wisdom and patience. I am indebted to Jim Kloppenberg and Karen Tani for many things, but their reviews of the penultimate version of this manuscript for the press were models of professional scholarly engagement that inspired me through final revisions (which, among other things, involved the elimination of some 50,000 extraneous words). I would also like to acknowledge the excellent editorial recommendations of Pamela Haag, Brian Ostrander, and Matthew Perez, as well as the research assistance of William Chorba, Andrew Clopton, David Frisof, Nash Hall, and the dedicated staff of the grand University of Michigan Law Library.

Early versions of the chapters in this book were presented at innumerable convenings over the past many years and benefited in countless ways from the wisdom and generosity that define the law and history communities. I cannot list all the workshop, symposia, and conference attendees who advanced this project, but a few friends have been close confidants for the entire journey. I have known Steve Pincus since we were graduate students, and he remains a model of devotion to historical craft. I have known Sally Gordon since we were first trying to become legal historians together, and she has been a constant source of sage advice, professional counsel, and personal guidance ever since. And then, well, there's Steve Sawyer and Jim Sparrow. From Hyde Park to Haymarket, from Ann Arbor to South Haven, from Paris to the Périgord, we have nurtured a rousing and vital conversation about history, the state, democracy, the university, and all the rest of it, which has been one of the profound pleasures in my life.

One of the disadvantages of taking a long time to write a book is that some of those with whom you would most like to share it are no longer with us. That is sadly true about my greatest teachers: Carl Ubbelohde, Morton Keller, Willard Hurst, Alan Brinkley, and Louis Novak. As I completed this volume, my mother, Elizabeth Novak, was ninety-five years old and still living in our childhood home without the aid of medication. Her example of will, fortitude, and sheer perseverance has not been lost on this project.

Max Novak and Gabriel Novak were marvelous little boys when I first started working on *New Democracy*. They are now remarkable young men with their own prodigious talents, careers, and life projects. It has been the privilege of my life to watch them grow. Frequently authors thank their children for reminding them that there are more important things than this book, and that is certainly true in this case. But that honor is also shared with Connie and Mike Powall, who have consistently reminded us of the inestimable values of friendship, family, and so many other very important things.

Margie Sikon and I met when she was sixteen and I was nineteen years old. She has been an intimate part of my heart and mind and soul every day, every jot, ever since. This book is dedicated to her wondrous spirit, which made everything possible.

INDEX

Page numbers in italics indicate tables.

commissions, regulatory (*continued*)
of Railroad Commissioners, 126–128;
National Association of Railroad and
Utilities Commissioners, 137; power
of, 128, 130–131; public utilities and,
202–203. *See also* administration; Interstate Commerce Commission (ICC); public
utilities; regulation, administrative
Committee of Social Hygiene, 173
common carriers, 113, 117, 135. *See also*
police power; public utilities; railroads
common law, 6, 13, 14, 28, 69, 154, 186;
in antebellum American state, 69; critique
of, 159–160; economic control and, 192;
individualism of, 154–155; lack of access
in, 137; public callings in, 113–115; public
utility idea and, 117; regulation and, 117;
shift away from, 90–91, 96, 97–98, 156,
176, 179, 214, 224–225, 249, 256; shortcomings of, 96–97, 159–160; vs. statute
law, 90–91; unfair trade and, 207; workers'
injuries and, 256
Commons, John R., 106, 109, 160, 254;
administration and, 244, 249, 257;
institutional economics and, 187; labor
reform and, 221; *Legal Foundations of
Capitalism*, 193
Commonwealth v. Alger, 93, 116, 138
communications, 108. *See also* public
utilities
competition, unfair, 184, 197, 204–210, 214,
217. *See also* regulated industries law
complaints/petitions, 127, 130–131,
137
Comstock Act of 1873, 101
Comte, Auguste, 74, 84
concubinage, 18–19
Connecticut, Crandall's school and, 53–54
Connor v. Elliott, 36
conservatism, 23
Constant, Benjamin, 11, 38
Constitution, US: Adequate Constitution
theory, 66; Bill of Rights, 35, 41, 62;
Civil War and, 27–28; comity principle
of, 51; Fifteenth Amendment, 28, 55, 65,
66; Fifth Amendment, 41, 139; national
citizenship concept and, 34–35; originalist,
13–14; privileges and immunities clause,
34, 44, 48, 49, 51, 52; secession issue and,
26–27; slaveholder, 25; Thirteenth Amendment, 28, 55, 57, 59–60, 63, 65, 66, 249.
See also Fourteenth Amendment; slavery
Constitutional Convention, 34

constitutionalism, laissez-faire, 103, 106–107
constitutional nationalism, 65–67. *See also*
citizenship, national
constitutional revolutions, 264. *See also*
transformation
consumption, 2
contract, liberty of, 80–81, 102, 103, 268.
See also *Lochner v. New York*
Cooley, Charles Horton, 152, 165, 189
Cooley, Thomas M., 65, 137, 182
Corfield v. Coryell, 36, 60
corporate charters, 115, 117–120, 140,
214, 242–243. *See also* public utilities
corporations, 129; as artificial persons, 39;
attempts to control, 108; cities and, 243,
247; in Delaware and New Jersey, 196,
214; economic power of, 265–266; number
of, 214; public service, 108, 109–113
(*See also* public utilities); relationship with
citizens, 130. *See also* antimonopoly/
antitrust; business; monopolies; public
utilities; railroads; regulated industries
law; regulation, administrative
corruption, 221, 237–240, 242, 265,
266–267
Corwin, Edward, 13, 15, 103, 106
Crafts, Wilbur Fisk, 164
Cram, Ralph Adams, 17
Crandall, Prudence, 47, 53–54
crime, war on, 167, 170
criminality, 161, 162, 167–179. *See also*
social police
criminal justice, 167–179, 253
criminology, 147
critical realism, 4, 13, 85, 86, 187, 236
Croly, Herbert, 77, 82, 227
Crooker, John Henry, 161
Cruikshank, United States v., 64
Cullom, Shelby, 136
Cullom Report, 136–137
cultural policing. *See* social police
Cushman, Robert E., 100, 136
Cyclopedia of Law and Procedure, 200

Daniels, Josephus, 178
Dartmouth College v. Woodward, 118
Davies, Joseph E., 208
Davis, David Brion, 85
Davis, Kenneth Culp, 110, 219
defect, 162, 248. *See also* social police
Delamare, Nicolas, 94
Delaware, 196, 214
delinquency, 162, 248. *See also* social police